The	Munson	Library	
**********	Your	Special	Code	**********
Please	mark the	space	below to	record
that you	have	read	this	book

OPERATION WHISPER

BARNES CARR

OPERATION WHISPER

THE CAPTURE OF SOVIET SPIES

MORRIS AND LONA COHEN

ForeEdge

ForeEdge
An imprint of University Press of New England
www.upne.com
© 2016 Barnes Carr
All rights reserved
Manufactured in the United States of America
Typeset in Garamond Premier Pro

Library of Congress Cataloging-in-Publication Data

Names: Carr, Barnes, author.

Title: Operation Whisper : the capture of Soviet spies
Morris and Lona Cohen / Barnes Carr.

Description: Lebanon NH : ForeEdge, an imprint of University Press
of New England, 2016. | Includes bibliographical references and index.

Identifiers: LCCN 2015043614 (print) | LCCN 2016002603 (ebook) |
ISBN 9781611688092 (cloth) | ISBN 9781611689396 (epub, mobi & pdf)

Subjects: LCSH: Kroger, Peter. | Kroger, Helen. | Spies—Soviet Union—
Biography. | Espionage, Soviet—United States. | Espionage, Soviet—Great Britain.

Classification: LCC UB271.R92 K733 2016 (print) | LCC UB271.R92 (ebook) |
DDC327.47073092/2—dc23

LC record available at http://lccn.loc.gov/2015043614

5 4 3 2 1

This book is for JOHN CURTIS CARR, brother and friend

CONTENTS

PART III MASTERS

Illustrations follow page 152

PREFACE

The subject of this book came to me on a morning that seemed to have been modeled from childhood memories, moist and green, smelling of jasmine and wild onions. I was sitting under the big oak in my backyard in New Orleans, drinking coffee and searching the paper for something interesting. But it was a slow news day. I was about to move on to the sports section when I noticed a story buried at the bottom of an inside page.

A famous spy for the Soviets had died in a KGB nursing home in Moscow. His name was Morris Cohen, eighty-four years old, born in the Bronx. There was something odd about this. I knew that Americans had spied for the Russians, but how many had actually got on a plane and defected to the workers' paradise?

And just how famous *was* he? The story went on to say that Morris and his wife Lona had run a Soviet spy network in the United States and Canada during World War II. They stole atomic secrets from the Manhattan Project and put Russia on a fast track to building its own nuclear arsenal. The Cohens, and not the Rosenbergs, had delivered a complete diagram of the first A-bomb to Moscow. That, I had to admit, was an impressive set of bona fides, as they say in the trade.

The story also said that Morris had worked as a sports writer for the *Memphis Press-Scimitar* before the war. That's when I sat up. I had worked as a reporter for the *Press-Scimitar*. It was my first major-market journalism job. A Russian spy was an alumnus of the *Press-Scimitar*? I put the paper down. Was that why some people used to call us Reds on the *Press-Scimitar*? I poured another cup and read on.

Morris had served in an international brigade in Spain and fought against Franco's army, the obituary said. He was wounded in battle and recruited for spying while recuperating in a hospital. I put the paper down. The Cohens sounded like a good subject for a feature story or an essay in a historical journal.

I obtained a copy of their FBI file, which included interviews with people who had known them in America at different times in their lives. I began mining sources at libraries, archives, museums, and additional government offices. I found that the Cohens, after leaving America, went on to atomic spying in England. But when I started checking British sources, I hit a wall. Nobody had ever heard of the Cohens. What was I doing wrong? My course was finally corrected by a helpful soul in the morgue (library) of the *Sunday Times*.

"Who?" he said.

"Morris and Lona Cohen," I replied. "Famous spies for the Soviets."

"In Britain? Never heard of them."

"It was the Portland spy case."

"Oh! You mean Peter and Helen Kroger. Bloody Yanks."

Things really opened up after that. I collected British news stories about the Cohens, and memoirs and reminiscences written by the spies they worked with, and the spy catchers who caught them. I contacted people who had known them, and located some good published interviews, including one conducted by KGB historians.

The Cohens and their London spy ring were finally captured in a joint effort by the FBI, CIA, RCMP, MI5, and Scotland Yard. When I found that out, I knew there was a book in all this. The roll-up was called Operation Whisper. The case featured all the elements of a Hitchcock thriller: chases, blackmail, threats of assassination, secret drops, secret meets, secret knocks, secret codes. Nocturnal beach landings and shots in the dark were included, along with a double-agent femme fatale. The Scotland Yard detective who arrested them was called Moonraker. I especially liked that.

One thing I noticed early on was that Americans who had written about the Cohens offered little information about their later work as the Krogers in England. And British writers who wrote about the Krogers seemed to care little about their previous incarnations as Americans. Thus, in this book I have tried to bring together a narrative history of the Cohens' "two lives" on both sides of the Atlantic.

Equally, I've described how police and security agents in the United States, Canada, and Britain systematically tracked down the Cohens, clue by clue. Writers often concentrate on the political ideology of spy cases and ignore the work of the spy catchers. But in a chase, I think the role of the hound is just as thrilling as that of the hare.

In the course of my research I learned a lot about spying, about the Spanish Civil War, the two world wars, and some truly fascinating characters I would like to have had a drink with. At times, the well ran dry. Other times, there was a flood. That's why I like research. But most of all, I like the writing.

I don't agree with what the Cohens did. But I do think they led intriguing lives. I've always believed that contradictions in character are the things that make people interesting. You'll find plenty of those in these pages.

OPERATION WHISPER

INTRODUCTION THE LONG TWILIGHT STRUGGLE

Imagine that a trusted colleague bursts into your living room one steamy afternoon and informs you that you must give up the life you now enjoy. Not to die, at least not in the foreseeable future, but to immediately abandon everything and disappear. You refuse. This is your hometown. You have a job and a comfortable apartment in a quiet neighborhood. You have favorite cafés, parks, theatres, sports teams. You have your books, your clothes, your favorite records and photographs, a lifetime of memories here. Most of all, you have your family and friends.

But here's the problem: You and your wife consider yourselves as American as football and fried chicken, yet you have spent most of your adult lives stealing American military secrets for the Soviet Union. That makes you both spies of the first order. Not killers or saboteurs, but thieves, and good ones. You've never been arrested or even suspected of doing anything illegal, but now your amazing run of luck has ended. Your fellow agents are being rounded up.

Your apartment might be bugged, so your friend, who's also one of your Soviet control officers, issues orders to you by writing notes, which your wife then burns in the bathroom. He tells you that your building might be watched, so when you and your wife leave you must carry nothing but your wallets in your pockets and the clothes on your backs. You'll never be able to see your friends and families again, or even contact them by letter or telephone.

You'll board a succession of trains and buses to get clean of surveillance, and eventually you'll land in Mexico City, at least for a while. Beyond that, you have no idea where you'll end up. You can't seek refuge in Russia. You're Jewish, and the Soviet Union is run by a megalomaniac who's on another one of his witch hunts for Jewish "traitors." But you have no choice. Here in New York City, federal agents are in your neighborhood right now, knocking on doors.

The bottom line: You and your wife spied against your own country in wartime. So did your associates, Julius and Ethel Rosenberg, the well-fed, idealistic, working-class Lower East Side couple dedicated to Communism and to spying for Mother Russia. The Rosenbergs have just been arrested, and the prosecutor says he'll ask for the death penalty. Do you want to face the same fate?

So go now. Leave the lights on, walk out, don't look back.

THAT WAS HOW Morris and Lona Cohen were forced to flee the United States in 1950 as the Rosenberg spy ring was being rolled up by the Federal Bureau of Investigation. The Cohens were a New York couple who ran a North American spy network that in 1945 was the first to deliver a complete diagram and description of the Allied atomic bomb to the Russians. That made them members of a select society of spies, the crème de la crème of espionage. They continued spying for the Soviets into the sixties, through some of the most turbulent decades in espionage history.

The Soviets gave the Rosenbergs money and ordered them to leave the United States just before they were formally charged. They took the money and refused to go. With that, the Soviets wrote them off and moved on to save the Cohens. The Rosenbergs were assigned to the scientific/industrial—not the atomic—line of Soviet spying in North America. Ethel did recruit her brother David Greenglass to steal product from the Manhattan Project, the Allied atomic bomb program, but he delivered only pieces of the puzzle. The Cohens ran the only Soviet network dedicated to atomic spying, and the product they turned in completed the puzzle, allowing the Russians to save years in the development of their own A-bomb. That made the Cohens eminently more valuable.

Spying is seldom a glamorous life of casinos, Aston Martins, and Beluga caviar. Mostly it's a mundane world occupied by ordinary people who work at ho-hum jobs to cover their covert work. For volunteers such as the Cohens the pay is somewhere between low and nonexistent, the hours long, the street corners cold and spooky. Most of all, it's a life based on deceit. Lies must be created every day, then more lies piled on to cover those lies. George Blake, a British agent who doubled for the Soviets, said you have to have a split mind to keep up with it all.[1] The rewards you get are the pride in doing your job well and the satisfaction of making a contribution to whatever you consider the greater good.

The Cohens maintained that they did not spy on the Manhattan Project in order to harm their homeland but rather to assist a wartime ally, Russia, in attaining nuclear parity so that a balance of power could be assured and another world war prevented. The atomic bomb was the most fearsome weapon ever devised. Stealing its secrets was the holy grail of espionage.

But the spy war between East and West did not end with the theft of the Bomb, or the capture of the Cohens or Blake or dozens of other spies, or with the implosion of Soviet Communism in 1991. This quiet war of lies, denials, and murder is still going on. The United States, Canada, Britain, Australia, and New Zealand operate a worldwide satellite surveillance system called Echelon that vacuums in data from phone calls and Internet traffic. Paris uses a similar program, Frenchelon, and Germany has Project 6, coordinated with the U.S. Central Intelligence Agency. Russia relies on its SORM (System of Operative Investigative Measures), and China conducts spying and hacking through Unit 61398 of the People's Liberation Army.

"Nothing has changed," cautioned Sergei Tretyakov, who defected in 2000 after running Russian intelligence operations out of New York. "The SVR [Russian foreign intelligence] rezidenturas in the U.S. are not less but in some respects even more active."[2] *Rezidenturas* are spy stations in countries outside Russia. The one in New York has traditionally been called Station One.

Tretyakov's warning means billions of dollars are being spent by each of those countries, every year, on spying. And each new year brings ever larger budgets, with no end in sight.

When did it all begin? And why?

Did it start with the Cold War? What exactly was that?

THE TERM "COLD WAR" was first used by financier Bernard Baruch, an advisor to presidents as far back as Woodrow Wilson. "As the Soviets thwarted an atomic agreement, lowered their Iron Curtain in Eastern Europe, and broke one promise after another in those early postwar years, it became clear that they were waging war against us," Baruch wrote in his memoirs. "It was a new kind of war, to be sure, in which guns were silent; but our survival was at stake nonetheless. It was a situation that soon came to be known as the 'cold war,' a phrase I introduced in a speech before the South Carolina legislature in April, 1947."[3]

The term made good copy. The media used it to represent the increasingly hostile relations between the Union of Soviet Socialist Republics and the Western alliance led by the United States, France, and Britain after the Second World War. But it wasn't really a new kind of war. And the guns had not always been silent. It began as a hot war, albeit one that had not been formally declared. It started in Russia, in the ashes of the First World War, that misunderstanding that the belligerents thought would be wrapped up by Christmas its first year but that went on to become what President Wilson called the worst disaster in history.

The first player to take the stage was Vladimir Ilyich Ulyanov, who used the nom de guerre of Lenin in his role as chairman of his Bolshevik Party in Russia. The Bolsheviks (the British called them Bolos) were a breakaway group from the Russian Social Democratic Labor Party, which advocated a Marxist revolution through long-term radicalization of the proletariat, the industrial working class. Lenin thought that process too slow. His government would be directed by an educated, disciplined party elite using mass terror to speedily achieve its aims. He, of course, would lead the charge.

But Lenin wasn't content to see himself simply as comrade chairman of just another noisy herd of Russian political rabble-rousers. He had a nobler vision. After his older brother Alexander was hanged in 1887 for plotting to assassinate Tsar Alexander III, Ilyich had grown up bitter and vengeful, obsessed with the idea that he had the right to be tsar himself, though he would never be so gauche as to use that title in public. Still, he liked it when his entourage called him Batyushka (little father), a form of address that had been reserved for the tsars.

Lenin was a small, balding man with Oriental eyes, a thick peasant's body, and a red Vandyke beard that hid his weak chin. He had German and Jewish ancestry, spoke English with a German accent, and churned out political tracts that probably were a little over the heads of many of his followers. Lenin adored Beethoven's *Appassionata*, and he once wept at a performance by Sarah Bernhardt. But the darker side of his soul devised a "beautiful plan" to "cleanse" Russia of his enemies, including the bourgeoisie, the priests, and the kulaks, the land-owning peasants. This he would do by continuing tsarist tactics of mass arrests and executions of political opponents.[4]

The Russian Revolution of February 1917 (March in the Western calendar) saw Imperial Army generals forcing the abdication of Nicholas II and a provisional government being formed to rule Russia until a constituent assembly could meet to decide the nation's future. The new premier was Alexander Fyodorovich Kerensky, a moderate socialist revolutionary. Kerensky called the new government the Russian Revolutionary Republic and kept the country in the war on the side of the Allies.

Lenin had other plans. He had secretly financed his Bolshevik Party with German money as far back as 1915, and he had cut a deal with Berlin to take Russia out of the war if he could seize power.[5] Lenin was not in Russia for the February Revolution; nor was Trotsky or Stalin. In April 1917 the Germans delivered Lenin back to his homeland in a so-called sealed train, and in July he attempted a Bolshevik coup d'état with a street mob. But Lenin, like Kerensky, was a great talker who possessed few realistic skills in military strategy. Lenin's "July Days" operation failed miserably, and he was forced to flee the country disguised as a woman wearing a poorly fitting wig after the provisional government publicized his ties with Germany.

Lenin sneaked back into Russia for a second act, in October 1917. This time he was successful. Millions of Russian soldiers were deserting the eastern front and killing their officers, and the Russian Provisional Government was on the brink of collapse. Kerensky dropped the ball and Lenin scooped it up. He called it the Great October Socialist Revolution, though it was not a general uprising of the Russian people but simply a coup staged by a few hundred street fighters. In Petrograd, the capital, some Red Guards landed two artillery shells on the Winter Palace, defended in part by Colonel Maria Leontievna Botchkareva and her First Russian Women's Battalion of Death.

After that "bombardment," the provisional government ministers and the women soldiers surrendered, and a mob looted the palace, leaving feces in the bathtubs as calling cards. Russia was then in the hands of the Bolsheviks.

There was little loss of life in Petrograd; eight Bolsheviks were killed, six of them by bullets fired by their own comrades. Lenin later admitted that his Red Guards mostly argued the opposition out of business. The Red Guards were replaced by the Red Army, later called the Soviet Army.[6]

Lenin kept his bargain with Berlin by signing a separate peace with the Central Powers at Brest-Litovsk (now in Belarus) on March 3, 1918. That shut down the eastern front, taking Russia and eight million of her soldiers out of the war. Germany and Austria-Hungary were then free to start shifting divisions over to France. The result was the Russian Civil War, with Lenin and the Bolsheviks defending their shaky new government against a mélange of Socialist Revolutionaries, anarchists, Czechs, Poles, tsarist White armies, Allied and German agents, and roaming gangs of highwaymen.

With the collapse of the Russian front, the Allies feared defeat in France, the main battleground of the war. London and Paris quickly drew up a plan to invade Russia and get the country back in the war as soon as possible.

THE ALLIES CLAIMED they were simply going to occupy a military supply depot in the North Russian port of Archangel and protect it from German forces in neighboring Finland. And while they were at it, they were also going to rescue the Czech Legion, a pro-Allied force of sixty thousand stranded along the Trans-Siberian Railway. But the wider Allied strategy was to raise a new Russian army and restore the eastern front.[7]

President Wilson, a former president of Princeton University and re-formist governor of New Jersey, carefully considered the operation that Paris and London were proposing. Wilson was not a well man. He had headaches, nausea, and nervous exhaustion. He was sixty-one years old, suffered from hypertension and arteriosclerosis, had survived a stroke that left one arm weakened, and was nearly blind in one eye. But he saw clearly enough the dangers of invading Russia.

For one thing, Wilson did not trust any of the belligerents in the war. He was convinced that after the war was over, Britain, France, and the other victors would try to carve up Europe like a Christmas turkey. He also feared that an invasion would bring on war with Russia. The United States had been the first country to recognize the Russian Revolutionary Republic and had lent them millions of dollars in war aid. But meddling in Russia's internal affairs would be a violation of Wilson's Fourteen Points, specifically number 6, which called for Russia's independent determination of her own political development and national policy. Wilson changed his mind after a visit to the White House by Colonel Maria Botchkareva.

Botchkareva, also known as Yashka, had fought on the eastern front for the Imperial Russian Army, had been wounded, and had received several medals for heroism. She was a stout peasant woman of little education but was endowed with an almost fanatical patriotism toward Mother Russia. She wore her hair in a men's brush cut and carried herself in a military manner.

The Bolsheviks had deemed Yashka a threat to Soviet national security and put her women's battalion out of business, so in 1918 she toured America and England to drum up support for an Allied intervention against the Reds. By the time she got to the White House, in early July, she was a celebrity, and Wilson couldn't help feeling a certain excitement in her presence. Wearing her dress uniform with sword, she marched into the Oval Office and described to Wilson the atrocities being committed in her beloved motherland. She told the president that the Bolsheviks and Germans had dragged Russia through the dirt, and all that loyal Russians asked was a chance to redeem themselves.[8]

"If the Allies will come, even with a small force, with the Americans in the lead, they will flock around them by the hundreds of thousands," she said. "But they must come quickly."

The interview left Wilson in tears. Within weeks he agreed to join an Allied expeditionary force to North Russia.

The AEFNR landed at Archangel on August 2, 1918. Compared to the huge armies fighting on the western front, it was indeed a small force: 13,100 British; 4,820 Americans; 2,350 French; 1,340 Italians; and 1,280 Serbs— with 11,770 Russian volunteers including Cossacks coming on board later.[9] Around 8,000 Soviet soldiers and sailors, supported by Germans, met the Allied force. Commissar of War Lev Davidovitch Trotsky announced that a state of war existed between Soviet Russia and the Allies. With his pretty face, bushy black hair, and comic-opera uniforms, Lev was a darling of the press, and his war claim was printed worldwide. Lenin quickly denied it, but it was no use. The smell of gunpowder and the roar of warplanes were in the air.

The Allied Intervention in the Russian Civil War, as it is popularly known, was actually a two-pronged operation. The second part was to kidnap Lenin, ferry him off to England to stand trial for treason, and install a pro-Allied government in Moscow. London's top conspirators in the plot were Robert Bruce Lockhart, British consul in Moscow and a special agent for the intelligence section of the British Foreign Office, and Sidney Reilly, an agent for MIIC, the British Secret Intelligence Service, also known as MI6. Washington was represented by Xenophon Dmitrevich deBlumenthal Kalamatiano, an American agent for the Bureau of Secret Intelligence of the Diplomatic Service of the U.S. State Department.

Kalamatiano—Kal to all who knew him—had been born in Austria, the only son of a Greek father and Russian mother. After Kal's father died, his mother remarried and the family emigrated to the United States, becoming naturalized citizens and settling in Bloomington, Illinois. Kal was a language scholar and track star at Culver Academy and the University of Chicago. An expert hunter and horseman, he was a handsome fellow with broad shoulders and thick dark hair. His glasses, his cane and gloves, and his Old World manners lent him a Continental charm.

Kal grew up hearing stories from his mother about exotic Old Russia, and in 1908, when he was twenty-six years old, he went over to seek his fortune. He sold farm implements in Odessa for the J. I. Case Company of Racine, Wisconsin, and later went into business for himself.[10] He moved to Moscow and enjoyed a robust social life. He married a Russian and they had a son. When war came, he was hired by the State Department as an American agent in Russia for the Bureau of Secret Intelligence.

Secretary of State Robert Lansing had created the BSI in April 1916 as America's first nonmilitary overseas spy agency. But its governmental status was debatable. The BSI was financed by private funds, had no congressional oversight, and was peopled by dollar-a-year cowboys (a popular term at the time meaning enthusiastic volunteers who worked for little or no money). The Washington and New York offices consisted of less than a dozen staffers. Their index system was the memory of the oldest relic in the office, and a joke was that he needed help to get in the door. Nevertheless, Kal was assured that no matter what happened, the U.S. government would back him up. He saw it as his Great Adventure in the Great War.

British consul Bruce Lockhart was a Scot, a little younger than Kal, low and stumpy, with skin toughened by years of service on a colonial rubber plantation in Malaya. After arriving in Russia, Bruce played soccer with the proletariat from a factory team in Moscow while enjoying the nightlife of a bon vivant. He was attracted to exotic women, and his open affair with a beautiful Russian aristocrat, Baroness Moura Budberg, was not appreciated by his wife, or his controllers back in London.[11]

Sidney Reilly was born Salomon Georgievich Rosenblum, of Russian Jewish origin, but he claimed a variety of names and nationalities. He was a cool, creative, elegantly dressed adventurer who collected an assortment of lonely women, at least half a dozen of whom thought they were married to him. Sidney was small and trim, almost a figurine of a man, with a hooked nose, thick lips, a closely cropped artist's beard, and the big wet eyes of a bulldog. Photos of him show a striking resemblance to the actor Humphrey Bogart.

Reilly was a linguist and a former Royal Flying Corps officer whose skills included forgery, counterfeiting, war profiteering, murder and, in a jam, selling patent medicine. Sidney was in spying for the money, and at times found himself working for Britain, America, Russia, Germany, and Japan, raking in big paychecks for his services. After he took up morphine and Christianity, he had visions of himself as the Napoléon of Russia, then as Jesus Christ. Captain Mansfield Smith-Cumming, the legendary "C" of MI6, didn't trust Reilly.[12] In fact, Reilly's letterhead read *Mundo nulla fides*, trust no one.[13] Smith-Cumming nevertheless hired him because of his many contacts in Russia.

The British would later call their Moscow coup attempt the Lockhart Conspiracy. The Russians saw it as the Envoys' Plot. Then there are those who say it was the Reilly Plot because Sidney might have been secretly planning his own coup in Moscow, which would allow him to do some browsing in the captured Soviet treasury. Taking all that into consideration, a more equitable term would be simply the Lenin Plot.

Like many secret ops, the Lenin Plot undoubtedly looked good on paper. Cooking up ambitious schemes was, after all, what spies and diplomats were paid to do. But then the human factor intervened, as it usually does. Allied agents were traveling all over Russia promising millions of dollars, francs, pounds, lire, and rubles to anyone with a workable plan for overthrowing the Bolsheviks. Double agents, triple agents, agents provocateurs, flimflam men, and dictator wannabes all had their hands out. Under pressure of time, Lockhart and Kalamatiano, along with their French and Italian associates, made some poor choices.

Lockhart's first mistake was succumbing to the charms of Baroness Budberg, an elegant, smoky-eyed femme fatale struggling to survive under the Soviet régime. Moura might have been a *seksot* (informer) for the secret police, the Cheka, as suggested by her later friendship with Lenin and Stalin. Then again, she might have been a double employed by the Allies, or the Germans. The jury is still out on that.[14]

Lockhart's second mistake was to join Reilly in inviting Boris Viktorovich Savinkov into the Lenin Plot. Kalamatiano, too, had interviewed Savinkov, and went along with this recruitment. Those mistakes were further compounded by the plotters meeting in the office of DeWitt Clinton Poole, U.S. consul general in Moscow, which was under surveillance by both Russians and Germans.

The plotters hired Boris Savinkov because he was an independent Socialist Revolutionary who operated an anti-Bolshevik underground army called the Union for the Defense of Motherland and Liberty. Savinkov had devoted his life to killing both tsarists and Bolsheviks. Known as the General of Terror and Bloody Boris, he was a slight, catlike man with a Mediterranean complexion and mystically slanted eyes. A journalist once wrote that his eyes suggested he was the issue of a Jesuit priest and a Turkish seer.

On one hand, Savinkov was a traditional Russian *barin*, an educated and cultured gentleman—a journalist, a novelist, a playwright, a former deputy minister of war for the provisional government. Because of his penchant for Cadillacs, Brooks Brothers suits, and hot jazz, the police gave him the code name *Amerikanets* (American). Savinkov was also one of the most dangerous international terrorists of his time—a bomber, a torturer, and a fast draw with dagger or pistol.

The Bolsheviks had murdered Savinkov's sister and her husband, so Boris had no interest in merely kidnapping Lenin. He wanted to kill him. Shoot him, stab him, whatever. Trotsky too, if they could find him. Then Savinkov would rule Russia as imperator for the Allies until the war was over, at which time he would give up his dictatorship, though that, of course, was negotiable.

As it turned out, the Allies' Lenin Plot was a sting operation set up by

Lenin and Felix Edmundovich Dzerzhinsky, head of the Cheka.[15] The conspiracy collapsed in disaster after Savinkov gave a pistol to Fanny Kaplan, the battle name of Fanya Yefimovna Roitman, terrorist daughter of Jewish schoolteachers who had left Volhynia for the United States.

Kaplan, a Socialist Revolutionary believed, as did Savinkov and the Allies, that the Bolshevik coup of October 1917 had ended the legitimate revolution that began the previous February. So, on August 30, 1918, a hot, dusty afternoon in the south end of Moscow, Kaplan took Savinkov's pistol and reportedly shot Lenin at the Mikhelson armaments factory.[16]

Two bullets struck Lenin. That ended the Allies' pretensions of giving Comrade Chairman due process of law in a courtroom. In those few seconds the Lenin Plot was transformed into an assassination attempt on a head of state. It was international terrorism in its rawest form.

Lenin was gravely wounded but managed to walk up the steps of the Kremlin to his apartment. He survived, but his health declined after that until a series of strokes left him in a wheelchair with a grotesque expression on his face. Meanwhile, Dzerzhinsky used the assassination attempt to step up the Red Terror. It was said that the reptilian-eyed Iron Felix wept as he signed the death warrants.

Cheka agents were known as headhunters. They wore leather jackets and brogans with Mauser automatics tucked into their belts. Some people swore that the acronym for the agency was phonetically similar to the sound of a Mauser being cocked—*che-ka*! But headhunters didn't kill people. It wasn't politically accurate to say that. The official expression was "entered under outgoing."[17] That organization would evolve into the NKVD (later called the KGB and now the SVR), the employers of Morris and Lona Cohen.

Fanny Kaplan was arrested and murdered in a greasy garage, Cheka style, with a bullet to the back of the head. She was twenty-eight years old and had spent more than a third of her life in tsarist prisons. Savinkov and Reilly escaped to the West but were lured back to Russia years later for arrest, and died in Cheka custody. Lockhart was locked up, then freed in a swap.

When Kalamatiano was arrested, he denied spying on the Soviets. He told the Cheka he was a businessman who operated a harmless "information service" for commercial clients back in the United States. But when his walking cane was opened, Chekisti found a codebook, a list of Kal's thirty-two Russian assets, and notes on money paid to them.

Alexander Orlov, a former army warrant officer who was about to go into guerrilla service for the Cheka, later wrote: "Kalamatiano no longer resisted, and gave candid testimony about himself and his network."[18] The suggestion is that Kal made a full confession. We will meet Orlov again later, in Spain, as the Soviet intelligence officer who recruited Morris Cohen to spy against the United States.

Kalamatiano was dragged before the Supreme Tribunal of Soviet Russia, in Moscow. Contrary to its earlier promises, the Wilson administration claimed no responsibility for him, and he had to pay for his own legal defense. Two French co-conspirators, Consul General Joseph Fernand Grenard and Colonel Henri deVertement (also spelled Verthamon), head of French intelligence in Russia, were freed after Premier Georges Clemenceau threatened a naval bombardment of Russian ports on the Black Sea.[19]

Kal's day in court was a circus for the world press, and it foreshadowed the Stalinist show trials of the thirties. The courtroom was the Mitrofanov Hall of the Kremlin, filled with Bolsheviks smoking, drinking, and spitting on the floor. The prosecution admitted that their case against Kal was weak, but the decision had already been made to make an example of him. Thus, on a cold, rainy evening in December 1918 the young American and his main asset in the Red Army, Colonel Alexander V. Friede, were convicted of treason. The sentence was death. Friede was promptly shot, but some financially minded mandarins in the Kremlin intervened on Kal's behalf.

Russia was flat broke, starving, suffering from epidemics, and bogged down in civil war. Kal's sentence was commuted to a prison term so he could be used as a hostage in bargaining for postwar assistance from the United States. But Kal was not told that. He was locked up on death row, beaten, and subjected to psychological torture consisting of nightly mock executions, with him never knowing when the firing squad might be armed with live ammunition. He wasn't released until 1921, during Russia's Great Famine, when Herbert Hoover, director of the American Relief Administration, insisted that America would not open her pocketbook to help the Soviets until all Western prisoners were freed.

The Lenin Plot was a colossal embarrassment to Washington, Paris, and London. They had gone to war against a former ally and tried to murder her leader. Worse yet, their sophisticated, modern invasion force was defeated by Trotsky's ragged Red Army at the battle of Shenkursk in January 1919 and driven out of Russia in shame.

Lockhart was praised and promoted in London, and later knighted. Kalamatiano was dismissed by Washington as a failure, a relic from another time. His controllers paid him off and put him on a train for Illinois. Two years later, his health broken, he died in obscurity.

But during his incarceration, Kalamatiano had continued to collect information about the Communists, the name the Bolsheviks had adopted in 1918, and when he was debriefed in Washington he warned that America had replaced Britain as the main adversary of Soviet Russia. It was both a prediction and a warning. And it turned out to be accurate.

Western intelligence agencies dismissed the Lenin Plot as just a sideshow that had gone bad. They tied it off and moved on. But the Russians saw it as proof that the West was out to destroy the Soviet state. Dzerzhinsky made the case a part of the curriculum at his spy school in Moscow. Succeeding generations of Soviet bosses used it to justify whatever mischief they could cook up against the West.

If the term "Cold War" can be defined as an attempt to defeat another nation politically, economically, or militarily without a formal declaration of war, then the Lenin Plot was the true beginning of what President John F. Kennedy would call the "long twilight struggle."

THE COHENS AND THEIR SPY RING were rounded up in London in 1961 and convicted of conspiring to violate the British Official Secrets Act. It was one of the high-profile spy cases of the sixties, a decade that would bring George Blake, Kim Philby, John Vassall, Robert Soblen, the Christine Keeler affair, and the U-2 incident into living rooms everywhere. And those were only the cases that intelligence agencies allowed the public to know about.

Morris and Lona had finally been tracked down by the British Security Service (MI5), assisted by Scotland Yard's Special Branch, the CIA, the FBI, and the counterintelligence agencies of several other nations. The Cohens had once again been plying the trade they knew best—stealing atomic secrets for Russia, this time by operating a spy network inside a North Atlantic Treaty Organization base in Britain. The media dubbed it the "Portland Spy Ring" and the "Naval Secrets Case." The roll-up of the Cohens' organization was called Operation Whisper first by Scotland Yard, then by the other agencies involved in the investigation.

In the passing years, the theft of the secrets of the Bomb has resulted in arms races many times more dangerous than the ones that preceded both world wars. The stain of that original crime continues to spread as the capability to build nuclear weapons is pursued by terrorists and tin-pot dictators who probably shouldn't be entrusted with electric can openers.

That's where the real problem lies today—not in a nuclear attack by a presumably responsible nation, but rather by some tribe of paranoiacs with an agenda to destroy everyone who doesn't happen to agree with their particular spin on history. A theft of nuclear weapons is something the major powers have been warning about for years. That includes the Russians, who, after all, were the first atomic thieves. And the Cohens, Moscow was proud to announce, were their best pinchers.

Some might say that just one of their projects, stealing atomic secrets from the Manhattan Project, was the greatest spy caper in history.

PART ONE **RECRUITS**

1 SECURITY MATTER C

The hunt for Morris and Lona Cohen began in New York City in 1953 after "an informant of unknown reliability" but who was "in a position to know" told FBI agents that the Cohens were "very radical Communists" who had conducted party meetings in their home.[1] The New York report arrived at FBI headquarters in Washington—the seat of government, as Director John Edgar Hoover called it—on November 13 and summarized the findings of five days of preliminary investigation.

The wording of the report was interesting. The FBI often collected information by hearsay, bribery, mail interception, warrantless wiretaps, and illegal entries, so code words such as "informant of unknown reliability" were used to signal to other agents that certain product had been obtained by methods the bureau would not want to explain in open court. But it's also possible this informant was simply someone who had heard about the Cohens' activities. Either way, by this time Morris and Lona had earned their stripes as master spies for the Soviets, and conducting party business in their home was a serious breach of security.

The report on the Cohens was sent to headquarters by FBI airtel. In an airtel, information was typed into a standardized report document and then simply mailed. The fact that this initial report on the Cohens was sent by regular mail rather than special delivery or telex suggests that the bureau was investigating a large number of "Red tips" at the time and that this one would be dutifully added to the pile.

Soviet Communism today is considered a failure, a neutered and defanged old idea once perpetrated by party functionaries throwing around terms such as "dialectical materialism" that most of their intended audience probably did not understand. So why was the FBI so obsessed with Communists? Hadn't Russia been an ally of the Western powers in two world wars? Yes, but Russia had abandoned the Allies in the first war, and in the second war it was more a case of enemies holding their noses to unite against a common threat. Strange bedfellows might be a better term.

GOVERNMENTAL SUSPICION of Soviet intentions in the United States dates back at least to January 1919, the same month that Allied forces were defeated at Shenkursk in North Russia. On the twenty-first of that month, a New York City police inspector and former military intelligence officer named Thomas J. Tunney told a U.S. Senate subcommittee a revealing story about Leon Trotsky. Trotsky had lived in New York for a while in 1917, editing a Russian newspaper and giving lectures on revolutionary socialism before going back to Russia to convert to Bolshevism and raise the Red Army. As Trotsky was leaving New York, Tunney said, he left instructions to his American followers: "I want you people here to organize and keep on organizing until you are able to overthrow the damned, rotten capitalistic government of this country."[2]

Two months after Tunney's testimony, the Communist International (Comintern) was founded in Moscow. This was during the time when the defeated Allied force in North Russia was waiting for a fresh troop surge from Britain and while Kalamatiano was being tortured in prison in Moscow. The Comintern was a Soviet-sponsored association of international Communist parties set up to stoke violent revolution throughout the world. "Setting off Red fireworks" was the expression used. The preferred method was to stage a *propagande par le fait*, a propaganda by the deed, against an established government. This involved committing a high-profile political crime in order to provoke an even harsher response from the state. Theoretically, it in turn would radicalize the population and catalyze a revolution, counterrevolution, civil war, or coup.

As if on cue, the first such deeds were executed in the United States barely seven weeks later. But most of them were committed not by communists but by anarchists. In April, a mail bomb was delivered to the office of Seattle mayor Ole Hansen, who had threatened to use martial law and military intervention to end a general strike of workers in his city. The bomb was defused and no one was hurt, but the next day a similar device exploded in the Atlanta home of U.S. senator Thomas Hardwick, injuring both his wife and his housekeeper.

Then postal inspectors in New York opened some suspicious-looking packages and disarmed thirty-six additional bombs. All were apparently intended to blow up on May Day, the international workers' holiday. John D. Rockefeller, cofounder of Standard Oil, an icon of capitalism, had been a target. So were banker J. P. Morgan in New York and a number of public officials in Washington, including Attorney General Alexander Mitchell Palmer. They all shared the common sin of having publicly denounced anarchism.

In June, bombs were detonated in eight more cities. Again the targets were government officials who had opposed anarchism and supported deportation of radicals. This time Palmer's house was hit. He was not injured, but the bomber, an anarchist newspaper editor named Carlo Valdinoli, was killed in the blast. Apparently the overweight Valdinoli had tripped on Palmer's doorstep with the bomb in his hands. One of his body parts landed across the street in the yard of Assistant Navy Secretary Franklin Delano Roosevelt. Two more inept bombers, along with a night watchman, were killed that night in New York in the bombing of a judge's home. Anarchists openly claimed responsibility for those attacks, but because of a lack of evidence, no arrests were ever made.

Anarchists, it should be noted, were not the same as communists, though both ideologies preached violent revolution and employed terrorism. The main difference was that communists, like capitalists, favored a strong central government; anarchists believed that all governments and laws were oppressive. Also, communism differed from socialism in that most Western socialists believed in running for office through free and open elections. But back then, all leftist organizations, including radical laborites such as the International Workers of the World (Wobblies), tended to be grouped together under the umbrella term "Reds." Today "national security threat" is preferred.

Two months after the second round of bombings, Palmer established a new Radical Division within the Justice Department. It was closely aligned with the Justice Department's Bureau of Investigation, forerunner to the

FBI. The Bureau of Investigation had been created in 1908 by Charles Joseph Bonaparte, secretary of the navy and attorney general in President Theodore Roosevelt's cabinet. Known variously as the Imperial Peacock and Souphouse Charlie, Bonaparte was a grandson of Jerome, younger brother of Napoléon I, making him probably the only member of royalty to ever reach high office in the U.S. government.

Palmer appointed Hoover, an efficient and ambitious attorney in the Justice Department's Alien Enemy Unit, as chief of the new Radical Division. Hoover was twenty-four years old, the same age as the recently departed Carlo Valdinoli, and lived at home with his parents. His family had been in government service for two generations, and he was born and raised in the shadow of the Capitol.

Two institutions at Central High School in Washington had left a profound influence on young John Edgar. From the debate team he learned how to think logically and match wits with opponents. From the military drill team he learned discipline and respect for order. His boyhood nickname was Speedy because of his quickness in delivering groceries. He worked his way through the National University School of Law, later absorbed by George Washington University.

Hoover would have a succession of love interests, including the actress Dorothy Lamour and the mother of Ginger Rogers, and he considered marriage at least once. But like a priest committed to his vows, he saw service to God and country as his calling in life, and marriage would be an unacceptable diversion from his mission. After his mother died, the woman closest to him was his personal assistant, Helen Gandy, who stayed with him for fifty-four years. She never married, either.

The thing that impressed Palmer about Hoover was that the young man was a progressive like himself. The word had a different meaning back then than it does now. These days, "progressive" usually means "liberal." But in Palmer's day, both liberals and conservatives called themselves progressives if they believed in honest and efficient government that was free from political hanky-pank. Theodore Roosevelt, a Republican, was a progressive. So was Woodrow Wilson, a Democrat. The progressive ideals fit young Edgar like a favorite pair of old house shoes.

Hoover's new "Red squad" collected information on radicals from the Bureau of Investigation, the Department of Labor, the consular service, military intelligence, local police, and patriotic organizations such as the American Protective League. Hoover's marching orders were to crack down on politically dangerous individuals and groups. He would do that as field commander of the headline-grabbing Palmer Raids.

Legislative authority for the Palmer Raids lay first in the Espionage Act of 1917. It mandated imprisonment or death to anyone convicted of obtaining information on national defense that could be used to the injury of the United States or passed on to the advantage of any foreign nation. It also prohibited mailing anything advocating treason, insurrection, or forcible resistance to any U.S. law. The second law was the Immigration Act of 1918. It called for the deportation of aliens who believed in, advocated, or taught the violent overthrow of the U.S. government, or who simply belonged to any organization supporting those ends. Only a night sky in winter could have been wider in scope.

The Palmer Raids began in November 1919 and ran through January 1920. More than ten thousand communists, anarchists, and fellow travelers (sympathizers) were arrested in dozens of cities, but in the end most were released because they were not aliens, and only a few hundred were actually deported. It wasn't a big haul, considering the money and manpower devoted to the operations. But the mainstream media, for the most part, cheered the raids.

Those were stormy times for America. In addition to terrorist bombings, there were crippling labor strikes. In all, four million went out that year, a fifth of America's industrial workforce. Then there were the riots. During the war there had been student riots, antidraft riots and anti-German riots, along with race riots in East St. Louis and Houston. Now in the summer of 1919, twenty-six cities got caught in a new wave of race riots.

A common thread was a fear by returning white veterans that blacks who had migrated north during the war were taking their jobs and integrating their neighborhoods. In Chicago the riot was touched off by the drowning of an African American boy when he wandered into the white section of a beach. The fighting went on for seven days, resulting in 38 deaths and hundreds injured. In Washington, white veterans in saloons on a hot Saturday night heard that the police had released a black suspect questioned in an attempted sexual assault case against a white woman, the wife of a navy man. The white veterans, already angry about the shortage of jobs, invaded an

African American neighborhood. Armed black veterans counterattacked. President Wilson had to send in 2,000 soldiers and marines to restore order. After four days, 39 were dead and 150 injured by mobs on both sides.

Red Summer, the newspapers called it. Red flags seemed to be everywhere. It came to be known as the nation's first Red Scare. As would be the case later on during the fifties when the Cohens and other communists came under official scrutiny, many Americans feared that the very fabric of the nation was being shredded and burned by forces beyond their control. And the violence continued. Another anarchist bombing, in September 1920, killed 38 and injured 143 on Wall Street in New York. At the same time, the Ku Klux Klan was resurrected as a nativist organization opposed not only to African Americans but also to Jews, Catholics, and immigrants, especially Reds.

With all that was happening, and with local authorities either unable or unwilling to control matters, federal intervention could not be put off any longer. Hoover began reviewing hundreds of field reports every week on radical activities. He tapped into intelligence resources of the War Department, the State Department, the British embassy, the Royal Canadian Mounted Police. He studied *The Communist Manifesto* and the Comintern, and absorbed articles in radical sheets. Using his experience as a former clerk at the Library of Congress, he created a card-file system and kept tabs on two hundred thousand suspected subversives. He became the government's preeminent authority on radicals, whether they were Italian, Russian, German, or American.

Rooting out subversives was to become Hoover's lifelong obsession, especially in the years after the Second World War when a Georgian named Iosif Vissarionovich Dzhugashvili, alias Joseph Stalin, began to grab countries in Eastern Europe that he had not already occupied. Stalin's march toward the Atlantic was stopped after he failed to run the United States, France, and Britain out of West Berlin, which had the misfortune of lying in East Germany, the Soviet zone of occupation. Uncle Joe blockaded the city in April 1948, and the Western Allies countered with daily airlifts of food, coal, and medical supplies. President Harry S. Truman also deployed B-29s to Europe, the same model of plane that had dropped atomic bombs on Japan. Stalin took the hint and lifted the blockade.

But then China, the most populous nation in the world, with more than half a billion people, fell to Communist forces after a civil war that had been fought off and on for over twenty years. With Stalin and Mao Zedong at the helms of Russia and China, almost a third of the world's population lay trapped under Communism.

To many Americans, though, that was all a world away. In a nation insulated by postwar prosperity and complacency, the political adventurisms of Stalin and Mao were mostly just wire copy in the newspaper. They were interesting, for a few paragraphs, on the way to the sports page and the grocery ads. A long, hard war was over. Enemies on two continents had been roundly defeated. America was now protected by reliable allies and a growing nuclear arsenal. What could possibly happen that would upset the quiet suburban lifestyles of folks who preferred to spend their ample spare time with Jackie Gleason on TV and Bob Hope at the movies?

The answer came in August 1949 as the Russians tested their first atomic bomb in the Kazakh Soviet Socialist Republic. The test was detected when a U.S. spy plane flying over the area detected a sudden spike in radioactivity in the atmosphere, which could only have resulted from an atomic explosion. Western scientists called the Russian bomb Joe-1. Photographs showed it to be an almost exact copy of the Fat Man bomb the U.S. Army Air Forces had exploded over Nagasaki four years earlier. Now the Western alliance no longer had a monopoly on atomic weapons. Nuclear proliferation had begun.

That new threat was exploited in America by patriotic air-raid sirens such as Republican senator Joseph R. McCarthy, a pudgy, hard-drinking former Marine and judge from Wisconsin who claimed to possess a list of 205 known Communists employed in the U.S. government. Tail Gunner Joe never did name all the names he was supposed to have, but that didn't matter to his supporters, who blamed a decline in traditional American values on the liberal policies of Roosevelt and Truman.

McCarthyism, as it came to be known, coupled with the arrest of Manhattan Project spy Klaus Fuchs in Britain and the resulting roll-up of the Rosenbergs' network, all combined to create an atmosphere of fear in America that would be worsened by still another wave of bad news: the Korean War. The United States and Britain joined other United Nations forces to assist South Korea in turning back an invasion by Communist North Korean troops reinforced by China and the Soviet Union. Russia contributed 20,000 troops to North Korea, along with 300 tanks and 1,450 warplanes.[3]

With Korea, relations between East and West went full circle back to Old Bolshevik days. The Cold War was hot again. The spread of the international Communist conspiracy, as it was called, became the top national security priority for NATO and its counterintelligence agencies, including the FBI and MI5. It foreshadowed today's war on international Islamic terrorism.

THE ACCUSATION against the Cohens—the claim that they were radical Communists who had held party meetings in their apartment—was vague at best. It came with no apparent supporting evidence, and as hearsay or the product of an illegal wiretap, probably would never have seen the inside of a courtroom. But the FBI had a case to investigate, and they proceeded against Morris and Lona on the grounds of two statutes.

First was the Smith Act, also called the Registration Act of 1940. Advocating the violent overthrow of any government in the United States or belonging to any group encouraging such action was made a federal offense. The second law was the McCarran Act of 1950, which required Communist organizations to register with the U.S. attorney general. Additional ammunition came in President Truman's expansion of the FBI's authority to investigate espionage, sabotage, and subversive activities affecting American national security.

The case of the Cohens was classified as a "Security Matter C" (Communist), and all information about them was stamped secret. Since the first report on the Cohens had come from the New York division, it was designated the office of origin for the case. New York, with advice from headquarters in Washington, would direct the investigation in the months and years to come and would send out leads for other FBI offices to pursue.

The FBI espionage squad in the New York office drew the assignment to investigate the Cohens. The office had just moved to 290 Broadway from the federal courthouse two blocks away at 40 Center Street in Foley Square. This was the lower end of Manhattan, within sight of the Brooklyn Bridge, a neighborhood that used to be called Five Points. The Broadway location was the old Dun & Bradstreet Building, and some of the agents considered it a dump, but at least it got them out of the noisy courthouse. The size of the New York division had recently been increased from seven hundred to a thousand agents because of an increase in national security and criminal cases, and that was also a factor in moving to larger quarters.

The special agent in charge of the New York office in 1953 and supervisor of the Cohens' case overall was George P. Baxtrum Jr., who had been with the bureau since 1946. His methods of spying on Reds would later get him into trouble as he and other government employees were sued by the Socialist Workers Party of New York. The SWP alleged a "systematic campaign" of harassment including excessive interrogation, warrantless electronic surveillance, unauthorized mail covers, and burglaries dating back to 1938.[4]

The special agents working the Cohen case fit into the mold created by Director Hoover: college educated with a degree in law or accounting, though those requirements were relaxed in wartime or whenever the bureau needed men with special skills. In the thirties, when gangsters were terrorizing the Midwest, Hoover had hired numerous local cops, including an Oklahoma Indian, who were good at shootouts with criminals.[5] Later on, a young man was hired because of his athletic ability. He was assigned to a quiet field office and given a workload that allowed him time for personal training so that he might represent the bureau in the Olympics.

Special agents investigating the Cohens came from both urban and rural backgrounds. They were overwhelmingly male, white, Christian, middle class, and conservative. No beards or mustaches were allowed, no long hair, no earrings, no tattoos. Hoover barred homosexuals from employment because they would be vulnerable to blackmail from enemy agents. That policy was exploited by a Soviet embassy official in Washington who conducted late-night meets at a gay bar with journalists looking for confirmation (or denial) of leaked news tips.

"The FBI won't follow us in here," the Russian assured one reporter. "Hoover doesn't like his boys to go into queer joints."[6]

At the same time, Hoover wouldn't hire recruits with extreme political views; nor did he like men with moist palms or who somehow didn't fit in with the conformist image of the FBI. One agent was fired because Hoover thought he looked like a truck driver.

Special agents assigned to the Cohens had been taught how to conduct investigations, gather evidence, and testify in court in a direct, businesslike manner. When interviewing someone, the rule was to be courteous, respect-ful, and patient. Heavy-handed techniques, even cursing, were verboten, though agents were trained in hand-to-hand combat and firearms, and were ready to defend themselves if attacked. An old adage in the bureau was to never draw your weapon unless you intended to use it, and then shoot to kill.

Agents investigating the Cohens worked in pairs, as was bureau practice. Each agent took notes, and when they wrote their report they compared their data for accuracy. They wore what came to be known as the FBI uni-form: snap-brim fedora, dark business suit, white shirt, and conservative tie of a color that matched the lining of the jacket. And the jacket was not supposed to be taken off in public, even in the dog days of summer. Bu-reau cars—budget models of Fords, Chevrolets, and Plymouths in varying shades of black—were equipped with Motorola two-way radios, the same model used by taxis. That meant that anyone with a scanner could eavesdrop on their calls, so code words were used when talking on the air. Pay phones were preferred for the most important calls, and since the cars weren't air-conditioned and the plastic seat covers tended to heat up, getting out to drop a nickel on the office was a blessed relief.

Work was begun on the Cohens' case when a pair of agents walked over to the New York Police Department and had the Bureau of Special Services and Investigations run the names of Morris and Lona through their files. Older agents usually drew routine assignments like that—the cigar squad. But the NYPD didn't have anything on the Cohens. No complaints, no arrests, no prosecutions. Not even a parking ticket. Nor were they listed as having participated in any public demonstrations. No photographs, no fingerprints, no driver's license.

At the same time, other agents (these younger) started knocking on doors on East Seventy-First Street around Second Avenue in Manhattan, where the Cohens were reportedly residing. The Upper East Side was not a district known to be a hotbed of radical activities. It was a sun-dappled neighborhood of trees, limousines, and uniformed doormen where good, solid Republican stock resided in posh apartments and townhouses. They gave cocktail parties, read the *Herald Tribune* and held on to their "I Like Ike" buttons.

Making the rounds of the neighborhood, the agents used the standard bureau procedure of introducing themselves courteously, showing their badges, and asking questions without revealing exactly why they were curious. Some respondents were cooperative, though agents from small towns often discovered that when it came to interviewing New Yorkers, hospitality might not be the rule of the day. Don't know nothing, ain't seen nothing, ain't heard nothing.

Then the agents had to use whatever powers of logic, charm, or humor they possessed. If that didn't work, and the interviewee became verbally abusive, the agents might suggest a chat downtown. Anybody who listened to *Gang Busters* on the radio knew what that meant: a hard chair, a bright light, a long night.

Meanwhile, New York informants in the Communist Party of the United States of America were questioned about the Cohens. By the early fifties, the CPUSA had been infiltrated so thoroughly that some cells included a high percentage of FBI spies. Across the river in Newark, the secretary of the Communist Party and his wife were FBI operatives and won a new car after writing the winning essay in an Americanism contest.[7]

Tipsters usually met with agents in the usual places frequented by people who had secrets to peddle—subway stations, parks, automats, coffee shops down shady side streets. Some of those contacts confirmed that Morris and Lona were indeed committed Communists. But if they were, why hadn't they been seen at the party halls? Were they intentionally keeping a low profile for some reason?

Finally somebody provided the agents with an exact address for the Cohens: 178 East Seventy-First, an aging brownstone four blocks from Central Park and a ten-minute walk from Hunter College. Not luxurious like some of its neighbors, but still a comfortable old heap. Residents of the building reported that Morris and Lona had moved out two or three years before, without leaving a forwarding address. No one seemed to have any idea where they went. They just up and left one night. Walked out and never came back. Didn't take their clothes, Lona's jewelry, or even their toothbrushes. The landlord said that Morris's father came over later to clean the place out.

Back to the sidewalks, then. Visit more fruit stands, delicatessens, laundries, snowball stands. Each FBI team was assigned a certain number of streets to cover each day, and the inquiries were conducted as late as they could find people awake. All leads had to be checked, and like infantrymen tramping across Europe in the war, the agents did a lot of hoofing. Where to now? Eight blocks down, six blocks over. No buses in sight, no taxis. Where did we park the car? Sometimes there were no streetlights. Many buildings didn't have elevators. But most of them had only five or six floors, more or less. Walk to the top and work your way down. Good for the heart.

The days got short, the nights turned cold. Autumn rain was followed by winter snow. Phone books and other public records were used in checking out leads. A pretext phone call was the quickest way to make an initial contact. The agent might introduce himself as a representative of the public library with a claim that they were holding a book for Morris Cohen. Sometimes a pretext call was productive. Sometimes it wasn't. You say there's no Morris Cohen at this number? Do you happen to know—hello?

Hit the streets again. Check that building you checked last week, and the week before. Say hello again to the same grumpy old men, suspicious women, mean dogs. This place smells the same way it did last time. Still noisy, too. How can anybody sleep up here? Day after day, night after night, the agents fulfilled that odd destiny that cops seem to have with doors: unmarked doors, wrong doors, slammed doors. Thank you ma'am, give us a call if you hear—

Somebody said the Cohens had moved to New Jersey. The Newark office pursued that lead. Agents over there found an abundant supply of Cohens, and one in particular looked promising. M. Cohen was written in pencil above his doorbell. But he wasn't the one they were looking for.

Just how many people named Cohen *were* there in New York and New Jersey? Census records from that time show dozens of residential addresses occupied by Cohens in New York City alone. If two or three Cohens lived at each address, then the total figure would run into the hundreds.

The new year shuffled in. The case was going nowhere. New York was the biggest office in the country and they had bank robbers to catch, kidnappers to track down, and twenty thousand military draft and deserter investigations dating back to 1940. "Old dog cases" was the term. But leads on the Cohens trickled in and were dutifully checked. In February 1954 a source reported that Morris had been in the army. Why hadn't somebody thought of that before?

Two gentlemen from the cigar squad pulled on overcoats and galoshes and tramped down to the Veterans Administration office at 252 Seventh

Avenue. There, in a bound volume found on a shelf in the records room, the bureau at last got a real break. Morris Cohen was indeed in the VA's register. A creak of a file cabinet, and his file was dug out. It included a record of Morris's army service in World War II, along with his description: five feet nine, 155 pounds, forty-three years old, brown eyes, and brown hair turning gray. There was a photo of Technician 5th Class Cohen, a set of his fingerprints, a sample of his handwriting, information on his wife, and the name and address of his mother and father.

At last, after two months of communing with dial tones, greasy asphalt, and mildewed stairwells, the agents had solid leads to work. Now they could speed up the laborious process of putting together a history of Morris and Lona Cohen. Their inquiries were about to spread into other states, and other countries. At the peak of the investigation the bureau would send wanted fliers to all NATO member nations and to embassy legations in Asia and Latin America.

2 STUDENT RADICAL

Harry and Sarah Cohen, Morris's parents, lived in the Bronx at 2020 Walton Avenue, apartment 6G, according to the VA file. An FBI agent made a pretext phone call and Harry answered. In response to the agent's questions, Harry said he did not know where his son was and had not seen him in some time. That wasn't much to go on. A mail cover was ordered. But the inspection of letters delivered to the Cohens' address didn't yield much useful information beyond the fact that Morris was receiving government disability checks. Apparently he had suffered frostbite during the war. The VA was sending him $15.75 (about $122.00 in today's money) each month, and none of the checks had been returned.

Following the pretext call, a couple of agents drove up to Walton Avenue, a classic Bronx pushcart neighborhood of newsboys, street peddlers, produce stands, and horse-drawn wagons.[1] The building at 2020 wasn't fancy, just another redbrick walk-up with rusty fire escapes clinging to the outside walls. It was a tenement, but not a slum. The apartments were built for working folks, sturdy but basic, heated by steam radiators. Air-conditioning was provided by electric fans and open windows, and on really hot nights people slept outside on the fire escapes. Some of the kitchens still had iceboxes instead of electric refrigerators. A man wearing leather on his shoulder lugged in a block of ice every day and loaded it into the top of the box.

A few tenants had black-and-white television sets, but shows that would soon be popular on TV—including the *Jack Benny Program*, *Amos 'n' Andy*, and *Gunsmoke*—were still on the radio. That was AM radio, which sizzled with static whenever a thunderstorm passed overhead. And people read.

They read a lot. The fifties were the glory days of magazines: *Life, Look, Time, Newsweek, Redbook, Photoplay, Ladies' Home Journal.* Hemingway and Faulkner were still writing novels. So were Steinbeck, Michener, Kathleen Winsor, and Daphne du Maurier. And New York had more daily newspapers than most cities today have TV stations. The giant was the *Daily News*, America's first tabloid. Its circulation of two million daily and four million on Sunday rivaled that of the London mass-appeal papers such as the *Daily Mirror* and the *Daily Express.*

Harry Cohen invited the two FBI agents into his apartment. He was a handsome, amiable sort, elderly but well-groomed, with gray hair, an engaging smile, and bright, confident eyes. Dressed up in a suit, he looked like a Wall Street banker. He had come to America in 1905 from Tarashcha, Ukraine, which had been part of the Russian Empire, a land so vast and so devoid of modern roads and bridges that it took months to drive across it in a car. Tarashcha was an important Jewish shtetl; Boris Thomashefsky, the Jewish American actor and singer, was born there. The entire *oblast* was under the protection (some said under the thumb) of the Cossacks, the traditional Russian national army that operated separately from the Imperial Army. The lovely old town had suffered its share of anti-Semitism when Harry was growing up there, but things got really nasty in 1905, the year of the first Russian revolution.

Nicholas II, who looked like his first cousin, King George V of England, suppressed the revolution in the cities first. Then he dispatched punitive expeditions to snuff out resistance in provincial towns like Tarashcha. The failure of the Russian Revolution of 1905, along with continuing pogroms, drove millions of Russians and East Europeans to the West in search of new lives. Harry Cohen might have been involved in revolutionary activity in Ukraine, perhaps making speeches or handing out revolutionary literature. Or maybe he was just sick of the same old, same old in imperial Russia. Either way, he simply left.

Harry settled first up in East Harlem, where a recession had made new housing available to immigrants at attractive rates. Harlem had been a center of Jewish and Italian culture for years, a diverse neighborhood of delicatessens, sweatshops, famous theatres, and opulent apartment buildings standing shoulder to shoulder with firetraps. Harry began peddling fruit and soon met Sarah Matlowski, a smart, attractive brunette two years younger. Sarah, also known as Sonya, had come over from Vilnius a year after Harry arrived.

Vilnius was the capital of Lithuania, and almost half the city was Jewish. Vilnius had more than a hundred synagogues and prayer houses, and six daily Jewish newspapers, giving it the nickname the Jerusalem of Lithuania. But when Sarah was growing up, the country was under the yoke of Nicholas II. The same conditions that drove Harry out of Ukraine undoubtedly forced Sarah to leave Lithuania. And like Harry, she brought to America a revolutionary zeal.

Sarah was a determined, focused woman with plump cheeks and a Kewpie-doll mouth. After a short courtship, she and Harry married and moved into an apartment at 40 East 100th Street, a narrow East Harlem thoroughfare dominated by five-story brick buildings. At night in the rain, the haloed streetlamps marched in surveyed lines toward a distant point of convergence at the East River, beyond which the Cohens would soon find their permanent home. Morris was born July 2, 1910, at the 100th Street address, and the family might have preferred to stay there indefinitely. But with the extension of a subway line into Harlem, the demographics changed. Cultures clashed. Race riots followed. The Cohens joined the Jewish migration across the East River to the Bronx, where Harry opened a larger and more profitable fruit stand.

In those days the Bronx was still the kind of quiet, shady village that Harlem had been a few years before. There were few automobiles. Trolley cars, wagons, bicycles, dogs, and shoe leather ruled the streets. Many of the blocks were still undeveloped, with occasional apartment houses sprouting up amid vistas of meadowland. People kept chickens, goats, and cows in their yards, which undoubtedly contributed to the sweetness of the air. The Cohens lived at 241 East 169th Street before moving to 1244 Grand Concourse, the wide thoroughfare built during the turn-of-the-century City Beautiful movement and designed to be the Champs Élysée of the Bronx. Then they moved to Walton Avenue, three blocks off the Grand Concourse. Walton Avenue would be the family's last address in the borough.

In the autobiography he later wrote for his personnel file at Soviet intelligence headquarters, known in the spy trade as Moscow Center, Morris said that when he was growing up, Russian immigrants often gathered at his family's apartment to listen to records they had brought to America.[2]

They sang folk songs and danced the polka and the *gopak*, the Cossack dance from Ukraine that involved much clapping, shouting, kicking, and jumping, which the neighbors on the floor below surely appreciated. Then the old folks told stories told about mysterious and loving Mother Russia. For the rest of his life Morris would remember those tales. Like Xenophon Kalamatiano, he grew up with a fascination for a country he revered like an exotic relative he had never met. And since Harry and Sarah were dedicated Communists, there were also impassioned political discussions.[3] One time when Morris was very young his parents took him to hear a speech by the radical journalist John Reed, which left a lasting impression on him.

Nostalgia for the old country aside, Jewish immigrants in America discovered early on that they had escaped one form of evil—Russian anti-Semitism—only to encounter its cousin in the New World. The United States was a segregated nation, but in older cities like New York it went beyond just racial partition. There were Italian neighborhoods, Irish neighborhoods, Spanish neighborhoods, German neighborhoods, and Jewish neighborhoods, and for self-protection, each group staked out its own claim. Hank Greenberg, the baseball player, described it this way: "Kids down in the Village thought the national pastime was beating up kids of other nationalities. On one of the nearby blocks was a group of Irish families. When their kids weren't fighting each other, they were fighting us Jewish kids."[4]

Other affronts had to be endured: many jobs, restaurants, hotels, apartment buildings, schools, recreation clubs, and vacation resorts were not open to Jews. So they took whatever work they could find and spent the rest of their lives trying to provide a better life for their children. Enter the Communist Party, which offered immigrants from Russia and Eastern Europe, many of whom couldn't speak English, something to supplement their lives beyond the daily grind.

There were different kinds of Communists, just as there were different kinds of Democrats and Republicans. Some were the fiery revolutionaries that Moscow doted on, absorbing all the rhetoric of the Comintern and looking forward to the day when the oppressive, imperialistic, capitalistic régime in Washington would be toppled by an inflamed proletariat and a USSA, United States of Soviet America, installed in its place. Other Communists were restless refugees from the left wing of various socialist and labor parties, or adventurous liberals who admired the CPUSA for defending the union movement and promoting civil rights. And some went to the meetings simply to get away from the wife, or the husband, for a while.

The *Daily Worker* and the *Jewish Daily Forward* were available for those who could read English; for others, there were *Russky Golos* (Voice of Russia), Soviet newsreels, and Eisenstein movies. The party joined in New York's big May Day parade, and a Labor Day dance gave singles a chance to get acquainted. The party also rallied to help members in need, taking up collections for comrades in the hospital and throwing rent parties to save families from eviction.

But party meetings also had a reputation for being long, boring affairs, hot in summer and cold in winter, sometimes dominated by crackpots and windbags who seemed to have nothing else to do than ramble on about obscure topics that would drive a hangman to distraction. Then there were the committees. They met and they met and they met. There was a committee for almost every occasion. Your husband was threatening to drop out of the party? A committee was convened to investigate. And just to be sure nobody got to go home early, committees met to plan agendas for committee meetings the next day. All this was available to members for only ten cents a week in dues.

Boria Sax, son of Saville Sax, a courier for Theodore Hall, a spy in the atomic network that Morris and Lona would later run, said the New York Russian Jewish community of his parents' day had its own expectations and deliberately set itself apart from the culture of its adopted country.[5] Like other immigrant groups, many Russian Jews hid behind fond memories of the old country and forgot the suffering they had left back there. "They tended to be very suspicious of American society at large," Sax said. "They identified mainstream society with their former persecutors and just didn't want to have too much to do with it." Communism, he said, was a sort of "substitute Judaism."

That profile didn't fit Harry and Sarah Cohen. Not exactly. While they did retain their Jewish and Communist identities and a nostalgia for bygone days, they also assimilated their two boys into American life by speaking English at home and foregoing a religious education for them. Morris and Abner were enrolled in public schools where they joined other American kids in singing the national anthem, reciting the pledge of allegiance, and discovering jazz and comic books and Yankee Stadium on spring afternoons.

It seemed to work, except that Morris would have trouble later with the part about the pledge of allegiance. It wasn't that he turned his back on that vow of loyalty to his country. But as time went on, he took other pledges of conflicting loyalties that pulled at him just as strongly. From the time he was nursed on his mother's lap, his soul was a house divided.

THE REPORT written by the special agents who drove up to Walton Avenue for that first interview with Harry Cohen in 1953 did not mention Sarah. She had been in bad health and apparently was not available. Harry did the talking. He said he had no idea their son was in trouble. Morris had been a substitute teacher in city schools, a man of good reputation. What had he done?

The agents were dependably vague on that. But this was right after the execution of the Rosenbergs, and surely Harry knew the agents were in his living room because of the past Communist Party ties of Morris and his wife. Their other son, Abner, had never bought the party line. He was in New Jersey operating a wholesale grocery business.

Harry reported that he and Sarah had received several letters from Morris in the weeks after he and Lona left New York suddenly in 1950. Morris had written that they were working on a small farm somewhere between Los Angeles and Fresno, and that he had done some private teaching. After that, the letters stopped.

Harry said his son's long, unexplained absence had been a source of considerable sorrow for him and Sarah, and was a contributing factor to their declining health. He said Morris had always been a fine son and a good boy, and he could not explain why he had just up and left. Since he and his son had always been on good terms, it would seem logical that he should know something, Harry said. But he didn't. Harry insisted that he himself had a good reputation personally and professionally, had always tried to be a good and loyal citizen, and would help the bureau if he could.

It wasn't a lot to go on. But the Los Angeles, Sacramento, and San Francisco FBI offices were notified and they searched California state records. But no driver's license, teaching certificate, or voter registration could be found for either Morris or Lona Cohen. More leads were pursed from Cohen's VA file. One of them took agents to the high school Morris had attended.

James Monroe High, just south of the Bronx Zoo, opened in 1924, the year before Morris enrolled there after attending a lower school for fast learners. Monroe High was a big five-story brick sun blocker built at Boynton Avenue and East 172nd from blueprints used for construction of several other city schools. Monroe would go on to achieve a notable academic and artistic reputation—Leon Lederman, the Nobel laureate in physics, was a graduate, as were jazz musician Stan Getz and editorial cartoonist Jules Feiffer. A Monroe alumna, actress Estelle Reiner, in the movie *When Harry Met Sally*, delivered that immortal line: "I'll have what she's having."

But Monroe in the twenties was better known as a sports powerhouse, and its gridiron was where Morris Cohen excelled. He was overweight for his height, but he was strong and had sturdy legs and that made him perfect as a lineman. He started at guard on the Monroe football squad that won the Bronx championship in 1927, only the second year they fielded a team. One of Cohen's teammates, Edward Lending, said that while he personally was "trying" to play football, Morris was the "real thing."[6]

Morris acquired his first nickname while playing football at Monroe. The story was that when an opposing player hit him, he made an "oink!" sound. This evolved into "Unk." His coach was Joseph "Doc" Weidman, a former football and lacrosse star at New York University. Weidman would go on to coach for years and would be remembered as one of the great mentors of high school athletes in the Bronx.

Hank Greenberg played football his senior year with Morris. "I was an end, and most of the plays went through the middle where you had to do a little blocking," Greenberg wrote in his autobiography. "Defensively, you had to protect for the end run, but it wasn't my type of game. It was all brute strength and a lot of bruises. . . ."[7] Hank went back to baseball, and after graduation he ignored religious taunts from fans as he fought his way up in the major leagues to achieve fame as a power hitter for the Detroit Tigers. Hammering Hank, they called him.

Morris took the usual courses in high school—English, history, arithmetic, and civics, along with music and drawing. He graduated in 1928, after three years, though his grades weren't much to brag about. Dr. Leo Weitz, principal of Monroe, remembered Morris as maintaining about a 70 average. But he added that Morris liked to talk up sports and made friends easily. In an argument, Weitz noted, Morris always seemed to take the side of the underdog.[8]

Morris enrolled at New York University in the autumn of 1928. With an enrollment of forty thousand it was the largest urban university in the country. When it was founded in 1831, NYU's announced mission was to offer education on the new European model that was both modern and classical. An endowment fund was established to keep it independent of religious or political pressure, and by the end of the nineteenth century NYU was open to women and blacks. More importantly for Morris Cohen, it did not impose a Jewish quota the way the Ivy League universities did.

Morris took mostly business courses at the Washington Square College campus in Greenwich Village—accounting, economics, contracts, management, and marketing—along with one semester of journalism theory under Assistant Professor Whipple, meeting Tuesday and Thursday afternoons for an hour. But as before, academics were not Morris's forte, as evidenced by his grades at NYU—mostly Cs, with a few Ds and Fs. Other than politics, his passion as always was sports.

Being an avid fan, Morris would have grown up reading sportswriters Harry Cross in the *Herald Tribune*, Sid Mercer and Garry Schumacher in the *Journal*, and Joe Williams in the *World-Telegram*. Bronx broadcaster Ted "Mile a Minute" Husing called Yankee games on CBS, and Tennessean Grantland Rice narrated "Sportlight" in Paramount newsreels. Morris knew the teams, he knew the players, he knew the stats. How many home runs did Babe Ruth hit last year? How many RBIs? Morris could tell you in a snap. He was a walking copy of *Sporting News*. When he had time, he continued to play pickup games in Grotona Park, and he retained ties to his alma mater by visiting Doc Weidman during afternoon practice sessions at Monroe. He also served as an officer of the Monroe Varsity Club.

Morris and his brother Abner worked as waiters in upstate resorts during the summers, and at odd jobs in New York City and New Jersey the rest of the year. But the economy had imploded with the stock market crash of 1929, and during the resulting Great Depression, money got tight for the family. That forced Morris to drop out of NYU. It might have seemed his college career was over. But then he went south, literally, and began a new chapter in his life.

IN 1931 MORRIS WON a football scholarship, probably through the efforts of Doc Weidman and the old coaches' network, to Mississippi Agricultural & Mechanical College, which a year later would become Mississippi State College (now Mississippi State University). It was in a part of the country where the local accent sounded like a foreign language to a boy from the Bronx, and in summer the sun was blinding, the heat staggering, and the humidity heavy enough to serve as gravy.

When Morris arrived, the school had an enrollment of twelve hundred and offered mostly agricultural, science, and business courses. But it was expanding rapidly. It had the largest state appropriation of any college in Mississippi and claimed the biggest cafeteria in the world, serving six thousand pounds of steak a week.[9] The Opéra Comique Company of New York performed at MSC while Morris was there; so did the Chicago Civic Opera. The Shakespearean Players of London came over to stage *The Merchant of Venice*, and the Avon Players followed with *Hamlet*. Touring black gospel shows were popular, as were Chief Big Snake and his Pueblo Indians dance show, and Herby Kay's jazz band. The MSC debate team took on Cambridge University, to no decision, but the maroon-and-white rifle team shot down the opposition from the U.S. Military Academy and the New York Stock Exchange. However, when the MSC drill team paid a visit to the campus of their blood rival, Ole Miss, they were assaulted with rotten fruit.

Mississippi State was located in Starkville, county seat of Oktibbeha County, just east of Delta country. Except for the courthouse and a few stores, the college was the town's main reason for existence. Starkville had a population of thirty-six hundred and was surrounded by thousands of acres of cattle, cotton, and pine trees. The main industries in town were a dairy and a cotton mill, but the college offered plenty of jobs to locals, a welcome thing during the Depression. Oktibbeha County, like the rest of the country, was legally dry, though bootleggers could always be found to minster to the needs of thirsty students. Downtown at the Rex Theatre, a matinee ticket cost twenty cents. For fine dining there was fried chicken at Peoples Café, ice cream and blueberry pie at the Bell Café, and barbecue at Watts Pig Stand. One main highway came through. They had one traffic light, and it was turned off at night. All in all, a *Last Picture Show* kind of place.

As at most southern schools, football was virtually a religion at Mississippi State, more popular than anything the churches could offer the day after a big game. But State had been struggling for years to remain competitive in the tough Southern Conference, which was about to split into the Southeastern Conference and the Atlantic Coast Conference. Morris, coming from a big-city championship team, seemed like a promising recruit for the rebuilding Bulldog football program. In return, Morris looked forward to playing against some of America's powerhouse teams, Alabama, Tennessee, and Tulane.

Unk joined the freshman football team, which was scheduled to play five games that season. Their coach was hard-driving K. E. "Cotton" Klindworth, an A&M graduate and former semipro baseball player. The Baby Bulldogs defeated East Mississippi Junior College, 14–13, in their opener, but Unk hurt his knee in the game and that ended his playing career.

Somebody in the proverbial front office liked Morris, though, and he was kept on scholarship as an athletic trainer. He ran the big modern training room in the new athletic dormitory, and during his second year he added duties as manager of the boxing team. After the Bulldog fighters won ten of sixteen matches, Morris was awarded a letter M to sew on his athletic jacket. The boxing coach was Russell Crane, a physical education instructor from Illinois. He might have influenced Morris to go on to graduate school later at the University of Illinois.

Unk's sports background also landed him a job as a writer for Mississippi State's sports information office. Dr. Ben Hilbun, former public relations director at MSC, remembered Morris as a fast-paced, good-natured boy who liked to talk. Not just a talker but a "great talker," Hilbun said.[10] Morris's new journalism job got him additional work as a sports correspondent for a daily newspaper in Tennessee, the *Memphis Press-Scimitar*.

The editor of the *Press-Scimitar* was Edward J. Meeman, who in earlier years had been a rising talent in the Socialist Party of Indiana. His mentor was Eugene Debs, who had been grooming Meeman to eventually take over the party. But after touring with Debs in his presidential bid, Meeman said goodbye to all that and signed on with Scripps-Howard, a middle-of-the-road, old-money Republican newspaper chain matched in size nationwide only by the populist Hearst group. When Morris went to work for the *Press-Scimitar*, Meeman had just returned from a fact-finding tour of Nazi Germany with other American editors. What he saw over there appalled him, and the *Press-Scimitar* became one of America's crusading antifascist papers, a situation that undoubtedly was not lost on Morris.

Several of Morris's former classmates at Mississippi State later told FBI agents that Cohen never mentioned politics. Others recalled that he was quite outspoken in his support of the Communist Party, which would not have been an unusual thing, since Depression America was rife with radical college politics. And alternative political ideas were not just confined to campuses. Three counties away from MSC, some Mississippians had organized a socialist commune.

With his prestigious status as a trainer/manager, Morris got his own room in the athletic dormitory. He was active in the drama club and in 1934 was one of the organizers of Sigma Phi Zeta, the first Jewish fraternity at Mississippi State. They didn't have a house, so their first mixer was held at the Young Men's Christian Association. Later they organized a picnic attended by both students and townspeople.

Morris was a student in the College of Business and Industry at MSC, and his grades began to improve as soon as he arrived at Starkville. In his first year he made mostly Bs and Cs, with a few As. The next two years he took twenty-eight courses and made A in twenty of them. He was awarded a bachelor of arts degree on May 29, 1934. His graduation picture in the *Reveille*, the MSC yearbook, shows a handsome young man in coat and tie, smiling pleasantly. He has slimmed down and he looks confident and well groomed, the very image of an ambitious business-school grad on his way to corporate success. After graduation he remained an athletic trainer for another year, and enrolled in graduate school, taking courses in French, English research, and political theories.

In 1935, Morris's last year at MSC, the Bulldogs had their first winning football season in thirteen years, going 8–3 with big wins over Alabama and Army. Morris's picture in the 1935 yearbook shows him wearing an athletic department sweatshirt, smiling as always. His nickname at State was Abe, short for Abraham, which in Hebrew means "father of a multitude," which fit his role as boss of the training room.

"Abie was so efficient in his work as trainer that when he got through with a charley horse it looked like a mere mosquito bite," the photo caption reads. "He was always on the job and is largely responsible for the success the team met with."[11]

Morris's years at Mississippi State were good for him. He was on his own, away from the security of his home turf, and he developed both intellectually and professionally. He had probably known no one at Mississippi State before he arrived there and he learned to not only survive but also to prosper in a strange environment, relying on his wits and the amiability he had picked up from his father. But now, with a business degree and a year of grad school under his belt, it was time to move on.

MORRIS SPENT THE SUMMER of 1935 the way he had for the past two years, waiting on tables at Jewish resorts in the Catskills. Hundreds of those summer places dotted the landscape in upstate New York, mostly in Sullivan and Ulster counties—the Borscht Belt, named after the cold beet soup popular with Jewish diners. Some of the hotels were middling in quality. Others were ritzy with swimming pools, tennis courts, candlelit dining rooms, and nightclubs. Many of the performers at the clubs had come out of vaudeville. Some, such as Sid Caesar and Danny Kaye, would go on to fame in radio, television, and the movies. But among all this talent and luxury there was still a working class that was paid petty wages to clean up after the guests. And this being the thirties, some of them inevitably were political radicals. All of which offered Morris still another opportunity to sharpen what the Communist Party called agitprop (agitation and propaganda) skills. He did this by joining, possibly organizing, a couple of strikes by hotel employees up there.

But that summer was different in a significant way for Morris. Before leaving the Bronx again in September to continue his graduate studies, he joined the National Student League. They were conducting a "school for preparation" in New York, and he was probably recruited there. It's not clear when he went to full membership in the CPUSA. At times he said it was 1935, then 1936.

The National Student League had been formed in New York in 1931 after some students at City College of New York (CCNY) got suspended for their antimilitarist activities. The NSL was a child of the Young Communist League, and like its parent it demanded lower tuition fees, academic freedom, abolition of compulsory religious services and Reserve Officers' Training Corps programs, political equality for "Negroes," unemployment insurance, and student control of student affairs.[12] But most of all, the YCL and NSL and their Socialist Party counterpart, the Student League for Industrial Democracy, stood foursquare against war.

The National Student League had formed chapters at high school and college campuses across the country and sponsored a nationwide strike of fifteen thousand students during a Student Anti-War Week in 1934. It wasn't a general strike in the organized labor sense, but a one-hour walkout from classes. Some speeches were made, and the Oxford Pledge was read. That was a vow, borrowed from Oxford University in England, not to support the government in any future war. Larger NSL walkouts would follow in 1935 and 1936, the latter drawing at least half a million participants.

The National Student League billed itself as a militant action group participating in working-class struggles. It followed the Comintern line in claiming that the USSR was the first country in the world where the basis for modern imperialistic war, the drive for capitalist profits, had been abolished. The NSL also opposed fascism on campus. That was a safe position to take. But they further wanted to abolish college sports programs. Apparently that didn't deter Morris, who owed most of his college career thus far to an athletic scholarship.

IN THE AUTUMN OF 1935, Morris headed west to the University of Illinois at Urbana-Champaign. Like Mississippi State, Illinois was a land-grant institution offering courses in science, engineering, military science, and agriculture. Indeed, they prided themselves on their famous corn and hogs. But there were differences. Illinois's enrollment of 10,362 was much larger than that of Mississippi State. And Illinois had women students, and a few black students, which MSC didn't have. There was also a campus radio station and a daily student newspaper that didn't hesitate to publicize campus radical activities, few as they were.

Urbana-Champaign, with 389 retail stores and a population of twenty-three thousand in 1935, was a two-and-a-half-hour ride from Chicago on the Illinois Central's mainline Illini train.[13] The university was surrounded by vast farmland, as hot as the South, but drier, with a spaciousness that left you parched and lethargic. Sunsets over the prairies were close to spiritual experiences, though, and cool weather did arrive on time.

When viewed together as one community, Urbana-Champaign appeared to be a typical small American city of the time, with shady lawns, a bandstand, a water tower, a Main Street patrolled by quaint turn-of-the-century brick buildings.

But life in this neck of the woods had a certain edge to it. This was the middle of the Midwest in the middle of the thirties. John Dillinger, Baby Face Nelson, Ma Barker, and "Creepy" Karpis had terrorized the region with submachine guns and souped-up getaway cars. (A Caddy was faster flat out, gangsters claimed, but a Ford was better on hills.) The local police were on constant lookout for mobsters slipping in from Chicago, and while Morris was a student there the cops collared six characters who arrived in a stolen car, apparently intent on making a large withdrawal from a local bank.[14]

Morris enrolled in graduate school in English on September 13 as a nonresident. Townspeople operated private rooming houses for students, and Morris moved into a Victorian pile at 104 East John Street in Champaign. It was a pleasant, tree-lined drive a few blocks west of the campus. It was also just south of the local red-light district, which got raided several times that fall by local vice officers—in student argot, the pussy posse.

Morris's new acquaintances at his rooming house gave him his third nickname—Ape—because of his heavy body hair. Morris took out a mail subscription to the *Daily Worker*, a small Stalinist foghorn published by the CPUSA in New York, and immediately got on the house telephone to start making contacts for various National Student League political-action projects he envisioned. Other students in the house complained that he was monopolizing the phone and ruining their social lives.

Morris and his NSL comrades at Illinois were a small minority of the student body, just a few pesky flies on the screen door. But they felt that their strength lay not in their numbers but in their sense of history and purpose. They bubbled with passion and were tirelessly confident in their worldview. They lived to argue. They argued with students and they argued with professors, always with the kind of "facts" that their opponents would have a hard time disproving, such as the claim that Russia had abolished capitalist profits.

Young Communists like the NSL troops turned their noses up at the idea of a university as a community of independent thinkers investigating issues in a fair and disinterested way. That smacked of liberalism. Communists hated liberals. Liberals stood for tolerance, moderation, and compromise, a surrender of revolutionary principles. The NSL recruits went to college to do political work, to confront, to organize, to make noise. It was their mission, just as other comrades might be sent to organize strikes in factories. The University of Illinois did not have a background as a politically aware place, so for Morris it was a cake waiting to be cut.

Morris's organizing efforts quickly showed results. While fraternity and sorority students were running around in nighttime pajama races and cheering the Fighting Illini in their big game with Southern Cal, Morris and his NSL comrades were enlisting some religious groups to help them sponsor a "We Don't Want War" rally. The meeting drew a good turnout the night of October 10 at the Wesley Foundation, the Methodist Church on campus. Speeches were made by Jewish, Catholic, and Baptist clergy, and the audience voted to send a letter to President Roosevelt commending him on his recent embargo of arms to Mussolini's Italy.[15]

Morris's next big project was a peace mobilization meeting to be held on November 11, Armistice Day. The NSL and six other campus groups had tried to organize a student strike for peace the previous year on that date, but after what the press called a violent discussion, the strike was called off.

The NSL's petition for official university recognition had been turned down by a student senate committee in 1934. Charges of communist sympathies and radicalism were not denied by the organization, it was reported at the time. But a lack of recognition didn't seem to mean much more than the fact that the group could not meet in university-owned buildings or receive university financial support. The NSL continued to operate openly on campus and now, in 1935, they announced they were going to stage another mass meeting.

Morris was named to head up a National Student League committee to contact people and drum up participation in the planned peace rally. Under his direction they got more than twenty campus and town organizations to endorse the program. Those included several women's groups such as the American Association of University Women, Alpha Kappa Alpha sorority, the Cosmopolitan Club, the Baptist Women's Missionary Society, the Young Women's Christian Association, and the Women's International League for Peace and Freedom.

As the day for the mobilization approached, students at a number of other campuses across the country staged large peace demonstrations. More than a thousand turned out for a boisterous rally at the University of Chicago, shouting "Down with war!" In Champaign a minor riot broke out as a crowd of students, some of whom might not have been too sober, formed a two-block long snake line and danced their way down Wright Street into the town's business district. Actually, it wasn't a war protest, but a football pep rally. But after the celebrants broke a bus window and rampaged through a movie theatre, police arrived with riot batons to break up the festivities. Reporters said the cops went about their work with enthusiasm.[16]

The business-district invasion had been preceded by a riot of Urbana high school students eleven days earlier after a Halloween party got out of hand. Three people had been hurt, one seriously, and a number of windshields were smashed.[17] So tensions were a little high as Armistice Day approached. Urbana and Champaign police were standing by to assist the campus cops, as were sheriff's deputies and state troopers.

As it turned out, the peace rally was a peaceful one. A modest-sized crowd of three hundred, including students, faculty, clergy, and townspeople, gathered at eight o'clock on the chilly night of November 11. Because the rally had so many respectable sponsors, the student senate allowed it to be held inside Smith Music Hall as long as no resolutions were passed and no political propaganda was allowed.

The meeting was a curious mixture of calls for both peace, and force.[18] A minister implored the audience to eliminate the spirit of hate from the hearts of men to expose the horror, selfish greed, political perfidy, and economic motives of war. A more hawkish political science professor countered that Mussolini would back down if he knew that America was against him. All in all, it was a civilized meeting, with no radical demands for a bombing of the ROTC building. The hated liberals had prevailed.

But then, eight days later, the university administration saw yet another red flag raised. Joseph P. Lash, national secretary of the Student League for Industrial Democracy came to campus to shake Morris Cohen's hand and announce that their two organizations were going to merge and form a new group, the American Student Union.[19] And despite previous denials, they were indeed going to organize a student strike at the University of Illinois.

Lash, a twenty-five-year-old Columbia graduate wearing a three-piece business suit and a look of radical zeal in his eye, was a full member of the

Socialist Party. Lash told a reporter that the ASU would strive toward an ultimate reexamination of the basic social structure but would not advocate what means should be followed.

What exactly did that mean? He was going to provoke a riot, then slip out the back way? University officials were furious. Lash didn't go into further details, and he departed the campus without leaving any noticeably smoldering debris in his wake. Presumably, further plans would be revealed after the SLID and NSL merged. The university administration remained on red alert.

Morris's next project was to recruit some other activist students to help the members of two black fraternities, Alpha Phi Alpha and Kappa Alpha Psi, to open a racially integrated café. It would replace Boyd's Café, 615 South Wright Street, which had closed on account of bankruptcy.[20] Aside from the university cafeteria, Boyd's had been the only place on campus where black students could eat.

Morris and his comrades pitched in to renovate the café and reopen it in January 1936 as a nonprofit, nondiscriminatory cooperative for students and faculty who paid a $2.50 membership fee. Morris, representing the National Student League, was a member of the board of control of the café. In an inaugural dinner for the new eatery, he made a short talk praising the co-op as a distinct forward movement toward the actual tackling of student problems.

Joseph Lash's earlier rhetoric on campus did produce an event that could have been classified as a student strike, more or less. It was organized by the new American Student Union, which predicted that a thousand students would take part. But only about one hundred showed up, along with a couple of hundred onlookers. The crowd gathered on the steps of the university auditorium on the afternoon of April 22, 1936, and listened to speeches. There was some scattered heckling—"Heil Hitler" and "On to Moscow"—as ASU speakers harangued the campus ROTC program. One student in an ROTC uniform showed up to strut around for a while. He drew a few laughs, then left. After an hour or so, the crowd dispersed peacefully.

But Morris Cohen, the energetic, fast-talking, radical charmer who had been in the news so much lately for his campus organizing, was not mentioned in any of the press reports. Where was he?

Prior to the strike, Morris had been tacking up posters promoting the planned strike with the fervor of a call to man the Parisian barricades. He did this at night, before sunrise. But the sounds of his hammer in the pre-dawn silence found their way to the campus police station. An officer was dispatched to investigate. He followed Morris around, taking the posters down as fast as they were put up.

"I hung and he tore," is the way Morris described it.[21]

This cat and mouse game didn't go on very long. Morris was summoned to the office of the university president, Arthur Cutts Willard. Here was a tight-lipped, sober-looking academic who leaned toward dark suits and bow ties, sometimes offset by a sweater vest that didn't quite match. Willard's background was in engineering. His research on mechanical ventilation had made possible the construction of the Holland Tunnel between Manhattan and Jersey City. Now he was a university president with a big responsibility to procure operating funds to keep his institution open. But with the Depression, the university was going through a rough patch. State funding had dried up. So had private donations. The university was also reeling from some earlier financial shenanigans that might be dragged out in court for years. That meant big legal fees would have to be paid for a long time.

Willard's only recourse was to try and get as much federal aid as he could. But all this radical activity lately didn't look good in the newspapers. Communists, socialists, antiwar rallies, student strikes, riots. And young Morris Cohen seemed to be in the middle of so much of it, madly stirring the pot. There were even stories that Cohen had been making speeches in a park promoting equal rights for Negroes.

As Cohen told it, when he arrived at the president's office he found not only Willard but also some university trustees waiting for him. The president of a student fraternity was there, too. Apparently he had filed a complaint against Morris. Had Morris's posters disturbed somebody's pajama race?

It was a nice office, well heated, with pictures on the paneled walls, potted plants by the windows, a handsome clock ticking as the sound of typewriters in the outer office punched holes in the quiet ambiance. The trustees were representatives of some of the biggest businesses in Illinois. They represented money, and authority, and good solid Republican virtues of loyalty and patriotism.

Besides the cigar smoke in the room, there was a smell of suspicion, resentment, psychic injury. Illinois was a peaceful university. That peace had been shattered by Morris Cohen's subversive activities. Cohen was a Communist Jew from the Bronx who had come here by way of four years in Mississippi. What kind of background was that? All eyes stared down at him. He might have felt like Caesar confronting Brutus in the Roman senate.

Willard told Morris he had to stop his radical activities. Morris, ever the gentleman, politely declined. He might have raised issues of constitutional rights to free speech and assembly. Either way, as Morris related it, the president told him:

"If you do not stop your activities, we will get rid of you."

Presumably that meant suspension, not assassination. Again, Morris refused. He turned and left the office intent on continuing his agitprop activities. He had accrued first-semester credits in Old English, research in special topics, seventeenth-century literature, and nineteenth-century prose writing, but he didn't make it into the second semester. He never said whether he withdrew voluntarily or was kicked out, but his transcript shows he left the university on January 17, 1936. A pesky fly had been swatted.

Morris's experiences at Illinois had matured him, despite the fact they had ended on a disappointing note. He had gained experience and confidence as an organizer, and that met with approval from the NSL and the ASU and the YCL and the CPUSA. Morris had graduated from the working class to the middle class but was still dedicated to social revolution. That delighted the party bosses.

The Comintern in Moscow was planning a Popular Front movement in America, and they no longer automatically disdained the bourgeoisie. To the contrary, the CPUSA planned for the current student movement, a mixture of working-class radicalism and middle-class conformity, to produce tomorrow's educated, articulate, elite Communist leaders. They in turn would lead to acceptance of a new Communism by mainstream America, along with more donations to the cause. Or so the theory went.

But that was all in the future. For the time being, it was back to the Bronx, and the old neighborhood, for Morris.

3 SPAIN CALLING

When Morris Cohen got home in 1936 he moved back in with his folks at 1244 Grand Concourse, near East 168th Street, a twenty-minute walk north of Yankee Stadium. It was a brick tenement too old to be new any longer but not old enough to claim status as a historic landmark. It stood shoulder to shoulder in dulled monotony with other five-story stacks that sealed off the broad concourse like the walls of a fort. Snow lay glazed on the sidewalks beneath a Bronx sky the color of iron dust, everything locked together in the cold like ice cubes in a tray.

Morris left behind the screams of children playing in the street and climbed the steps to his family's apartment. The creak of the stairway, the sound of a radio playing, voices laughing behind closed doors—the familiar sounds of the building settled on him like his old woolen football jacket. A click of his key in the lock admitted him into the warmth of his living room. There it all was again—the hiss of the radiators, the winter light breaking through the windows to polish the hardwood floors, the smell of cooking in the kitchen. In his room he found his books and his records waiting for him, along with his clothes, his desk, his bed. Everything was just as he had left it. It was if his room had been sleeping while he was away, and now a snap of the light switch woke it up again.

Most of all, home meant being with his parents and his brother Abner again, and his old friends in the neighborhood. Morris was twenty-five years old, with a business degree and a year and a half of grad school, but despite FDR's alphabet soup of recovery programs, good jobs were still scarce. So Morris went back to working as a waiter around town while playing football in the park and visiting Doc Weidman at Monroe High. According to his FBI file, he also sold display advertising for the Pioneer News Company.

A check of the Manhattan White Pages shows there was a business by that name at Eleventh and Broadway in Greenwich Village, which in those days was home to several radical political sheets.[1] Pioneer was a word the Soviets liked to use. It conjured up visions of dedicated Communist explorers hacking their revolutionary way through jungles of imperialistic capitalism. Young Pioneer clubs were organized for children, and a party publication, the *New Pioneer*, was sold at Communist rallies.

When Morris joined the CPUSA it was probably at one of the branches in the Bronx. After the World War of 1914–18 ended, more than a dozen Jewish, Hungarian, Russian, and Lettish halls had opened in that borough alone. Total party membership in the New York area was around twenty thousand, with nearly half of them Jewish. In a questionnaire he completed later in Spain, Morris supplied his reason for joining: "Realized that the CP is the vanguard of the working class which is directing the path toward revolution and an international soviet; i.e., the building of a better world for the masses."[2]

It was the party line, straight from the Comintern. His moving up to full membership in the CPUSA surely met the approval of his always supportive parents, who that year would again enroll with the New York Board of Elections as Communist voters.

After Morris settled in back at home, he linked up with Edward Lending, his old football pal from Monroe High. Ed lived down the street. He was two years younger than Morris and had the same brown eyes and hair, and impressive athletic build. And like Morris, he had an enduring passion for sports, an agreeable sense of humor, and a personal commitment to Communism.

Ed's parents, Nathan and Helen Lending, were Jewish immigrants from Russia, and the family lived in a building at 520 West End Avenue. Nathan was an umbrella manufacturer and an early member of the Zionist Organization of America. Ed had attended CCNY for a year and NYU for two years, taking business and journalism courses without graduating. Now he was working for the federal Works Project Administration, teaching remedial reading classes and offering counseling to jobless, out-of-school youths for $23.86 a week (about $388.00 in today's currency).[3]

"In the mid-thirties we discovered ties that bound us," Ed later wrote of his renewed friendship with Morris. "We were both branch organizers for the Communist Party, I in the Northwest Bronx, Morris—Morris Picket now—in the lower West Bronx, on the Grand Concourse. We met at the frequent party enclaves, debated passionately—party problems, programs and prospects."

The national economy was at last improving in 1936. People were going back to work, moving into better apartments, shopping for new clothes and new cars. Vacations in Europe and Cuba were hot again. *Life* magazine ran pictures of Ivy League football weekends and pretty suntanned girls in swimsuits on California beaches. But it was mostly a middle-class recovery, and still as fragile as a politician's record of promises fulfilled.

Workers, those souls who mopped floors and picked up garbage, as invisible to a passerby as a potted palm, were still suffering. In the thirties, America was the most powerful industrial nation in the world, but the people who owned the factories resisted giving raises to the employees they hadn't laid off. This, despite the fact that everything was going up: rent, utilities, food, streetcar fares. God help you if you got sick and had to pay the doctor and the hospital.

After a failed campaign to promote rent strikes, the Communist Party bosses were forced to put on a less threatening mask in their drive for public acceptance, which in turn would hopefully bring in fresh members and new donations to the cause. They turned to campaigning for politicians sympathetic to the party program of higher wages, shorter hours, unionization of workers, and jobless relief. The press called it a Red New Deal.

Like other experienced agitprop organizers, Morris and Ed were undoubtedly among the most eager of the volunteers in that campaign. One of the party's strategies was to try and pressure a U.S. representative from the Bronx to introduce a bill in Congress setting up unemployment insurance. Canvassers worked the tenements to get signatures on a petition for those benefits, working at it until the ten o'clock radio news was over and people went to bed. Rain, sleet, snow, leaky shoes, it didn't matter. They were on a mission.

They would knock on a door. Somebody inside would open it, just a crack. An eye would settle on the figure standing out in the hallway. This boy didn't look like a cop, or a lawyer from the landlord. What did he want?

We're circulating a petition to get our congressman to introduce a bill for jobless benefits, the canvasser would announce (or words to that effect). We think it's the right thing to do. Is anybody in this family out of work?

That was often answered with a growl of anger and sometimes a stab at cynical humor. "I ain't seen work since Christ was a corporal" was a popular saying.

The canvasser replied that he, too, was out of work. Millions of Americans were jobless. Everybody knew that. Some were sleeping under bridges and in landfills. If it hadn't been for the soup kitchens, many would have died of starvation.

We want the government to provide us with work, the petitioner would say. If they won't, then they should support us.

But you're asking for socialism.

We're asking for either jobs, or money.

Sometimes the canvasser got a signature on the petition. Sometimes the tenant smelled something more threatening than just another socialist in the hallway, and slammed the door. Sometimes his departure was encouraged by a dog, the poor man's security system.

Organizers got better press when they played the milk card. They got a crowd of women together, each pushing a carriage with a baby inside, and they invaded the Bronx Borough Hall, accompanied by a reporter and photographer from the *Daily Worker*. The babies squalled as the women demanded to see their alderman. Then after disrupting the outer office, this parade of mothers marched into the politician's inner sanctum, left, right, left, right, chanting: "We want milk! Milk for the children!"[4]

Who could resist a show like that?

IN APRIL the last of the ice melted on the Grand Concourse. The air softened, the trees blushed green again, and sunsets the color of bruised fruit lingered in the evening sky. As spring warmed to summer, Morris packed his bag and headed upstate again for another three months of work at Jewish resorts in the Catskills. And for the third year, he joined a strike of hotel employees up there. This added to his growing reputation as a skilled agitprop organizer. It also brought him to the attention of Earl Browder, general secretary of the CPUSA. Browder was a member of the executive committee of the Comintern in Moscow and a New York spotter of talent for Soviet espionage.

While the local party halls tended to be badly heated, poorly lit, cheaply furnished, and smelly, Browder ruled his domain from comfortable head-quarters in a stately old townhouse at 23 West Twenty-Sixth Street in Manhattan. The Soviet state security and foreign intelligence agency, now known as the NKVD (*Narodny Kommissariat Vnutrennikh Del*), had given Browder the *klichka* (code name) of *Rulevoy*, which meant "helmsman." This no doubt was homage to Stalin, who called himself the Great Helmsman.

Browder came from a family that had settled in Virginia before the American Revolution. He grew up in Wichita, Kansas, and learned so-cialism from his father, a country schoolteacher. Earl later claimed he led fights for students' freedom of expression while in school, but that might have been an apocryphal story, since he dropped out at age nine. He took a succession of clerking jobs, joined the Socialist Party, and was arrested twice for opposing the draft. He served three years in Leavenworth, 1917–20, and after his release he became a CPUSA member and worked as a Comintern agent in China. He and his sister Marguerite traveled to Russia to study Communism, and after he returned to America he took over as boss of the CPUSA in 1930.[5]

Publicity photos showed Browder as a lean, handsome man with sharp features, slicked-back hair, and a pipe in his mouth. With his studious ex-pression he looked very literary. Indeed he was a writer, but a dull one. His speeches, too, were not guaranteed to keep people awake for very long. He was also dictatorial. During a party meeting he would listen patiently to different sides in a discussion, then issue his ruling, after which he would allow no dissent. He followed the Comintern line and the Comintern kept him in power. Elizabeth Bentley, an ideological recruit to Soviet spying in New York and a critical observer of party personalities, saw Browder as a spiteful man who liked to settle old scores on the sly; a cheap, tawdry figure, a low, conniving politician who was out for himself.

Browder's Russian wife Raïssa had been a Soviet agent since Bolshevik days and a powerful figure in the former GPU (*Gosudarstvennoye Politich-eskoye Upravleniye*), a successor to the Cheka. Bentley considered Raïssa a dangerous woman with an air of arrogance and thinly veiled cruelty. In addition, Earl's niece, Helen Lowry, was married to Iskhak Abdulovich

Akhmerov, one of the Soviet control officers of Yakov Naumovich Reisen, known in America as Jacob Golos, an organizer of spy activities run through the CPUSA.

But despite the various criticisms aimed at Browder, he was important to the Comintern as one of the local CPUSA officials who were recruiting volunteers to fight in the Spanish Civil War. Browder's selection of Morris Cohen would have a decisive influence on the young man's future career as a spy against his own country.

MOSCOW'S INTEREST in Spain can be traced back to Hitler's ascension to power in Germany in 1933. The Comintern at first went into a state of denial, holding out hope that Hitler would eventually lose power. Then it would be the Communists' turn to rule Germany. But Hitler was just as brutal as Stalin; his power was absolute, and it was growing. So was the military strength of his new Nazi Germany, which was rearming in viola-tion of the Treaty of Versailles of 1919. Mussolini and his Fascist Party had acquired a similar stranglehold on Italy. Stalin saw that he had to adapt to this new dual threat.

At their seventh congress in Moscow in 1935, the Comintern revealed a new strategy: organizing a worldwide People's Front against fascism. The term People's Front evolved into Popular Front. It suggested a coalition of Communists with their traditional adversaries, socialists and middle-class liberals, with radical laborites and other fellow travelers allowed in for good measure. It sounded wonderful in speeches—former enemies now united in a common struggle against the evil of fascism. That was another umbrella term. Fascism came to include not just members of the Italian Fascist Party but also German Nazis and any other groups from the extreme right of the political spectrum. In America that meant organizations such as the Klan and the German American Bund, which paraded around with both American and Nazi flags.

An attempt to form a Popular Front in Britain and Italy failed, and the one established in France was shaky. The Comintern was more successful in Spain, which like Russia was a nation mostly of peasants and workers. The Popular Front promoted what they felt was the coming of a modern New Spain governed somehow by a witch's brew of Communists, socialists, anarchists, syndicalists, Catalonians, Trotskyists, and liberals, everybody with his own agenda. Trotskyist—or Trotskyite, as the NKVD called them—was another categorical term. Originally it had meant Marxists who shared Trotsky's ideas of permanent revolution abroad. But Stalin wasn't interested in world revolution. He was desperate to solidify his personal power at home, and anyone who opposed him was branded a Trotskyite, a traitor fit for execution. Moscow Center's code name for American Trotskyites was Polecats.

The National Front in Spain stood at the other end of the political dial from the Popular Front. The Nationalists were loyal to the Old Spain of landowners, army, Catholic Church, and bourgeoisie. Franco was not a member of any fascist party; he was a conservative, a traditionalist. But he accepted the support of the German Nazis, the Italian Fascists, and the Spanish Falange, made up of young fascist men and women marching in proletarian blue shirts and calling one another comrade. That led to Franco being pigeonholed as a fascist. But he simply used the fascists for his own purposes, the way the Comintern would use the international brigades.

In Spain's general election of February 1936, the Popular Front won by a margin of about 1 percent. It was a narrow victory, but a legal one. In June, Manuel Azaña y Diaz, a liberal and one of the founders of the Popular Front, was elected president. One of his first acts was to fire General Francisco Franco y Bahamonde from his position in the War Ministry because of his suppression of a leftist uprising in Asturias two years before. Franco was shuffled off to the Canary Islands, a move comparable to an FBI agent being exiled to Butte, Montana.

Contrary to Azaña's promises, the transition to a new government turned out to be anything but peaceful. Violent elements on the left could not be controlled, and warring tribes within the Popular Front went on a rampage of riots, strikes, church bombings, and murders of nuns and priests. Newspapers were sacked, political centers wrecked. Peasants seized land, trade unions traded gunfire. There was no longer one Spain, new or old. Now there were dozens of Spains, and they all seemed intent on destroying one another.

The country fell into chaos. A hundred thousand were reportedly killed in one month alone.[6] People who could afford it fled to France. They included businessmen and financiers who took their money with them, which didn't help the collapsing value of the peseta. Finally some army generals stepped up to say the only way to save the nation was to overthrow the government and restore order with an iron fist. General Franco emerged as leader of the plot.

Franco was a short, fat man with a weak chin, a forty-four-year-old staunch traditionalist married to a devout Catholic from Asturias. Franco had naval ancestry on both sides of his family but had chosen instead to go to the infantry academy. He was the youngest officer ever to be promoted to general and had commanded the Spanish Foreign Legion and the Moorish Regulares in Africa for fourteen years. He was a brilliant organizer and tactician, a cautious and patient man, and also a cruel disciplinarian, as evidenced by his repressions in Asturias in 1934. But the fact remained, if you were going to stage a coup, Franco was your man.

Franco appealed to Germany and Italy for military assistance, and got it. Both Adolf Hitler and Benito Mussolini saw great strategic value in turning Spain into an Axis power. France was already blocked on the east by Germany and Italy. If Spain fell to Franco, France would be further hemmed in from the south. Seizing Spain would also offer Berlin and Rome a chance to grab Gibraltar away from Britain. If that maneuver succeeded, then Germany and Italy could control the militarily significant entrance to the Mediterranean. Franco's forces were called Nationalists, or Rebels, or Fascists. Franco was *el Caudillo*. It meant "dictator," Spain's own Führer.

Stalin, at the same time, sold Soviet military aid to the legally elected Spanish government in order to defend the struggling republic against fascism. At least, that was the line from the Comintern's propaganda office. But Stalin had little interest in the downtrodden peasants and workers of Spain. He wanted to add Spain to his own sphere of influence. At the very least, that might persuade France and England to include Russia in a military front against Hitler.[7] But more than that, a Soviet régime in Spain would give Stalin the same kind of strategic control of the Mediterranean that the Axis powers coveted. Aside from guns, tanks, and warplanes, Stalin sent two thousand Red Army troops to Spain to be held in reserve, away from Spanish troops.

Franco's Army of Africa invaded mainland Spain from Morocco in July. That set off pro-Franco uprisings of military garrisons in Barcelona, Valencia, and Madrid. Azaña's forces—known variously as Loyalists, Republicans, Leftists, or Reds—counterattacked. A wobbly front was soon established that ran down the middle of the country. The Loyalists defended the eastern part of Spain, including the biggest cities, while the Nationalists held the western regions and tried to move east but were blocked at Madrid.

THE SPANISH CIVIL WAR quickly shaped up as the first shots of a new world war that many people had feared—but denied—was coming. Morris Cohen, though, refused to consider Spain in geopolitical terms. In his mind, it was no chess game. He saw Russia simply as the only one of the Allied powers from the last war to directly help the new Spanish republic in her struggle against Franco, Hitler, and Mussolini. In that summer of '36 the world was shocked by news of the atrocities committed by both sides in Spain, but Morris saw only the sins of the Nationalists and continued to quote the official line from Moscow.

"In 1936, when fascism was rampant in Spain, there took place an instant polarization of forces in the world," he wrote in that personal questionnaire he filled out in Spain. "On one hand there were the forces of peace, progress and democracy, and on the other hand, the adherents of reactionary forces, the oppressors and tyrants. Everyone was to make a choice on which side he was."

His convictions seemed to have shifted dramatically in a matter of months. At Illinois, he had been one of the leaders of an antimilitarist campaign on campus, campaigning for peace. Now he was all for war. What happened?

It was simple. The Communist International wanted a pro-Soviet Popular Front government in America, and one of the platforms of that movement was the fight against international fascism. That meant assuming a warlike posture.

But what chance did the CPUSA really have for taking power in Washington? The closest a leftist candidate had ever come to getting elected president was Eugene Debs of the Socialist Party when he polled 925,000 votes in 1920. Still, Earl Browder did as he was told, and ran for president in 1936. First, he stopped calling Roosevelt a fascist. Then he declared that he, Earl Browder, was a progressive, a clever allusion to two of America's most revered presidents, the Republican Teddy Roosevelt and the Democrat Woodrow Wilson.

"The Communist Party does not advocate force and violence," Browder said in a radio interview. "It is a legal party and defends its legality. Communists are not conspirators, not terrorists, not anarchists. The Communist Party is an open revolutionary party, continuing under modern conditions the revolutionary traditions of 1776."[8]

That meant the CPUSA was actually a patriotic old Yankee party, as American as apple pandowdy and sour mash bourbon. Why hadn't you noticed that before? Suddenly the United States flag was hung at party meetings and waved in parades. American holidays such as the Fourth of July were observed. Receptionists at party halls were now pretty girls wearing fashionable dresses. "Welcome, comrade," they chirped brightly to visitors. The media called it Browderism. The public didn't buy it.

In the general election, FDR was reelected with 27,000,000 votes while Socialist Party leader Norman Thomas polled around 187,000. Browder took home 80,000, hardly enough to get him into the Bronx Borough Hall, much less the White House. It was irrefutable proof that a Communist-led Popular Front strong enough to legally elect a radical national government simply did not exist in America. It confirmed that most Americans saw their salvation from the Depression not in some fringe party that took its orders from Moscow, but in FDR's New Deal programs of jöb creation, bank protections, and old-age pensions.

On to Plan B then for the party: full-press support for the Loyalists in Spain. What could be more American than a campaign against Fascists and Nazis?

During a visit to Moscow in September 1936, Maurice Thorez, leader of the French Communist Party, had suggested that the Comintern instruct their party affiliates around the world to recruit volunteer soldiers to go to Spain and fight Franco. Stalin liked the idea. Soviet-sponsored international brigades would create great publicity for world Communism. They could also serve as a Soviet force to eventually seize control of the Spanish government and then perhaps assist those two thousand Red Army reservists in capturing Gibraltar.

That summer, an international-brigade recruiting office opened in New York. Soon they had signed up almost a thousand men, and the line on the sidewalk was getting longer. The first two battalions bore the patriotic names of George Washington and Abraham Lincoln. They were sent to Spain to join the international brigades being formed with volunteers from Russia, England, Ireland, Germany, Italy, and other European countries.

Ed Lending was one of the early American volunteers. He said later that he and Morris had found themselves incessantly at philosophical and tactical odds lately about the future of their work for the party. Ed was still a communist at heart but he was tired of peddling petitions for party candidates who had little chance of getting elected. He saw that the real struggle of his generation was going to be against fascism. He wanted to be in the action. Like Kalamatiano's experience in the Russian Civil War, Spain would be Lending's Great Adventure.

Ed went down to the international brigade recruiting office at 100 Fifth Avenue and talked to a recruiter.[9] The recruiters worked for the NKVD, though that was not publicized. Ed filled out an application for a passport and they ran a background check to be sure he was who he claimed to be. After Ed received his passport, on February 10, 1937, he was assigned to the George Washington Battalion.

The major world powers had earlier agreed not to intervene in Spain, so new U.S. passports were stamped Not Valid for Spain. That didn't bother Ed. He wrote on his application that he was going to France to visit relatives. From France he could slip into Spain. Other volunteers claimed they were going to France as tourists, or students, or to brush up on their mountain climbing, or whatever.

Ed sailed on the *Ile de France* and arrived at Le Havre on February 26. Despite France's official nonintervention policy, troops and war matériel were being shipped to the Loyalists from French ports, just as American oil was being openly sold to Franco by the Texas Company (Texaco).[10] Immigration officials at Le Havre gave Ed and his American comrades a wink and a nod and waved them through.

Morris, though, didn't move that fast. His agitprop work in Illinois and New York had given him confidence. Despite his truncated student career at Illinois, he had scored some successes out there that had not gone unnoticed by the CPUSA. Now he was looking forward to a career of party activism in New York. He, too, saw fascism as the great evil of his generation, and wanted to do something about it. But he was also comfortable where he was. He was tied to his party work, to his family, to his friends. Going to Spain would be an awful wrench.

But as the new year arrived, some things happened that would cause him to put his ideological beliefs on the line in a life-and-death struggle thousands of miles away. He wouldn't know it until he got there, but his own adventure was going to come close to killing him.

4 DANGEROUS CROSSING

In the spring of 1937, party activists were ordered to campaign energetically to promote the cause of Loyalist Spain among seamen and longshoremen on the New York docks. Morris Cohen and Ed Lending, two of the star organizers for the party, were probably assigned as group captains in the campaign. Campaigners posted Lincoln Battalion recruiting posters on warehouse walls and café windows. They went aboard ships and solicited donations for the Loyalist army.

At the same time, the party organized a Cultural Front of writers, artists, teachers, scientists, clergy, and Hollywood luminaries to oppose Franco in Spain. The CPUSA had been organizing Soviet fronts in the United States since the early thirties. They published magazines such as the *Anvil*, the *Blast*, and the *Cauldron*, which featured short stories for the American proletariat. They sponsored the League Workers Theatres, the Workers Music League, and the Young Workers Dance League. Motion pictures were also a favorite tool. Lenin had been a great believer of the propaganda effect of movies. He admired *The Birth of a Nation* because that film's depiction of the Klan as an effective terrorist group supposedly justified the use of such methods by the Bolsheviks. By the thirties, seven New York movie houses were showing Soviet propaganda films.

Writers carried much of the weight of the Cultural Front. This was before television. Radio brought fast-breaking news to the public, but for depth of coverage, people relied on newspapers and books. In 1937 a group of notable writers released a statement condemning the forces waging war on the legally and democratically elected republican government of Spain. The signers of the statement included personalities as diverse as Max Eastman, Dorothy Parker, Sinclair Lewis, Carl Sandburg, Upton Sinclair, Thornton Wilder, Suzanne La Follette, and William Faulkner.[1]

Some in this group, such as Eastman, were fellow travelers. They believed in at least some of the aims of Communism, just as some Americans on the other side of the great political divide found inspiration in the Black Legion or the Silver Shirts or the Bund. Still others saw Cultural Front politics as simply fashionable. Cocktail Communists, they were called. But since the party did not tolerate independent thought, few actually joined up. Playwright Lillian Hellman later said she was a member for two years, then flip-flopped and claimed she had just attended a few meetings as an observer.

Ernest Hemingway adopted the cause of the Loyalists in Spain. This was curious indeed, since Ernie had never shown much interest in politics before. He had been an ambulance driver in the First World War, was wounded, and afterwards blamed politicians for the carnage of what at the time was called the Good Cause. Aside from being a prominent journalist, Hem was best known as author of *A Farewell to Arms*, one of the great tragic wartime love stories in literature. Basically, he was a romantic, an innocent, as were most of the young internationals recruited to fight in Spain. He had bought and equipped two ambulances for the Loyalists, and in March 1937, Ernesto set out for Spain again, to cover the war as a correspondent and help produce a Loyalist propaganda film, *The Spanish Earth*.

Morris Cohen, meanwhile, was caught up in the spirit of two big events in New York that drew attention to Spain. The first was a May Day parade across Union Square, a center of radical politics in the city. It drew seventy thousand marchers and ran for ten hours. The first group to march was a CPUSA unit, followed by representatives of labor unions. Norman Thomas, head of the Socialist Party, read a cablegram he'd received from the Soviet Union: "Give greetings to United May Day celebration from Moscow. Let the workers' strength be the answer to fascism."[2]

While the May Day parade in Moscow was mostly a lockstep display of Stalin's new tanks and warplanes, reporters found the New York crowd loose and good-natured. They ate ice cream, drank sodas, and joked with the two thousand cops assigned to the parade.

The second big event was American Week for Spanish Democracy, sponsored by the North American Committee to Aid Spanish Democracy, one of twenty-eight front organizations set up by the Comintern to rally support for the Loyalists fighting Franco. Speeches were made in Chicago, San Francisco, and New York. The CPUSA sent demonstrators to picket the German and Italian consulates in Manhattan and demand a withdrawal of their forces from Spain. Rallies for Loyalist Spain were held in factories and union halls. African Americans were courted in separate events.

Morris Cohen's friends knew he was prone toward suffering an occasional black chill of depression, but the success of those two events in May undoubtedly improved his mood and made him more receptive toward the idea of actually going to Spain himself, even though in the meantime bad news had been coming in from that quarter. The U.S. recruits in Spain were cheap sources of manpower, and the international brigade commanders were throwing them into combat as shock troops against well-trained, superbly equipped professional soldiers from Germany, Italy, and the Spanish Foreign Legion. Americans, in effect, were being used as suicide squads.

In the Battle of the Jamara Valley, 450 men fought in the Lincoln Battalion and 120 were killed, with another 175 wounded. Most of their officers were lost at Jamara. Then at the Battle of Brunete, the Lincoln and Washington losses were so heavy that the two battalions had to be merged. Oliver Law, a black Texan who had commanded the Washington Battalion, was killed, along with a high number of Jewish American troops. Insubordination broke out in the ranks of the internationals. A cavalry commander deserted. There was a mutiny. A commander shot a mutineer and barely escaped with his own life.

After Brunete, 500 Americans had been killed of the approximately 1,700 who had enlisted thus far.[3] That was a KIA rate of over 34 percent, and it didn't include those wounded, sick, captured, or missing. It was the kind of mindless slaughter that in the First World War had brought down the Russian imperial government and caused mutinies in the French army. The passports of the dead troops were seized and sent to Moscow. There cobblers (forgers) used them to create boots (false passports) for future Soviet spy ops against the United States. To add insult to injury, thirty thousand of Franco's troops now wore U.S. Army uniforms bought as military surplus.

Further bad news came when Morris picked up a newspaper on Saturday, July 10, and read that his old friend Ed Lending had been shot at Brunete. Not killed, but seriously wounded, and hospitalized in Madrid. Ed and the some of the other wounded men told a reporter that what they wanted most were American cigarettes. And books in English. Not detective stories, but serious books.

The wounding of Ed Lending; the desperate need for reinforcements in the international brigades; a growing support for Loyalist Spain by ordinary Americans; and most of all, the horrible prospect of a Fascist and Nazi victory in Spain—those were undoubtedly factors that drove Morris to finally decide to commit himself to the Loyalist side in Spain. But when he later filled out that questionnaire in Spain, he put a party spin on it:

> I realized the necessity from the outbreak of the uprising [by Franco].
> It was principally a question of leaving my parents. But when I heard
> Phil Bard speak at a meeting of Bronx County functionaries, I decided
> that my duty lie where liberty was in greatest danger—in Spain. I feel
> that, as Dimitrov said, the central commission [committee] of the CI
> [Communist International] is my highest judge, and its analysis of world
> events points to where our highest duty lies.[4]

Morris went public with his commitment to Loyalist Spain on Monday night, July 19, 1937. The North American Committee to Aid Spanish Democracy had rented Madison Square Garden, New York's largest indoor arena, for a huge rally to mark the first anniversary of the fight against Franco in Spain. People began gathering in the Garden early that evening. When the show began at eight o'clock, they were still streaming in. At nine o'clock, the seating capacity of twenty thousand was reached, and the fire department closed the Garden doors, turning away two thousand more. "Take me in," an old lady pleaded with a reporter. "Take me in as if I were your mother."[5]

People who got shut out staged their own rally outside. Inside, Vito Marcantonio, a former member of the American Republican Party and now a popular radical speaker, took the stage to shake his fist at the Franco government and predict its downfall.

"And after Franco," he shouted, "the people of Italy will proceed to the overthrow of Mussolini and the people of Germany to the overthrow of Hitler and the establishment of complete democracy in those lands!"

The crowd loved him. "Viva Vito!" they shouted. They waved the Spanish tricolor. "Abasso Mussolini! Abajo Franco!"

Truth was, the crowd loved all the speakers. Major Huberto Galleani of the Garibaldi Battalion in Spain was on hand, along with Girolamo Valenti, editor of New York's antifascist Italian daily, *La Stampa Libera*. Roger Nash Baldwin, director of the American Civil Liberties Union, waved a telegram he was going to send to President Roosevelt protesting Washington's neutrality policy. Baldwin was a fellow traveler who had visited the Soviet Union several years before and written an article proposing a workers' dictatorship in America, even if it required what he termed violent tactics.[6]

Dr. Edward Barsky, a New York member of the CPUSA who had volunteered for the Communist-sponsored Medical Bureau to Aid Spanish Democracy, told the crowd that six hospitals had been set up on the Loyalist side. On this night he collected more than five thousand dollars for more medical supplies. Three months out, Morris Cohen would find himself in one of the Loyalist hospitals.

Norman Thomas and Earl Browder took the stage to charge Britain and America with shameful conduct for not arming Loyalist Spain. Browder declared that the Spanish people had given a rallying cry to all the people of the outside world: "No passaran!"

The stage was decorated with the colors of Loyalist Spain and a huge portrait of General José Miaja Menant, the former antirepublican who had come out of retirement to command the force defending Madrid against the Nationalists. It was a steamy night and the big electric fans in the Garden did little more than shift the heat around, but the audience was oblivious to such inconvenience. They sweated and shouted. They whistled and clapped and passed wine skins as they sang patriotic Spanish songs and gave the clenched fist salute of the international brigades. The place never quieted down. Applause rolled back and forth across the auditorium like the ebb and flow of ocean waves.

It was a tight, skillfully produced show, as professional as any of the religious revivals for which the Garden was famous. At the conclusion, an appeal was made for converts to come forward and join the cause. Morris was in the group who got up to cheers from the crowd and made the long walk down the aisle to the altar of the Spanish Republic. "I had no other choice but to stand of my own free will for the defense of the Spanish republic," he later wrote in that questionnaire in Spain. "I was just being true to my convictions."

But was there a woman involved in his decision to volunteer on this particular night? Was he perhaps trying to impress her, just a little?

BEFORE THE RALLY, Morris and some friends had gone to a cafeteria to have coffee and talk about Spain. There they met some other party members who were going to the rally. Morris was introduced to Leontina Petka, who used the diminutive Lona. She was twenty-four years old, in the pink of young womanhood, and Morris was smitten by her honey-blonde hair, her dazzling blue eyes, her trim and alluring figure.

"Lona looked great in her sky blue suit and little white hat," Morris recalled. If she had a shortcoming, he said, it was that she looked too pretty, like a bride drawing too much attention at a wedding.[7] She could disarm a man with just one of her seductive looks.

"That came in mighty useful to her later, however," Morris added. "And although I was the direct opposite of her, perhaps too modest and indecisive, I set my mind firmly on winning that girl's favor."

Lona had joined the Communist Party in '35. But unlike Morris, she didn't come from a Communist family. Her conversation with Morris, though, confirmed her commitment to the cause. At the same time, she was miffed by Cohen's behavior toward her. A little cold-blooded was the word she used.

"When our eyes first met, Morris turned away for some reason, either out of embarrassment or out of indifference, as I thought then," she said later. "That amazed me because until then all I could see in the eyes of each man looking at me was admiration. My womanly pride was hurt. I considered myself irresistible to men, and got awfully offended with him. I must confess, though, that Morris also impressed me at first sight. He had pleasant features, an aquiline nose, and his brown eyes were so kind!"[8]

In other words, it was love at first sight. For the time being, though, that was as far as it went. They exchanged phone numbers, and after the rally, Morris went off to war.

THE INTERNATIONAL BRIGADE RECRUITERS in Manhattan put Morris on a fast track to Spain, undoubtedly because he had the backing of Earl Browder. When he signed the enlistment papers he listed his nationality as American, his occupation as journalist, his address as 1244 Grand Concourse in the Bronx. Upon enlistment, each volunteer was assigned a nom de guerre. Cohen's was Israel Altman.

The FBI later tracked down the real Israel Altman, who told them he had gone to the recruiting office, volunteered to serve in Spain, and filled out an application for a passport. But he was rejected after a physical exam. The twenty-eight-year-old Altman (the real one) then walked out of the recruiting office, never to see Spain from a rifle's point of view. Why had he been disqualified? He considered that none of the FBI's business.[9]

Nevertheless, Altman's application was used to obtain passport number 458513, in his name.[10] The international brigade recruiters then assigned that passport to Morris, with his photo on it. He wore glasses and a false mustache as a disguise in the picture.

The recruiting office also obtained documents for volunteers through Jacob Golos, a Russian Jew who had come to America in 1907 and was one of the founders of the American Communist Party, predecessor to the CPUSA. Golos worked more for the CPUSA than the NKVD, and since 1930 had specialized in procuring passports. He developed an asset in the Brooklyn office of the U.S. Passport Bureau who would take an application, with birth certificate, both submitted by Golos, and then send the documents to Washington. The Passport Bureau apparently trusted the Brooklyn clerk's work since he was presumably a loyal federal employee. Each application was processed in Washington and mailed to the applicant at the address he had provided. The whole process took around three days. This Brooklyn clerk could also obtain valid U.S. passports in the names of dead people, illegal immigrants, or those who had left the United States.

After Golos's death, his spy network would be taken over by Elizabeth Bentley, the NKVD's courier on the important New York–Washington run. Her defection to the FBI would be one of the key factors in the collapse of Soviet spy nets in North America, including the one run by the Cohens.

When Bentley was first assigned to Golos she found him to be rather colorless and shabby, a sad-looking little man wearing a battered hat, cheap suit, and worn-out shoes, all in tired shades of brown.[11] She later revised her opinion, describing him as powerfully built, with a large head, broad shoulders, and strong square hands. She liked his blue eyes, his red hair, and the shape of his mouth, which reminded her of her mother. She also decided that his mind was quick, keen, and incisive. Having revised her opinion of him from cold to hot, she became his lover.

Morris was given minimal military training while waiting to be deployed to Spain. Volunteers were usually taken to a rundown warehouse district and up a flight of stairs to a big second-floor room in an old building where other recruits sat on benches listening to lectures on battle formations delivered by a former U.S. Army sergeant. A two-week course in military drill was offered at a camp out in the country, but Morris wasn't in town long enough to attend. He was taught the International Brigade salute, though—clenched right fist touched to the temple.

Jacob Golos was useful to the recruiting efforts in a second way. He managed a travel agency, World Tourists Inc., a Communist roof (front) in the Flatiron Building in Manhattan, and this office provided Morris and other volunteers with steamer tickets to France. Just before embarking, the recruits were given a little money and sent out to pick up a few personal things for their trip. They bought cardboard suitcases at a pawn shop and some military items from a surplus store. But no firearms.

Morris was assigned to the Mackenzie-Papineau Battalion, a Canadian outfit that had been formed in Spain on July 1 and named for two nineteenth-century patriots who rebelled against British rule. Canadians had been serving in American battalions from the very beginning, but in the name of national pride they wanted their own outfit, and the Yanks supported them. At first the Mac-Paps had Canadian officers, but as time went on, most of their commanders would be American. That was due to the high mortality rate in battle and the fact there were more Americans than Canadians available with military experience.

Volunteers in Canada were recruited by the Canadian Committee to Aid Spanish Democracy. They were officially banned from Spain by the Foreign Enlistments Act passed by the Parliament in Ottawa, but that act, like the U.S. ban, was routinely ignored.

Morris was assigned to the Mac-Pap because there weren't enough Canadians to fill out the ranks. The battalion was divided into three infantry companies and one machine gun company. Their battle flag was red and gold, with the inscription "Fascism Shall Be Destroyed."

Cohen and seventeen other Mac-Paps sailed together for France on July 21, barely two days after that rally at Madison Square Garden. Morris's group elected him their leader. They traveled on the twenty-five-year-old SS *Berengaria*, a creaky but still luxurious Cunard liner that once had been the biggest ship in the world. World Tourists had provided the boys with the cheapest accommodations available, which meant third class or steerage, down by the ship's noisy and smoky engine room. But they got plenty of fresh air up on deck, playing games, mugging for photographs, drinking beer, and trying to impress girls. They also amused themselves looking for other recruits on the ship. That probably wasn't difficult. All they had to do was look for other guys about their age wearing old clothes and carrying cheap suitcases.[12]

Upon arrival at Cherbourg two weeks later, the *volontaires d'Espagne* found out that the border with Spain was indeed closed, technically, and that a few Americans had even been arrested for trying to slip across the frontier. The punishment was usually light, a few days in jail, but once they were released, the men could be deported. So Morris and his flock stayed together and kept their heads down. If one of them got arrested, even on a minor charge like public drunkenness, he might let slip some information that could blow the rest of the group.

A French Communist arrived with tickets, and the Mac-Paps boarded a train to Paris. After arrival at the Gare du Nord they checked into budget hotels and went to the headquarters of the Paris control committee of the international brigades. The office was located in a three-story, block-long building that housed a trade-union headquarters in the Avenue Matherin-Moreau, a narrow, shady thoroughfare of shops and apartment buildings on a steep hill. At that time, the neighborhood was called the Quartier du Combat. It was in the 19th arrondissement, a northeast corner of Paris adjoining the Red Ring of Communist suburbs. The Combat Quarter was infamous for the public hangings conducted there before the Revolution of 1789 replaced the gibbet with the allegedly more humane guillotine. Communist Party headquarters were nearby in the Place du Combat.

The Mac-Paps found the front yard of the union hall filled with other volunteers running on in different languages. A commissionaire in the big hallway on the ground floor directed Morris and his flock back to the office handling Canadian recruits. There the men were interviewed in order to verify their identities and their commitment to serving in Spain on the Loyalist side. That was also the last chance to weed out any problem cases such as drug addicts, drunkards, or psychotics.

After going through another physical exam, the men were issued tickets to a big, noisy cooperative restaurant where they could get two meals a day. They were also free to explore the boulevards, the bistros, and the Paris Exposition for a day or two while arrangements were made to transport them down to Spain on one of the underground railroad systems the Communists were running. The cafés featured coffee with hot goat's milk, cheap Champagne and, for an additional charge, pretty girls offering *l'amour*.

On their last day in Paris, Morris and his group were instructed to turn in their suitcases and any spare clothing they had. Those were stored at a depot and later issued to volunteers who had arrived without sufficient clothing, and to wounded men coming out of Spain. The Mac-Paps were told to keep just what they could wear, and if they didn't have a sturdy jacket, then go buy one. They were also advised to stock up on tobacco.

Finally it was time to move out. Hotel bills were paid by the control committee, and the Mac-Paps reported to the Rue Mathurin Moreau for the last time. They were taken to an assembly room where they were briefed on the route they would take to Spain and the routine they would have to follow. That information was extremely important. One false move and somebody might get arrested, or shot. Some of the volunteers would be smuggled into Spain on freighters sailing out of French ports on the Mediterranean. Morris and his group were going to hike across the Pyrenees Mountains.

That night, Morris and his comrades enjoyed their last dinner in Paris. Afterward, they went to some shops and bought bread, sausage, and wine to take on the train. Then they piled into taxis and took off for the Gare de Lyon. Separating into smaller groups, the men boarded the PLM train (Chemins de fer de Paris à Lyon et à la Méditerranée) and settled into their compartments. A twelve-year-old girl was assigned to ride with them on their "Red Express" down to Perpignan.

"The French Communist Party had everything prepared," Morris said.[13]

That night the train raced past the lights and smells of a France that North American tourists seldom saw—villages and small towns, occasionally a city, provincial and changeless, protecting private lives of old songs, old traditions. The Mac-Paps arrived at their destination, Perpignan, on one of those green Mediterranean mornings when the sunlight was a taste of moist and measureless distance.

Perpignan was an ancient Roman settlement surrounded by lush green farmland, defined by its endurance, its adaptability, its survivability. It used to belong to Spain, and a dialect of Catalan was still spoken there along with French. It was a factory town, a popular resort, a city with a cathedral and a palace and mildew-stained stucco tenements standing alongside ancient mansions of honey-colored stone cut from local quarries. Narrow streets, shady gardens, smoky cafés—all were bonded together by the blinding sun and the sour smells of black soil and overgrown vegetation. But a pleasant town, for all that, plump and content with itself.

Recently Perpignan had become popular as a place where young men from foreign countries came for a bit of mountain climbing. But despite the fact they all went up, none seemed to come down. How odd, visitors might have remarked. The locals, though, knew what they were up to. They smiled and waved to them as they passed.

At dusk the Mac-Paps were bussed out to a farmhouse that served as a safe house in the foothills of the mountains. There they waited for darkness, eager to move on and at the same time apprehensive about the unknown that waited for them somewhere out there. They sat, they paced, they talked. Finally it was time to go. They pulled on Spanish sneakers and started their long hike, led by the young girl who was their guide.

It was a moonless night, as dark as death itself. As they climbed they left behind the cottony warmth of the summer night below them and ascended into the dry cold air of the higher altitudes. They kept at it, hour after hour, the thin soles of their shoes fighting the rocks on the trail. Sprains were a constant danger, along with falls into unseen and stunningly cold streams.

They followed one of the smuggling routes across the mountains. If a man fell from exhaustion, he was left there and helped back to Perpignan later. Each climber's world was narrowed to the fellow in front of him and the one behind him. They held hands for safety and blindly followed their guide. No time to stop and eat. Too dangerous to build a fire and warm up.

They climbed all night. Their legs hurt and they were weak from fatigue and hunger. They passed a border station and were ignored by the French guards. Finally at dawn they reached a plateau and stopped to rest. Below them lay the fields of Spain and in the distance the mirrored water of the Med. They had made it. Later they would find out that a group of 245 volunteers that left for Spain earlier on a ship out of Marseilles had not been so fortunate. They were torpedoed by an Italian submarine off the coast of Barcelona. Half the crew of the ship and 160 recruits were lost.

But on this morning, on that mountaintop, beneath a warming sun and a wind that brought the smell of pines and the bleating of sheep from the slopes below, Morris and his squad were elated that they had completed the opening chapter of their odyssey. Below them lay the thrill of their great expedition. To mark the occasion, they broke out singing the Communist anthem, the "Internationale."

5 THE ELITE OF THE INTERNATIONALS

A cool haze fell off the shoulders of Morris Cohen and his group as they descended the mountain into the close warmth of the foothills on the Spanish side of the frontier. They found the dirt road they were looking for and walked until they came to a Loyalist outpost. They showed their papers from the committee in Paris and were given a ride in a truck to Figueres. It was another ancient village, a cluster of squat cottages, home to two or three thousand peasants with their attendant goats, dogs, and bullfight posters, all bowed before the local Catholic church.

Richard Wright, an American writer who passed through this neck of the woods, remembered a bleak, seemingly diseased, and inhospitable landscape that grudged a few patches of scrubby vegetation growing amid vast humped mounds of leprous-looking rubble.[1] But Figueres had two claims to fame. It was the birthplace of Salvador Dalí, and it had a castle, Sant Ferran, built barely ten years before the American Revolution, which made it a fairly modern military installation, by Spanish standards.

San Ferran got bombed frequently by the Nationalists, but still it stood baking in the sun, immovable, indomitable, a symbol of the peeling Spanish grandeur that Franco hoped to restore. Morris and his group spent the night inside the safety of Sant Ferran's massive stone walls and then boarded a train for the port city of Barcelona, the largest Loyalist stronghold on the Spanish east coast. In the crowded station there, within the sight of elegant flowered boulevards and the noise of braying mules that seemed to be parked on every corner, they helped themselves to coffee, bread, and butter offered by the Red Cross. Refreshed, they continued on to the south along the coastal plain, and then inland again.

Albacete was their destination, waiting for them on a dry, brown, almost treeless plateau. It used to be a quiet feed and seed town until the war came along and turned it into a raucous army camp. Like Perpignan, Albacete was a provincial capital, with its own cathedral and palace. The stone and stuccoed houses in its medieval streets were a sonnet to Spanish order and austerity. But Albacete's claim to fame was Miguel de Cervantes Saavedra. A nice old casa here was where Cervantes wrote most of *Don Quixote de la Mancha*, his novel of an errant knight attacking a windmill with his lance. The house was still standing. If you asked, someone would give you a tour, for a modest fee.

Albacete's tactical importance lay in its position as a highway and rail hub, and as headquarters of the international brigades. It was surrounded by training camps, and the main base of the Loyalist air force lay nearby in Los Llanos. Morris and his squad gathered first in the Albacete bullring to register. All the battalion recruiters wanted English speakers and they bickered with one another like buyers at a cattle auction. But the Canadians and the Yanks managed to stick together. The Mac-Paps were officially designated the 60th Battalion of the 15th International Brigade. Aside from the Linc-Wash, other battalions in the 15th came from Britain, Latin America, and Yugoslavia. The Mac-Paps were the last international battalion to come in.

Most veterans of the last war were appointed sergeants. At the quartermaster store the men were issued poorly made brown twill trousers and tunics. No hats, socks, boots, or helmets were available yet, though there were a few greatcoats and ponchos.

Since the international brigades were a Comintern show, there had to be commissars. Morris was elected a part-time commissar, or political officer, for his group. His duties included tending to the men's personal needs, seeing that they had soap, towels, writing paper, and medical care, and explaining, over and over again, that there was no tobacco here because the cigarette factories were in enemy territory.

Morris was also responsible for making inspirational speeches on the men's mission in Spain, but with a darker side to his duties: he had to make sure that everyone, even those of higher rank, made politically correct decisions in line with Stalinist doctrine. He was also instructed to keep an eye out for spies, saboteurs, and malingerers in the ranks. For entertainment, there was a cinema, an occasional bullfight, and cafés that offered the dependable wartime diversions of wine, women, and American jazz on the record player.

Albacete was in La Mancha, a district fat with farms and ranches run like corporations, and for a while the shops in town stocked copious quantities of cheese, fruit, cognac, and marmalade. But enemy bombings had destroyed warehouses and disrupted delivery systems, so that by the time Morris and his group arrived, the army was desperate to get what it could. No butter, eggs, sugar, milk, or real coffee were on the menu. Most meals consisted of hard bread along with rice fried in recycled olive oil. One day the diners discovered some kind of mystery meat had been thrown in. Investigation revealed it was bombed mule, courtesy of enemy warplanes. Chronic diarrhea became common. Some men passed blood every day, causing a weakness they would have to endure throughout their stay in Spain. The only treatment was to eat charcoal tablets. At least the local wines were served at meals. They were raw and sour, but fortifying.

Morris and his group were trucked out to basic training at Tarazona, about eighteen miles from Albacete, on August 4. Like most of the older settlements in eastern Spain, Tarazona traced its lineage back to Roman times. Many of the buildings were terraced along the bluffs above the flood stage of the Queiles River. The campanile of Santa Magdalena Church was the tallest structure in town, commanding a view for miles in every direction. Some Nationalists had installed a machine gun in the tower for a while, and before being evicted they had held the entire city to ransom. Tarazona had once been home to a vibrant community of Jews, until they were expelled like the Muslims before them. A building in the old quarter still had an ornately carved wooden door that might have included part of a Torah.

The infantry camp outside Tarazona where Morris and the Mac-Paps reported for training wasn't so historic, or scenic. The barracks were little more than log cabins built like those at Siberian labor camps, and the mess hall was a barn. The merciless sun kept the earth parched, the winds dusty. There was a well, but no plumbing in the camp. Latrines were trenches in the ground. A bath was a swim in the river. Recreation included volleyball, wrestling, and soccer, with national teams playing one another, and big sing-alongs at night. Off the base, small wine shops could be identified by a green bough nailed to the front door.

There was one pub in town, and its main attraction was a radio tuned every night to a station out of Salamanca that broadcast propaganda speeches from officers on the Nationalist side. One of them was always talking about who was allegedly sleeping with La Passionaria, the revolutionary name of Dolores Ibarruri, a Spanish Communist and former sardine peddler who broadcast impassioned Loyalist speeches at night over Radio Madrid. The Mac-Paps called the Salamanca broadcaster the Pornographic General. He was an early version of Lord-Haw, who would go on the air for the Nazis in the coming second world war.

Because some of the international battalions had been plagued by setbacks—defeats in battle, cowardice, desertions, insurrection, and defeatist attitudes—the Comintern was determined to impose rigorous training on the fresh Mac-Paps and send them into battle as a shining example of how a real combat outfit was supposed to fight. Responsibility for their training and conduct was put on the shoulders of André Marty, son of a French revolutionary from the days of the Paris Commune. As a machinist in the French navy in 1919, he had refused orders from Paris to support a force of Whites during the Russian Civil War and then led a mutiny of the French Black Sea Fleet. He joined the French Communist Party in 1923 and rose to the top. Marty had been appointed one of the top three commanders of the international brigades on the basis of his military background and his favor with Stalin.

Early on, Marty had been an impressive figure. He welcomed new recruits with enthusiastic speeches and appeared to be a pleasant, confident man, secure in his mission, fully in control of his faculties. He sat with the privates in the mess hall, ate the food they ate, and sang with them in the evenings. He abolished saluting and told the officers and men to address one another as comrade. His wife sewed aprons for the barbershop.

But by the time Morris arrived, the pressures of one defeat after another had sent Marty into mental decline. He marched from one flyblown training ground to another, railing at the American volunteers while sniffing out fascist spies he seemed to see hiding under every rock. He was an almost comic figure, short and fat with a puffy, sagging face and a graying mustache beneath a big floppy wool beret, strutting around like a bantam rooster. He thought the North Americans were spoiled brats who should be sent home. Moscow disagreed. They were a cheap and enthusiastic source of bodies for death battalions.

Marty had two sources of security enforcers. One was the NKVD, installed by Moscow and run by Colonel Alexander Orlov, who had been one of the interrogators of Kalamatiano in 1918. The other was SIM (Servicio de Investigación Militar), the military intelligence agency and kill squad for the Loyalists.

Orlov was a career Soviet spy, one of the Old Bolsheviks who had been in service for the Reds since 1917. He was born Leiba Lazarevich Feldbin, a Russian of Jewish ancestry from Byelorussia (now called Belarus). He had been sent to Spain in July 1936 after his lover shot herself in front of the Lubyanka, home of the NKVD, because Orlov refused to divorce his wife and marry her. Orlov was a handsome, solidly built man with groomed black hair, a mustache, and a take-charge manner; a talented journalist, skilled hunter, and hard drinker in the Hemingway tradition, equally at home with generals or gangsters.

Orlov spoke French, Spanish, English, and German, and wore Western clothes. He was thought by many to be a charming man, as killers often are. Like Sidney Reilly, he trusted no one, including his own NKVD chiefs in Moscow, and so he carried a concealed pistol. Orlov and Hemingway became instant friends in Spain. They dined together and Hem took a tour of one of Orlov's training schools where they tried to outshoot one another on the firing range while knocking back shots of vodka. Orlov later said he was the inspiration for the character Varloff in *For Whom the Bell Tolls*, Hemingway's novel of the Spanish Civil War.

Orlov always claimed he was merely a Soviet advisor to Loyalist forces in Spain.[2] In reality, he was operational head of the NKVD in Spain and ruthlessly targeted not only fascist spies but also Trotskyites, anarchists, and any other kind of political deviants he found inside or outside the international brigades.[3] General Jan Berzin, former head of Red Army intelligence, charged that Orlov and the NKVD treated Spain as if it were already a Soviet colony.[4] Orlov assigned Soviet "advisers" to help the Loyalists set up SIM. After that, SIM agents ran concentration camps, torture chambers, and execution rooms in the NKVD tradition.[5] Their headquarters was at La Tamarita, a small villa that backed up to the Soviet consulate in Barcelona. Both SIM and the NKVD used terror in Spain the way Stalin used it in Russia: government by firing squad.

Through the NKVD and SIM, André Marty reportedly had droves of his enemies, either real or imagined, executed. "He purifies more than

Salvarsan," Hemingway wrote.[6] No one can say precisely how many Marty ordered killed. Marty reportedly claimed it was only five hundred or so.[7] By the time Morris Cohen met him in late 1937, Marty was a tired man, paranoid and obsessive, worn out before his time. The Butcher of Albacete, he was called. Soldiers tried to stay away from his headquarters, the way Muscovites avoided walking past the Lubyanka. Hemingway wrote that Marty's face looked like it had been modeled from the waste material you find under the claws of a very old lion.[8]

AS PLANNED, Morris and the Mac-Paps received disciplined and thorough training at Tarazona. The day started with reveille at five. After a wash and a couple of cups of ersatz coffee brewed from burnt barley, they drilled for four hours, got another four hours off for lunch and rest, then attended blackboard lectures. Following a final drill session they went to supper. Singing after that, and taps at nine or ten. Coming into the war late, they had one great advantage: they benefited from the company of seasoned combat vets from hard-fought battles such as Jamara and Brunete.

But many of their Russian training officers could not speak English or Spanish. Some of the Russian instructors were efficient; others were incompetent, or drunkards who resented being sent there. The language problems were never ironed out. Orders were given in a multilingual polyglot called the Spanish Gargle.

During weapons drills, the men used rifles manufactured in Mexico in 1917 on U.S. contract for sale to the Russian Provisional Government. But after the Bolsheviks seized power, the rifles had sat in Mexico until the Soviets bought them and resold them to Loyalist Spain with a hammer and sickle engraved on each barrel. Mexicanskis, the troops called them. After a few shots, the bolts jammed up and had to be hammered free with a stone, so they were just about useless for anything other than training.

Morris was sent to machine-gun school. Like the rifles, the machine guns used in training were antiquated and far from combat quality. Nor were there unlimited amounts of ammunition available for practice.

Despite the fact the international battalions were a Communist show, barely half the North American volunteers were actually party members. The rest were an energetic collection of socialists, anarchists, left-wing writers and intellectuals, radical laborites, seamen, and military adventurers who tramped from one war to another. Many had simply been unemployed and needed a job, or just wanted to get away from home for a while. Nevertheless, they realized they had to serve under Soviet commanders, and accepted that. It didn't matter. They were all together on a crusade. They saw themselves as liberators.

During Morris's training period, the total strength of the 15th International Brigade was around twenty-five hundred men, about two-thirds its designated strength. Major Robert Merriman was chief of staff for the 15th. He was the officer who originally approved creation of a separate Canadian company, which then evolved into the Mackenzie-Papineau Battalion.

Merriman was an economics graduate of the University of Nevada with an ROTC commission as a second lieutenant. He had joined the Communist Party after spending a year studying international economics in Moscow on a scholarship from the University of California at Berkeley. He was tall and broad-shouldered, with skin bronzed by the sun. With his introspective manner and his round, black-framed eyeglasses, Merriman was a dead ringer for the actor Harold Lloyd. Robert Jordan, the protagonist in *For Whom the Bell Tolls*, is based on Merriman.

Bob Merriman had an analytical mind, but unlike most Communists he was also fiercely independent. In Moscow he had admired some of the features of the Soviet system that he thought could improve life in Depression America, and in that regard he was an idealist. But after touring Russia and hearing about the murders committed en masse by Stalin, he was determined not to become a sycophant for either Uncle Joe or his martinet in Spain, André Marty. Merriman refused to see the current fighting in Spain as a civil war. Like Hemingway, he saw Spain as a prelude to something far more sinister. "Hitler is blooding his troops in Spain for a larger world war," Merriman told a friend.[9]

At first, the North Americans in the 15th IB were a restless, unruly lot, fighting with each other and bitching about regulations. But the Mac-Paps admired Bob Merriman and responded to his training sessions. Bob got them organized and disciplined. He got them to read their training manuals and attend his lectures on tank and trench warfare. He showed them how to pull on gas masks and throw grenades, and how to read maps, which unfortunately were in Spanish and sometimes outdated.

Merriman taught Morris and the Mac-Paps to take apart and reassemble their weapons blindfolded. They went out on maneuvers and learned simple security rules such as not lighting a cigarette while on night patrol. They learned when to shoot and when to duck. Unlike the Russian officers in Spain, Merriman had not come here on orders from Moscow. He was here on an ideological mission to fight fascism, writing in his diary at one point that he was willing to die for his ideas. He was a commander the Americans and Canadians could trust. Bob spoke their language, literally.

While in training camp, Morris wrote a friend back in the Bronx and urged him to join the Loyalist cause right away. "We have been involved in intense campaigns to push back the fascists," he said. "From these battles we have felt the pulse of fighting against enemies of the people, against fascists and Nazis who want to suppress everyone and control the world." Some fifty thousand Germans and hundreds of planes had been sent to Spain, he wrote, and they "raised havoc over our heads for days on end and killed thousands of innocent women and children who were not carrying any arms at all." The internationals, he said, required arms, which America would not sell them. He implored his friend to join the "forces for peace and democracy" that were fighting in Spain. He warned him not to wait until fascists started shooting in New York the way they had in Europe. "You as a Jew are in double danger," he added.[10]

Actually, Morris had fudged the truth, as he did from time to time. He had not been involved in any campaigns against the enemy so far, except for the fact that he belonged to a brigade that indeed had seen intense fighting in past months. But finally his time came. On September 5, 1937, the Mac-Paps were called up for deployment to the front.

FIRST, a parade was held in the Plaza de Tarazona. Townspeople turned out to cheer the troops as they lined up for inspection by their officers. Speeches were made by generals, commissars, and politicians. A band played, and patriotic Spanish songs were sung. Victory was in the air.

"*Salud! A la frente!*" the locals shouted.

It had been drilled into the Mac-Paps over and over again that they were the elite of the internationals. They had trained hard and had been given every advantage that Bob Merriman could get for them. Most of all, they had not known defeat in battle. They were energetic and optimistic. But still, that all came with a certain sense of anxiety caused by the sight of Linc-Wash survivors from Brunete.

"Thin to the point of emaciation; bloodshot, pus-running eyes; facial bones sticking out prominently; and in response to questions, brusque to the point of rudeness," Ronald Liversedge wrote in his memoir. "So we saw what a battle did to men in the Spanish war. I could not recall seeing men so drained of all vitality in France in the First World War."

Some of the men of the Linc-Wash, in turn, were not too impressed by the Mac-Paps. The Linc-Wash veterans were exhausted. Some were despondent. They had no patience with the gung-ho Mac-Paps and their constant rifle practice and bugle blowing. Finally somebody stole their bugle.

At last it was time to move out. The Mac-Paps were loaded into Russian Sturka trucks in near darkness like figures in an El Greco painting. They rode down to the station at Albacete and got on troop trains to begin the long haul northward through the Valencia region along the Med. They sat up in day coaches and slept in their seats. They crossed rivers and passed long stretches of orchards and citrus groves and miles of flat brown earth devoid of anything green. The villages were the same color as the earth, and as the train approached them they seemed to pop up like apparitions. But peasants everywhere turned out to wave as they passed.

The trains entered the Aragon region and the men began to see things that foreshadowed what lay ahead. They passed bombed-out towns, some of them still burning, and columns of soldiers marching, their faces and tunics powdered with dust, and convoys of trucks carrying ammunition and big guns. The men ate the food they had brought with them on the trains. They played cards. They told stories. They sang a tune about the battle of the Jamara, set to the melody of "Red River Valley:"

There's a valley in Spain called Jamara,
That's a place that we all know so well,
For 'tis there that we wasted our manhood,
And most of our old age as well.

Jamara was the battle where the Lincoln Battalion lost most of their officers along with 120 men, and another 175 wounded, a staggeringly high casualty rate for an outfit of only 450. Some of the European soldiers on the train didn't appreciate the song. They couldn't understand why Americans would sing that way about a disaster.

Three days and nights later, Morris and his battalion arrived at Huesca. The turnover of officers in the Mac-Pap Battalion continued. Their new commander was an American, Major Rollin Dart, a former U.S. Army Air Corps officer who gratefully moved reveille back from five o'clock to six. Dart was soon replaced by still another American, and then another. But Bob Merriman was always there, updating the men on the shifting battle situations around them.

Huesca had once been famous for its silver mines, and one of its local monasteries held the tomb of King Alfonso I of Aragon. But the city was noted more as the hometown of San Lorenzo, also known as Saint Lawrence, who was martyred by the Romans—burned on a grill, legend had it. Hence the symbol of San Lorenzo was a grill. You could find them all over town, in window glass and carved on doors.

Huesca was in the hands of the Nationalists but under siege by the Loyalists. Outside the city, the front was rough, hilly, dry, and treeless. Hardscrabble, like the Dust Bowl that many of them had left behind in the United States and Canada. The Huesca front wasn't well defined the way it was in Madrid, where you could take a streetcar to a certain street and there the enemy was. The opposing trenches below Huesca were sometimes a mile apart. Artillery was fired and patrols went out, but no ground attacks were ordered.

In addition to the diarrhea they had brought with them, some of the men came down with colds, pneumonia, pleurisy, and jaundice. Everybody had lice. The army treatment was to touch a lit cigarette to the skin and incinerate them.

Morris and his unit heard about a devastating battle that had been fought to the south at Belchite. The internationals had to take the town house by house with hand grenades. Once the shooting was over, only about one hundred men of the Linc-Wash were left standing. The battleground was littered with hundreds of corpses rotting in the sun and had to be burned in huge pyres. A grim joke ran through the internationals: "Tomorrow we'll have coffee in Huesca."

Morris and his battalion had been held in reserve at Huesca with the idea of gradually acclimating them to combat situations. On October 8 their trucks took them south to Albalate, an old Moorish town presided over by a Gothic castle that resembled a grain elevator. Their convoy inched its way through streets so narrow that the trucks scraped the fronts of houses. Children ran laughing alongside the column while old women in shapeless black dresses watched from doorways and windows. Hundreds of supply trucks were in the convoy. Seventy-five flatbeds hauled Soviet tanks painted in green and yellow camouflage patches. Thousands of Spanish infantry marched behind a battalion of republican cavalry that itself was a mile long.

The Mac-Paps took four days to reach Zaragoza, on the Ebro River, just east of Belchite. It had a population of over two hundred thousand, making it one of the biggest cities in Spain. Franco planned to mount a major offensive at Zaragoza, break through Loyalist lines, and rush eastward to conquer the key Mediterranean port cities of Taragona and Barcelona. If successful, that maneuver would cut the Loyalist territory in half. Zaragoza also had an emotional appeal to the Nationalists, especially the Catholics, since Saint James the Greater, brother of John the Evangelist, was buried there. He had arrived in Zaragoza to preach the gospel forty years after the death of Christ. Some believed he saw the Virgin Mary there.

The Loyalist strategy was to first send the 15th International Brigade up to attack the village of Fuentes de Ebro, eight miles away. That was a small but formidable Nationalist position that protected Zaragoza from the southeast. After taking Fuentes, the internationals would then move sixteen miles upriver for a major assault on Zaragoza. But it was a big gamble, as offensives often are in wartime. A defeat at Fuentes de Ebro just might spell the beginning of the end of the republican cause.

On the night of October 12, Morris and his battalion rolled out again. Winking lights in the distance marked enemy campfires around Fuentes de Ebro. Morris's machine gun section had better Russian weapons now, heavy Maxims and lighter Maxim-Tokarevs. The Maxims had a wheeled carriage, along with a front shield. Both Maxims and Tokarevs were considered antiques by the Soviets, and they had unloaded them on the Loyalists at a tidy profit. Still, they were formidable weapons. They were belt-fed and could fire standard Russian 7.62-millimeter ammunition at 600 rounds per minute. With a range of 1,000 meters, roughly the length of eleven football fields, they were valuable also as antiaircraft guns. A machine-gun squad was made up of eight or so men. If they had a Maxim, two of the men would pull the machine gun along on its clunky wagon wheels while the others ran behind, toting steel boxes of ammo.

The infantry sections also got improved weapons, Russian Mosin-Nagant 7.62 mm rifles left over from 1918. With the needle bayonet attached, they were almost seven feet long. Everybody got proper shoes at last but socks were still a problem. Some men wrapped their feet in rags Russian style. At least there were enough helmets for all—French, Italian, Spanish, Russian, German—many of them taken off the bodies of casualties. The most popular helmets were German. Their coal skuttle shape protected the ears and neck from shrapnel.

Morris ran into Edward Lending before the battle. Ed had been fielding questions from the green Mac-Paps about what combat was like. How had things gone at Belchite? How many got killed? Wounded? How did the Nationalists fight? How did their equipment compare with that of the international battalions?

"I brushed them off," Ed wrote later. "I had lost too many precious comrades. Wanted no new ones to lose. And then I recognized Morris, not twenty yards away."

"Moishe!" Ed shouted.

Morris stared at Ed a moment, at first not recognizing this bedraggled soul as his old schoolmate and football chum. Then he grinned and went up to him.

"Oh, Ed, did you hear about the new Bronx aldermanic district program we've organized? It's slick. Next election, we're gonna cream 'em!"

Ed was furious. He had heard nothing from Morris about the situation that faced them at that moment. They were both going into a big battle. This time tomorrow they might be dead. And there Morris was, obsessed with some petty election back home.

"A strange echo from a distant, irrelevant past," Ed said. "I turned, walked away."[11]

FUENTES DE EBRO sat on top of a high ridge in a district known for its caves and alabaster quarries. The walls of the local church and the houses around it formed a fort, behind which lay the Ebro River and the railroad. An arroyo, a gulch, was out front. Below the gulch was a steep, treeless plain that sloped for a mile down to the highway. All in all, a pretty barren place. Hemingway had written in a short story that the hills around there looked like white elephants.

The planners of the Loyalist attack intended to stop their trucks with the lights off just short of Fuentes and slip into the trenches that had been dug in front of the village. The internationals would relieve the Catalonian troops laying siege to Fuentes, and then at dawn, zero hour, the Loyalist air force, la Gloriosa, would bomb the enemy trenches around the village. After that, Soviet tanks would lead the infantrymen in their attack on the village walls. Undoubtedly it looked good on paper. But it was a blunder from the very beginning.

First, a massive nighttime traffic jam developed on the road up from Quinto. It was fully daylight when Morris and the Mac-Paps finally jumped out of their trucks and ran for the narrow, shallow trenches that spread out from the road like feather vanes to a quill. Three-quarters of the men in the battalion were still exposed on the road as enemy machine gunners opened up. Many were cut down right there. Zero hour came and went, and the bombers didn't arrive.

Second problem: The Mac-Paps were not properly acquainted with the layout of the battlefield. Hearing firing from their right, they thought they were under attack from enemy forces over there. They returned the fire. But it was the Linc-Wash Battalion. Finally everybody was ordered to stop shooting and redirect his fire toward the village.

Still the Loyalist planes had not appeared. The men lay in their trenches, exposed to the pitiless sun. They were short on water and they knew there would be no food coming up until nightfall.

Zero hour was set again, for noon. Finally the Loyalist planes did arrive. They flew up from the south, fifty light bombers glinting in the sunlight. The pilots banked and swooped down on the enemy trenches in a long continuous line. The antiaircraft fire was heavy but the pilots held steady. The bombs fell like silver petals, leaving behind blooms of fire on the ground. The earth trembled with the force of an earthquake. Then the smoke and dust settled as the planes withdrew.

The delayed air strike was followed by the fourth blunder of the day. The tanks were late. The men in the trenches waited. Time slowed to a mortal crawl across the broiling battlefield. The Moors and Italians were able to repair their trenches and bring up more men, machine guns, mortars, field artillery.

Ambulances stood by behind the Loyalist lines. Some were mobile blood transfusion trucks that had been developed in Spain by a Canadian surgeon, Norman Bethune. An ambulance driver later recalled blood being drawn from dead soldiers for use as transfusions into wounded men. It was a Soviet technique and had to be done quickly before the blood in the corpses coagulated.

"Their bad luck was our good luck," the doctor said.[12]

Finally, an hour and a half later, the Loyalists cheered as the Soviets' International Tank Regiment appeared. They drove new, light BT-5 tanks, equipped with machine guns, flamethrowers, and 45 mm cannon. The BT-5s roared over the tops of the Mac-Pap trenches. One soldier panicked and tried to crawl out and was nearly crushed. Some Spaniards of the 24th Battalion climbed on the tops of the tanks. Apparently somebody had seen that in a movie. Most were quickly shot down.

With the tanks leading the way, a bugler blew the order to charge, and the Mac-Paps scrambled out of their trenches with a collective roar. The Linc-Wash and the British battalions joined the mad scramble up the hill. The men tried to catch up with the tanks and use them for cover, but BT-5s were independent, deep-maneuver vehicles not designed for infantry support. They roared up the plain at more than twenty miles per hour, leaving the infantrymen behind. Still, the men on foot bravely charged—kneel, fire, and advance; kneel, fire, and advance—but were caught out in the open and picked off like blackbirds on a telephone line.

Some of the BT-5s fell into the gulley and flipped over. Others got stuck in mud. Of the forty-eight tanks committed to the attack, nineteen were destroyed by enemy guns. Behind them, Joe Dallet, chief commissar for the Mac-Paps, was hit by a bullet and was dead before he hit the ground. A witness said he had been walking up the hill, smiling and smoking his pipe, when he caught it.

Morris and some of the other machine gunners dived for low hummocks on the field and were able to set up return fire. But soon they ran out of ammunition. Stretcher-bearers were killed trying to reach wounded men lying bleeding out in the open.

With most of their officers killed or wounded, the Loyalist force had no one to tell them what to do next. The entire offensive stalled at the foot of the village. No reinforcements came. No artillery support. No more tanks, planes, or ammunition. The exposed men could neither advance nor retreat. The only thing they could was dig into the ground with their dinner plates. Then they waited, in their pitiful holes, in the baking sun, with no food or water, while enemy gunners shot at them. After dark, they crawled on their bellies back down the plain to their own trenches.

In a word, it was a slaughter. Some blamed the Soviets for hastily planning the operation at the last moment. Delays, missed orders, old maps, no clear orders. One thing after another. The attack was an exercise in incompetence and achieved absolutely nothing. Two days later, the Nationalists broke through the Loyalist lines, and that signaled the beginning of the fall of northern Spain to Franco.

The small Mackenzie-Papineau Battalion lost sixty dead and two hundred wounded in that one battle, a casualty rate of over 50 percent. Morris Cohen was hit on October 14. He was taken off the battlefield with a machine gun wound to each thigh. He was twenty-eight years old.

6 CODE NAME LUIS

A few days after the disaster at Fuentes de Ebro, Edward Lending was down in Murcia, southeast of 15th International Brigade headquarters at Albacete. Casualties from Fuentes had been treated at field dressing stations in the north and were now being brought here to the Hospitale Universidad, run by Edward Barsky, the doctor who spoke at the rally for Spain that Morris Cohen attended in New York. Ed went from room to room looking for pals. He found Morris.

"A chunk of his thigh was gone," Ed wrote later. "The blood had seeped through his bandages, soaked the bedding, and was still oozing."

He asked Moishe how he was doing.

"Just great!" Morris replied.

The answer, Ed noted, came with the beatific look of pure sainthood.

Again, Lending was disgusted. He had been through four of the worst battles of the war—Jamara, Brunete, Belchite, and Fuentes de Ebro. And there Morris was, acting as if combat were just some kind of party function back in the Bronx.

Ed had grown to realize what others had already concluded about what was going on in Spain. Saving the country from the evils of fascism looked good in the world press, but Stalin was here to show off his new weapons and sharpen his knives for the coming big war with Germany. Hitler and Mussolini were doing the same thing. Idealistic young men like Ed and Morris, whether they had fought for the Loyalists or the Nationalists, had been sent on a fool's errand.

The Soviets were losing the war. That was obvious. But the Russian pilots, tankers, and commissars would be welcomed home as heroes of a great patriotic struggle. So would the international brigade volunteers from Russia. They would receive medical care at government expense. Their dead would be buried as war veterans. But for the volunteers from the Western nations, it was a different story.

Men from Germany and Italy faced arrest and concentration camps if they went home. Survivors from the United States and Canada in the Mac-Pap and Linc-Wash battalions would, at best, be ignored. A few would be arrested in America for violating the Logan Act 1799 in connection with recruiting volunteers for Spain.

The American and Canadian volunteers had fought the nations that would be the enemies of the Allies in the next war, but no veterans' benefits were waiting for them, no ticker-tape parades. Ed didn't even have his passport. It had been taken from him three months before. That was the Comintern's way of keeping the internationals from leaving Spain.

Ed talked with Morris a while longer. But he was sick of Cohen's fierce dedication to his unshakable Stalinist illusions. Ed changed Morris's bandages, then got the hell out of there. "Throughout the war, Morris remained a preeminent member of our widely disdained political Boy Scout faction," Lending wrote later.[1]

Murcia wasn't a bad place to be if you were wounded. It was a sunny regional capital tucked away in the mountains of southeast Spain, a short drive from the beaches on the Costa Blanca. The city was famous for the fruit and vegetables grown in its orchards and vineyards. Some Americans thought the farmland looked like Southern California.

Murcia was an old Muslim settlement built around Platería and Trapería streets, center of its ancient Jewish silver and garment trade. The city had survived an earthquake, a flood, and the bubonic plague, and now it was dealing with air raids, enemy spies, and thousands of casualties from the north. The cafés were overrun by rich young Spanish men with oiled hair wearing French suits and American sunglasses after buying their way out of military service. Shouted insults from wounded soldiers were not uncommon.

Morris Cohen took four months to recover. As soon as he was able to get out of bed and walk around the English-speaking ward on crutches, he resumed his agitprop work for the party. He read to patients, wrote letters home for them, ran errands, made inquiries on their behalf. Those were things that people liked about him, in addition to the fact he always seemed to have the latest sports news from back home.

Oscar Hunter, one of the American commissars at Murcia, wrote a glowing report of Morris. Oscar was an African American from New Jersey who had played football at West Virginia State College (like Morris, on athletic scholarship) and studied journalism at Northwestern University. He had joined the John Reed Club in Chicago with Richard Wright and Nelson Algren, and later went into the CPUSA. After he was wounded himself in Spain, he joined Morris at the Murcia hospital. But Oscar wasn't just another patient. He was trusted by certain people at 15th International Brigade headquarters. He sent them reports that the Comintern might find useful.

"His work while in the hospital has been of the best," Oscar wrote of Morris. "He has a fine sense of what the comrades want and how to develop the work around their needs." His ability to organize things to produce results was an example to others, Hunter said in his report. "And that is most important—the comrade has been developing steadily and is much more mature in his judgments and approach to people than he was in the beginning of his work."[2]

Morris also caught the eye of local spotters for the NKVD. One of those was Jack Bjoze (né Goldstein), a young Jew about Morris's age from the Bronx. Bjoze had been born in Poland and became an American citizen through his father's naturalization. He arrived in the United States around 1923, traveled to Russia in 1933, and joined the CPUSA in 1935. He volunteered for Spain two months before Morris. They met in the hospital early in 1938 and became fast friends.

"Our shared ideals [concerned] the conditions in the United States on employment, bread lines, no jobs, and the danger of Hitler coming into power," Bjoze recalled later. Morris was a very charming person who could smoothly engage strangers in political discussions without offending them, he added. Bjoze also admired Morris for his athletic skills. "We had a soccer game in which we took part, and our opponents were Germans. Morris was the best athlete in our team."[3]

It was quite a compliment, considering Morris had a football knee and machine gun wounds to both legs. Perhaps the German players were in worse shape.

That questionnaire that Morris had filled out upon first arriving in Spain in August 1937 was also useful to the NKVD's evaluation of him. Morris had been asked in the questionnaire to explain the most outstanding thing he had noticed since leaving the United States. He replied that it was the maturity of the Popular Front and the labor movements in France and Spain as compared to those in the United States.

"This is even reflected in the education of the little children, in their conduct on the streets or at the stations when our train approached, as well as the progress of their parents and the latter's organizations," he wrote. "This is coupled with the change in the institutions in Spain. Here is a former church, shorn of every ecclesiastical vestige, transformed into a House of the People, with union meeting halls at the sides, a platform for speakers, posters depicting speakers, and slogans reflecting the historical events of the day. . . ."

But accompanying that ideological transformation, Morris said, was an economic hangover in Spain that one could see in the "primitive manner of threshing wheat, dependent upon the wind, still prevailing as a heritage from the feudalistic reign of King Alfonso and his reactionary successors." When ideology and culture were revolutionized, he added, mechanical ways of production would follow. "It is these parallel rails of progress whose course can never be stopped, which struck me most powerfully."

Propaganda skills aside, Morris had provided another answer on that questionnaire that was even more interesting to his watchers. Asked what he intended to do after the war, he replied: "When the war is finished, I would like to return to activity in the American labor movement. However, if circumstances require my presence elsewhere, similar to the Spanish struggle against fascism, then I would go there."

Here was new talent, begging for an audition.

An official evaluation was sent to the Comintern by some members of the Central Committee of the Communist Party of Spain. Comrade Cohen's "general political attitude" was praised, along with his "disciplined, steady" devotion to the Communist Party. A good agitator, a good organizer, "a very good party member," the evaluation concluded.[4]

Morris was discharged from the hospital in March 1938 and assigned to work as a security guard at 15th International headquarters in Albacete. Now he was watched even more closely. How was he holding up psychologically? Had he turned defeatist because of his wounds? Was he beginning to question Communism? No, that wasn't Morris Cohen. As always, he toed the party line.

After a while, he was summoned to Barcelona for an interview. Up until now, there had been two pivotal moments in Morris Cohen's life. The first had been when he joined the Communist Party as a full member and dedicated his life to the cause. The second had been when he volunteered to leave everything behind in New York to fight in the Spanish Civil War. Now he was about to encounter a third crossroads in his life.

THE ADDRESS he found in Barcelona belonged to a big villa set back from the road and surrounded by a dusty stone wall. Like Spain herself, it had once been grandiose and proud but was now used for a more earthly purpose—as a school for guerrilla and sabotage training. It was listed as a Spanish Army facility but in fact was operated by the NKVD.

A handsome, muscular man wearing a mustache and a plain uniform without rank or unit designations met Morris at the gate. With impressive English he introduced himself as Compañero Brown. He said Morris had been recommended by 15th IB headquarters for training here.

KGB historian Vladimir Chikov believes that Compañero Brown was Alexander Orlov, one of the Chekists who had questioned Xenophon Kalamatiano in Moscow after his arrest in 1918. Orlov had fought with the Reds in the Russian Civil War and the Soviet war against Poland. He was a hardened revolutionary and a ruthless counterintelligence chief who had witnessed the defeatism and infighting that had plagued the Loyalist side in the war. But he supported Soviet intervention in Spain because he felt that Germany was eventually going to attack the Soviet Union and perhaps a show of strength here might deter Hitler, at least for a while. It had been Orlov's idea to send the passports of dead international volunteers to Moscow for use by Soviet spies who would be posted later to Western nations.

Orlov operated six guerrilla-sabotage schools in the Madrid, Valencia, and Barcelona areas.[5] They trained men and women to slip into enemy territory and attack bridges and airfields, derail trains, and cut phone lines. Robert Jordan would be on that kind of mission in Hemingway's *For Whom the Bell Tolls.* In ten months, Orlov's schools had trained sixteen hundred regular guerrillas and fourteen thousand partisans. Jack Bjoze had already been picked to attend one of the schools.

Morris recounted this meeting later, saying that Orlov took him for a tour of the grounds of the villa and asked him about his feelings toward Russia.[6] Morris replied that he felt the USSR was leading the way in building a "free society" and that he was committed to worldwide Communist revolution. The Soviet Union, he added, was the only major power so far to fight the "brown plague" (fascism).

Then it was Morris's turn for a question. He asked Orlov about the purges that Stalin had been carrying out in Russia. Was Stalin a Russian Franco?

"Yes," Orlov replied, "Stalin is a tragedy for our country."

Stalin feared the intelligent and talented Russians around him, Orlov explained. They were threats to his power because they knew that the secret document called Lenin's Testament had not clearly named Stalin as Comrade Chairman's successor. Millions of Russians, Orlov said, particularly Old Bolsheviks like himself who had known Lenin, were being purged by Stalin, either sent to labor camps or executed without trial. But those were topics that one did not discuss openly in Russia. There was an old saying that curiosity killed the comrade.

Morris had to be impressed by the fact that he could ask Orlov about those things and get frank answers. Orlov, in turn, was undoubtedly flattered by Morris's trusting him enough to inquire about them in the first place. In short, the young and still innocent recruit, and the wizened old killer who was about to become his mentor, hit it off from the start.

In his report to Moscow on Morris's recruitment, Orlov wrote that his new charge knew exactly what he was doing when he volunteered to help out the Soviets in the future. Orlov said he was convinced that Morris was not driven by a sense of adventure but by political ideals of liberty, democracy, and peace; world revolution, too (which sounded a tad Trotskyist). But what else was it about Morris Cohen that had prompted Orlov to recruit him? Specialized training was expensive. Candidates had to be chosen carefully.

First of all, Orlov believed that the best recruits were those who were in it for the money, or who were ideologically committed. Those who were pressured through blackmail were simply not dependable, he warned. Mor-

ris fit neatly as an ideological recruit. Also, he had arrived in Spain with
Earl Browder's recommendation preceding him.

Always on the lookout for promising talent, Orlov had watched Morris
from the day he showed up at Albacete. Comrade Cohen was an affable,
popular young man, of good character, with no police record, and well
versed in Marxist thought. He came from a modest background, the son of
a fruit peddler, but was now a university graduate and conducted himself
as a gentleman. One foot in the working class, the other in the bourgeoisie. Perfect. His final test of grit had been his bravery in combat against a
superior enemy force.

In a word, his bona fides were impeccable.

Because of his battle wounds, Morris was not offered guerrilla and sabotage training. He simply was not up to the physical demands of mountain
climbing and long marches with a heavy pack on his back. Instead, Orlov
wanted to train him as a radio operator at a separate intelligence school in
Barcelona. If everything panned out, Orlov would offer him his own secret
mission. Morris accepted immediately.

The scout had found his master.

ORLOV'S SPY SCHOOL at Barcelona might have been the first established
by the Soviets outside Russia. Its code name was Construction. The curriculum was based on that used by the Central Military School in Moscow
where Orlov had taught before coming to Spain.[7] Construction was operated secretly. The students were registered by coded numbers to defeat
government recruiters who came in looking for the names of men they
wanted for further combat service. Orlov was grooming his young men and
women for a higher calling. They were going to be sent back to their home
countries to operate underground in a clandestine war against international
fascism—that is, spying for the Soviet Union.

Morris would operate as a *nelegal* (illegal) agent for the NKVD in America. That meant he was not a Soviet citizen legally accredited by Washington
to work in the United States for the USSR. A spy who was a legal conducted
his espionage work out of a Soviet consulate, embassy, trade office, or news
agency, and used his official job as cover for his clandestine work. An il-

legal was an independent operative who maintained a cover job such as a shopkeeper away from the official spotlight.

Orlov is often credited with originating the idea of illegals. As an important section chief of the intelligence directorate in Moscow, he had concluded early on that the main reason why Russian legals got caught abroad was because they worked out of Soviet offices, which were under surveillance by counterintelligence agents. Thus, it only made sense to create an illegals directorate. That firewall of secrecy would also serve another important purpose: offering Moscow two independent sources—legals and illegals—for double-checking intelligence product coming in to the Center.

Illegals were emphatically ordered to stay away from Soviet embassies or consulates. They were told not to visit them, phone them, or send them mail. The penalty for spying against the United States was thirty years in prison, or death, so the strictest rule for an illegal was to keep low. If a legal got blown (exposed), he or she would simply be deported. If an illegal got arrested, Mother Russia would never claim him. Someone at an NKVD *rezidentura* might discretely make some phones calls to find him a lawyer, but that was about it.

Morris had to have been thrilled at being personally chosen by the legendary Alexander Orlov. True, Morris considered himself a dedicated Communist, an idealist, a romantic. But there was that other thing he had experienced—the reality of the battlefield, the dry-mouthed, throbbing fear and elation of a wild infantry charge across an open field into the chuckle of enemy machine-gun fire. He had been scared. Everybody was. That was one of the things that kept you alive. But he had performed without complaint, had been seriously wounded, and had survived. His calmness in battle confirmed him as one of the elites of the international brigades. Now, as a reward, he had been handpicked to join Orlov's special cadre of intelligence agents.

MORRIS AND THE OTHER STUDENTS at Construction were first taught the basics of *konspiratsia* (tradecraft). It started with learning to maintain absolute secrecy about your work. You could never confide in friends or family, except for your spouse. At the same time, you had to divorce yourself completely from the Communist Party. Stay away from the party halls, don't subscribe to any party publications, don't sign any petitions, don't register to vote as Communist. Most of all, don't get involved in public demonstrations that might draw the attention of the police or the media. When investigating a subject, counterintelligence officers always started with police files. Even if you never got arrested, you still might be identified by a photo.

Morris would be assigned a control officer. They would both work at cover jobs. The NKVD was notoriously cheap, so Morris, as an ideological recruit, would not be paid a salary but would receive compensation for expenses. If you were an especially valuable agent, Moscow Center would provide seed money for you to start up a roof for your spy work, but otherwise you were expected to support yourself. Some operatives made good money with their start-ups, placing them squarely in the capitalist camp.

All outside contacts between operatives had to be preceded by a process of getting clean of surveillance. It involved taking a long taxi ride, ducking out the side doors of stores, or playing musical chairs on a succession of subway cars. It took hours but it was necessary. You also needed a cover story for your trip, in case you were stopped. You might pretend to be going to a movie or ball game, or to the dentist.

Once you were sure you were clean, you moved on to the actual contact. To transfer documents, agents used a *dubok* (dead drop), or a pass. A drop was safer than a pass. A favorite place for Soviets drops was a darkened movie theater. Your asset would go in first. He would take a certain seat toward the back of the auditorium. He would watch the movie for a while, tape his envelope of documents under his seat, then get up and leave. It was recommended that he do this at an exciting moment in the movie when everybody was watching the screen and paying no attention to you as you came in, sat in the same seat, and retrieved the documents.

A pass was faster, but more dangerous, and it required more skill and nerve. In a brush pass, you approached your asset on a crowded sidewalk or inside a busy store. First, you both looked past each other's shoulder to see if anyone was following. Then you transferred the documents as you brushed past each other.

There were also automobile passes. You got into your car in a parking garage. Your contact pulled in beside you and tossed the documents in through your window. Then you drove off with the goods. But regardless of which type of pass was used, Russians liked an additional layer of security: after receiving the documents in a pass, you walked or drove around the corner and passed the documents again, this time to your assistant, who then disappeared with them.

If the documents had to be returned right away, your backup would photograph them at the *rezidentura* and then rejoin you at a busy café or automat where you were innocently eating a sandwich. The man or woman who happened to be sitting across from you at the table drinking coffee and reading a newspaper was your agent who had slipped you the documents in the first place. After a while, your assistant came in and sat down with you. The newspaper he casually placed on the table was identical to the one being read by your agent. Then you and your assistant got up and left. Your agent waited a minute, and went out by another door. He had switched newspapers. The paper he carried under his arm was the one your assistant had brought to the table. It contained the documents that had to be returned.

Seasoned operatives were often suspicious of both drops and passes. Too many things could go wrong. If the drop was in a park and snow was on the ground, your agent might bury the package in the wrong place. Or a dog might come along and dig it up. And squirrels often hijacked strange objects tucked into knotholes of their trees. That's why face-to-face meetings were preferred.

Morris and his control officer would have two kinds of meetings. First, there were regular meets taking place at a prearranged time and place—for example, at 2:00 p.m. on the second Sunday of each month in front of the lion cage at the Bronx Zoo. If either party didn't show, the meeting was automatically moved to another time according to a backup schedule.

Regular meetings were for routine business such as comparing notes, making new assignments, and discussing assets to be recruited.[8] They also served as venting sessions. Your operative might complain of faulty equipment or murky instructions. He might add pleas of neglect, or broken promises, or poverty. You would pretend to make suggestions, and he would pretend to listen. Then you would take him someplace cheap for lunch, assure him that Mother still loved him, and send him on his way with batteries recharged.

Then there were special meetings. They were called for urgent business such as relaying new instructions received from Moscow Center. They were set up by a signal. Over the years, Hollywood seems to have thought that the only signal ever used by spies was a chalk mark scratched on a wall or a mailbox. Orlov taught Morris and his other students to be more discreet. A favorite signal was a thumbtack pressed under the wooden shelf beneath a certain pay phone.

A phone call was allowed for scheduling a meet, but only with caution. One way was to call your contact from a pay station. You identified yourself by a code name and suggested meeting for coffee to talk about last weekend's football game or some swell new platter just released by Louis Armstrong. Then you set a day and time on a "plus" system. For example, you might ask for a meeting at four o'clock on Thursday. Using two plus, that meant six o'clock on Saturday. Adding "my place" or "your place" was code for a certain café or tavern. Another system was for you to call your contact, apologize for ringing the wrong number, and hang up. That was the signal for him to go out to a certain public phone and take a call from you.

If Morris had never met his contact before, he would be supplied with a description. First, a general sketch would be given: say, a man, about forty years old, five feet eleven, 200 pounds, with black hair, mustache, and glasses. Then more specific details were added: a gray suit with a red tie, and something different in each hand—a newspaper, a tennis ball, a new book by Bennett Cerf. Once you recognized your contact, you approached and engaged in a prearranged dialogue called a parole.

But blind contacts like that were the most dangerous of all. Orlov told his students about a young Soviet operative in Berlin who was instructed to proceed to a certain bus stop, meet a courier, and hand him a small box of talcum powder that contained a roll of secret film. Arriving at the bus stop, the agent spotted a man who fit the description of the courier.

"I am here as a tourist," the Soviet agent said. "I admire your beautiful country."

"Yes, it is beautiful," the other man replied. "I am also a tourist."

Every word of the parole was correct. The Soviet agent was about to hand over the film when—

"That's my bus!" the stranger declared. With that, he bounded onto the bus and roared off, leaving the Soviet agent dumbfounded.

Sometimes long meets were required. Those might take place in a safe house rented by the NKVD through an asset who could not be traced back to Station One. But safe houses, in time, could draw surveillance. A safer venue was a weekend in the country.

On a trip out of town, you took your own car, which gave you mobility for losing a tail, or you rode a train or bus. If you flew, you would have to give a name, and renting a car required a driver's license. In a final flourish of operational security, you and the agent you were meeting took your families along for the trip. Then upon arrival in the great outdoors, all of you just happened to run into one another in the woods. Props were helpful—a tent, a fishing pole, a flashlight.

Most important of all, though, were communications with Moscow Center. As an illegal operating outside diplomatic channels, Morris could never communicate directly with the Center by telephone, telegram, or diplomatic pouch. In the United States, his control officer would take care of all his messages to Moscow. Later on, in England, he would contact the Center directly by shortwave radio.

Today's average FM broadcast station uses a transmitter the size of a couple of refrigerators, has a maximum power of one hundred thousand watts, but can throw a primary signal out for only about seventy miles. Spies use high-frequency ham radios. A dependable model is the size of a small suitcase and can send a shortwave signal bouncing around the world with less than a hundred watts.

But the radios that Morris learned to operate in 1938 were more complicated than those in use today. Older radios required a dozen or more adjustments be made before each use: antenna and secondary condensers, antenna and secondary inductance, the coupling, the tickler, the filament current, the plate current, and so on.

Morris learned to take apart and reassemble his radio, and to repair it. Spy radios were custom-built in Moscow, and the parts had no identifying marks on them. For that reason, if Morris took his radio into a repair shop, the technician might get suspicious and contact the Federal Communications Commission. They in turn would call the FBI. Then men in suits and snap-brim fedoras would be waiting when Cohen came back to pick up his set.

When operating his radio, Morris would transmit in international Morse code. A metal key was used to tap out a series of dots and dashes over the air. The duration of a dash was three times that of a dot; individual letters in a word were separated by a short space, whole words by a longer space. Morris became a star pupil in his radio class, learning to send thirty or more words per minute.

Each sender had his own personal style of transmitting, called a fist, which was as distinctive as the sound of his voice. If Morris got arrested and an FBI agent attempted to send a message on his transmitter, the listener in the radio room at Moscow Center would know immediately that it wasn't Cohen's fist. Moscow would also listen for the safety signal that was supposed to be included in each message. It was something subtle such as a back shift in the fourth group of numbers. Safety signals were standard operating procedure for intelligence services. Inclusion of the safety signal confirmed that the sender was not transmitting under duress.

While learning Morse code, Morris was also taught ciphers. They were not the same thing. Morris would first convert his plain-text message into code by looking up the words or phrases in a codebook organized like a dictionary. But instead of a definition, each entry was assigned a four-digit number group. The message "Documents arriving Thursday" might read as 4459 2398 2239. Simple coding was not enough, though. Even before computers, an experienced code analyst could sit down with an enemy message, consult his file of previously intercepted signals from that source, do some mathematical calculations, and figure it out. Thus, encoded signals were taken one step further. They were enciphered.

Russia, Britain, France, and Germany all used the one-time pad (OTP) system for enciphering. The OTP obscured the coded message by use of additives. The Soviet OTP was a tablet about the size of a booklet of today's Post-It notes. Each page contained columns of five-digit numbers—the additives. You added the additives to the original four-digit coded numbers, then transmitted the totals.

The receiver of the message had an identical copy of your OTP and you would both be using the same pages from the pad. First the receiver looked up the numbers of the additive in his own OTP. Then he subtracted the five-digit OTP additives from the totals he had received from you. That revealed the original four-digit coded numbers. A check of the codebook put the message back into clear text.

But here was the essential part: Both Morris as the sender and Moscow

Center as the receiver were supposed to use each page only once, then tear it off. Because the additive numbers had been selected randomly, were different for each message, and were not supposed to be used again, the system was considered unbreakable. The U.S. Army, though, would later prove that to be a false assumption.

Morris was also taught how to make microdots. A microdot is a photograph that can be reduced to a size smaller than the period at the end of this sentence. You photographed a document with a standard 35 mm camera—the Soviets preferred Leicas—fitted with a special lens that operated like a reverse microscope to make the image smaller, not larger. Morris was taught to hide the developed negative inside the spine of a book, and that was the system he used later in Britain. But a microdot could also be pasted on top of a certain letter in a certain word on a certain line on a certain page of the book.

Except for the camera, which was supplied by the NKVD, Morris could purchase the rest of the supplies he needed from any photo shop without attracting attention. Only a simple darkroom was required. A small bathroom with the window blacked out worked fine.

The ancient art of secret writing was another subject Morris studied. Using milk, lemon juice, or urine for invisible ink was considered the mark of an amateur. Morris was taught to use hydrochloric acid, potassium nitrate, and acetate, which were shaken or stirred according to instructions. Silver bromide was also popular because it could additionally be used to coat clear Cellophane for use as microfilm. Those were all common chemicals that could be bought at hardware stores or supply houses that catered to science students.

Morris was also taught how to mix chemicals for steaming open sealed envelopes. But many of the chemicals used in the steaming were toxic, so students were warned: Do not inhale fumes.

ALEXANDER ORLOV left Spain before Morris Cohen. For the Loyalists, the war was lost. They had attempted to negotiate peace with the Nationalists, to no avail, and it was just a matter of time before Franco's forces overran the remaining republican territory. Stalin was seeking an alliance with Germany in order to avoid or at least postpone war for a while, and the international brigades were withdrawn to appease Hitler. That was a shattering blow to idealistic volunteers like Morris, though it was welcome news to Loyalist government officials who had resented the Soviet presence from the very beginning.

Stalin's purges had spread from the Red Army to the NKVD, and during 1937 alone, more than three thousand intelligence officers were liquidated in Russia. One by one, Orlov's NKVD colleagues in Spain had been called back to Moscow and never heard from again. In July 1938, he received a cryptogram from Moscow Center ordering him to go to Antwerp and board a Soviet ship for a meeting with some unnamed person to discuss some unspecified plan of some unrevealed importance. Orlov smelled an assassination plot.

Orlov walked out of his office and never went back. His squad of hand-picked German bodyguards escorted him to the French border, and in Paris he obtained Canadian visas for himself, his wife, and his daughter. A couple of weeks later, at the American legation in Ottawa, a friendly officer who had worked in Spain issued the family temporary visas that got them into the United States.

After that, they simply disappeared. Orlov had a small fortune in his possession that allowed the family to live underground under assumed names for more than a decade. Orlov was never clear on where he got his fortune, but he had directed the transfer (some said theft) of the Spanish government's gold supply to Russia. The family's presence in America came to light only after they ran out of money and Orlov published an exposé on Stalin's crimes in order to raise cash. The FBI had no idea that one of the top *chefagents* (spy bosses) in the history of Soviet intelligence had been hiding under their noses all that time.

Meanwhile, Hemingway was working on *For Whom the Bell Tolls*, which would become an all-time best seller. As it turned out, Ernie had not been as gullible toward the Communists as his critics had suggested. His reportorial skills were as sharp as ever, and his book would be brutally honest about what he'd seen in Spain, causing him to be roundly denounced by Reds everywhere as a traitor to the cause.

After completing his intelligence training, Morris was placed in reserve by the NKVD in Spain. But with Orlov gone, he had nothing to do but wait around for further orders, which never arrived. André Marty was at the station to see the Mac-Paps off when they left Spain. He stood on a platform, glaring down at them, accusing them again of cowardice. He spotted one of the soldiers lighting a cigarette.

"Spy!" Marty screamed. "He's signaling the fascists!"[9]

He sent his security enforcers to arrest the man. But the soldiers laughed so hard the agents were called off.

Morris and his battalion left Spain through the Pyrenees, not over them. Their trains left from Portbou, a pleasant seaside village in the Costa Brava region close to the point where Cohen had originally arrived in Spain. A short run through the railway tunnel in the mountain deposited them in Cerbère, France, a small town whose main reasons for existence were its rail yard and border checkpoint.

It was a sad ride for the survivors of Spain. But at least they were alive and they were going home. From Cerbère, they took other trains up to Cherbourg and boarded the SS *Ausonia*, another grand old Cunard liner soon to be converted into a British warship. Morris and Jack Bjoze disembarked in New York five days before Christmas. Carrying a valid passport (in the name of Israel Altman), Cohen had no trouble getting through customs.

But before he left Spain, Morris had been given a final briefing. He was told that someone would contact him in New York and give him his first espionage assignment. He was handed half a broken comb. His contact would have the other half. They would match the two pieces as an identifier. Moscow Center had assigned Cohen a code name: Luis.

With that, he was officially in the game.

PART TWO **PROFESSIONALS**

7 VOLUNTEER ACTIVATED

This time after Morris Cohen got home to the Bronx he stayed away from party activities altogether. He engaged in no organizing, no canvassing, no demonstrations. He also avoided the office of the Veterans of the Abraham Lincoln Brigade, the inflated name that had been given the Linc-Wash Battalion. At the same time, Ed Lending and some of the other returning veterans resumed their party activities. With intensity, Ed later wrote:

"But a few of the quintessential Boy Scouts—the 100 percenters, we otherwise called them—had mysteriously disappeared. So out of character for these pious activists. It was bewildering. Then rumors proliferated. They had been fingered for Soviet agentry. Their instructions, the grapevine had it, were to lay low, abandon all party activity, await the next phoned instructions."

"Wonder what's happened to Moishe Cohen?" somebody in the VALB office asked.

"Oh, he's still waiting for his phone call."[1]

They laughed at what Ed called the persistent naïveté of their star activist. Then after a while, the memory of Morris Cohen, alias Morris Pickett and Israel Altman, aka Unk and Abe and Ape and comrade assistant commissar, ebbed away.

Which was exactly what Morris had in mind. Indeed he was following instructions to maintain a low profile. To keep him on hand until he got his call from the NKVD, he was given low-paying work in the Soviet pavilion at the 1939 New York World's Fair. But a Soviet spy recruit working openly at a high-profile Russian tourist attraction while awaiting his first espionage assignment was the sort of tradecraft that Alexander Orlov would have warned against.

The World's Fair had been built in a swampy area of Flushing Meadows, Queens. It didn't have the glamour of the recent Paris Exposition, and Flushing Meadows wasn't the City of Light, but there were some impressive exhibits, including the one where Polish girls in topless mermaid suits swam around in a big tank of water. The Soviet pavilion was the largest exhibit, a nine-story, U-shaped edifice with a white marble façade built in a brutal Soviet social-realism style eerily similar to Italian Fascist architecture. Tall columns offered bas-relief profiles of Stalin and Lenin. Inside, a full-scale mockup of a Moscow subway station awaited visitors.

The pavilion was built around a courtyard. From the courtyard rose a blood-red granite tower 188 feet high, topped by a 79-foot-tall steel statue of a Soviet worker heroically holding aloft a big illuminated red star. Worker Joe, the press called him. Some people complained that the tallest structure in the fair was a symbol of Communism that could be seen for miles at night. Others protested that Worker Joe stood taller than the American flag that flew over the fair, and that the entire pavilion was a political taunt.[2] So the flag was raised, and the pavilion closed at the end of the year after months of declining attendance.

Still using the name Israel Altman, Morris waited on tables in the pavilion's lunchroom. As an English speaker, he also might have served as a guide or security guard. It was just cover work. His assignment there coincided with the arrival in New York of two important NKVD officers.

First there was Pavel Panteleimonovich Pastelnyak, also known as Klarin, just in from Moscow. His NKVD cover name was Luka, and his street name was Pete. Pastelnyak was a short, stocky Russian with a florid complexion, pockmarked face, and thick brown hair swept back in a pompadour. He had a hard look in his eyes and appeared older than his thirty-six years. His wife and two daughters would soon join him in New York, but for the time being he rented a room from a lady near the fair. His English was so accented he would have to take language lessons.

Pastelnyak told the U.S. government he had worked as an economist for the All-Union Chamber of Commerce in Russia and as a senior economist for the People's Commissariat of Agriculture.[3] His job at the World's Fair, he claimed, was head of the agriculture section at the Soviet pavilion. That kind of cover might have been original at one time, but after a while it seemed that every other Soviet spy was claiming to be a news correspondent or agricultural consultant. Perhaps they were taunting the FBI. Catch us if you can.

Pastelynak's real assignment in the United States was to contact Russian émigrés and turn them into Soviet agents. When he and another NKVD officer took a potential asset to lunch, the frugal Pastelnyak would pay only for the guest's check. Nevertheless, Pastelnyak would go on to develop large networks of agents and install them in high places in American organizations. He also acquired passports and sneaked illegal agents into the country.

Pastelnyak was a career soldier and had served as a border guard in Russia. That qualified him for his second cover job at the fair, as the Soviet pavilion's boss of security. In that position, and as a high-ranking NKVD officer, Pastelnyak was probably Morris's chief watcher at the fair. Perhaps they had training sessions with Pastelnyak lecturing Cohen on more advanced tradecraft.

The second key NKVD officer arrived at the fair one day when Morris was sitting at a table in the dining room. He was a pleasant-looking man about Cohen's age. He sat down, started a conversation, and showed Morris half a broken comb. Morris then produced his half. They matched. Morris now had his first control officer in America, no doubt with an approving nod from Pastelnyak.

Control was Semyon Markovich Semyonov (also spelled Semenov). His NKVD code name was Twain, and his street name was Sam. He was a baby-faced Lithuanian Jew with thick brown hair, a mellow voice, a shy smile, and big eyes as restless as a radar scanner. Sam Semyonov had a soft spot for Robert Frost, spoke English almost without accent, and liked to maintain the image of a smiling, ambitious Russian businessman who admired the United States. He was said to be a warm and compassionate man, and a fine drinking companion. He dressed well and liked to take his attractive wife out to dinner where they could make business and social contacts he might be able to exploit in his spy work. Developing assets, it was called.

Developing assets was the kind of work that Morris would spend most of his time doing in the future. It was time-consuming, and often boring and frustrating. But it had to proceed calmly and confidently, like a well-planned seduction. Patience and timing were the keys. It was all technique—what restaurant or café to suggest, what to talk about, what to eat and drink. And then, when the time was right, he would make his pitch.

Cohen's recruiting would be aimed at people who had important jobs at industries doing work for the U.S. government. Did the recruit have access to blueprints of top-secret government projects? Was he Jewish? Cohen would remind him of what would happen if the Nazis ever got a foothold in America: Russia is the only country standing up to them, you know. But we need help. No, you wouldn't be harming America, not at all. But you would be helping, in a very big way, the defeat of international fascism. History will thank you.

But what exactly did Morris Cohen know about his new control officer? After all, an agent's control was supposed to be not just his supervisor but also his comrade and workmate, a man who could help him in countless ways. Semyonov revealed that he had been sent to America to study at the Massachusetts Institute of Technology. It was actually an NKVD infiltration mission. Semyonov imbedded himself in American life at MIT while making contacts and laying the groundwork for future science and technology spying in the United States. In time, he would be one of the first Soviet agents to identify many of the scientists working on the Manhattan Project.

Sam Semyonov was still a student at MIT when he went down to meet Morris at the fair. By all accounts, Sam and Morris got along well. Perhaps that was because they were both young and were learning the spy game together, with Sam being ahead of Morris by only a year or so.

After the Soviet pavilion closed at the end of 1939, Pastelnyak went to the Soviet consulate as vice consul and assistant to Gaik Badalovich Ovakimian, the New York *rezident* (chief of station). The consulate was an elegant building with a sculpted stone front at 7 East Sixty-First Street, one of those Manhattan side streets so narrow it admitted direct sunlight only around lunchtime. The FBI had teams of watchers—known as the bucket squad—in a room across the street in the Pierre Hotel, and they used 35-mm newsreel cameras to film people entering and leaving the consulate. Some of the NKVD and FBI agents frequented the same coffee shop around the corner that offered a hot dog and coffee for a dime.

The top three floors of the consulate housed the NKVD *rezidentura* (Station One), the control center for Soviet spying in North America. After

Semyonov finished his studies at MIT in 1940, he was listed as an engineer for the Amtorg Trading Corporation, the Soviet government's purchasing office in New York, but he also had an office at the *rezidentura* with about a dozen other NKVD officers.

Following the closing of the Soviet pavilion, Morris was given work in the kitchen at Amtorg, which allowed him to work more closely with Semyonov. He also did some substitute teaching in the public schools. Sending Morris to work openly at Amtorg was another risky move by the NKVD. Amtorg employed more than five hundred people, about half of them Americans, but the place did have a checkered history that made it a continuing security concern for U.S. agents.

Amtorg was one of Stalin's most important projects. After Lenin's death, Stalin had continued the Bolshevik practice of conducting widespread terror and refusing to pay financial debts to Western nations. As a result, the West refused diplomatic recognition. But Stalin desperately needed to import machinery and technology for his ambitious five-year redevelopment plans, so he set up trade agencies in the 1920s to purchase Western products. In New York it was called Amtorg; in London it was Arcos Ltd. Those agencies negotiated contracts with British and American companies. Their buyers were allowed to visit factories, chemical plants, and military installations. Amtorg and Arcos served as substitutes for formal diplomatic ties.

Amtorg and Arcos buyers were also spies. They asked questions, made sketches from memory, and took photographs with tiny spy cameras. At Ford Motor Company in Detroit, Amtorg representatives were caught trying to bribe a manager for trade secrets. That resulted in fifty-one of them getting barred from the facility.[4] Other U.S. companies selling goods to Russia were pressured by Amtorg agents to pay kickbacks. Finally a former Amtorg employee went on record confirming to Congress that the agency was indeed running an elaborate spy operation out of its offices.

One of Amtorg's most effective schemes was to grab copies of practically every new industrial, chemical, and military patent on file with the U.S. government.[5] Legally, U.S. patents were public knowledge—open intelligence in an open society. A Soviet agent or anybody else could simply walk into the U.S. Patent Office in Washington and plop twenty-five cents down on the counter for a copy of the design of a new tank or artillery shell. Copies of the patents were also available at eighteen New York public libraries. Access to patents would be restricted later on during World War II, but by that time, the Soviets had walked off with hundreds of thousands of American patents and not offered one Russian patent in return.

Throughout his spy career, Morris Cohen enjoyed remarkable luck by his association with some of the NKVD's most effective agents abroad. First there was Browder, then Orlov, Pastelnyak, and Semyonov. Pastelnyak and Semyonov were known as "cadre men," field officers who ran networks operated by "assistants" such as Cohen. Cadre men trained their assistants, sent them out on assignments, and stood by to receive the incoming product. Now, under Semyonov's control, Morris was trained as an "athlete," a term that included duties such as recruiting new assets and acting as a cutout (intermediary) and a courier. After he gained experience and developed his own subnetwork, he would be known as a *gruppovik* (group leader).

ALL THE STATION ONE SPIES, including Cohen, were ultimately answerable to Moscow Center, headquarters of what was probably the world's largest espionage service. It was still in the Lubyanka, the same place it had been since Cheka days. The Lubyanka was a big yellow and orange building built in an ornate Russian imperial style facing a downtown square that for many years held a statue of Dzerzhinsky, first boss of the Cheka, until the effigy was torn down and scrapped after the fall of Communism.

In Old Bolshevik days, Cheka agents were often criminals or army deserters. At one time, many Cheka headhunters were Jews, recruited because of their hatred of tsarism. In time, though, Jews would be purged from the Russian intelligence and security services, and new recruits carefully screened.[6] Exceptions were made in the thirties and forties because Jewish agents such as Semyonov were useful in recruiting American Jews, who were fiercely opposed to fascism.

Recruiters in Moscow looked for college graduates and party members who had an aptitude for intelligence work.[7] Until World War II, most of the training took place inside the Lubyanka. Recruits studied party history, international politics, and anti-Stalinist and deviational movements such as Trotskyism. They learned the language of the country where they were likely to be sent and they practiced their conversational skills in small groups. They took courses in observation, report writing, and organization of agent networks. Much time was devoted to tradecraft—locks and picks, audio and visual surveillance, and flaps and seals (surreptitiously opening and resealing envelopes).

The Lubyanka had originally been built for an insurance company, and the accommodations above ground were modern, warm, and sunny. In some ways, the Lubyanka was just another government building, with offices, conference rooms, classrooms, and commissaries. Bureaucrats pored over field reports and section chiefs lobbied for more money. But the Lubyanka also housed an NKVD prison guarded by security troops with submachine guns. The torture chambers and execution rooms were in the basement.

Beatings, drugs, electrical devices, and surgical tools were used to extract confessions from prisoners regardless of whether they were innocent or guilty. Then they were sent off to labor camps or simply executed. The killings were performed Cheka style with one shot to the back of the head. At one time, the Moscow municipal authorities had complained that so much blood was running out the Lubyanka sewers that it was polluting the river. There was a saying: The Lubyanka was the tallest building in Russia because you could see eternity from the basement.

Despite all that, some of the NKVD officers who trained in the Lubyanka carried reputations as gentlemen. Semyonov was one of them. So was Ovakimian, his station chief in New York.

Before they left Spain, Alexander Orlov instructed Morris Cohen to stay in touch with fellow veterans who might have access to U.S. military or economic information after they returned home. In a later report to Moscow, Semyonov confirmed that Morris did that, though he didn't name any assets that Cohen recruited.[8] Cohen was also instructed to gather information on the local German colony in New York.[9] Morris didn't say much about that in later interviews. It probably wasn't a good idea to begin with, since the FBI had infiltrated most pro-Nazi groups in the tristate area, and Morris might have drawn the attention of a bureau operative.

A more urgent assignment for Cohen and other agents working out of Station One came in the wake of events now racing across Europe at the speed of a runaway train. Hitler had already been on the move militarily, annexing Austria and Czechoslovakia, and in August 1939 a news story broke that prompted people all over the world to read the report again and again in disbelief: Germany and Russia, formerly blood enemies, had signed two treaties. One was a mutual friendship pact. The other was a nonaggression agreement.

Stalin had gotten into bed with Hitler? What about all those anti-Nazi sermons the Soviets were preaching? Russia is the only country standing up to Germany. Stalin needs your help. Suddenly thousands abandoned the Communist Party in the United States. The Cultural Front of Stalinist sympathizers collapsed.

Only true believers like Morris Cohen defended Stalin's moves. It was difficult, though. American Communists found old friends turning on them, accusing them of being traitors and fools. A labor organizer with whom Morris had worked in the past denounced him as a dirty Red. But he refused to back down. His rebuttal was that Stalin was simply buying time to build up the Red Army.

"My Uncle Joe is very smart," he said. "He'll smoke his pipe and he'll watch."[10]

But this was world politics on its most dangerous level, and things were not exactly as they appeared. That nonaggression treaty between Germany and the USSR called for the partition of Poland, with one part under German control and the other under Russian domination. The Poles, of course, were not consulted on this. In addition, a secret protocol of the pact essentially divided up all of Eastern Europe into Soviet and German spheres of domination. That would allow Stalin to recover countries from the old Russian empire that had been lost after 1918.

On September 1, 1939, nine days after the nonaggression treaty was signed, Hitler invaded Poland from the west. Stalin invaded Poland from the east on the seventeenth. Britain, France, Australia, and New Zealand quickly declared war on Germany. But Roosevelt kept his distance, merely condemning the USSR as an absolute dictatorship and imposing what he called a moral embargo on certain goods to Russia. If Spain had been the dress rehearsal for a new world war, then Poland was the first act of the main show. And that's where the orders to New York for that urgent assignment came in.

Station One was ordered to send its agents out to gain access to military weapons being developed in America. Roosevelt had not shown much inclination toward handing over the War Department's most guarded secrets to

Stalin. The information FDR did allow Stalin was of low priority. Chicken feed, it was called. The Soviets felt they had a right to America's military secrets. If the Americans wouldn't share them, then they should be stolen.

A good part of U.S. military and industrial research and production was done in the manufacturing corridor running from Maryland to Massachusetts. Station One was geographically in the middle of that, and all hands were sent out on wide-ranging fishing expeditions. In 1940, Cohen began working the New York waterfront and defense plants up and down the East Coast.

In an assignment like that, he would contact a longshoreman, a factory worker, or a technician who was already an active Soviet asset, a party member, or at least a fellow traveler. The name of the contact might have been supplied by another field agent, by the CPUSA, or by a controller at Station One. Sometimes a new source was a walk-in.

Morris would seek out the contact at some place away from his work-place—a café, a sandwich stand, a bar. He would open with a casual conversation, perhaps about sports, and then bring up politics. Most everybody had an opinion about politics. Morris had known that all his life. Morris might have a newspaper handy and make a comment about the war, then segue into the topic of Stalin. If the contact seemed to be a supporter of Stalin, then the next step was to ask if he would help out the war effort by making a contribution. Not in money, but in something much more useful—information.

It might take several meetings in order to convince the source to take that final step of actually handing over the goods. It might be a report of U.S. military supplies leaving secretly on a cargo ship for Britain, a list of the employees at a munitions plant, or a new chemical formula. Then a date was set for the transfer, again away from the source's workplace.

Returning to New York, Morris would turn the product over to Sam Semyonov in a dead drop or a brush pass. A favorite Soviet place for a pass was out on the busy sidewalk in front of Madison Square Garden during Friday night fights. Morris often acted as Semyonov's backup, the assistant who took the goods after Sam received them from an asset.

Morris gradually built up his own network of agents, code-named Volunteer because of his service in Spain. Coded NKVD messages would later refer to him individually as Volunteer. But life was not all work for him after his return to New York. Despite his busy schedule working at Amtorg and his teaching and spying, he managed to pick up where he had left off with the lovely Lona Petka.

During their courtship, Morris and Lona went to movies, dined together, took walks along the river, attended concerts in the park, and talked about their mutual commitment to Communism. Lona kept up her party activities while Morris followed orders and stayed away from the halls.

Morris had his mind set on another kind of commitment, which he hoped would coincide with his spy work. Moscow Center encouraged their spies to get married. Having a wife or husband to whom you could confide your fears and frustrations was good for controlling stress. For your spouse to actually help you on your missions was even better. There was also a measure of legal protection in marriage. If you got arrested, your wife or husband could not be compelled to testify against you.

"I found him unchanged upon his return from Spain," Lona later told a Russian friend. "He was as composed, correct, and invariably polite as I remembered him." But she noticed that Morris was very particular about what he said and how he behaved, and that he was extremely wary of everything. She gave him some advice: "Please be yourself, restrained but not too much so." Those who were too secretive, unsociable, or excessively cautious drew attention to themselves, she said, especially if they disappeared too often and for too long.

"Then I guessed he was engaged in some kind of secret work," she said.[11]

But what kind? Was he working for a criminal organization? Was he running numbers? Was he selling drugs? Did he have a honey in Philly?

Morris knew that Lona shared his commitment to Communism. He was additionally committed to spying for the Russians, for the rest of his life. But with things getting serious between them, he knew he couldn't keep his secret indefinitely.

He had to tell her. But when? And how would she take the news? Would she break off their affair? Would she have an attack of patriotism and denounce him to the FBI?

Here was another crossroads in his life. Could he bear to make a choice between his work and the woman he loved, if that's what it came down to?

All other decisions he had made up to now seemed to pale in comparison.

8 GHOULS AND DEAD DOUBLES

Lona Cohen liked to say that she had always been a revolutionary. A better word might be a rebel. Even her birthplace—Adams, Massachusetts, in the beautiful Berkshires—had an aura of rebelliousness about it as the hometown of abolitionist and suffragist Susan B. Anthony. The town was founded before the American War of Independence and named for Samuel Adams (the patriot, not the beer).

Around thirteen thousand people were living there when Lona was born, on January 11, 1913. Despite its small size, the town had an enviable supply of fine homes, churches, and schools, all connected by paved streets, trolley cars, and Yankee thrift. Adams lay along the Hoosic River in the shadow of Mount Greylock where, according to legend, iron was mined for construction of the USS *Monitor*, the navy's first ironclad battleship. It was a river town, a farming town, and a mill town. There was great hunting and fishing around there, and a lot of snow, too. People were known to get caught in blizzards and never be heard from again.

Adams was a factory town in the New England tradition. It had more industries than some towns that size had automobiles. The biggest was Berkshire Cotton Manufacturing Company, a massive complex of buildings four and five stories tall. One of the buildings contained nine acres of floor space. That was bigger than some of the farms around Adams. The factories kept Adams and North Adams alive, offering year-round employment to thousands of workers who made shoes, paper, cotton goods, and woolens.

When Lona's parents, Wladyslaw Petka and Marja Czupryna (Walter and Mary) came over from Poland in the 1890s, there were no child labor laws to speak of. It was the era of sweatshops and exploitation of children. With no federal oversight, industrial accidents were common. Some lost a hand, an arm, or an eye; others, their lives. Nor was affordable health insurance available. Walter arrived in 1896 and was seventeen years old when he went to work as a weaver at Berkshire Cotton.[1] Mary arrived two years later and was fourteen when she started there, also as a weaver. They met and married in Adams.

There was nothing radical in the Petkas' background except the fact that after they were married, Walter was arrested four times for liquor violations during national prohibition. Mary delivered Lona (née Leontyna) in an apartment at 4 Bellevue Avenue in Adams, a plain, two-story wood house shaped like a military barracks in a modest Polish working-class neighborhood. There was no sidewalk there, just a stretch of gravel for parking off the street. As they labored at the mill, Walter and Mary saved their money and bought two houses as rental properties, and then a couple of vacant lots in a subdivision. They also donated to the establishment of a new church, Saint Stanislaus Kostka.

With their increased income as landlords, the Petkas moved to 7 Albert Street, a big comfortable Victorian-style house with shutters and a long front porch ideal for sipping lemonade on summer afternoons. Their new address confirmed that the two peasants from the old country had succeeded in joining the American bourgeoisie.

Lona grew up on Albert Street. She had five sisters and attended the Renfrew School in Adams. But beyond their newfound comfort in Adams, Walter and Mary had long shared a goal—to own a farm. That was their vision of the American Dream. So, in 1923, when Lona was ten years old, they sold their Adams properties and bought a small spread outside Taftville, Connecticut. Mary also might have thought that the country air would be therapeutic for her husband's drinking.

Taftville was another traditional New England factory town, home of Ponemah Mills, built on the Shetucket River, about thirty miles north of New London. With more than a thousand employees, Ponemah Mills was to Taftville what Ford was to Detroit. Ponemah rented housing to its employees, and like cotton plantations, ran a company store where workers could go shopping (and into debt) between paychecks. But Ponemah had made a notable contribution to the scenery around there: the huge main building was an impressive imitation of a French palace, complete with towers and cupolas, a Versailles for the working class.

After five years at Taftsville, Lona decided she wasn't destined to spend the rest of her life staring at dirt clods and empty bottles. She left home at age fifteen and headed for the lights of New York. There she moved in with a sister in Greenwich Village, got a sweatshop job, and joined the Socialist Party. That would have been around 1928.

Lona fell in with radicals and freethinkers in the Village, rebelling against conventional society by practicing free love and frequenting Roaring Twenties speakeasies. She also rebelled against her family's Catholicism by declaring she was an atheist. No doubt about it, a friend of hers later told the FBI, Lona had a "hell of a good time" in the Village. She rebelled against the Socialists, too, after being groped by some men at a party hall. She went over to the Communist Party after that. Presumably they didn't condone lechery during regular hours.

When Morris returned from Spain, fit and sun-tanned and handsome with his broad shoulders, chestnut hair, and winning smile, he was twenty-eight years old and Lona was twenty-six. Her job situation had improved considerably. She was now working as a governess for a wealthy family on Park Avenue. She was in charge of their son, playing with him and taking him to Central Park. The family liked her and paid her well. She bought stylish clothes and learned how to conduct herself as a lady, when she wanted to. Lona was no Jean Harlow, but she had blonde hair, bright blue eyes, legs that would have caught Michelangelo's eye, and a certain élan that drew men like flies to honey. Her natural style, though, remained loud and brash.

George Blake, the British mole for the Soviets during the 1950s who was arrested in London in 1961 around the same time as the Cohens, thought Lona might have been the dominant one in her relationship with Morris. She was a "very, very resolute woman, very determined," with a style just the opposite of the easygoing Morris, Blake said.[2] Jack Bjoze, on the other hand, didn't like her at all. "She was too chatty," he recalled. He didn't even think she was pretty. Her shoulders were too wide, he said, and she drank too much. "Not my type of woman," he said.[3]

WHEN MORRIS AND LONA started dating, Station One had barely a dozen Russian intelligence officers working in New York, and their most important American sources numbered only a few more than that. But the number of assets was rapidly growing and would soon surpass two hundred. Stalin's purges of the NKVD had forced the agency to quickly bring up younger officers such as Sam Semyonov to build new networks almost from scratch.

For a while, things went well for the NKVD in North America. One of their cleverest operations was to send CPUSA members, usually women, into graveyards to get the names of people who had died young. They then went to New York public libraries and applied for copies of birth certificates in the names of the deceased they had found. After that, the birth certificates were used to procure U.S. passports for use by Soviet intelligence. The same system was used by spies in many countries. The passports were called dead doubles, and the people who did the cemetery searches were known as ghouls.[4] The system worked because death records were kept separate from birth records, and detecting a passport obtained fraudulently required a lengthy comparison of records stored at different locations. The practice was still in use as late as 2010, when Andrei Bezrukov, one of the ten Russian agents arrested on the U.S. East Coat, obtained a dead double Canadian passport in the name of the late Donald Howard Heathfield.[5]

The NKVD also stepped up recruitment of sources in U.S. government offices. Few if any of the assets were actually party members. Many were hangers-on from the defunct Cultural Front who still believed the Soviet Union was a perfect society with no unemployment, no anti-Semitism, no racism, and no imperialism, a system far superior to the capitalism that had produced the Great Depression.

But despite Station One's gains in developing new assets, trouble was brewing.

Having chopped up Poland together, Stalin and Hitler pursued their secret protocol to conquer Europe. Russia overran Finland in 1939, followed by Estonia, Latvia, Lithuania, and Bessarabia in 1940. Also in 1940, Germany seized France, Belgium, the Netherlands, Denmark, and Norway. Britain was still standing, but no one knew for how long. It was becoming imperative that the United States enter the war on the side of Britain and France. The FBI turned its counterintelligence focus more sharply on both Soviet and Axis activities in America.

President Roosevelt in 1936 had given J. Edgar Hoover the authority, through Secretary of State Cordell Hull, to investigate Communist, Nazi, and Fascist groups in the United States. With the arrival of war in Europe in 1939, Roosevelt further strengthened Hoover's powers by a presidential directive allowing the FBI to specifically investigate Soviet and Axis subversion at home. Wiretaps were illegal in those days and not admissible in court. Thus, if Hoover intended to use them, as he had been doing for years, along with black bag jobs (burglaries), Roosevelt didn't want to hear about them. A former FBI agent said FDR told Hoover:

"John, I want you to know that to be good, you have to look good."[6]

That meant don't get caught.

In 1939 the FBI had around seven hundred special agents. That figure would more than double in two years, and then in another year double again. The bureau set up round-the-clock surveillance of Russian, German, Italian, Japanese, and French embassies, consulates, news agencies, and trade organizations. Anyone who walked out of the Soviet embassy in Washington was photographed, then tailed and quietly identified. The FBI agents often got a traffic cop to help them. The officer would stop the subject in question, accuse him of something like jaywalking, and demand to see identification.

The John Dillinger and Machine Gun Kelly days of the FBI were over. With America on the threshold of war, Hoover increased the number of special agents working general intelligence, especially in New York and Washington. At least one agent trained in defense-plant security was placed in each of the FBI's forty-two field offices. Agents with technical training were assigned to work undercover in munitions plants, shipyards, aircraft factories, and engine manufacturers. In addition, civilian informants were recruited at more than twelve hundred defense plants.[7] In one Ohio city, the FBI had more than a hundred tipsters working in a single factory. Hoover further got fraternal organizations such as the American Legion to report suspicious activity.

The bureau amassed security cards on ten million people, including many foreigners, living in the United States. By 1940, the FBI Identification Division was operating around the clock processing the twelve thousand new sets of fingerprints coming in every day from field offices, police agencies, and defense employers. The bureau was also operating radio stations to intercept messages sent from secret transmitters in the United States to foreign nations. One of those FBI stations could pick up radio waves carrying impulses transmitted from specially designed Teletype machines that weren't readable by regular intercept units.

Those were the kinds of counterintelligence measures that Morris Cohen and other new Soviet agents had to face as they built their networks. It would be tough going for them, but they had a distinct advantage in that they had no memory of slower, easier times when the FBI was largely leaving Soviet spies alone. Morris had to learn quickly how to deal with U.S. agents who were just as smart, resourceful, and dedicated as those on his side.

As far as Cohen's work was concerned, any day might turn out to be an emergency. Examples would be the later arrests of Klaus Fuchs, Harry Gold, David Greenglass, and the Rosenbergs, and the defections of Igor Gouzenko to the RCMP and Elizabeth Bentley to the FBI. In most of those incidents, arrests would come suddenly and without warning to Station One, like a shot in the dark.

DESPITE HER SUSPICIONS about Morris's secrecies and unexplained absences from New York in 1939 and 1940, it was actually Lona who was seeing someone else at the time, a lawyer. She couldn't make up her mind between the two men. The party always needed money, and the lawyer had plenty of it. If she married him, she would be able to donate to the cause. What did Morris have—a kitchen shift at Amtorg, a substitute-teaching job at some inner-city school too poor to buy gloves for its baseball team?

Lona sought the advice of a party official she trusted. He told her that if she married the lawyer she would have everything she needed and she would forget about Communism. Marry the poor guy, he suggested, and work together with him for Communism. She mulled over it and finally decided in favor of Morris.

They got married July 13, 1941, in a civil ceremony at Norwich, Connecticut, near the Petka farm. She gave her name as Lorna Therese Petka, of Lisbon, Connecticut, employed as a governess. Morris's occupation was listed as a steward (dining-room worker). Just a few Petka family members were present. Lona still didn't know Morris was a spy.

That quickly changed. Hitler had suddenly turned on Stalin like a starved wolf and invaded Russia on June 22. The codename for the invasion was Operation Barbarossa. Now it wasn't just the Allies who were in trouble. The Wehrmacht, supported by the Luftwaffe, crossed the Polish border and marched on Moscow. The Germans had good weather and the element of surprise on their side, while the Russians were still reeling from Uncle Joe's purges of the Red Army and the NKVD. The country could fall at any time.

"My husband sank into melancholy," Lona recalled. "He remained in a state of depression for days. Then he brought a bouquet of roses one night and furtively put it on a hall table. I could see that he wanted to tell me something but could not speak his mind."

Morris admitted that it took it a long time to decide whether to draw Lona into his secret work. "I realized, of course, that there was no playing hide-and-seek with her," he remembered. "She would have found me out anyway. And besides, Moscow had already decided on Lona and me fulfilling its assignments together. There is nothing like a good and reliable married couple."

When he finally told her about his espionage work, she was appalled. She accused him of everything but high treason.

But Morris insisted he was not anti-American, only antifascist. "I had to explain to her that had I betrayed America for money, or, say, betrayed the party, my convictions and conscience, relinquished the ideas which constituted my creed—that was a different matter. But upholding and fighting for universal truth and justice in good faith was not treachery at all."[8]

So Morris Cohen was not a traitor. He was fighting for universal truth and justice. He was acting in good faith. No treachery was intended. That was the political mantra he would chant for the rest of his life.

Lona finally calmed down. Her attitude toward this new European war was more emotional than political. As a child she had seen American soldiers returning from the first war with horrendous wounds. It was an experience that left her a committed pacifist. So she thought things over and agreed to join Morris in his spy work as her own way of fighting against the whole idea of war itself. In that way, she felt she could save American lives. She declared that they would have both a "love marriage and a spy marriage."[9]

Moscow Center, as expected, was delighted. They gave Lona the code name of Leslie. Her street name would be Helen, which she would use for the rest of her spy career. In time, the Cohens working together would be known as *Dachniki*. The word translates as "cottage dwellers," meaning those who spend their vacations in a country house, a *dacha*. By extension, it means "vacationers," a term that would fit the Cohens' later jet-set espionage style.

RUSSIAN FOREIGN INTELLIGENCE had undergone another name change. As of February 1941, it was the Office of the NKGB (*Narodny Kommissariat Gosudarstvennoye Bezopasnosti*).[10] The Cohens worked to expand the number of assets that Morris had already recruited for his Volunteer network. Their first mission together was to obtain specimens of new weapons—not just plans or sketches or photos, though, but the real thing. They soon made their first score.

Lona, as Helen, met a young engineer—her report called him Allen—working at an aircraft plant at Hartford, Connecticut. She turned on the charm and got him to tell her about a new machine gun his factory was developing. Reportedly it would dramatically increase the kill power of a fighter plane. Moscow Center told her to get the actual components of the gun.

Lona went back and asked Allen if he could smuggle one of the guns out of the plant. She knew that defense plants were protected by tight security. All employees had to wear ID badges and were watched by guards as they signed in and out. Allen's plant would be dripping with FBI informers. And everybody knew that the plain-looking panel truck parked outside the front gate contained an FBI photo team. The odds seemed insurmountable.

But Allen was confident. He agreed to do it, for two thousand dollars. That was a lot of money in 1941. For two grand, you could buy a small house. Moscow Center okayed the money, but there were still two major problems.

First: How could Allen smuggle the biggest part of the gun, the barrel, out of the factory? Smaller parts weren't a problem. But a machine gun barrel was long and heavy. It wasn't something you could hide in your lunch pail. Moscow Center put on its thinking cap and came up with a plan. Lona had described Allen as a tall, wide man, so Moscow suggested that he tie the barrel over his shoulders, rest it against his back, and walk out with it under his coat. This, of course, while trying not to look too much like the Hunchback of Notre-Dame.

It worked. Morris was waiting outside the plant to receive the barrel.

He put it inside an empty carrying case for a bass fiddle and hauled it back to New York.

Then the second problem: How could Morris get his package into the Soviet consulate? The place was under twenty-four-hour surveillance by the FBI bucket squad in the hotel across the street and by cops on the sidewalk. The NYPD was ostensibly there for consulate protection. Their duties included stopping and searching suspicious-looking characters who walked up. A dead drop was out, too. Lugging a fiddle case into the Paramount Theater just might attract a little attention.

Morris came up with the solution. He took the fiddle case up to Harlem, his first New York neighborhood. He knew an African American gentleman there who could be trusted. He was also unemployed, so financial remuneration was a factor in their talks. The man took the fiddle case to a Harlem flea market. There he was approached by a man who wasn't hard to spot. He was wearing lilac-colored trousers and a long checkered gray coat, and holding a conductor's baton. This might have been Cohen's control.

"How much is your music box?" he asked.

Those were the passwords. Some money changed hands and the fiddle case was loaded into the trunk of a car that probably belonged to a consulate employee. When the car approached the consulate's driveway, the guard would simply open the gate and wave it in.[11]

A few days later, the gun found itself packed in a crate bound for Moscow under protection of the diplomatic pouch law. It was quite a coup for Luis and Leslie. They had organized the mission, taken the risks, used their imagination, avoided detection, and fulfilled an important assignment within a reasonable amount of time.

As it turned out, though, it was a wasted effort. Roosevelt by that time was anticipating war with Germany, not Russia, and the embargo against the Soviets had been lifted. Soon warplanes containing that very model of machine gun would be provided to the Soviets by the U.S. War Department.

NEXT, MORRIS COHEN would be a major figure in the theft of a much more valuable piece of military hardware than a machine gun. The receipt of planes, tanks, and artillery under Roosevelt's Lend-Lease program had relieved the Soviets of the need to spend a lot more time and money sending out valuable agents to steal ordinary weapons. Russia was not an industrial giant like Germany or the United States. For survival, they needed to become a technological nation in the Western mold as fast as possible. Moscow Center decided it was time to go after one of America's most closely guarded military secrets: radar.

Radar was one of the most important developments of the war years. A radar transmitter sent out radio waves that hit objects and bounced back in the form of echoes displayed on a screen. Radar could detect squadrons of bombers approaching from hundreds of miles away, giving your civilian population time to take shelter while your fighters scrambled to intercept the enemy planes. With underwater radar, called sonar, your submarines could track enemy ships and torpedo them before they knew you were anywhere near. It worked the other way, too. Surface ships could track subs just as effectively.

The Soviets hit the radar jackpot after a recently recruited asset working in a U.S. defense plant was turned over to a newly arrived Station One control officer, Alexander Feklisov. The source that Feklisov inherited was a French electrical engineer who had fled to America following the fall of France in June 1940. Moscow Center assigned him the code name Antelope.

In his memoirs, Feklisov wrote that he approached the Frenchman first on a social basis. They had dinner with a friend, they hit it off, and they exchanged cards. Then Antelope invited Feklisov to some antifascist receptions given by French exiles. Feklisov never named Antelope other to say that he was a Gaullist and aggressively anti-Nazi, a socialist who sympathized with Russia's struggle against Germany.

"You can help our Cossacks get all the way to Berlin," Feklisov told him. "And therefore shorten the time when General de Gaulle will enter Paris." When Antelope asked how he could help, Feklisov replied, "The instruction manual for radar would be very useful to all antifascists, not just the Americans."

The Frenchman delivered a radar instruction manual, and for two years after that he passed on what Feklisov called extremely valuable material. "He was so committed that I often had to slow him down," Feklisov said.[12]

The American agent working out of Station One who had first recruited Antelope was later identified as Morris Cohen.[13]

Cohen worked as Semyonov's assistant in running another radar source.

In a report to Moscow Center on Volunteer (Morris), Sam Semyonov explained:

> Before going into the army he [Cohen] was used to receive materials
> from me at meetings with Emulsion and as a talent spotter, as well as
> for covering the activities and studying former members of the Lincoln
> Brigade in Spain. A lead was received from him and the highly valuable
> agent Relay was recruited with his help. He [Cohen] is fully aware of
> whom he's working with, he is sincerely devoted to us, ready to carry
> out any assignment for us. Exceptionally honest, mature, politically well
> versed. Ready to dedicate his whole life to our work. Upon returning from
> the army he should be used as our full-time illegal. He can be used along
> the following lines: a) as a courier; b) to select illegal operatives from
> among former veterans; c) to arrange safe houses and covers. He knows
> the restaurant business well; he could open a small snack bar that would
> serve as a meeting place to pass materials, letters, etc. Volunteer should be
> given full trust.[14]

That first agent mentioned, Emulsion, has not been identified, but was obviously a technical source of some importance. The code name of the second agent, Relay, was later changed to Serb. Semyonov identified him as Joseph Chmilevski, twenty-six years old, born in the United States. His mother was Polish, his father Ukrainian. He and his wife Helene had one child. Chmilevski had been a party member since 1937. He was a volunteer in Spain from January to October 1937. He was wounded, his right leg was amputated, and thereafter he used a wooden prosthetic.

Despite Chmilevski's shattered nerves, apparently a result of the war, Semyonov told the Center that he provided valuable materials on radio, especially radar technology. "A radio operator and a junior engineer at a sonar laboratory in Camden," Semyonov's memo said of Chmilevski. "Recruited in Aug. '42 by Volunteer [Morris Cohen]."

UP TO THIS POINT, technical and industrial spying had been the primary focus of Morris Cohen and the other agents working out of Station One. But now they were about to begin a new operation that would make all other matters seem petty by comparison. A commission of Soviet scientists in 1940 had heard reports that some kind of super uranium bomb was being developed by the Allies, but they decided it was only a theoretical idea. However, Leonid Kvasnikov, chief of scientific intelligence for Moscow Center, ordered all stations in Great Britain, Scandinavia, and the United States to watch for any news of such a weapon.

Two years later, Donald Maclean, a member of the Soviets' Cambridge spy ring working as a mole inside the Foreign Office in London, sent a sixty-page report to Moscow revealing that the British felt they could build a uranium-235 bomb of staggering destructive force within two years. Lavrenty Beria, head of the People's Commissariat for Internal Affairs, sent the message along to Stalin.

Just before the war, Stalin had been shown a letter predicting that uranium fission could lead to such a super bomb. Stalin had no idea what uranium fission was, and took no action. But two months after Maclean's report reached Moscow, some mathematical calculations involving U-235 were found on a German prisoner of war, suggesting that Hitler was on the case, too.

Then another sensational message came in from London. This one was from Anatoly Gorsky, head of the Soviet intelligence station there.[15] It said that a shortage of money had forced Britain to shelve its plan to build an atomic-bomb factory in Canada and that those two nations were going to partner with the United States. The Americans were now in charge of the Allies' atomic project, and the first A-bomb could be ready before the end of the war. With that, Stalin had to do something. He created Russia's own project to build an atomic bomb, with Beria in charge.

Thus began what the Soviets called Operation *Enormoz* (enormous), Moscow's plan to steal the secrets of the atomic bomb from the West. The Cohens' Volunteer network would soon become the only one in North America dedicated completely to atomic espionage.

But first, a major interruption arrived for the Cohens and their Volunteer network. After Japan attacked Pearl Harbor on December 7, 1941, and after Germany and Italy declared war on America four days later, America began a massive mobilization. Peacetime industries that once manufactured cars and household cleaners now set about turning out tanks and explosives. An army of ten million was being raised and more would be called up if needed.

Morris received a letter from his local draft board. It began with "Greetings" and concluded with an order for him to report for induction.

9 THE AGENT WHO NEVER WAS

Morris Cohen was drafted into the army on July 8, 1942, and two weeks later reported to Fort Jay, an old defense base on Governor's Island in New York Harbor, a short ferry ride south of Manhattan.[1] Morris seemed to have no hesitation in taking up arms and going off to fight yet another war and risk getting shot again. To the contrary, he seemed proud to get into a second fight against Nazis and Fascists, this time in the ranks of what was to become the most modern and well-equipped fighting force in history.

Morris was interviewed, inoculated, photographed, and fingerprinted at Fort Jay. He took the eye test and the stress test and offered up samples of bodily fluids for laboratory analysis. He filled out forms in triplicate, demonstrating that he could read and write English, and stood in lines for hours for seemingly indefinable purposes. Finally he raised his right hand, faced the flag, and swore to protect his country and his president against all enemies. Copies of his fingerprints were kept on file permanently, a move that would come back to haunt him later.

Cohen's university degree, graduate work, and combat experience in Spain should have made him a natural candidate for officer training. But to the War Department, all the volunteers from Spain wore red underwear. They were classified as PAFs, premature antifascists, and were assigned menial work in the lower ranks. Morris was promoted, from recruit to private, and assigned kitchen duties in Company C of the new 241st Quartermaster Service Battalion. After previous kitchen duties at the World's Fair and Amtorg, he might have wondered if he was destined to a life of peeling potatoes.

Morris and Company C were loaded on a train and sent up to Camp Edwards, Massachusetts, home of the 26th Yankee Division, for basic training.[2] Edwards was one of America's biggest and most important bases, built on 200,000 acres of Upper Cape Cod. It had 1,300 buildings, two airstrips, a rail line, a highway, and barracks for 30,000 men. Amphibious engineers at Edwards developed one of the most useful medical aids in military history: the seasick pill.

After arrival at Edwards, Morris began a boot-camp schedule of getting up at six in the morning to learn again what he already knew—how to march, stand at attention, salute, and shoot. He was issued a .30-caliber Enfield from the last war and taught that a rifle was not called a gun, not in this man's army. A gun was one of those big artillery pieces that fired an explosive shell that could change the molecular structure of a courthouse. A sergeant would emphasize that by holding an Enfield in one hand, patting the fly of his trousers with his other hand, and teaching his men the old infantryman's poem: "This is my rifle and this is my gun; one is for fighting, the other for fun." As a reward for their outstanding training development, the men were given their first nighttime guard duty.

At first, Morris and the rest of the men bunked in comfortable barracks near the post service club. At the end of October they were moved to wood and tarpaper buildings at the edge of camp and taught the quartermaster skills of loading trucks, unloading trucks, issuing clothing, and digging. They dug to clear brush for a landscaping project. They dug to bury garbage. They dug trenches. Bulldozers were better suited for that kind of work, but in the quartermaster tradition, the men learned to do it with shovels, picks, and gloves. Soon they were in great physical shape—trim, alert, and sunburnt.

A 1942 Christmas dinner menu notes that Morris was one of the cooks for the traditional meal of turkey and dressing served to the 241st. He also seems to have received another promotion, to private first class.[3] After the holidays, the men got their orders to move out. They boarded a troop train on January 29, 1943. Keeping with wartime security, the company was told destination unknown.

THE MEN CROSSED the entire North American continent on that train, and five days later entered British Columbia. They reached the end of the Northern Alberta Railway line on February 6 and got off at Dawson Creek, a windy prairie railhead and farm town in the Peace River district. There were no barracks there, just tents. Each tent had a pot-bellied iron stove, though no fuel was yet available. But on that first night the temperature was only forty-three below.

Just a few months before, Dawson Creek had been a quiet village of five hundred or so, a good number of them Canadian Indians and war refugees relocated there from Sudetenland. Downtown was six blocks of wood-frame buildings. The town had electricity and barrooms, but no running water. The main street was a gravel path. But now the United States had begun a massive project to build a two-lane highway through here up to Fairbanks, Alaska, so that military forces could rush to the Aleutian Islands in case of Japanese invasion. It was called the Alaska Highway, or the Alcan (Alaska-Canadian). Dawson Creek was mile 0, the starting point.

The U.S. Corps of Engineers was in charge of building the Alcan. Civilian contractors, truck drivers, and soldiers, including three African American regiments, poured in to work on the 1,543-mile-long road. The engineers boasted that the Alcan was one of the top ten construction projects of the twentieth century. Punsters called it the Oil Can Highway because of the thousands of empty petroleum drums the engineers dumped along the way as they forged ahead on their eight-month building schedule.

The morning after their arrival, Morris and Company C were served hot coffee and a big breakfast. Then they drew their first assignment, to go out and procure supplies for their base, a good way to get some exercise after that long train ride. The snow was up to their knees, but at least the sun was out.

They spent the next three months exploring the backwoods in trucks, mule trains, dog sleds, and a pokey narrow-gauge train, the Cannon Ball Express, as they searched for coal, gravel, and water. The 241st helped build three sawmills to produce lumber for the construction of bridges across two hundred rivers. They also cut thousands of trees for corduroy (log) roads. The hardest work was clearing dense forests with handsaws and axes while they waited for bulldozers.

Morris and Company C were enlisted for emergency duty one evening when fire consumed nearly a full block of downtown, including the venerable Dawson Creek Hotel, a historic landmark that meant as much to British Columbia as the Château Frontenac did to Québec. The fire broke out in a former livery stable where tons of dynamite, blasting caps, chemicals, and tires were stored for construction of the Alcan.[4] The fire spread to an adjacent building containing hundreds of fifty-five-gallon drums of gasoline and oil. Thousands of onlookers crowded into the narrow street to watch. They got dangerously close. Military police drew their pistols and tried to move them back. Other soldiers used wet burlap bags to save nearby buildings.

Suddenly the dynamite, gasoline, and oil exploded, sending fire and smoke hundreds of feet into the air. People standing in the street were felled like wheat before a sickle. Five were killed. More than 150 were injured. Some of the wounds were horrendous. The army used trucks to rush the injured to a clubhouse the Red Cross turned into an emergency hospital. Soon the floors and walls of the building were smeared with mud and blood. Women of the town went in to mop the floors during the emergency surgeries. Morris and his company spent that night containing the fire, then salvaged property the next day and guarded against looters. The post commander commended the 241st for their efforts.

Morris had been in Dawson Creek almost four months when they got orders to move out again. On May 30 they boarded Greyhound buses and headed north on the highway they were still in the process of building. They got as far as Fort Nelson, at mile 300. There they found that a bridge up ahead had been washed out by heavy rains. They couldn't go back to Dawson Creek, either. A section of the highway behind them had collapsed.

Company C sat at Fort Nelson for a month, back in their tents, surrounded by mud, snakes, and mosquitoes that descended in thick clouds like a biblical plague. They were serenaded day and night by moose, goats, wolves, coyotes, foxes, and lynx. Bears were a particular problem; they thought nothing of wandering into camp at all hours in search of tasty garbage. Fort Nelson had originally been a trading post and was called the Gateway to the Rockies. Like Dawson Creek, the main street was a gravel road. The post office was a one-room shack. There was not a lot to do around there on Saturday night unless you had a deck of cards or a radio.

Finally Morris and his unit were airlifted out on cargo planes from a nearby army airfield and delivered to Whitehorse, in the Yukon Territory, on July 1. There they faced more woodcutting duties. But at least they could bunk in comfortable Quonset huts, semicylindrical buildings built of galvanized steel paneling. Military Quonset huts were used all over the world during the war. Each one came prefabricated and could be put together in half a day. They were hot in the summer but immune to rain and termites.

Whitehorse was another old gold-rush town, once infamous for its saloons and gunfights, now enjoying new prosperity thanks to construction of the Alcan. Whitehorse was at mile 918 of the Alcan, on the west bank of the Yukon River. With a wartime population pushing ten thousand, it was the territory's biggest settlement. One of its notable native sons was Robert W. Service, who wrote "The Cremation of Sam McGee," a poem about a prospector who's so cold in the Yukon that he wants his remains burned after he dies. Then he rises from the ashes of his cremation and announces it's the first time he's been warm since he left Tennessee. The men of Morris's unit would remember Whitehorse because it was there, on September 23, that the 241st Quartermaster Battalion was broken up. Cohen's unit was renamed the 3233rd Quartermaster Service Company.

Four months later, Tech 5 Cohen and the 3233rd got traveling orders again. They boarded a train on a narrow-gauge line and lurched and bounced 110 miles north to Skagway, Alaska, another old prospecting town whose glimmer had faded over the years but which was shiny and expensive again with the arrival of the horde building the Alcan. Skagway, too, had a literary history. While panning for gold around there, Jack London wrote *The Call of the Wild*, the grandfather of talking-dog stories. On January 25, 1944, the 3233rd got new orders. They boarded a boat, the *Eli D. Hoyle*, for a trip down the Yukon River and out into the Pacific. It was a rough trip and most of the company got seasick.

They went down the coast and disembarked at Prince Rupert, 350 miles north of Vancouver, on January 26. It was a small, picturesque fishing town, the western terminus of the Canadian National Railway and home to several U.S. army forts, along with Port Edward. Snowfall there is rare, and the port is ice-free year-round. At Port Edward the men were treated to milk and ice cream, which they had not seen for months, and on February 3 they boarded a troop train for the return trip to Massachusetts. They arrived at Camp Edwards on February 8, 1944. Morris went on four-week furlough before reporting back to Camp Edwards to await further orders. While on leave, many of the men saw themselves in a Paramount newsreel about the building of the Alcan.

LONA COHEN TOOK OVER the Volunteer network after Morris went into the army. The technical, scientific, and industrial espionage the Cohens had been conducting was categorized by the Soviets as Line X work.[5] Lona ran seven main agents in the eastern states, taking buses and trains as far south as Baltimore and north to Rochester to pick up documents. Then she brought them back to New York and turned them over to Sam Semyonov in meets at various locations, including their old favorite, the Bronx Zoo.

Lona was also assigned to go down to the docks and make contact with seamen from Europe and South America smuggling film or paper documents into the United States for Station One. Sometimes a guard at the gate would stop her. Then she had to turn on the charm to get past him, pleading that she wanted to see her boyfriend on a certain ship. Just for two minutes. Just two minutes. Lona had a certain reputation as an actress, and might have capped her appeal off with a forlorn look and a flutter of the eyelashes.

Line X work was not considered an exciting, glamorous game. There were no cocktail parties with a visiting maharajah, or polo with some prince on a tour of the colonies. That was what they did in the days of Sidney Reilly and Xenophon Kalamatiano, when spies were products of the best schools, dressed to the nines, and made contacts over baccarat at casinos. In the thirties and forties it was plodding, proletarian work, sometimes boring, more often frustrating.

The asset you were trying to recruit might be frightened to the point of making a stupid mistake and endangering both of you. He or she might be rude or condescending, and you had to force yourself to try and get along. So you dug in, pasted on a winning smile, and conjured up all your powers of persuasion, which might include a couple of subtle threats. Just a reminder, comrade: the information you gave us last time alone was enough to send you up if the feds ever found out about it. You're in it with the rest of us whether you like it or not, so relax, trust me.

Take several hours to get clean of surveillance before a meet: that was the rule. Then, on a cold street corner, in the dark, you walked up to some stranger you hoped would be your contact. But if your asset had turned you in and it was an FBI agent standing there wearing the cap and leather jacket of a dockworker, how would you explain what you were doing here, in the middle of the night, in this neighborhood, in this city, hundreds of miles from your home? What's that you've got under your raincoat? Just some papers? What kind of papers?

Lona Cohen made mistakes the way all novices do, but when Sam Semyonov later wrote an appraisal of her, he praised her devotion to Soviet spying and noted that she had been used for maintaining contact with an agent code-named Link.[6]

As it turned out, Link was undoubtedly the most successful Soviet mole to ever penetrate American intelligence. The damage Link did was so catastrophic and embarrassing that U.S. intelligence agencies would spend half a century refusing to comment on him. As far as they were concerned, he was the agent who never was.

LINK WAS WILLIAM WOLFE WEISBAND. His parents were Jews from Odessa. At times, he claimed to have been born in either Odessa or Cairo. The family was living in Egypt before they emigrated to the United States in 1925 and became naturalized citizens.[7] William's two brothers, Harold and Mark, had earlier entered America illegally as stowaways on a ship. William worked at the family jewelry store at 8016 Third Avenue (later at 8320 Fifth Avenue) in Brooklyn. He also worked for the Stork Club and several hotels, including the Waldorf Astoria, apparently as a bookkeeper. The Waldorf Astoria did not allow Jews in. When William told management that he was a Jew, they fired him.

Weisband was possibly recruited as a spy in the midthirties during a trip to Russia to study Communism. Aside from Link, he also used the code name Zhora. Most of the time he seems to have worked quietly without attracting attention. But he had a close call with the police in the autumn of 1938 after he and a Russian rented an apartment together in New York. Weisband later claimed he had met the man at a pool hall in Philadelphia and noticed that he had a Russian accent. The Russian said he had worked as a mechanic in Detroit and was looking for work and a place to live in New York. He also had several thousand dollars on him. Weisband wanted to get out of his parents' apartment, so the two men rented an apartment together on Haven Street.[8] Weisband had been a student at the Radio Corporation of America Institute in New York since 1936, and he continued there, studying radio and Morse code.

Weisband's Russian roommate might have been a new illegal sent from Moscow, or he might have been an agent that Weisband himself recruited. But his value, whatever it was, lasted only six weeks. The two men got into an argument with the landlady over the rent and she had them arrested. The Russian was taken to Ellis Island and examined. He convinced them he was crazy and was released, whereupon he disappeared. The FBI later confirmed that he was indeed a Soviet agent. Weisband was booked with harboring an alien, but the charge was dropped.

Two illegals rooming together like that had been very risky. The arrest of one implicated the other. But then Weisband made another major blunder. He told one of his girlfriends that he was engaged in some kind of secret work for some unnamed organization, for which he was being paid well. She accompanied him on several dead drops. Weisband would later tell the FBI he had just been shooting off his mouth to impress the girl. But if Moscow Center had found out about her, Weisband's usefulness undoubtedly would have been terminated with the speed of a radio thrown out a window.

Weisband worked at the World's Fair in 1939, when he was thirty-one years old. Since Morris Cohen was there at the same time, perhaps the two spies got to know one another in the shadow of Worker Joe. Weisband was drafted in September 1942 and worked as a Teletype operator at Gardner Field, California, before going on to officer-candidate school at Fort Monmouth, New Jersey.

Fort Monmouth was an important listening base for monitoring radio traffic, and a good place for an up-and-coming signals officer to get specialized training. Weisband went into the army's Signals Intelligence Service, predecessor to today's National Security Agency. He was assigned temporarily to the SIS at Arlington Hall, Virginia, across the river from Washington. There he received further signals training.

In 1943, Second Lieutenant Weisband was deployed to the Mediterranean as a cryptologist for the Army Signal Corps. He sharpened his skills under Colonel Harold Hayes, a top signals intelligence officer. Weisband was a polyglot, speaking German, Spanish, Italian, Arabic, and French in addition to his native English and Russian. He was assigned as a liaison officer with the French Expeditionary Corps in Italy, monitoring their radio messages for security violations. While he was doing that, the U.S. Army gave him an assignment that debunked the old adage that gentlemen (or at least wartime allies) do not read one another's mail: he was told to steal the French military codes, which he did.

In 1945, after the war, Weisband returned to Arlington Hall, an antebellum style mansion that once had been a private girls' school. The building and grounds were so picturesque that the army used picture postcards of them for recruiting new staff. The army had started a project called Venona, a made-up name with no particular significance. Venona was a top-secret Anglo-American operation. Its existence was so closely guarded that the public didn't find out about it until fifty years after the Manhattan Project was revealed. Venona was an operation that would be a key factor in the eventual roll-up of Soviet spies in America and the forced flight of the Cohens.

Arlington Hall was an important target of Soviet spying. Moscow Center knew the Americans and British were deciphering Russian messages but they had no idea how extensive and damaging the Venona program really was. Indeed, Arlington Hall cryptanalysts were looking at all Soviet diplomatic cables that had been sent between the United States and Russia by telegraph companies such as Western Union and RCA. Authority for that had come from President Roosevelt the day after Pearl Harbor. He had ordered that a copy of every cable sent in or out of the United States be delivered to a government censor. If they were in code, they were forwarded to Arlington Hall. Soon warehouses were required for storing all the paper.

Venona deciphered the Soviet traffic for information about Amtorg and Soviet intelligence. Most of the analysts at Arlington Hall used hand-cranked calculators and the kind of card-sorting machines that had been employed by the U.S. Census Bureau since the nineteenth century. Workers sat at wooden desks in big open offices and used mathematics, earlier decoded messages, tips from various sources, and personal hunches to attack the Soviet ciphers on big worksheets. In the dog days of summer, the work sheets stuck to their hands.

Weisband was assigned to the Russian Section as a linguist adviser. Fellow workers at Arlington Hall remembered him as a good-looking, plump man with thinning hair and a vivified manner—lively, but not brilliant, like a jolly maître d'hôtel. He had drinking and gambling problems but was popular because he threw lavish parties for his friends.

But how could Bill afford such entertainment on his army salary? One way he raised cash was by visiting New York and bringing back jewelry that he sold at Arlington Hall.[9] But people still wondered. Weisband also had a knack for appearing in office areas where he had no business, but never seemed to get into trouble for it. Although he didn't work directly on the Venona project, he learned a lot about it by peeking over shoulders.

Then the roof fell in. Little by little, the Soviets stopped using the ciphers that Arlington Hall had been breaking. Moscow Center started using new ciphers, and all the previous systems went dark. Years of identifying Soviet spies in the United States and Britain ended as quickly as ink drying. It would go down as one of the worst intelligence disasters in Anglo-American history, ranking up there with the thefts of radar, the proximity fuse, and the atomic bomb.

What had happened?

It took a while for the army and the FBI to figure it out, but clearly somebody inside Arlington Hall had tipped off the Russians. They had a clue that the mole spoke Arabic. Weisband was interviewed by the bureau on April 28, May 9, May 11, and May 13, 1950, and denied spying for the Soviets. A Soviet agent named James Orin York (Needle) had already been questioned by the FBI, on April 10, and said he had dealt with a Soviet agent known only as "Bill" about ten times in Los Angeles, in 1941–42. York said he received around fifteen hundred dollars for photographing documents at Northrup Aircraft. Then in August 1950, while in the custody of FBI agents in Los Angeles, York saw "Bill" on the sidewalk outside the courthouse. It was William Weisband.[10]

One way Weisband had delivered information to the Soviets was by putting it into an ordinary envelope and mailing it to a woman, in care of one of his brothers. The woman would then go to the brother's house and ask for "her" mail. She was in fact a Soviet courier on a pickup for Station One. After receiving "her" mail and dodging questions posed by the curious brother, she delivered the product to her control in New York.

Who was that woman?

It was Lona Cohen.

After Weisband blew the Venona program, he asked for asylum in Moscow. But the Center considered him one of the Old Masters from Russian spying of the thirties and they didn't want to discontinue a valuable American agent unless he was in imminent danger. So they dragged their feet about rescuing him. Then it was too late. The government didn't have enough evidence at the time to prosecute Weisband, but he and his wife were suspended from Arlington Hall on suspicion of disloyalty and he was sent to prison for a year after ignoring a subpoena to testify about Communist spying.

Bill Weisband's son later confirmed that his father had spied on Venona. He also described Weisband as a gentle man, a loving father, and an American patriot who taught his son that the United States was the greatest nation in the world. According to the son, Weisband seemed to believe that passing his country's secrets to a former ally was simply the right thing to do. Like the Cohens, he was a man of divided loyalties.

Weisband ended his days selling insurance door-to-door in Virginia. After he lost a leg due to hernia surgery, his son would go out on calls with him, knock on customers' doors, and announce that Mister Weisband the insurance man was there. Most of his clients were African Americans. Fifty of them appeared at his funeral.

"Mister Weisband taught me how to sign my name," one mourner said.[11]

10 A BALANCE OF TERROR

With Morris away with the quartermaster corps, Lona established a cover for her spy work by joining another army—the civilian work force of eighteen million women employed in war industries. In 1942 she worked as a machine operator at Publix Metals, which made taps and dyes at 100 Sixth Avenue in Manhattan. In 1943 she went out to Aircraft Screw Products, a factory in Long Island City that made fasteners for warplanes. One night she was seriously injured when her hair got caught in a machine and her scalp was torn. She also received some dental work that turned out badly, leaving her with a gap between her front teeth.

Publix Metal and Aircraft Screw were defense plants, which made Lona a proverbial fox in the chicken house. At one point she was a union steward on the night shift and entertained her fellow workers with so many antimanagement harangues that her bosses blamed her for an outbreak of sloppy work bordering on sabotage. Another supervisor said she was preaching Communism on the job. She did make an effort to publicly distance herself from the CPUSA by registering to vote for the American Labor Party, but it had been taken over in Manhattan and Brooklyn by Communists, which didn't offer her much insulation. Lona was one-half of an important spy couple, and such behavior was not wise for a secret agent who was supposed to be secret.

Lona started wearing men's shirts and slacks, which for safety reasons were the norm for women working at industrial jobs. Away from work, she added sunglasses and a beret to her ensemble. She had lived with Harry and Sarah Cohen for over a year after Morris went into the army, but ultimately she wasn't able to get along with her mother-in-law. Lona's spy work required her to stay out late at night and sometimes to disappear for days at a time. That apparently led Sarah to suspect she was running around with other men. Lona's not wearing a wedding ring probably added to Sarah's suspicions. There also might have been some lingering resentment that Morris had not married a nice Jewish girl. Arguments ensued. Lona moved out.

On November 15, 1943, she sublet apartment 3B in an old brownstone at 78 East Seventy-First Street in Manhattan. It was a three-room flat, a walk-up, not at all fancy. But it was in the Central Park neighborhood from her days as a governess, and she felt comfortable there. A neighbor later quoted Lona as saying she had been kicked out of her previous address.[1]

Despite Lona's lapses in operational security, she was about to prove her worth as a key operative in Moscow's Operation Enormous to infiltrate the Manhattan Project. The project's name came from the fact that it was managed by the Manhattan, New York, district of the U.S. Army Corps of Engineers. Ground zero for the Manhattan Project was a new atomic research facility the army was building on the grounds of the former Los Alamos Ranch School, which it had purchased. The school was located on a mesa in the Jemez Mountains about sixty miles north of Albuquerque, New Mexico.

Los Alamos was going to be the Cohens' most valuable target in their North American spying for the Soviets. It had been a small boarding school operating on Teddy Roosevelt's conviction that a boy's education should be complemented by a vigorous outdoor life of camping, hiking, and riding. The buildings were big and sturdy, constructed of logs and stone. Sometimes bears hibernated under them. The writers Gore Vidal and William S. Burroughs had been students at Los Alamos for a while. Only four young men were in the senior class that graduated just before the army took it over in February 1943.

The Los Alamos site was chosen because of its isolation. No airfield, train station, or bus depot was anywhere around, and the only way to get up to the site was on narrow, winding mountain roads. If snoopers showed up, their dust trail would be spotted while they were still miles away. Public safety was also a consideration. Early on, the bomb designers didn't know exactly what an atomic explosion would do. Would it change the climate by melting the polar ice caps? Would it electrify the soil and spur crop production? Or would it set fire to the earth's atmosphere? For all they knew, fire and radioactive fallout might spread across the North American continent and leave a charred wasteland. They hoped that the remoteness of the Southwest would keep that kind of disaster from affecting major cities on the East and West Coasts. If the winds were right, the poisonous fallout would be a problem for Mexico, not the United States.

A team in France—Fréderick Joliot, Hans von Halban, Lew Kowarski, and Francis Perrin—had first designed an atomic bomb in the thirties. They called themselves the Paris Group, and they obtained a bomb patent that they secretly transferred to the British Royal Navy ahead of the fall of France. In England the A-bomb project was called Tube Alloys, a code name for uranium. But the British, too, feared a German invasion, and began moving their project over to their Commonwealth partner of Canada. That was why the French, British, and Canadians were ahead of the United States and Russia in the early race to build an A-bomb. But it was only a paper dream. Building a working bomb would require huge research and production facilities and tons of cash. The United States Treasury and the Manhattan Project would fill that need.

Albert Einstein had tipped off President Roosevelt to the potential of an atomic bomb early on, so FDR made the Manhattan Project a major military program and took over the research on behalf of the Allies. His speed in doing so was influenced by reports (later shown to be exaggerated) that Germany was also building an A-bomb. The Soviets would give the Allied atomic bomb the code name Balloon. At Los Alamos they called the first one the Gadget. The first bombs used in the war were nicknamed Fat Man and Little Boy.

The Manhattan Project would end up costing 2 billion wartime dollars. That's 2.58 trillion dollars in today's currency, making it probably the most expensive single military project in history, outside of maybe the Great Wall of China. Security was so tight that the U.S. government did not admit the existence of the Manhattan Project. Various excuses were given for all the land bought and construction done, all the scientists hired away from their regular jobs. Folks who lived around Los Alamos watched as heavily loaded trucks lumbered up to the site every day, but came back empty. One rumor had it that a pregnancy camp for unwed WACs was being built.

Ultimately, Los Alamos alone would become home to nearly forty-five thousand employees and dependents. As the facility grew with Quonset huts, muddy streets, cheap wood barracks, guard towers, barbed-wire fences, passes, badges, and vehicle inspections, some Europeans at Los Alamos compared it to a concentration camp. Soldiers in Jeeps and on horseback patrolled the grounds, mail was censored, and outside phone calls prohibited. Employees were allowed to leave the reservation one day each month, on Sunday, for shopping in Santa Fe, which was closer than Albuquerque.

The director of the Manhattan Project, Major General Leslie Groves, a portly West Pointer, a patient bureaucrat and a talented writer, knew that some of his Los Alamos whiz kids were lefties, and he ordered them tailed by army security agents whenever they left the reservation. That made Los Alamos, in effect, a think tank with bayonets. The army designated it Project Y. People who worked there called it the Hill. The Soviets gave it various code names: Nature Preserve, Camp-2, or simply the Camp (Camp-1 was Oak Ridge, Tennessee, a site used for uranium enrichment).

Despite the temporary wartime cooperation between the Allies and the Soviet Union, Roosevelt knew that after the war the United States would again emerge as Moscow's main enemy, so Manhattan Project scientists were forbidden from sharing their research with Russia. But even the British and French complained that the Yanks didn't always come clean with them. And the Canadians were bitter because the U.S. Army downgraded their atomic research facility at Montréal and muscled in to take over Eldorado, the privately owned radium mines at Port Hope, Ontario. Eldorado gave the Manhattan Project a virtual monopoly on North American uranium production.

At first, Station One in New York had trouble locating the site of the Manhattan Project. They were told it was somewhere in Mexico. Then once they did find it, in *New* Mexico, they faced a greater problem: how to crack it. As it turned out, the answer was simple. Recruiters for General Groves were grabbing all the top physicists in America that they could, regardless of their age or politics, and Station One was able to cut a hole in the Manhattan Project's security net by exploiting some of those idealistic employees who were communists or fellow travelers, appealing to their sympathies for what they saw as America's unjustly ignored ally.

Ideological recruits didn't cost much. That made them the best kind of agents, Alexander Orlov always said. The most helpful volunteers turned out to be Klaus Fuchs and Theodore Alvin Hall. Hall would soon work in the Cohens' Volunteer network, with Lona as his field officer and courier. He would be their main contact inside Los Alamos, the first agent to give the Soviets a complete diagram of the first A-bomb.

Fuchs would never meet Morris and Lona, but he would later verify for Moscow Center the accuracy of the information that Hall stole. Fuchs's capture would also turn out to be a major disaster for both the Rosenberg and Cohen networks.

But the Fuchs affair was a little bit down the road. For the moment, Ted Hall had the highway all to himself.

TED HALL GRADUATED from Townsend Harris Hall, a public school in Queens for academically gifted boys, founded by a diplomat who had helped establish the Free Academy of the City of New York, later CCNY. Ted was fourteen years old at graduation. Many kids that age were still wearing beanies and knickerbockers and reading Captain Marvel comic books. But Ted was an algebra and physics prodigy.

Ted was born in Far Rockaway, Long Island, son of Jewish parents, Bernard Holtzberg and Rose Moscowitz, another couple who had come to the United States to escape imperial Russia. When Bernard's furrier business failed in the Great Depression, the family had to give up their comfortable suburban house and move into a small apartment in Washington Heights, Manhattan. That's where Ted grew up, playing ball in the street and sledding in winter on the traffic ramps up to the new George Washington Bridge.

Ted's brother Ed was eleven years older and would soon take two engineering degrees at CCNY and serve in the army air corps during the war. In order to avoid anti-Semitism, Ed Anglicized his name, and Ted's, to Hall, over their parents' objections. Like Morris Cohen, Ted Hall was a popular boy, healthy and athletic, and an expert in sports statistics, with the Yankees as his team. As his family prepared to celebrate his bar mitzvah, Ted didn't want to participate because he was an atheist. The rabbi patiently talked him into cooperating, but Ted still found a way to express his irreverence. When it came time for him to make a little speech at the ceremony, he shocked the congregation by including a dig at a local transit line he hated.

"We must eliminate from the world," he said, "poverty, greed, intolerance and the Sixth Avenue El."[2]

Townsend Harris Hall had an impressive academic reputation. Its alumni included Herman Wouk, Bennett Cerf, Ira Gershwin, Jonas Salk, and a couple of Nobel Prize winners in math and physics. After Ted graduated, he tried to enter Columbia University. They told him he was too young and suggested he travel for a year. He enrolled instead at nearby Queens College, a new branch of City University of New York (CUNY). The fact that Queens was a free public school fit in well with Ted's financial situation.

Queens was just three years old, a commuter college with only a few hundred students. It did have a chapter of the Young Communist League, which Ted joined. Ultimately, though, he was disappointed in the narrow-mindedness of the YCL leadership. He was troubled by the prospect that if Communism made everyone's life good, then people might lose the incentive to fight, and their interests would be reduced to the level of petty personal ambitions, resulting in spiritual atrophy. Like Morris Cohen, Ted was a Stalinist, a defender of Uncle Joe's treaties with Hitler.

Ted was a top student at Queen's College. But aside from his YCL membership, he didn't find much of interest there. Ed knew what was wrong. Queen's amounted to just another high school, he said. Ted needed a real challenge. Ed demanded that his little brother apply to Harvard. He did, and was admitted as a junior in the autumn of '42. He was sixteen years old. That was also the year that Townsend Harris was shut down, ostensibly for budgetary reasons. But there was a story that Mayor Fiorello LaGuardia ordered the blackboards dusted for the last time because a relative of his was refused admittance.

WHEN TED ARRIVED in Cambridge, Massachusetts, old Harvard had cast off its collar of pacifism and joined the war effort with the vigor of a draft dodger who's just been chased down by his selective service board. Dormitories were turned over to a U.S. Navy officer-training program, and the loudspeakers and bells installed in the hallways were loud enough to be appreciated by students trying to sleep late in nearby digs. An air-raid siren was installed atop the library and tested every day during classes, a welcome way to cover up some bad readings of Chaucer. Flagpoles were erected, military columns marched across the Yard, patriotic movies opened at the local theatres, and an outbreak of saluting swept the campus.

Ted at first roomed with Jake Bean and Barney Emmert, two cheerleaders for the John Reed Society at Harvard. The club had only about a dozen members, and the wisecracking Bean and Emmert at times seemed to think the whole thing was a joke. Nevertheless, Hall joined up, though he noticed that the other members didn't seem to know much about Marxism. Ted contributed to the cause by doing some organizing work for the United Steelworkers' Union at the Bethlehem Steel factory at Fall River, Massachusetts.

He took courses in math, physics, and German, but thought his professors were pompous, humorless windbags. Again he lost interest in academics. He found solace in military courses: fundamental issues at stake in the war, guerrilla training, parachuting behind enemy lines. He decided he wanted to be a paratrooper, when he wasn't playing Ping-Pong. His grades dropped—a surprise to no one. When he went home for the holidays he told his parents he wanted to drop out. They gave him a kick start and sent him back.

In January 1943, Ted's second semester at Harvard, he took advanced courses in math, physics, and quantum mechanics. For the first time, he felt he was firing on all cylinders. He also studied Marxism more deeply, wondering if an economic system could be defined in terms of mathematical variables. He rejected outright Stalin's recent strategy of trying to appease Roosevelt by watering down American Communism into some pink shade of New Deal.

At the beginning of Ted's senior year, in September 1943, he roomed with Roy Glauber, a physics student from the Bronx who would later win a Nobel Prize. Soon another student, Saville Sax, moved in with them. There were only two bedrooms in the dorm suite, so Savy slept on the sofa.

Savy Sax is an important figure in the story of the Cohens' infiltration of the Manhattan Project because he would become Ted Hall's first courier. Sax and Hall would show that the Manhattan Project's security firewalls could be breached and that top-secret documents could be smuggled out of Los Alamos. In time, Savy's duties would be turned over to Lona.

Joan Hall described her husband Ted in those days as tall and darkly attractive, with big brown eyes and a soft, warm voice. But he was also pimply, badly shaven, and slovenly dressed. If his clothes got torn, he would just staple them together. He had thick coffee-colored hair, distinctively arched eyebrows, and a long face with a sometimes-moody expression. But when Joan met Ted and Savy after the war, she thought they were both charming, witty, and likeable.

A photo from that period shows Savy Sax as a grinning young man with wild-looking hair. He was unconventional, enthusiastic, and loyal to Ted, who became his best friend. But Savy's son, Boria Sax, later painted a darker picture. In an interview, he said his father was mentally ill, a nervous, unpredictable manic-depressive with wild mood swings ranging from anger to despair.[3] Savy had grown up in an insular Jewish family that, like Ted's folks, had fled to New York from Nicholas II's Russia. Savy's parents spoke Yiddish, idealized Russia and communism, and had little interest in assimilating into the American mainstream.

Savy Sax was disorganized. His table manners were a disaster. He was alienated and insecure and never quite seemed to fit in anywhere. But he was a talented writer and wanted to be a poet. Savy was the one who suggested to Hall that if his work at Los Alamos turned out to be some kind of terrible weapon, then he should tell the Russians about it.

Ted agreed. But he warned Savy never to mention it to anyone.

TED HALL WENT DOWN to Los Alamos as a junior physicist. He was eighteen years old and still technically a senior at Harvard. But he had finished his academic work, and that left him free to leave six months ahead of graduation. Forget about Rome or Acapulco. Building an atomic bomb was going to be his senior trip.

In its early days, Los Alamos was a dirty, smelly place. The new buildings were flimsy and overheated by coal-burning stoves that left a shroud of smoke hanging over the camp to stain laundry drying in the air. There were few sidewalks, and when it rained everybody had to wade through mud. They worked six days a week. Sirens were their factory whistle. Saturday night was party night. Square dances were held, with scientists dressed up like drugstore cowboys. Sundays were spent playing golf or baseball or going on outings. Poker games were popular. So was a certain women's dormitory that served as the local brothel.[4]

But the rest of the time there was serious work to be done, with the pressure of an assumed race against Hitler on the backs of the scientists. Research meetings were often raucous affairs with everybody passionately arguing his ideas. Should the A-bomb be shaped like an artillery shell? Or should it be an implosive device?

Hall was the youngest scientist working at Los Alamos. He was assigned to the laboratory of Bruno Rossi, an Italian experimental physicist. Ted helped build a radiation counter for measuring the fission of plutonium when bombarded by fast neutrons. Fission was essential to creating an atomic explosion, and the work in the Rossi lab might have been the most important single experiment leading directly to the design of the Gadget, the first atomic bomb, an implosion device with a plutonium core. The implosion bomb was the one that Hall would describe in the diagram he gave to Lona Cohen.

While he was working on the bomb, the army drafted Hall as a private and issued him a uniform. It didn't improve his sartorial habits. He walked around with muddy boots, an unbuttoned shirt and a skull cap rather than a regulation army hat. He never did seem to master the skill of saluting or saying "sir" to officers. But Rossi was impressed with his work and made him a team leader. As Ted progressed, he thought some more about telling the Soviets what was being done at Los Alamos. By October 1944, four months after he was graduated in absentia from Harvard, he had made the decision to pass information to the Russians.

After he married, Hall told his wife it had been a slow, deliberate decision developed over time.[5] He felt disgusted by the effects of the worldwide Depression—the rise of the Nazis in Germany and the Fascists in Italy and Spain, and the humiliating loss of his father's business. He thought the Depression in America had been relieved by the nation's going to a wartime economy, but he feared that hard times would return once the fighting was over. Then a racist, anti-Semitic government would emerge and use the A-bomb to dictate to the rest of the world. He thought that giving the A-bomb to the Russians, creating a balance of power, would be insurance against that.

Like Morris Cohen, Ted Hall did not see himself as a traitor for assisting the Russians. He would just be sharing information that had been unfairly denied to a wartime ally. But how to do it? And when?

"At a certain point I stopped dithering and decided to act," he said.[6]

Boria Sax, Savy's son, would later disagree with the presumption that the United States would do evil things with a nuclear monopoly after the war. That argument had an "eerily technocratic ring" to it, he said. Boria didn't believe that establishing a "balance of terror" between the Soviet Union and the West was the real reason Hall gave the Bomb to the Russians.

"My suspicion is that belief in the Marxist utopia might have been a greater factor than we are led to think," Boria wrote.[7]

DESPITE THE BRIGHT WARM SUNSHINE outside on October 22, 1944, they weren't having a good day at Station One in New York. As of April 1943, Soviet foreign intelligence was run by Department 1 of the NKGB, but still known as Moscow Center.[8] Infiltrating the Manhattan Project was the Center's absolute priority in North America, and they had found out that aside from Los Alamos, the U.S. Army had built larger atomic facilities at Oak Ridge and at Hanford, Washington, to process uranium into plutonium. Affiliated atomic research was also progressing in Canada. But Station One had not met the demands from the high Soviet leadership, code-named Echelon, to install a productive probationer (source) inside Los Alamos.

Klaus Fuchs, a German closet Communist working on Tube Alloys in England, had first offered to give British atomic secrets to the Soviets in London in 1941 after the invasion of Russia by Germany. He was sent to America in '43 to work in the Manhattan Project, and was turned over to Station One in New York. Then he seemed to have disappeared. Until he surfaced again, Russell McNutt (Fogel and later Persian) was the only source Moscow had in the Manhattan Project. McNutt was a Communist who had been recruited for spying by his friend Julius Rosenberg (Antenna and Liberal). But McNutt was an obscure civil engineer working in New York for Kellex, a contractor building a gas diffusion plant at Oak Ridge. He had given Station One some information about equipment being used in the Manhattan Project, but it was mostly chicken feed.

That's why Ted Hall was going to be so important to the Soviets. The young army private arrived in New York from Los Alamos that October on two-week leave. He looked up Savy Sax, told him about the A-bomb, and showed him a report he had written. They decided to look for a Russian to whom they could give the report. But they ruled out a visit to the Soviet consulate because they figured, correctly, that it was under surveillance.

There are different versions of what happened next.

The Soviet account says that Sax went to CPUSA headquarters alone and tried to see Earl Browder, but couldn't get past a secretary. Hall, meanwhile, went to see Nikolai Napoli, head of Artkino, a Soviet company in Times Square that imported Russian films. Ted said he wanted to speak to someone about an important military issue. In the past, Napoli had assisted Jacob Golos, head of covert ops for the CPUSA. Napoli had contacts in the NKGB but wasn't authorized to recruit assets or accept product himself. He sent Hall along to Sergey Kurnakov, an NKGB agent.

Joan Hall, however, said that Ted actually went to Amtorg first, and tried to talk to somebody there. He found an employee unpacking boxes. The man was horrified at the topic of Ted's visit, and pawned him off on Kurnakov.

Another version came from Boria Sax. He thought the initial contact with the Russians might have been made by Savy's mother, Bluma. "She didn't really seem like somebody who would be engaged in espionage, who would be involved with secrets," he wrote. "Later I began to think that perhaps she might."[9]

Boria didn't offer any evidence of Bluma's complicity other than her work for Russian War Relief, a Communist front. Boria said it was "at least conceivable" that Bluma set up contact with the Soviets for Savy and Ted through contacts she had at Russian War Relief and the CPUSA.

Nevertheless, the different versions do agree on one thing: Ted did find Kurnakov. His cover was military analyst for local Soviet news publications, which at least was more creative than trying to say he was an agricultural consultant in the middle of New York City. Ted found him at the *Russky Golos* office and quickly told him about a new secret weapon on which he was working.

Kurnakov was cautious. Espionage is based on deceit, not trust.

Where was Ted doing that work? he asked.

Los Alamos, Ted replied.

That caught Kurnakov's attention. He suggested they continue their conversation the next day at his apartment.

In that next meeting, Kurnakov found the young man sitting before him to be a sharp conversationalist, witty and somewhat sarcastic. He also noticed that Ted wore dirty socks that hung down over his muddy boots. Ted was nervous. Kurnakov, a drinker in the Russian style, tried to relax Hall by plying him with vodka. It didn't work. Ted kept biting his nails and looking miserable. Finally Kurnakov showed Hall a newspaper story about some missiles the U.S. government was developing. Was that what this visit was all about?

"No, it's much worse than that," Ted replied.

Hall described the Los Alamos secret weapon as an atomic bomb of colossal destructive capability.

"Do you understand what you are doing?" Kurnakov asked him. "What makes you think you should reveal the USA's secrets for the USSR's sake?"

"The Soviet Union is the only nation that could be trusted with such a terrible thing," Hall was reported to have replied. "The USSR ought to be aware of its existence and stay abreast of the progress of experiments and construction." That way, he added, Russia would not be subjected to "blackmail" at a peace conference after the war.

Kurnakov was still suspicious. Seasoned spies didn't trust walk-ins; there was always too much chance of them being agents provocateurs, operatives who enticed others to commit illegal acts, thereby exposing them to blackmail or arrest. A classic example of such a trap occurred in the Lenin Plot when Felix Dzerzhinsky sent two Cheka agents posing as Latvians to draw the Allies into a phony coup plot.

"Well, how do we know that you're not just an agent of the U.S. government trying to trap me?" Kurnakov asked.

"You don't," Ted replied.

"Well, why don't you just write up your ideas or whatever you want to tell us and give it to me?"

"I've already done that."

Ted pulled out some papers and dropped them to the table. They didn't contain many technical details—those would come later—but they did include a general overview of the A-bomb work, a list of scientists working at Los Alamos, and the locations of research sites.

"Show this to any physicist and he will understand what it's about," Hall said.[10]

Ted was now a teen-aged atomic spy.

Kurnakov was so shaken by the importance of this walk-in that he sent his wife outside to see if anybody had tailed Ted. She didn't spot anybody, but after Hall left, Sergey went out to walk around the neighborhood while his wife removed the report from the apartment. Meanwhile, Ted sent Savy to the Soviet consulate with a copy of the same report. Savy gave it to Anatoli Yatskov, New York chief of station.

With that, Savy joined the band, too.

Kurnakov would act as the boys' first control officer. Because of his youth—he had just turned nineteen—Ted was given the code name *Mlad* (young). Savy, almost two years older, was *Star* (old). Until Ted and Savy could be investigated further, Kurnakov didn't want to assign them a regular Soviet courier. For the time being, Savy would be Ted's courier for bringing in product from Los Alamos. To prepare for later couriers, Kurnakov got a photograph from Ted.

Ted Hall and Saville Sax would later spend years in fear of government prosecution for what they were about to do. When questioned by the FBI in 1951, they would both lie about their spy work. In the sixties, though, Sax would openly brag of his spy work, while Hall would not own up to it until much later, and then in only an oblique manner.

At times, though, when Boria was growing up in the fifties, his father suffered terrible bouts of suicidal depression. For a couple of months, Savy kept a revolver in the house and threatened to kill himself. In a mood of reflection, he wrote a poem:

> Judge the man you see before you.
> Look deeply past the appearance
> Till his cone absorbs your cone.
> See the government through you, through him,
> The sky, the sun, the streets, the avenues.
> Through you, through him, look deep
> And see what is in you is in him.
> Then as you condemn him, you condemn yourself.[11]

Morris Cohen (*left*) as a 1934 business graduate of Mississippi State, and (*right*) as head athletic trainer in 1935. (Mississippi State University)

Morris Cohen in 1941, during his second year of spying for the Soviets, and Lona in 1943, when she worked for U.S. defense industries. (Russian Foreign Intelligence Service)

Main gate at Los Alamos in the days of the Manhattan Project. (Los Alamos National Laboratory)

Los Alamos security officers searching vehicles leaving the reservation at the time of the Manhattan Project. (Los Alamos National Laboratory)

Ted Hall, the youngest physicist inside the Manhattan Project, had just graduated from Harvard when he passed to Lona Cohen a complete plan for the first atomic bomb. (Los Alamos National Laboratory)

Theordore A. Hall

Surveillance photo of Willie Fisher, aka Rudolf Abel and a host of other aliases (*upper left*), conducting a sidewalk meet with a contact, possibly Reino Hayhanen, his assistant in New York. (Federal Bureau of Investigation)

A U.S. marshal helps Willie Fisher exit a Black Maria at the federal courthouse in Brooklyn following his arrest in 1957. (Associated Press)

"How are Joann's murders?" This FBI report describes photos of Morris and Lona with paroles (passwords) written on them that were found in Willie Fisher's hotel room when he was arrested. The photos were the smoking gun that identified the Cohens as Soviet spies. The upper left corner of the report lists some of the aliases used by Fisher. (Federal Bureau of Investigation)

FBI assistant director Alan Belmont, the counterintelligence officer in charge of major cases for the bureau, spent seven years tracking down the Cohens. (Federal Bureau of Investigation)

The "house of secrets" operated by Morris and Lona Cohen, known in England as Peter and Helen Kroger, in a recent photograph. (Ruislip Online)

Security officers watched the Cohen residence, headquarters for the Portland spy ring, from the second-floor side windows of Bill and Ruth Search's house across the street. (Ruislip Online).

"Lonsdale's escape alley," the walkway at the bottom of Cranley Drive used by Soviet controller Konon Molody when leaving the Cohens' house. (Gay Search)

Three of the Portland spies were arrested on the sidewalk outside the Old Vic Theatre in London while passing stolen NATO atomic documents. This view was taken from the small park across the street, another place where the spies liked to rendez-vous. (MrsEllacot/ Wikimedia Commons)

Great Scotland Yard, the street outside the original headquarters of the Metropolitan Police in London. The Met moved to a larger HQ, called New Scotland Yard, on the Victoria Embankment, in 1890. Then they moved to a second New Scotlnd Yard, on Broadway, in 1967. (Paul Farmer/Wikimedia Commons)

Central Criminal Court in London (the Old Bailey), where major spy cases were tried in Britain, including those of the Cohens and their Portland ring, along with George Blake, Klaus Fuchs, and Alan Nunn May. (TBmurray/Wikimedia Commons)

MI5 officer Jim Skardon (*left*) and Special Branch Detective Superintendent George "Moonraker" Smith, chief British counterintelligence officers in Operation Whisper, leaving the Old Bailey. (Associated Press)

The Cohens' London control officer, Konon Molody, known in England as Gordon Lonsdale, enjoying a laugh in East Berlin after his release from a British prison in a swap. (Alamy)

The Cohens' fellow spies Harry Houghton and Ethel Gee reunited after serving terms in British prisons. (Corbis)

Wormwood Scrubs, historically one of Britain's most notorious prisons, where Morris Cohen served time. A friend of Cohen's said the name of Strangeways Prison seemed "almost romantic" by comparison with that of the Scrubs. (Chmee2/Wikimedia Commons)

The Cohens on a Champagne flight to Poland after their release from prison in England in a swap for three British subjects held by the Soviets. (Alamy)

The Cohens' apartment house in Moscow, in a swanky neighborhood near the American embassy, after their final return to Russia. (Christopher Marcisz)

"To love and to be loved" is the inscription on the Cohens' tombstone in the KGB cemetery in Moscow. (Christopher Marcisz).

11 MISSION TO ALBUQUERQUE

Squares of morning light warmed Lona Cohen's lap as the bus jostled her down a battered road past patches of scrubby grass. No trees were in sight, no shade, just a summer sun that shimmered like water on the sand and rocks that reached endlessly into the distance. It looked like utter desolation out there. But that was misleading. The New Mexico desert was teeming with a multitude of critters, from Gila monsters and rattlesnakes to centipedes and butterflies. One of the most lovely and deadly was the tarantula hawk wasp. The female, with her big blue-black body and orange wings, hunted tarantulas by smell. Finding one, she stung it with a poison that did not kill, but paralyzed. *Pepsis grossa* then dragged the helpless spider back to her burrow, refreshed herself by sucking fluids from its wounds, then laid her eggs on its body. When the eggs hatched, the baby wasps fed on the tarantula's body.

But Lona was not in New Mexico to commune with the local fauna and flora. With Morris still in the army in Europe, she was running their Volunteer network alone and she was on an urgent mission for Station One — to meet Ted Hall and pick up a very important report he had smuggled out of Los Alamos.

Savy Sax had made an earlier trip for the same purpose. But Savy had a habit of talking to himself and gesturing wildly as he walked — a mad Russian right out of central casting — and he was stopped and questioned by government agents. They wanted to know his citizenship and draft status. He produced a catalogue from the University of New Mexico and told them he was considering a transfer down here. He had even taken a bus all the way from New York in order to reinforce his image as a student on a budget.

Sax had picked up a handwritten report from Hall and returned to New York without further incident. But now the two young men had a new control officer, Anatoli Yatskov, who had taken over from the less experienced Sergey Kurnakov. Yatskov (aka Yakovlev) was not happy with the way Savy had handled his assignment. Sax had copied Hall's report onto the pages of a newspaper with milk as an invisible ink and then burned the original. Yatskov spent hours transcribing the report and still wasn't sure he had gotten everything right.

Yatskov decided to send another courier next time, a woman. He wanted one who could think fast and finesse her way through a checkpoint. The lovely Leslie (Lona) immediately came to mind.

Lona had been reactivated in January 1945 after having been put on ice four months earlier when Sam Semyonov, the Cohens' first control officer, was recalled to Moscow. Semyonov had been under FBI surveillance since an anonymous letter typed in Cyrillic was mailed to "Mr. Hoover" at bureau headquarters in Washington in the dead of night back in August 1943. The letter identified several high-ranking members of Soviet intelligence in New York, and denounced them. Semyonov was included.

He was accused of running agents in all U.S. industrial cities, in all aviation and chemical war plants, and in large institutes. Semyonov was "robbing the whole of the war industry of America," the letter said. "He works very brazenly and roughly. It would be very easy to follow him and catch him red-handed. He would be glad to be arrested as he has long been seeking a reason to remain in the USA, hates the NKGB, but is a frightful coward and loves money. He will give all his agents away with pleasure if he is promised an American passport."[1] The writer was later identified as Vassily Mironov, a disgruntled agent posted to the Soviet embassy in Washington who wanted to do some damage to Russia's spy apparatus in the United States.

Semyonov had been running not only the Cohens but also the Rosenbergs—he gave them an early crash course in *konspiratsia*—but now with the FBI following him around like hounds on the scent of a rabbit, Sam soon found it impossible to service any of his agents, and he was summoned back to Moscow.

Moscow Center blamed Semyonov and Gaik Ovakimian, the New York station chief at the time, for sending courier Harry Gold to New Mexico to meet with David Greenglass (Caliber), Ethel Rosenberg's brother, and pick up some sketches of high-explosive lens molds for the implosion bomb. But on the day when that trip was scheduled, Greenglass's regular courier couldn't go, so Gold was sent instead.

What was wrong with that?

The problem was that Gold was the regular courier for Klaus Fuchs (Rest), who had resurfaced and was now working as another important Soviet source inside Los Alamos. To send a courier for an agent in one network to pick up documents from an agent in another network was extremely risky. Discovery could blow two networks at the same time. It just wasn't done.

As it turned out, that one mistake involving Gold, that one bad decision on somebody's part, would be one of the factors leading to the exposure of some of Station One's most important spy networks. The Rosenbergs would be arrested, and the Cohens forced to flee the United States.

As a result of the Harry Gold affair, Semyonov was fired. Yatskov took over his agents at Station One. But it was Yatskov, not Semyonov, who had been Gold's control. Yatskov was the one who sent Gold to New Mexico. He had done that on orders from Moscow Center. One former high official in Soviet intelligence suggested that Semyonov was made a scapegoat for Moscow Center's own shortcoming because he was a Jew.[2] The Center had given Zionists the code name Rats.

Yatskov became the Cohens' most important control officer. He would prepare Lona for her very dangerous trip to New Mexico. He would walk her through the mission in advance, step by step, and stand by to send assistance if needed.

Yatskov had arrived in New York on February 4, 1941, telling immigration officials that he was a new clerk for the Soviet consulate. His wife Anastasia said she was going to work as a translator at Amtorg. They took an apartment at 3 West 108th Street in Manhattan and then Anastasia delivered twins, Victoria and Pavel, in Brooklyn.[3] Like so many Soviet intelligence officers now moving up in the ranks after Stalin's purges, Anatoli was a young agent. When he first walked in the door of the New York consulate, he was twenty-nine, just one year older than Lona. His code name was Aleksey. His street name would be John.

Aside from the Cohens, Yatskov began to run some of the other top agents working for Station One, including Hall, Gold, Fuchs, and the Rosenbergs. He also controlled Jacob Golos, the CPUSA operative who had supplied passports and transportation for Morris Cohen and other volunteers for Spain.

When Elizabeth Bentley, Golos's assistant and lover, first met Yatskov, she thought he was a bit of a klutz. She found a thin, pale, boyish-looking fellow just short of six feet tall, with thick brown hair that persisted in falling down across his forehead. He wore a badly fitting Russian suit and had a half-starved look that she thought was characteristic of new arrivals from the workers' utopia. Yatskov's English was so bad that Elizabeth had trouble understanding him, and despite his preparation at Moscow Center, he showed a certain ignorance of American life. She was amused by his stubborn and unshakable belief that American workers were so terrorized by the police that they had to carry revolvers to the polls on election day.

Further, Yatskov in New York seemed dangerously ignorant of even the simplest tradecraft. He forgot meets, he was late for meets, he neglected to put film in cameras. Once he missed a meet with Bentley, then called her office and asked for her by her code name, Miss Wise. Yatskov also seemed unable to spot surveillance, and during meets was nervous to the point of drawing attention. At first Bentley thought his anxiety was based on fear of the FBI, which Moscow Center had code-named Octopus. But then she realized that Yatskov, like so many Soviet agents, was terrified by his own organization.[4]

In time, Yatskov would improve his English, and his tradecraft. He bought fashionable American clothes, made important friends, and developed an image as a debonair and amusing dispenser of Old World charm. It was said that no diplomatic party was complete without the delightful Anatoli Ananovitch, a glass of Champagne in one hand and a cigar in the other, waxing eloquent on how much a friend Russia was to America.

Yatskov picked Lona for the big run to New Mexico because of her successful record as Morris's partner in the Volunteer network and her services individually as a mail drop for William Weisband and Klaus Fuchs. After her reactivation in January 1945, she was first sent on courier runs to Washington State and Canada to retrieve documents from other sources inside the Manhattan Project. A retired Russian intelligence officer later said that

Lona picked up an envelope at Niagara Falls that contained a powdered sample of uranium ore that was then sent along to Moscow.[5]

Two other couriers had been considered for the coming New Mexico trip, but then rejected. The first one was code-named Pylos and has not been identified. He had flubbed two meetings for trivial reasons. The other was Klibi, a play on Liberal. That was Julius Rosenberg, who said he couldn't bear such a long journey.

That meant Lona had a green light for this most challenging of missions.

BECAUSE LONA in the past had been a little casual in arriving on time for meets and remembering the required parole (passwords), Moscow Center insisted that Yatskov sit her down and give her a stern lecture on tradecraft before she was dispatched to New Mexico. This was wartime, and government agents and local police were checking buses and trains all across America. They were watching for spies or saboteurs carrying weapons, explosives, subversive literature, or suspicious-looking radio equipment. They were particularly on the lookout for stolen secret documents or photos. Experienced counterintelligence agents had developed an early warning system that was always scanning for elements out of place—strange movements, odd clothing, evasive looks, nervous tics. Before personal computers, memory banks were in the agents' heads. Sometimes they took people in for questioning just on a hunch. If Lona got caught with damning documents, she faced a long prison term, or execution.

Yatskov told Leslie that when she met Ted Hall she should get physically close to him, as if they were old friends, then stroll for a while in a natural manner while making the pass. If stopped for questioning, she should remain calm. Take control of the situation, Yatskov said. Be brave and tough, but cautious; use logic and common sense, not violence. Yatskov thought Lona had talent as an actress. He told her to use that gift.

Lona was instructed to rent a room in Sandia, a small mountain resort a few miles east of Albuquerque. She was to dress simply, to watch the other people staying there, and to blend in.[6] If anybody asked, she would say she had come to the hot, dry Southwest for her health. But she should not get into any political arguments with anyone. Act like an ordinary tourist, Yatskov told her.

After settling in at Sandia, Lona would take a bus on Sunday morning down to the small station on First Street sw in downtown Albuquerque, just off Route 66, America's most famous interstate highway. She would walk the seven short blocks south to the Cathedral of St. John, at Fourth and Silver streets, and meet Mlad (Hall) at one o'clock in the afternoon. The cathedral was built of stone and brick in traditional Episcopalian style and had a sidewalk in front. Lona could loiter there in the shade of the building without attracting attention, as if she were waiting for someone after the noon service. Once she received Ted's report, she should not keep it in her hotel room. She should get out of town as fast as she could.

After Lona's tutorial in tradecraft, Yatskov sent her to a doctor to complain of a persistent sore throat and cough. The doctor gave her a note diagnosing her condition as chronic bronchitis. Lona then showed the note, and a prescription from the doctor, to her boss at work and was granted sick leave.

Lona's mission was an urgent one because the first atomic bomb, the Gadget, had just been tested, on July 16, at Alamogordo, New Mexico. The test was called Trinity. There had been no way for the U.S. government to cover it up. The blast lit up the night sky brighter than the sun, and the shock wave was felt in Albuquerque, two hundred miles away. A blind woman fifty miles away was reported to have undergone a reverse effect: she saw light for the first time in years and said, "What's that?"[7]

But Station One was still in the dark. Other than what they had read in the newspapers, they had no information on the test. Nor did they know anything about plans to use future A-bombs in combat. Most of all, they needed a schematic of an operational bomb.

The surprise of the Trinity test prompted Yatskov to take the extraordinary step of personally intercepting Lona on her way to work. He ran up and slipped her a note telling her to leave the next day. In order to avoid surveillance, she was instructed to buy a train ticket to Chicago and stay there overnight. Then she would board a ninety-mile-an-hour Santa Fe Railroad Super Chief for the overnight trip to Albuquerque. The same route would be used in her return.

Then one last detail: If Lona had to contact Yatskov, she should send a letter or telegram to herself at her own address in New York. Someone from Station One would check her mailbox every day while she was gone.

Station One had allocated $400 for Sax's expenses in his trip to New Mexico—around $5,300 in today's currency—so that's probably what Lona got. Other than her cash on hand, she was armed with nothing but her own personal determination.

She immediately set out on her own Great Adventure.

LONA ARRIVED IN SANDIA in late July of '45. The following Sunday she took the bus down the mountain to Albuquerque and got to the cathedral an hour in advance. She didn't give her exact arrival date in later interviews, but the last Sunday of the month was the twenty-ninth.

To kill time, she walked around inspecting the low white mission-revival buildings with tiled roofs that fronted the narrow streets and sidewalks. There were almost no trees or flowers or grass, just hot concrete beneath a blinding sun. Across the street, a cafeteria was open, but other than that, downtown was a valley of near silence, a place where suspicion grew like cacti into grotesque shadows that clung to the stuccoed walls around her.

The appointed hour came. Ted Hall was not there. Agents were supposed to be at the right place at the right time for a pass. There was little margin for error in a business as dangerous as this. Lona waited ten minutes, then twenty. She crossed the street and walked around over there for a while. Had she got the day, or the time, wrong? She went back to the cathedral at two o'clock. There was still no Ted. Again she left. Again she returned. She finally gave up and went back to Sandia.

The following Sunday went the same way. Lona arrived at the cathedral at one o'clock and strolled about for an hour. Her mind raced with all sorts of scenarios. Had Ted gone to the wrong church? Was he ill? Had he been delayed by work? Had he been arrested? Being so young, he might not be able to stand up to questioning by security agents. If he had told them about Lona, she could be the target of a search at that very moment.

Lona walked over to the telegraph office and fired off a message to Yatskov: "Harry" (Ted) had not shown up for his "cure." She was burning up her sick leave. What should she do?

Yatskov replied that she should wait as agreed.

Now Lona was furious. She hated Ted Hall. She went back to Sandia and tried to keep her anger in check by doing some hiking and by chatting with other guests at the hotel. She tried to act normal. She kept to her cover story that she was there for therapeutic reasons. But some people suspected she was being stood up by her fellow. They thought the only therapy she needed was a good man. They offered to line her up with a helpful volunteer. Lona refused. Their laughter just made her feel worse.

The next day, on August 6, a uranium bomb called Little Boy was dropped on Hiroshima, Japan. It was a gun-type device with a blast equivalent to twenty thousand tons of TNT. Three days later, on August 9, a plutonium bomb, Fat Man, was dropped on Nagasaki. It was an implosion device of similar strength. The world found out that Los Alamos was bomb central, and tourists began pouring in to New Mexico for a look-see. That brought in more FBI agents and army counterintelligence officers. Everybody was watching everybody else.

On Lona's third trip to town she again went to the cathedral at one o'clock. Mass was over, and parishioners were talking outside on the sidewalk. Was Ted there somewhere? She had never seen him in person. She had to be careful.

Lona spotted a man in the crowd carrying a yellow paper grocery sack. That was the kind of bag that Ted was supposed to be holding as a recognition signal. But this man didn't look like the picture of Ted that Yatskov had given her. He was older, and heavier. But maybe Ted had sent him. She went over and looked him straight in the eye.

"Excuse me," she said, quoting the parole she had been given, "do you know which is the best resort for respiratory disorders, Sandia or the Rio Grande?"

The man, not knowing who this strange woman was, didn't answer. Lona stepped closer. She asked him if he was going to just stand there while the world turned.

According to historian Vladimir Chiko Ted was supposed to have a fish tail hanging out the bottom of his grocery bag. This man's sack didn't. Frankly, it wasn't a signal that made a lot of sense. A fish in this heat would stink and attract attention. Apparently somebody at Moscow Center had not consulted a weather report for New Mexico in the dog days of summer.

Lona quickly tried to think of a way to back out of this situation diplomatically. But the man could see that something was wrong. He asked if he could be of assistance. Lona decided to use the acting talent that Yatskov had noticed in her.

"No," she replied dramatically. "No one can do anything for me. I have to carry my cross alone."

The man pressed on. He told her he liked her. She had beautiful legs. Would she like to come with him? He touched her arm. She recoiled in disgust.

"What's this bullshit?" she said. "Damn you! I don't need you!"

She turned and strode away indignantly.

BACK IN SANDIA, Lona was not only angry but also desperate. She had come all this way and it seemed it had been for nothing. Had Hall experienced a change of heart? Had he realized the gravity of what he was doing and decided to wash his hands of the Soviets? Maybe he had been a double for the FBI all the time. That would mean big trouble for Lona and the Volunteer network.

But she had been to the cathedral three Sundays in a row and nobody had asked her what she was doing there. She hadn't spotted any men in sunglasses and snap-brim fedoras watching her with binoculars. Everything seemed normal—that is, hot and spooky. She decided to try one last time. Then she would go back to New York.

On the fourth Sunday, deep in August, Lona packed her bag and checked out of her hotel in Sandia. She took the familiar bus into town and walked down to the cathedral. As she neared the church she spotted a young man leaving the cafeteria across the street. He, too, was heading for the cathedral. He wore a white sports shirt, straw hat, and sandals.

He was carrying a yellow grocery bag with a fish tail hanging out the bottom.

Voilà!

He stopped in the shadow of the cathedral and looked around. He watched without expression as Lona approached.

"Excuse me," she said. "Can I ask you—"

"Yes, what is it?" he replied curtly.

He resembled the figure in the Ted Hall photo she had. Thin face, big eyes, a nice-looking boy who appeared sympathetic and trustworthy. She decided to forge on.

"You brought it?"

He seemed startled by the question. He turned the grocery bag to show the store's logo printed on the other side. If she was who she was supposed to be, she would recognize it as a warning to be careful.

"Yes, I brought something," he whispered, nodding down at the bag. She looked inside. It held a big catfish. And indeed it was starting to smell a bit ripe.

It was time for Lona to give the parole. But again her memory failed her. The young man stared at her. Lona shifted nervously. What was the parole? As always, it finally came to her.

"Excuse me, would you know which is the best resort for respiratory disorders, Sandia or the Rio Grande?"

"The place where the climate is the best is in the Rocky Mountains," he replied quietly. "There's a good doctor there."

Here, at last, was Ted Hall.

He took Lona's arm and guided her away from the cathedral. There were people around there. They needed to be alone. He suggested they go to the cafeteria that he had just left.

Suddenly Lona stopped him. "Where the hell have you been?" she demanded. "Every Sunday I came here—"

"Yes," he admitted. "It's my fault. I'm in the wrong month."

"All right. Did you bring anything?"

Ted reached into the bottom of the bag under the fish and brought up some papers. Lona smiled. They started walking again. Lona pressed against Ted, took the papers, and slipped them into her handbag. She asked his name.

"Just call me the man from another world," he said.

Lona wiped her face with the sweat towel she carried. They walked down the street, arm in arm like lovers. Ted told her he had to get back to Los Alamos. That was all right, Lona said. She had to catch her train in an hour.

She complained that she had been at the end of her tether. She had spent three Sundays walking around in that heat, waiting for someone, for something.

He grinned. "With what I brought you today," he said, "you could come back every day of the year."

LONA HAD OBTAINED the report she came for. But her mission was not complete. She now faced the final leg of her adventure and the most danger-ous part—her escape. Once she got on her train she would be able to relax a little. But between here and New York awaited a storm of possibilities that ranged from the merely threatening to the truly terrifying.

She walked back up to First Street, still carrying her purse and her towel. She retrieved her suitcase from a locker at the bus station, then went down to the train station. It adjoined the Alvarado Hotel, another impressive mission-style building, with arched walkways and towers facing the tracks. The Super Chief sat there steaming. She went to the ticket window and booked a compartment to Chicago. Then she turned and walked out on the platform.

And there she stopped.

Just ahead of her, passengers were lining up to board the cars. There was nothing unusual about that. But they were being questioned by men in suits, either local police detectives or federal agents. They were inspecting bags and purses.

What should she do, go back to Sandia? No, she had to get out of town. She needed to put as much distance as she could between herself and Al-buquerque. If she waited for a later train, she would still have to submit to a search. It was best to face this thing now and get it over with.

That report from Ted was, at that moment, the hottest sheath of papers in the world. Germany would have paid millions for it. So would the Jap-anese. They would have killed for it. She had it, and Moscow was waiting for it. Where could she hide it? She couldn't put it in her suitcase, or her purse. Inside her blouse wasn't a good idea either. If she were taken in for questioning, a female agent would search her.

She went over Yatskov's instructions. He had told her to always stay in control, to not give the opposition a chance to grab the momentum. Show your resourcefulness, your acting ability, he had told her. Yes, that was it. Now she knew what to do.

She would stage a little drama for the cops.

She went back into the station and found the ladies' room. Thankfully, it wasn't occupied. She took her ticket and stuck it in a book she was carrying in her purse. She had a box of Kleenex to support her claim of bronchitis, and she took a few tissues off the top and threw them away. Then she tucked Ted's report into the bottom of the box and adjusted the remaining tissues on top of it.

She checked her watch. Four minutes to go.

She ran out to her car. Up and down the line, porters were picking up the metal boarding steps. She tried to toss her suitcase into the doorway. The two agents held out their hands to block her.

"What's going on?" Lona demanded.

"Nothing special," the younger agent replied. "Just checking." They needed to see her ID and inspect her bags and her towel.

Lona fumbled around. The officers watched patiently. They were used to dealing with people who weren't quite fully organized. Lona opened her purse, pulled out her wallet, and showed them her identification and her medical prescription. She'd been here for her health, she said. She was going home now.

She opened her suitcase next. The older officer ran his hands through the contents and felt along the lining. Meanwhile, the younger officer gave Lona a smile and an admiring look.

"Got your ticket?" he asked.

Lona gave him a sudden look. Her ticket? Yes, it was here. It was here somewhere.

She shifted the Kleenex box from one hand to another as she went through her suitcase, tossing the contents around. She handed the Kleenex box to the younger agent. Hold this, she told him, hoping the box didn't smell of rotten fish.

The engineer blew the whistle. "All aboard!" the conductor called.

Now the cops got impatient. Where was her *ticket*?

She closed the suitcase and went through her purse again. It contained all the essentials a woman would carry, but no ticket was visible. Then she got the zipper stuck, and had to deal with that. The older agent spotted the book in the purse. What's this? He pulled it out and opened it.

There her ticket was.

"Thank you," Lona grinned. "I completely forgot."

"Oh, you're just like my daughter," he laughed.

Lona tossed her suitcase inside and the officers helped her climb aboard. The train began pulling out of the station. But she needed her Kleenex box. The young agent was standing there, still holding it, still smiling at her.

Lona faked a sneeze and held out her hand for her Kleenex box. The officer ran to catch up with the train and handed it to her. Then they waved goodbye.

When Lona got to New York, she left a chalk mark on a wall between two gutters as a signal to Yatskov that she was back. He went to her apartment and she made them coffee. Then she turned over Ted's document and told him the story about the Kleenex box. He was mortified. She had taken a wild risk. He had heard from her only once in a month. He'd been so worried he was about to send Harry Gold down to Albuquerque to see what was wrong.

But now he could relax. Lona poured him another cup. She had come through.

The Kleenex box incident became legendary in Soviet intelligence as an example of the resourcefulness that a good agent was supposed to show when caught in a dangerous situation.

Ted Hall had given Lona a complete diagram of the first A-bomb. Other agents such as David Greenglass had contributed crude drawings of parts of the bomb, but Hall's schematic contained all the parts of the puzzle. Fuchs would later verify its accuracy.

"The information we acquired enabled us to gain time in building our own bomb," Yatskov recalled later. "How much time we gained is hard to tell, but a few years at least. If it had not been for the information that other people were developing a bomb, we would not have started our own effort until the end of the war."[8]

Considering that, it would probably be safe to say that Ted Hall and Lona Cohen scored what undoubtedly was one of the greatest intelligence coups in history.

12 ALL NETWORKS BLOWN

After proving their mettle against moose and mosquitoes in the Yukon, Morris Cohen's quartermaster company finally got their chance to see frontline action in the spring of 1944. They sailed out of Boston on April 7 aboard the SS *Excelsior*, an army transport ship the length of five football fields. She occupied one of the coffin corners (remote positions) in a big military convoy across the North Atlantic, making her a prime target for enemy torpedoes. Day and night, commands went out over the loudspeakers: "Gunners to battle stations" and "Guards keep sharp watch—subs in vicinity." But the convoy was spared an attack, and after nine days at sea the 3233rd Quartermaster Company entered Scottish waters and sailed up the River Clyde to Glasgow. There Morris and his mates saw for the first time the face of the war they were coming over here to fight.

Glasgow was Scotland's largest city, a working-class northern town of two million, and one of the world's major shipbuilders. Waves of Luftwaffe bombers had blitzed Glasgow in March 1941. Their targets were the Clydeside ammunition factories and the shipyards where 1,500 vessels, including 3 aircraft carriers, had been built since the war began. But the bombers missed most of their military targets and hit residential sections. Hundreds of blocks of brick tenements were destroyed. More than 500 people were killed, 40,000 left homeless. By the time Morris and his company arrived, most of the rubble had been cleared, leaving stubbles of wrecked foundations covered with curiously beautiful pink flowering weeds. As the new shipment of Yanks and Canadians arrived, they were greeted by the peal of church bells.

Next stop for Morris and the 3233rd was Dursley, Gloucester, in south-west England. As they rolled into the old redbrick Dursley Station, local residents greeted them from behind the iron fence that separated the plat-form from the street. Adults waved as the troops got off the train. Kids ran up to them calling out the line that was soon to become a universal greeting all across Europe: "Got any gum, chum?"

Dursley was both a traditional English market town and a center of modern industry. Petters Limited in Dursley built internal combustion engines there; R. A. Lister and Company built trucks, tractors, and loco-motives. Both firms were getting fat on war contracts. Downtown, shops in ancient buildings huddled above narrow winding streets, while out in the residential neighborhoods, timber-framed houses stood protected by low stone walls. Just outside town lay the remains of an old Roman shrine. Closer in, more contemporary local ruins laid in wait for the new soldier boys at the pubs on Silver Street.

Morris and the other new arrivals built a tent city outside Dursley and spent the next two months in the company of English rain and Guernsey cows. Finally they got new orders. They were assigned to the 471st Quar-termaster Battalion of the U.S. First Army. On June 6 (D-Day) they got on another train, rode down to Southampton, and boarded U.S. Navy boats. But then they had to sit in the harbor for five days and try to deal with backed-up toilets, seasickness, and more rain. Finally on June 11 they were motored across the English Channel.

Destination: Operation Overlord, the invasion of France.

GERMANY'S FORTIFIED CONCRETE Atlantic Wall had been breached in the initial invasion of Normandy, but Allied troops were able to advance only a few hundred yards beyond the beaches before getting pinned down again by enemy artillery fire. The shelling was still so heavy that the navy could not land Morris and the 3233rd on any of the invasion beaches. They had to stay on their boats another day and take more Camp Edwards seasick pills until gunships and bombers cleared the way for them onto Utah Beach.

The 3233rd waded ashore, moved a short distance up from the beach, cleared an area of mines and booby-traps, and set up the first Allied salvage depot in France. They stockpiled incoming supplies and scoured their sector for abandoned weapons, Jeeps, trucks, and corpses. For the living, they cooked hot meals and brewed coffee around the clock.

Morris and his unit moved farther inland on June 28 and crossed the Vire River into Isigny-sur-Mers, an important port town that lay low in the base of the Cherbourg Peninsula, which was still a German stronghold. Isigny was famous for its oysters, caramels, and Camembert cheese, and the fact that Walt Disney's name came from there.

An Allied bombardment had destroyed most of Isigny, and now the 3233rd began clearing the road of rubble and building another supply depot. The Germans counterattacked, and the quartermaster corps had to perform their work as enemy shells blew up around them. Warplanes attacked them at night, and both Allied and enemy aircraft were shot down close to the depot. Sirens went off several times warning of chemical attacks. Shouts swept down the line—"Gas! Gas!"—and the men pulled on their masks. It was too dangerous to pitch tents. The men dug foxholes in a field and slept below ground. But unexploded artillery shells and mines lay all around them. Once they watched as a cow stepped on a mine and was blown into meat for the evening dinner.

That Isigny supply depot was vital to the taking of nearby St.-Lô in what became known as the Battle of the Hedgerows. St.-Lô was a major highway hub. The Allies needed to take the town so they could move out of the Normandy Pocket. Twelve divisions of the U.S. First Army, assisted by the British Second Army, attacked St.-Lô along a twenty-five-mile front and encountered bitter resistance. On one day alone, the men of the 3233rd counted more than 1,500 bombers and 150 fighter planes passing overhead to pound enemy positions. It took the Allies three weeks in July to take the town, and they had to destroy most of it in the process. But that battle allowed the deployment of thousands of tanks deeper into France. The race for Berlin was on.

Morris's last major stop in France was at Hirson, a small town in northeastern France on the Belgian border close to the area where the Battle of the Ardennes was fought in the First World War. Later on, in December, the German army would counterattack through the Ardennes in the Battle of the Bulge. But now, in August, the highway through Hirson into Belgium was requisitioned for the Allies' Red Ball Express, a name borrowed from the fast trains of the Santa Fe Railroad. A big red ball was painted on army supply trucks to signal that they were in special convoys rushing supplies up to the advancing front lines. Almost 6,000 trucks rolled every day, driven mostly by African Americans. On one occasion, Morris's unit loaded 5-gallon cans of gasoline onto 110 trucks for General George S. Patton's tanks. That was 150,000 gallons in one day.

In October '44, at Herbesthal, Belgium, Morris and his company were billeted in real buildings for the first time in four months and drew guard duty at the local supply depot that stood almost within sight of the Siegfried Line. At night they watched the lights of huge formations of Allied bombers flying over to bomb Aachen, Germany. But they were also under attack constantly by German planes and v-1 rockets, called buzz bombs because of the noise their engines made. v-1s were early versions of cruise missiles but had no guidance system. They were simply aimed toward the enemy, somewhere out there, and launched. The rule was that if you could hear a buzz bomb, you were okay; it was probably passing over. But once the engine ran out of fuel and went silent, that meant it was about to hit the ground and you should take cover.

In December, Morris crossed the frontier and rode into Germany atop a truck in the Red Ball Express. The towns rolled by like frames in a newsreel: Enzen, Duren, Marburg, Weissenthurm, Bad Wildungen. He and his unit finally landed in the eastern city of Weimar. It was a curious place. On one hand, Weimar was a symbol of Germany's highest cultural achievements. Artists who had worked there included Goethe, Schiller, Bach, Liszt, Weber, and Nietzsche. But the hills north of the city hid a nightmare of Gothic proportions—Buchenwald.

Buchenwald was one of the largest Nazi death camps. A quarter-million prisoners had been sent there—Jews, Gypsies, Jehovah's Witnesses, Communists, German criminals, military deserters, and others that Hitler's ss considered *Untermenschen* (subhumans). More than fifty thousand men, women, and children died in Buchenwald and their bodies were burned in crematoria. After Buchenwald was liberated by the U.S. Third Army, Patton rounded up the citizens of Weimar and marched them through the camp so they could see for themselves what had gone on there. When the 3233rd arrived, about six thousand prisoners were still in the camp, kept there so the roads would be clear for Allied tanks.

Buchenwald had been tidied up by the time Morris and his unit rolled in. But the air was still heavy with the caustic smell of the lye that had been used to clean the ovens of the human grease left behind by the cremations. Cohen was shocked by the sight of hundreds of bodies stacked up like firewood at Buchenwald. But he was favorably impressed with a "weird" but "striking" mural of Stalin in a white uniform that some prisoners had painted on a wall.

"The feelings of the people were that the Soviet Union had saved the world from fascism," he said in a later interview. Cohen thought Uncle Joe looked like a "movie star."[1]

The 3233rd helped out in the big army field kitchen and hospital that Patton had set up for the survivors in Buchenwald. The battalion was headquartered at Weimar when Germany surrendered. After being assigned next to the Ninth and then the Seventh armies, Morris and the 3233rd moved on to Potsdam for duties at the Big Three Conference on July 17, 1945.

Truman, Stalin, and British Prime Minister Winston Churchill reached reluctant agreements at Potsdam regarding German reparations and disarmament. They also proceeded to do exactly what President Wilson had warned against in the first war—to cut up Europe for their own purposes. Most damaging was the agreement allowing Stalin to keep Eastern Europe as his exclusive sphere of influence. That had been one of the deals Stalin struck with Hitler in '39. Truman and Churchill's appeasement of Stalin led to the installation of police states in the East that would last for forty-five years.

Truman had intended for the A-bomb to be a crucial factor in negotiations with Stalin for postwar concessions.[2] The first atomic bomb, Trinity, was tested the day before the Potsdam Conference began, and Little Boy would be dropped on Hiroshima a few days after Truman left Potsdam. Truman considered the A-bomb "the most terrible bomb in the history of the world." But when he told Stalin about it, Uncle Joe didn't seem interested, and the moment passed. Stalin, of course, knew all about the Manhattan Project through his North American spies. Lona Cohen had just arrived in Albuquerque to pick up a complete schematic of the first bomb from Ted Hall, and the American who had set up Stalin's only spy network in North America dedicated to atomic espionage was there at Potsdam as a U.S. Army guard—Morris Cohen.

After Potsdam, Cohen was assigned more guard duty, this time with the Army of Occupation in Berlin. He lived in an army-controlled apartment building with two women servants, hobnobbed with some Soviet soldiers, and counted his points for discharge eligibility. But before leaving Germany, Cohen was an earnest participant in what would be remembered as one of the most shameful episodes of the war.

At the Moscow Conference of October 1944 and the Yalta Conference of February 1945, Roosevelt and Churchill had agreed in a secret codicil to round up and repatriate all Soviet subjects found in enemy territory taken by the United States and Britain.[3] That number was estimated to be several million, and Stalin wanted to impress them into labor battalions to rebuild the Russian cities that had been all but destroyed in the war. The Allies called the roundup Operation Keelhaul. General Dwight D. Eisenhower, supreme Allied commander, was lukewarm toward the idea until it appeared that the U.S. Army could not feed the million or so refugees trying to flee into the American zone in Germany, and then he didn't oppose it. British Foreign Secretary Anthony Eden, who had opposed appeasement of Hitler in the thirties, enthusiastically supported Keelhaul as a way to appease Stalin.

Keelhaul is a nautical term for punishment in which an offender is bound with ropes and dragged underwater against the hull of a ship, down one side and up the other. If he doesn't drown, his flesh will be torn from his body by the barnacles on the hull. It was an appropriate name for the military operation that bore that name. More than five million men, women, and children were rounded up and screened by the NKGB and SMERSH (short for *Smert Shpionam*, death to spies). Some were Soviet soldiers captured by the Germans. Others were collaborators, deserters, refugees, forced laborers, or simply old anti-Communist émigrés. Many managed to escape and flee into Western Europe. A few made it to America, but in 1945 only thirty-nine thousand immigrants were allowed into the United States during the entire year.

Operation Keelhaul resulted in the forced return of more than two million people to Russia. Some were delivered in cattle trucks, trains, and ships. Others were forcibly marched across the frontier. In one case, Russian POWs in Germany resisting return had to be evicted from their barracks by American soldiers firing tear gas. Some of those POWs committed suicide by cutting or hanging themselves. In Russia, the returnees were considered to have been tainted by Western ideas, a dangerous thing in the Soviet state, and many were tortured and shot. One British observer reported 150 arrivals at Murmansk were taken into warehouses and behind sheds, and machine-gunned by executioners who appeared to be fourteen to sixteen years old.[4]

When Morris Cohen was assigned to Keelhaul his army group was given a list of Russian subjects in their sector to seize. Most of them were working on farms and at businesses in local towns. It took Cohen and his squad several days to arrest them all and load them into trucks for delivery to a Soviet colonel. Repatriation was a "good idea," Cohen later said. He praised it as a "concrete example of cooperation" with the Soviets.

MORRIS COHEN had looked forward to picking up where he had left off with Station One when he got home from the war. But he wouldn't know until he returned to New York that he and Lona had been deactivated. Every other Soviet agent and network in North America had also been put on ice. That shutdown would lead to a roll-up of the Rosenberg spy ring and the forced flight of the Cohens from America without any hope of ever coming back.

It could be called the great Soviet intelligence disaster of 1945 and it was caused by two very important defections.

Defector number one was Igor Sergeyevich Gouzenko, a cipher clerk at the Soviet embassy in Ottawa. Most urgent messages between spy services and their foreign stations were sent by encrypted messages in telegrams or by shortwave radio, and cipher clerks were the skilled technicians who ran the system. Their work was as important as that of today's computer-system administrators such as Edward Snowden, who blew the whistle on NSA surveillance in 2013 and fled to Russia.

But there was more to Gouzenko's position at the embassy. Gouzenko worked for Colonel Nikolai Zabotin, the military attaché who was running a vast spy network in Canada for Soviet military intelligence. That made Gouzenko privy to top-secret operations against Canada and, by extension, the United States and Britain. Igor was without doubt a dangerously knowledgeable young man.

At around 8:00 p.m. on September 5, 1945, while Morris Cohen was still in Berlin and Lona was settling back in New York after her run to Albuquerque, Gouzenko took more than a hundred documents out of his safe in room 12 on the second floor of the Russian embassy in Charlotte Street, a stately brick manor with a white wood solarium built along the side that faced the sunsets. The papers included copies of cables and some pages torn from Zabotin's diary showing that Canadian officials had been secretly passing documents to the Soviets. The short and tubby Gouzenko tucked them under his shirt, closed his jacket, and held his belly in so he wouldn't look like a pregnant camel as he walked out past the embassy security men into the warm, humid night.[5]

Gouzenko had been recalled to Moscow. Was it a routine rotation? Igor didn't think so. He had seen other cipher clerks recalled and never heard from again. One of them was shot for cheating on his expense account to the tune of fifty Canadian dollars. Gouzenko was not going to risk that. He was going to defect.

Igor was twenty-six years old, with high cheekbones and low eyebrows that gave him a stern Slavic look. But he was actually a quiet, courteous man who took his hat off when greeting someone. Igor had joined the Young Communist League in Russia when he was sixteen years old. He went to the NKVD code school and worked for the Main Intelligence Division of the Red Army before being posted to Ottawa. Igor and his wife Svetlana and their little boy Andrei lived in apartment 4 on the second floor of a low, boxy, drab-looking brick building at 511 Somerset Street in Ottawa. They couldn't afford a telephone or radio, so they were quiet tenants. The only thing that caught the attention of neighbors was the little boy's habit of peeing off the rear balcony.

The Gouzenkos kept a picture of Stalin on their living room wall in case someone from the embassy dropped by. But Igor was not exactly a dedicated Marxist. The person he admired most was Winston Churchill. What the Soviet system had meant to Igor was a chance to go overseas and work in a comfortable Western capital where his wife wouldn't have to stand in line all day for a loaf of bread. Igor had never had enough to eat in Russia. He and Svetlana often went to the IGA supermarket in Ottawa just to walk the aisles admiring the stocks of meat, vegetables and fruit. He wanted to give his family the good life in Canada. Those documents under his shirt were going to be their ticket to the show. But the USSR had technically been a Canadian ally in the war, and Gouzenko immediately hit brick walls.

At the *Ottawa Journal*, Igor told Chester Frowde, the night city editor, that Canadians in high places were spying for the Russians, and he had the evidence. "It's war. It's war. It's Russia." Frowde adjusted his green eyeshade, looked down at the odd little man who stood before him pale and sweating, and told him that Canada was not at war with Russia and didn't expect to be. Frowde later realized he had missed what would have been the biggest scoop of his career.[6]

Gouzenko also tried to see Louis St. Laurent, the Canadian minister of justice. He didn't have time to talk. Next day, Igor returned to the *Journal*. This time a woman in the office sent the Gouzenkos to the crown attorney's office. "If you want it so the Russians can't pick you up, get naturalized," she said.[7]

But at that office, Fernande Coulson, secretary to the crown attorney, told Igor and Svetlana they were not eligible for Canadian citizenship because they were not landed immigrants. Igor insisted in his stumbling English that he had documents proving that important Canadians were spying for Russia and that his life was in danger.

Mrs. Coulson was a young, attractive, and efficient secretary, politically savvy and very determined — the crown attorney's own Miss Moneypenny. She got on the phone to the Royal Canadian Mounted Police, the country's chief counterintelligence agency. But Igor had already been to RCMP headquarters, asking for protection. They thought he was having a nervous breakdown and sent him home.[8] Mrs. Coulson was a government employee of some standing, though. She told the RCMP she wanted a Mountie in her office right now.

An officer came over and interviewed Igor, but said there was nothing he could do. Next, Mrs. Coulson called Prime Minister Mackenzie King's office. But the PM was a weak and naïve man who considered Russia a friend to Canada and feared any kind of confrontation. He told her to send Gouzenko and his papers back to the Soviet embassy. King, too, would later regret his indifference as scandal from the Gouzenko defection tore into his administration.

By now, Mrs. Coulson had her blood up. Alternating between French and English and smoking one cigarette after another, she called some newspaper contacts. They wouldn't touch the story. She called her priest. He saved souls, not spies. She phoned the RCMP again. This time she found a sympathetic listener, Inspector John Leopold.

Leopold had tried to join the North-West Mounted Police Expedition-ary Force in 1918 and fight in the Allied war against Soviet Russia, but was turned down because he was too short. Then he worked for years as an undercover RCMP spy in the Communist Party of Canada and succeeded in bringing in eight convictions. He was known as Canada's chief Red hunter, the counterpart to Hoover at the FBI. Leopold told her to send Gouzenko around to his office the next morning.

That rest of that day was an ordeal for the Gouzenkos. Returning to their apartment, they spotted two men standing in Dundonald Park across the street watching their building. Then came a knock at their door. A voice asked for Gouzenko. It was a driver from the embassy. Igor and Svetlana took Andrei out on their rear balcony and gave him to their neighbors, Canadian Air Force Corporal Harold Main and his wife in apartment 5, for safekeeping. A prowler appeared at the back of the building. Corporal Main went for the police on his bicycle while the Gouzenkos took refuge with another neighbor, in apartment 6.

Ottawa Police Constables John B. McCulloch and Tom Walsh arrived and assured the Gouzenkos that they would park out front and watch the building all night. They told Igor to keep the bathroom light on in apart-ment 6. In case of trouble, he should turn it off as a signal.

Meanwhile, Staff Sergeant Cecil Bayfield of the RCMP's Special Branch was dispatched to the scene in plainclothes, apparently by Inspector Leo-pold. Bayfield took a seat on a bench in Dundonald Park across the street and watched from there. Constables McCulloch and Walsh, not knowing who he was, shooed him off. Bayfield left and slipped back into the park from another direction.

Soon four Russians climbed the rear stairs and pounded on the Gouzen-kos' door. Hearing no response, they broke the door down and ransacked the apartment. Constables McCulloch and Walsh rushed up the stairs with pistols drawn.

One of the Russians was Vitali Mavolv, head of the NKGB in Canada. He told the constables that Gouzenko had stolen papers from the embassy and they wanted them—and him—back. Mavolv claimed the Gouzenkos' apartment was Soviet property. The constables corrected him. The apart-ment was not Russian soil the way the embassy was. After a final round of futile arguments, the Russians withdrew.

By that time, word of the Gouzenko documents had swept through high circles. William Stephenson, the Canadian code-named Intrepid who ran the British Security Coordination Office in New York, phoned Norman Robertson, Canadian under secretary of state for external affairs, and advised him to ignore the prime minister and protect the Gouzenkos at all costs. Next morning, Igor met with Inspector Leopold and representatives of British MI5 and the FBI. He showed them documents that revealed the Soviets were stealing important defense documents from Canada. The Gouzenkos were secretly whisked away under guard to a distant safe house for protection. An investigation was begun, code-named Corby, named after the brand of Canadian rye whisky the RCMP officers liked.

Gouzenko identified a number of Soviet agents working inside the Canadian government, including Kathleen Mary Wilsher of the British High Commission and Harold Samuel Gerson of the Department of Munitions and Supply. A total of twenty-one people were prosecuted under the Canadian War Powers Act and accused of operating a Communist "fifth column" in Canada. It was a term coined by Hemingway when he wrote of the Spanish Civil War, referring to traitors who secretly aided an enemy power. Eleven were convicted on various charges. Fifty other Canadians were either demoted in their jobs or allowed to resign. More than two dozen Soviet officials were expelled from the country.

The biggest fish hauled in was Alan Nunn May, a British scientist who had worked on the Anglo-Canadian atomic energy project at Chalk River.[9] He had deep knowledge of all the Allied atomic research programs. His presence at Chalk River might have made him a contact for the Cohens on one of their runs up to Canada.

Also exposed were Soviet agents and fellow travelers high up in the Roosevelt administration, including Lauchlin Currie, FDR's economic affairs adviser; Harry Dexter White, chief economist in the Treasury Department; Nathan Gregory Silvermaster, chief of the division of economic analysis of the War Assets Board; and Victor Perlo, a member of the CPUSA since the thirties who served as a department head in both the War Production Board and the Office of Price Administration. J. Edgar Hoover ordered an immediate investigation.[10] But spy charges were not brought because that would have exposed the existence of the Venona program.

DEFECTOR NUMBER TWO was Elizabeth Bentley. She had grown up in Milford, Connecticut, and Rochester, New York, the daughter of strict puritanical parents.[11] Her interest in leftist politics had first been stirred up in the early twenties when she was outraged by the treatment of rioting steelworkers on strike in McKeesport, Pennsylvania, and by the Sacco-Vanzetti case. At Vassar College she briefly joined the Student League for Industrial Democracy, the Socialist Party activist group run nationally by Morris Cohen's friend Joseph Lash.

While a student at the Columbia University secretarial school, a friend persuaded Bentley to join the CPUSA. That was in 1935, around the time that Morris and Lona Cohen joined up. Elizabeth was in Columbia University Unit 1 of the party and paid the usual dues of a dime a week. She attended the Communist Workers' School at 50 East Thirteenth Street, was taught *konspiratsia*, and assigned a party name, Elizabeth Sherman. But like Lona (who had a bad habit of fumbling passwords), Elizabeth was not terribly efficient at tradecraft, and forgot her cover name.

At first, Elizabeth saw her party work as a reaction to her overly stern, old-fashioned New England upbringing. But she quickly discovered the seamy side of Communism. A Soviet agent, Juliet Stuart Poyntz, tried to pressure Elizabeth into doing some "special work" as an undercover operative in Italy. That meant running a honey trap—sleeping around to obtain information. When Elizabeth refused, Poyntz then accused her of being a Trotskyite and threatened to put her "six feet under." Poyntz was later accused of being a German agent, and disappeared.

Elizabeth Bentley was a tall woman, handsome in a tight-lipped, schoolmarm kind of way. She met Jacob Golos in 1938. The badly dressed but kindly little red-haired Russian who procured U.S. passports for Soviet agents was a welcome relief to her after some of the control officers she had suffered through. Bentley began making the courier run to Washington to pick up documents for Golos from the Silvermaster and Perlo networks. In addition to Miss Wise, she was also assigned the code names Good Girl and Myrna.

Golos's professional light was starting to dim, though, as far as the party was concerned. The CPUSA found itself strapped for cash in '42 and wanted Golos to return fifteen thousand dollars the party had invested in his travel agency. But his agency needed the money, and he resisted. The party then sent young, inexperienced people to deal with him. Like Xenophon Ka-lamatiano at the BSI after the first war, Jacob Golos was considered an old relic and treated in a condescending manner. He in turn complained to Elizabeth that Russians were stupid and cruel people. He developed heart disease and slipped into a pit of depression. As he weakened, he turned more and more of his agents over to Bentley. In 1943, after the party tried to take his best people away from him and demote him to a training officer, he died.

Bentley then managed full networks in both New York and Washington, making her an important Soviet handler. But her new control, Joseph Katz (Agent X), turned on her. He accused her of sloppy *konspiratsia*—failing to get clean of surveillance before a meet, using her apartment for meetings, and allowing members of her New York network to learn one another's identity. She was "precisely the type of person who should not be involved with this group, let alone controlling it," Katz told Moscow Center. He seemed to blame all this on her having been closely tied to the recently discredited Golos.[12]

In February 1945, Moscow Center and Station One took away the agents that Bentley had inherited from Golos and shuffled her off to a dead-end clerical job with United States Service and Shipping Corporation, a party front. Now it was Bentley's turn to feel angry and humiliated. She had also developed a drinking problem. In November 1945 she turned herself in to the FBI as a Soviet spy.

Bentley told the bureau that extensive spying was being carried out through the CPUSA and the Soviet embassy, consulates, and trade organi-zations such as Amtorg. She named names, a lot of names. Most of them were in the Silvermaster and Perlo networks in Washington. Hoover cre-ated Operation Gregory to investigate Bentley's claims. All pretenses of the USSR being an "ally" were thrown out, and hundreds of agents were assigned to the case. Heat was put on the embassy, the consulates, and the trade organizations in the form of close surveillance. Everyone going in or coming out was followed, openly, day and night, by agents on foot and in cars, buses, and subways. This surveillance got so heavy that one night agents in nine bureau cars found themselves parked in the same dead-end street in Washington.

Moscow Center wanted Myrna (Bentley) liquidated. At first it was sug-gested that a poison be put on one of her pillows or handkerchiefs. But

Station One complained that no one in the office had any poison. One of the station officers did have a couple of pistols, though. Moscow Center dismissed that idea. Gunshots would be too noisy. Elizabeth took the subway every day. How about pushing her under the train? No, what if the pusher got pulled down with her? Finally, Moscow suggested that Katz should pick the lock of her apartment one night, slip in, and stab her. Either that, or stage a suicide. Maybe a tumble out the window?

"That's unreliable, since M [Myrna] is a very strong, tall and healthy woman, and X lately has not felt well," a memo to Moscow said.[13]

Finally Boss Beria in Moscow, possibly shaking his head in disbelief at all this, told them to cease plans to kill her.

Alexander Feklisov, an assistant to controller Anatoli Yatskov at Station One during this period, later wrote that more than one hundred Soviet sources were exposed in 1945 because of the Bentley defection alone. All networks were shut down indefinitely, including those run by the Cohens and the Rosenbergs.[14]

It would be remembered as the year of the NKGB's greatest success, the theft of the secrets of the atomic bomb, and its greatest disaster.

Cold War II had arrived.

13 A GRAVE SITUATION

After the war, millions of men and women who had never been more than a few miles from the old homestead returned after years of traipsing through jungles and deserts, eating and drinking things they couldn't even pronounce, and found a world back home they hardly recognized. Before 1941, the United States and Canada had mostly been lands of farms and small towns. Only a few cities had more than a million people. Now new urban centers and highways were sprouting up like weeds after a rain, fertilized by defense industries retooling to turn out washing machines and station wagons for the suburban baby boom.

In the new North America, skirts were shorter, hats taller, cars lower. Freddy Martin and Bing Crosby were at the top of the music charts, but nightclubs across the country were making millions by offering the "race music" that radio stations outside the South didn't dare play before servicemen returned with broader outlooks. The best-selling novel continued to be Thomas Costain's *The Black Rose*, the story of a student expelled from Oxford for his participation in the 1273 riots at the university. Meanwhile, Alfred Hitchcock was filling up theatres with his spy thriller *Notorious*, the story of a German woman (played by Ingrid Bergman) who is sent by an American agent (Cary Grant) to spy on some of her father's Nazi friends in Brazil. But aside from escapist entertainment, the postwar period meant a return to dreams of progress and affluence that had been locked in the cellar during the long hard years of the Depression.

Morris Cohen was mustered out of the army on November 6, 1945, receiving an honorable discharge with battle participation stars for Normandy, Northern France, Rhineland, Central Europe, and the Ardennes Campaign. After he got back to New York, probably in time for the Hanukkah and Christmas holidays, he and Lona continued living in their small apartment on East Seventy-First Street, with a lease running until 1950. In those days before TV sit-coms and frozen dinners, people went out a lot. They went to movies. They went to ball games. They went to spaghetti houses where three courses with wine for two cost three bucks. The Cohens particularly liked the free concerts in Central Park, a fifteen-minute walk from their building.

A January 1946 victory parade down Fifth Avenue in New York offered the last hurrah of the war. Now it was back to basics—finding a job, a spouse, a place to live. Under the new GI Bill, veterans were offered unemployment compensation at the rate of $20 a week for 52 weeks—the 52/20 club—along with free college tuition. Morris chose Columbia University Teachers College and began work there on his master's degree in education in February. Most of the women who had worked in defense industries were being laid off as veterans returned, and Lona found a part-time job in a library. Morris and Lona lived frugally but were comfortable.

While the defections of Igor Gouzenko and Elizabeth Bentley had been major catastrophes for Soviet spying, they had also produced serious embarrassments for the FBI, RCMP, and MI5. J. Edgar Hoover was particularly stung. He considered his FBI to be the best counterintelligence (CI) agency in the world, ahead of even the French Sûreté. But there were key CI officers in the Western agencies who had not been napping while the Soviets played. One of them was Alan Belmont, assistant special agent in charge of the FBI's New York office. He would become the bureau's coordinating officer in the search for Morris and Lona Cohen.

BELMONT IN 1946 ran the major-case squad in New York, which included the office of spy catchers. Belmont had sent special agent Ed Buckley up to New Haven to interview Bentley and persuade her to come down to New York and confess. As early as 1940, Belmont had suggested that people who complained about secret Nazi and Fascist party meetings being held in their neighborhoods should be sent in to join those groups and report their findings back to the bureau. Hoover vetoed the idea, saying that all investigative work should be performed by regularly constituted law en-forcement officers.[1] In other words, it was back to the boys in the suits and fedoras who managed regular, trusted informants. But Hoover was coming around to Belmont's idea, and soon the bureau would be infiltrating the CPUSA so thoroughly that Washington would know what happened in local party meetings before Moscow did.

Alan Belmont was a rising star in the bureau. He was born January 22, 1907, in the Bronx, making him about three years older than Morris Cohen. Belmont's father was an accountant. During the Depression he had moved his family to Cincinnati and Flagstaff, Arizona, before settling in Ingle-wood, California. Alan came from a big family—three brothers and two sisters—and worked as a janitor to pay his way through three years at San Diego State Teachers College (now San Diego State University). He was a tall, neatly dressed boy, with blue eyes, brown hair, and an innocent, almost saintly face. He ran track, played football, baseball, and handball, and somewhere in all that he broke his nose. He also enjoyed recreational shooting and was an expert marksman from an early age.

Belmont transferred to Stanford University for his senior year, and cut grass and waxed floors to pay his tuition before receiving a bachelor's degree in accounting in 1931. Alan loved the West. During summers he panned for gold in the Rockies, managed a trading post in Alaska, and drove a bus at Glacier National Park. One day while he was grinding gears at the park he met Clyde Tolson, one of Hoover's top aides. After that, Belmont wrote a letter to Hoover offering his services. Two months later, in November 1936, he was hired. He was twenty-nine years old.

Al Belmont joined the bureau during the wanted-dead-or-alive gangster era, but didn't see much of that action. He started out as a special agent accountant in Birmingham. Working with numbers was his talent, and he impressed prosecutors with his expertise in fraud cases. His next post was Chicago, where he got into trouble for losing his FBI briefcase, a cardinal sin at the bureau. At headquarters in Washington he managed the FBI basketball team, to Hoover's approval, but was written up for failing to notice that the defroster on J. Edgar's limousine was not working properly. Nevertheless, Belmont rose quickly in the bureau, receiving a promotion and pay hike after each "aw shucks" reprimand from the director.

During the war, Belmont worked as an investigator in the FBI's National Defense Division, monitoring Nazis, Fascists, Communists, and civil rights cases. When Belmont's local draft board tried to draft him, Hoover informed them that he could not be replaced. It was also during the war that Alan finally got to see some of the G-man action he had missed. The occasion was the capture of Roger Touhy.

Touhy was son of a former Chicago cop. He had run a gang in Chicago in the early thirties and fought a turf war against Al Capone's mob. A short man with a big nose and wild hair, Touhy was an electrician by training, though his true callings were bootlegging, armed robbery, auto theft, murder, and kidnapping. Terrible Touhy, they called him. By the end of 1934, three members of his mob were dead, and the other eleven, including Touhy himself, were in prison at Joliet.

In August 1942, Touhy got a couple of pistols smuggled into the prison by a trusty. Then Touhy and six other inmates shot it out with guards, stole a car and more guns, and fled to Chicago. Touhy had been one of the most notorious mobsters of the Prohibition era, the kind of hoodlum that made the FBI—and Hoover—matinee idols. J. Edgar wanted to take over the case immediately. Unfortunately, the prison escapes were state offenses. But Hoover wasn't about to let that stop him. He ordered Touhy's new mob arrested for draft evasion, a federal crime.

Four months later, FBI agents tracked the gang to two apartment buildings in Chicago. Hoover flew to Chicago to personally take charge of the arrests. Veteran FBI shooters were brought in from St. Louis, Oklahoma City, Kansas City, and Saint Paul to augment the Chicago agents.

On Monday night, December 28, the operation began. The two buildings were surrounded and streets were blocked off. Belmont, who consistently scored a perfect 100 in submachine gun practice, was one of the agents who slipped into the two buildings and quietly evacuated everybody except the gangsters.

At 11:20 p.m., two of the mobsters returned to their room in the first building, on Leland Avenue. They found two FBI agents waiting for them, and were shot dead in a gunfight. Five hours later, just before dawn, the FBI turned on powerful floodlights to illuminate the other building, on Kenmore Avenue. Hoover got on a loudspeaker and ordered the remaining gangsters to give up.

The sound of that amplified voice terrified them. Like a warning from heaven, it came in through all the windows and doors. The gangsters quickly followed Hoover's instructions and backed out of the building one at a time with their hands up. Touhy was wearing hot red satin pajamas. When Hoover slapped the cuffs on him, Touhy said it was an honor to be collared by the "big Chief" himself.[2] For his work in the raid, Belmont was given another promotion and a commendation.

Belmont drew additional attention in New York for his handling of William Curtis Colepaugh, a young spy for Germany who was put ashore at Frenchman's Bay, Maine, from a U-boat during a snowstorm in November 1944. Colepaugh (code-named Walter) was an American from Niantic, Connecticut, a former merchant seaman who had defected to Germany. His partner was Erich Gimpel (Edgar), an experienced German spy. The two were sent to America to steal all the military product they could find.

But once they arrived in New York, Colepaugh had an attack of conscience and realized he had made a big mistake. He confessed to an old friend, who helped him get in touch with the FBI.[3] Colepaugh then led agents to grab Gimpel. Belmont spent long hours interviewing Colepaugh and learning the intricacies of German espionage he could never find in a textbook. His preparation of the FBI's case drew additional praise from Hoover.

Dozens of Nazi spies and saboteurs in America had been neutralized during the war. The biggest haul was in December 1941, when thirty-three members of the William Sebold Duquesne spy ring in New York and Florida were nabbed and sent to prison.[4] One of their assignments had been to plant suitcase bombs in Jewish shops. Then in 1942, six members of the George John Dasch ring were executed in Washington. Now that the war was over, the FBI shifted its focus back to Soviet espionage.

Belmont had six supervisors and more than two hundred agents in his major-case division in 1946. Some were native New Yorkers who had wrangled a transfer back home from remote offices like Butte, Montana, which was considered the Siberia of the bureau. New York was considered spook central for Soviet spying in the United States, and Belmont was told by headquarters to develop more informants and step up both physical and technical surveillance. That meant more black bag jobs, wiretaps and hidden mikes, and more cold nights on rainy streets tailing Soviet officials, even if they were just out for a night on the town.

A memorandum to Belmont from headquarters emphasized the "gravity of the international situation" in regard to Russia. "The entire picture of communism as it exists at the present time reflects a serious and tense situation not only from a domestic point of view but from the international aspect," the memo stated. "Consequently, the Bureau must be prepared to face an emergency which might arise at any time."[5]

That "emergency" meant only one thing: possible war with the Soviet Union.

Not only did the FBI get another big budget increase, but President Truman also signed an executive order setting up a federal loyalty program in which civil service employees were required to sign an oath swearing they had never advocated the overthrow of the government by illegal means. At the same time, the names of all known Communists were added to the FBI's security index. In case of war, they would be interned the way Japanese had been in 1942.

In the years to come, Alan Belmont would become one of the top men at FBI headquarters, two doors away from the director's office. As the man responsible for all major investigations by the bureau, he would spend years tracking the Cohens after they fled New York. Considering his dogged determination to stay on their case until he achieved satisfaction, it might be said that Belmont was the Inspector Javert of Operation Whisper.

MORRIS COHEN received a master's degree in education from Columbia on February 26, 1947, and began student teaching at Ben Franklin High School on Pleasant Avenue in East Harlem between 114th and 116th streets. It was a redbrick building with white columns across the front, looking more like a New England courthouse than an inner-city school. But that pleasant façade could not hide the school's internal problems. Two years before, Ben Franklin had been the scene of rioting between black and Italian-American students, but things calmed down after Frank Sinatra appeared on campus for a concert.[6]

Station One contacted the Cohens again in the spring of '47. Their last controller, Anatoli Yatskov, had been pulled out of the United States following Elizabeth Bentley's defection, but before he left in late '45 he instructed all his agents to cease spy activities, destroy any damning evidence they possessed, and not contact anyone at Station One. They were given passwords so they could be contacted in the future. They were also briefed on what they should say (nothing) if questioned by the FBI.

In the summer of '47 the Cohens were sent to Paris at Russian expense to meet with Yatskov, who was now assigned to the Soviet embassy there, and with Sam Semyonov, their first controller. They arrived in time for the Bastille Day celebration on July 14. It was a national holiday, and millions turned out to watch the big military parade down the Champs Élysées. The star of the show as usual was the long cavalry parade of the Garde républicaine, followed by sanitation crews running behind with shovels to clean up after the horses. It was a warm, sunny day, perfect for a holiday. After a blazing sunset, the lights on the Eiffel Tower were turned on, and the Cohens joined Parisians in drinking and dancing at cafés.

Morris was impressed with seeing some noted French Communists at the festival, including Jacques Duclos. He was a party delegate to the National Assembly who had written a letter in 1945 denouncing Earl Browder's endorsement of Roosevelt's New Deal. The "Duclos letter" then led to the removal of Browder as party boss in New York, something the U.S. government had not been able to do even after he was convicted in federal court of passport fraud in 1940 and served fourteen months in prison.

The Cohens were in Paris several weeks. They rented a house and tried not to appear too touristy, despite their heavy New York accents. They had been given expense money but insisted on eking out a proletarian existence on the cheap. That lasted until one of their Soviet comrades told them he was shocked at how thin they looked. They were starving to death, he said. Go to a black market restaurant that ignored the rationing laws and have a decent meal, they were told. They did, but still complained about the cost.

After Lona's success at Los Alamos, the Cohens were the Soviets' most valuable agents in North America. Despite the fact that Julius and Ethel Rosenberg would later be executed for atomic spying, their greatest accomplishment had been the theft of another one of America's most coveted secret weapons in the war, the proximity fuse. The proximity fuse was a battery-powered detonator fitted on the nose of an aerial bomb, rocket, or artillery shell. It sent out radio waves like radar and allowed a projectile to explode at an exact distance from its target. What this meant was that when shooting at an enemy plane, for example, you didn't have to actually hit it. All the proximity-fused shell had to do was pass close to it and explode.

The Rosenbergs were atomic spies only in the sense that they had received some Los Alamos sketches from Greenglass.

Klaus Fuchs, too, was an important atomic spy. But his written description of the atomic bomb didn't reach Beria until October 1945, after Hall's schematic had already been passed on to Moscow Center. And Fuchs's description left some unanswered questions regarding construction of an A-bomb. The Fuchs document was valuable in verifying Hall's report, but now, in '47, Klaus was no longer in the United States.

Feklisov later wrote that the three most important espionage operations run by the Soviets before, during, and immediately after World War II involved the Cambridge Five, the Rosenberg group, and the atomic spies. He added that the Rosenberg network was the "most active" in North America, but "secondary" in importance to the atomic spies.[7]

As of 1947, the top atomic spies had included the Cohens, Ted Hall, Savy Sax, Klaus Fuchs, Harry Gold, and Alan Nunn May. But Hall and Sax were out of the game for the time being, with their eyes on academic pursuits. Fuchs had returned to England, and Gold was about to go into business with a chemist friend. Nunn May was in prison, and David Greenglass, who had made a minor contribution, was disillusioned with Communism and about to vote as a Democrat.[8]

That left the Cohens as the MVPs of Soviet spying in North America. This was based on Lona's having delivered to Station One "the actual specific information" from Hall on how to build an atomic bomb.[9] Now Moscow had decided to reactivate the Cohens, so this was an important business trip for them.[10]

Even with the stolen information that Moscow had received so far on the Manhattan Project, Russia was still way behind the Allies in developing an atomic bomb. Because the Soviets were convinced the Allies were planning a nuclear war against them, building their own nuclear arsenal was a top priority for Moscow. And now there were reports the Allies were developing an even more fearsome weapon, a hydrogen bomb.

While an atomic bomb's blast effect was measured in thousands of tons of TNT, an H-bomb would be measured in *millions* of tons of TNT. The H-bomb would be so powerful that it would require an A-bomb to detonate it. The media called it the Hell-bomb. Beria in Moscow wanted more on the H-bomb and he wanted it now.

Ted Hall, with his Los Alamos contacts, would have been a natural for penetration of the H-bomb project. But he was out of the army and living in Chicago with his new wife while working on a PhD at the University of Chicago. How did Hall feel now about the work he had done for Station One during the war? Was he still loyal to the Soviet Union? Would he do some more work for Mother Russia? Soon the Cohens would be assigned to reestablish contact with him.[11]

WHEN THE COHENS RETURNED to New York from Paris at the end of the summer of '47, they had a new control officer, Yuri Sergeyevich Sokolov. He had entered the United States in March as press secretary to the USSR delegation to the United Nations.[12] That was his cover and it offered him diplomatic immunity while he conducted his spy operations.

Sokolov was a large man with curly black hair and a footballer's build—broad shoulders, and a jaw as wide as the Neva River. Big Yuri, they called him. He was a smoker, spoke English with a heavy Russian accent, and wore wire-rimmed glasses that lent him a studious air. Yuri was twenty-eight years old when he got to New York with his wife Valentina and their two daughters. That made him nine years younger than Morris. He was a graduate of the Moscow Aviation Institute and had served as a security officer at the Yalta Conference in 1947. His code name was Claude.

Morris was supposed to work under a separate control officer, but he had not arrived in New York yet. Until then, Sokolov would run both the Cohens. Sokolov was told to meet Lona twice a month, Morris less often. Yuri got a preview of Lona's tradecraft the first time they met. The rendezvous was on a sidewalk in the Bronx. Sokolov had a photo of Lona so he knew what she was supposed to look like.

A woman approached him. She might be the woman in the photo, Yuri thought. He started the parole by asking if she was waiting for Johnny, which had been Yatskov's street name. As usual, Lona couldn't remember the rest of the patter, except for the word "stinker." She was supposed to call Johnny a stinker. She did that. Yes, Johnny was a stinker, she told Sokolov. But Yuri had the presence of mind to double-check. He asked her about some things that she would know only if she had known Johnny. That way, she managed to pass the audition.

For the rest of that year and into 1948, the Cohens resumed their duties as couriers and recruiters of new assets, though available Soviet documents aren't too clear on exactly what they accomplished. They might have had trouble finding new sources, considering the U.S. government's crackdown on Soviet spying. But Ted Hall and Savy Sax were still on Moscow Center's mind. On April 27, 1948, the Center told Sokolov to have the Cohens renew their ties with Hall and Sax.[13] Moscow wanted Hall to go back to work at Los Alamos after he picked up his doctoral degree in May.

After that signal from Moscow Center, the notes on Soviet spying that Russian journalist and historian Alexander Vassiliev made while doing research at the KBG in the nineties make no mention of the Cohens in connection with Hall until later that year. In an October communiqué, Moscow complained that the activities of Hall and Sax after deactivation had caused a "significant weakening of their position" as agents for Russia.[14] That was a reference to their dabbling in leftist politics, including the campaign to get the name of former Vice President Henry A. Wallace, an admirer of the Soviet Union, on the ballot for the presidency. Ted was also criticized for having joined the CPUSA. That created a public profile that the Soviets had always warned their agents not to do.

That same October message admonished the Cohens for not following instructions to get Hall to stop working for such "progressive" organizations.[15] The note further reprimanded Sokolov for his "poor work" with the Cohens. To make matters worse, the note said the FBI was now investigating Hall's past activities at Los Alamos.[16]

Sokolov was replaced as the Cohens' control officer, apparently because of his alleged poor performance. Their new supervisor was William August Fisher, an agent older and more experienced than Sokolov. But in time, Willie Fisher's new American network would also get rolled up by federal authorities. And when that happened, Alan Belmont and the FBI would find the smoking gun that confirmed the Cohens were indeed Soviet spies.

14 AGENTS ON THE RUN

Growing up, Willie Fisher seemed to have three feet—one each in Germany, Russia, and Britain. But his fluency in the languages of those countries and his daring exploits as a top military spy resulted in his coming home to the Soviet Union in 1945 as a hero of what the Russians called their Great Patriotic War.

Like Morris Cohen, Willie Fisher came from a Communist family.[1] His grandparents—they spelled their name Fischer—had moved to Russia from Germany and prospered as workers. Their first son, Heinrich, grew up to become a proletarian intellectual. At Saint Petersburg he taught mathematics, developed an interest in Marxism, and at the age of twenty-two became acquainted with Lenin. To many Old Bolsheviks like Heinrich, just meeting Lenin once, just touching him, was a moment to remember for the rest of their lives. After getting into trouble for revolutionary activities, Heinrich was told to leave Russia. He and his wife, a fellow radical, moved to Newcastle-on-Tyne, the shipbuilding and coal-exporting city in the northeast of England. When Lenin had seventeen editions of his newspaper, *Iskra* (the Spark), printed in England, Heinrich smuggled them over to Russia on a ship.

Heinrich's son William was born in Newcastle in 1903 and became known by the German diminutive of Willie. He learned German from his father, Russian from his mother, and educated British English from his Newcastle mates. In 1921, during the recession after the war, Heinrich moved back to Russia, taking his family with him. Now that the Communists were in charge, Heinrich was highly regarded in Moscow, and the Fishers were given an apartment in the Kremlin. Willie's interests in art and music grew while his father wrote his memoirs and his mother worked as social secretary for the Old Bolsheviks Society.

Willie was a tall, thin young man with big ears, a long nose, a weak chin, and a modest smile, not particularly handsome, but gregarious and popular. He also had a secretive streak, which would serve him well later. He worked as a translator for the Comintern in the early 1920s and studied art at the Surkikov Arts Institute in Moscow. He also liked building radios, in the days when they were the latest thing in communications. In 1925, at the age of twenty-two, Willie was drafted into the Red Army and assigned to a radio battalion where he endured harsh discipline.

Willie was smitten with Elena Stepanova Lebedeva, a Russian who was studying harp at a conservatory. They were playing the piano together one day when Willie asked for her hand in marriage. Elena was hesitant. She thought Willie treated her as a student more than a lover, always demanding to know how much she had practiced. Did he really love her? Willie considered himself Russian now and gave her a Russian answer: Russians loved everything, he said, including painting, apples, and dogs. But despite his clumsy social skills and repressed emotions, Willie was a gentle man. He and Elena got past that day at the keyboard and were married. Their daughter Evelyn was born two years later.

Willie Fisher was a dedicated Communist, and in 1927 he went to work as a translator for the security and intelligence service OGPU (*Obiedinyonnoye Gosudarstvennoye Politicheskoye Upravleniye*), predecessor to the NKVD. Four years later he was sent on his first foreign spy mission, to Oslo. He worked as an illegal, running a radio shop as his cover while operating a secret transceiver for relaying messages between Moscow Center and Russian agents in Norway. After he returned to Russia he trained new agents, including Kitty Harris, the British-born Russian Jew who would go on to become Earl Browder's lover.

Willie's next assignment was London. There he worked for Alexander Orlov, the illegals *rezident* in the capital and Morris Cohen's future mentor. Willie built London Station's secret radio station but was recalled to Moscow after Orlov's cover was blown. One of Willie's best radio students was Rudolf Ivanovich Abel, son of a Latvian chimney sweep. Abel had been a Red Guard during the Bolshevik coup, and he and Willie joined the Cheka in the same year. The two men were different in appearance and temperament, but became fast friends. Willie would later take Abel's name in New York; after he was arrested, Fisher would continue to insist that he was Abel, and it took years for the FBI to discover his real identity.

During the war, Willie Fisher utilized his German language skills in working behind enemy lines in Byelorussia, posing as an officer of the Abwehr, the Wehrmacht's intelligence service. One day he was summoned to German headquarters to interview a subject who claimed to be a poor Byelorussian itinerant worker sympathetic toward Deutschland. The man had been picked up because his documents didn't seem to be in order. But Willie had been tipped off that he was in fact a Russian spy like himself. Willie interviewed him and offered him a job as a German agent operating against the Red Army. But first he would have to pass a physical exam. To the man's astonishment, Willie told him he had failed the exam. He was then released, and escaped exposure and execution.

That Russian double agent posing as a poor itinerant worker was Konon Molody, who would later surface as the Cohens' control officer in England and one of the Soviet agents rounded up in Operation Whisper.

Molody wrote of Willie Fisher: "This was my first introduction to one of the most remarkable men I have ever met in my life, who is indeed one of the most astute intelligence officers of all time."[2]

Willie was awarded the Red Star and the Order of the Red Banner, and in October 1948 he left his family in Moscow again and headed out for new assignments, this time in the United States. On the way, he changed identities twice. In Warsaw he was issued a dead double passport in the name of Andrew Kayotis, a Lithuanian American whose documents were seized after he died in a Copenhagen hospital. Then in New York City he became Emil Goldfus, who would have been Willie's age, if he had not died as an infant.

But before Fisher met with the Cohens he traveled to the West Coast and scouted locations on the Mexican border where safe houses could be rented, secret radio stations built, and explosives stored. With Russia convinced of a coming war with America, those explosives could be used in sabotage operations. Fisher also set up an escape route from the United States to Mexico City and then into South America for agents fleeing the United States. Finally, in the summer of 1949, he met with Yuri Sokolov at

Bear Mountain State Park, about fifty miles north of New York, and was given control of both the Cohens.

Willie met Lona first, at the Bronx zoo. Willie had a picture of Lona and tailed her to be sure she wasn't being followed. But Lona had a feeling she was being shadowed and took evasive action—changing trains and ducking in and out of stores—to lose him. It was no use. Willie was waiting for her when she showed up at the zoo. The master had arrived.

Fisher rented an apartment in New York, established himself as an aspiring amateur painter, and immersed himself in American life. It was all a cover for his assignment as the Cohens' new controller in New York. Morris and Lona liked Willie and his Old World charm. They spent time with him in the park and invited him to their apartment for a 1950 New Year's dinner, introducing him to friends as Milton. That, of course, was a supreme violation of *konspiratsia* on the part of all concerned. And they did it again a few weeks later, at another party, with Milt again as a guest.

Morris was still teaching as his cover job. There had been no arrests of Soviet spies lately in North America, no defections, no warning flags hoisted. The Cohens were apparently coasting, happy and content, rebuilding their old Volunteer network while enjoying life with their charming new comrade. Life must have seemed as sweet as a spring morning for them all.

But maybe if someone at Moscow Center had listened closely they might have heard the footsteps of another disaster approaching. If they did, they didn't warn Fisher or the Cohens or the Rosenbergs or their other agents in North America. This new catastrophe was going to be the result of an extraordinary series of events occurring at that moment, popping like a string of firecrackers.

It would mean that the time the Cohens had left in America was now down to a matter of months.

IT HAD ALL STARTED back when the RCMP was investigating leads in the Gouzenko case in Canada. Agents searched the residence of one of their suspects, Israel Halperin, and found a notebook with an entry: "Klaus Fuchs, Asst. to M. Born, 84 Grange Lane, University of Edinburgh, Scotland camp N.-Camp L."[3] A copy was sent along to MI5 and the FBI. But who was Klaus Fuchs? The name didn't set off any alarms, and the report was filed away in Washington, Ottawa, and London. That was in 1945.

Flash forward to August 1949, when that American plane flying over Kazakhstan detected traces of radioactivity in the atmosphere, indicating the Soviets had tested their first atomic bomb. To the FBI, this was a very curious situation. This first A-bomb explosion by the Russians had come four years after the Trinity test, but a vice president of Union Carbide, a key contractor in the Manhattan Project, had predicted a Soviet lag of seven years in bomb building.[4] Other sources thought it much greater.

What had happened? How had the Soviets caught up with the West so quickly?

Obviously they had stolen information from the Manhattan Project.

Who had been their agent—or agents—at Los Alamos?

In Washington, an FBI response team was formed, headed up by Special Agent Robert Lamphere. He and some MI5 officers were assigned as advisers to the U.S. Army's Venona program of deciphering Soviet cable traffic that had flowed in and out of the United States during the war. Kim Philby of MI6 would join them for a while, as liaison with the U.S. intelligence community, and as a Soviet mole.

Lamphere was an interesting addition to the bureau's growing cadre of spy catchers. He had grown up in Idaho, son of a mining consultant. He worked in the mines himself during summers and got into a few fights, but in the process learned how to get along with ordinary folk as equals. Bob worked as a clerical auditor at the Treasury Department in Washington while going to night classes at the National Law School, Hoover's alma mater.

Lamphere joined the FBI in 1941 at the age of twenty-three. He was a big, affable man, quick to smile, but also fast to complain and argue when the occasion demanded it. Overall, though, he believed what Hoover preached, that the FBI was an elite outfit built on hard work, discipline, and high moral principles, opposed to the four evil "isms"—gangsterism, fascism, nazism, and communism.

Bob Lamphere had taken on counterspy duties reluctantly. He preferred criminal cases. You investigated, you made an arrest, you testified in court, and that was that. But spy catching was frustrating. It seemed to go on forever. You spent years tracking down some unsub (unidentified subject) only to see him walk free because of diplomatic immunity or lack of admissible evidence. Lamphere also hated boring surveillance duty with its hot days and cold nights of sitting in a car watching some doorway for hours at a time. But he eventually found out that spy work demanded real ingenuity, such as switching briefcases with a subject, photographing the contents, then switching them back again before anything was suspected.

Lamphere and his MI5 associates were looking for the identities behind the code names they were finding in the Venona messages. Finally a picture of a certain mystery spy at Los Alamos began to emerge, slowly, like film developed in a darkroom.

First, there was a February 9, 1944, message from Station One in New York to Moscow Center describing a meeting between Soviet agents code-named Gus and Rest. It said Rest had arrived in the United States as a member of the British Mission to *Enormoz* (the Manhattan Project). He would be working on a process for separation of uranium isotopes.[5]

Second, Lamphere learned that Rest on June 15, 1944, had furnished the Soviets a part of a Manhattan Project document titled "Fluctuations and the Efficiency of a Diffusion Plant." The "MSN" label on the paper indicated that British scientists sent over to work on the Manhattan Project had prepared it. The paper was signed K. Fuchs.[6]

The names of all members of the British Mission were checked. Yes, a scientist named Klaus Fuchs was on the list. Lamphere then found in FBI files a captured Gestapo order for the arrest of a Klaus Fuchs who had been a member of the German Communist Party before the war.

It all added up to this: Soviet agent Rest was Fuchs. In England, Klaus was now head of the theoretical physics division of the Atomic Energy Research Establishment near Harwell. It was a very important top-secret job, just a couple of levels below the top job at Harwell. Beginning in July 1949, Fuchs's mail and telephone calls were monitored by MI5.

That was the way counterintelligence work was supposed to work, by methodically checking and verifying leads—in a word, research. Now the FBI, RCMP, and MI5 had their spy, or at least one of them. But notebook references and code names and a past association with Communists weren't enough. They had to find grounds for arrest and prosecution. In the absence of physical evidence of spying, a confession would do fine.

FUCHS WAS GERMAN, the son of a pacifist Lutheran parson who had gone over to the Quakers. Klaus joined the Communist Party while he was a student at the University of Kiel, and in 1933 got into a street fight with Brownshirts and was beaten and thrown in a river. He fled to Britain where he became a naturalized citizen and took his Communist activities underground. After he earned a doctorate in physics from Bristol University, he was recruited for Tube Alloys, Britain's early atomic bomb program. The next year, in 1941, he volunteered his services as a spy for Soviet military intelligence. He was sent to America to work on the Manhattan Project in 1943.[7]

Klaus Fuchs was a scholarly looking man who spoke with a German accent. He was thin and balding, with slitted eyes behind heavy eyeglasses. A reserved man; some said a cold fish. He was also a dedicated Stalinist who supported the purges of Old Bolsheviks.

The British Security Service (MI5) wasn't getting anywhere with their mail and telephone surveillance of Fuchs, so late in '49 they sent William James Skardon, known as Jim, to have a chat with him. Skardon told Fuchs he was just making some routine inquiries. There had been some reports of a security breach at Harwell, and since Fuchs's father was a resident of East Germany, British officials were naturally curious.

At first, Fuchs stonewalled Skardon. But Skardon was a patient man. He had to be, since he had not been supplied with any evidence from Venona that he could put on the table. Kim Philby's infiltration not withstanding, Venona was one of the most closely guarded secrets in the Anglo-American alliance, and the U.S. Army didn't want word of it to leak out to Skardon, Fuchs, or anybody else. That way, the army hoped to continue deciphering Soviet signals with impunity.

"My golden rule of interrogation is: never let a man get away with a lie," Skardon said later. "If he tells one, stop him, let him know that you know. If you let him tell a lie, he's stuck with it. He has to defend it, and then he'll be led further away from the truth."[8]

Skardon worked to win Fuchs's confidence and get him to open up. Finally Skardon told him, in December 1949, that MI5 knew all about his spy work.[9] He even hinted that Fuchs might be allowed to continue his very important work at Harwell if he would just come clean on the matter at hand. Fuchs became increasingly stressed. He started chainsmoking and walking with a stoop. He had betrayed the country that had given him refuge from the Nazis. He wanted to vent his conscience.

Their talks went on until their fourth meeting, in January 1950. Skardon took Fuchs out to lunch at a hotel, and Fuchs owned up to spying for the Soviets. He was charged the following month.

Fuchs told Skardon he knew his American courier only by his street name, Raymond. He described Raymond as a white male around forty-five years old, 5 feet 8, with dark brown hair, a round face, and a stocky build. That, of course, could have fit a few million members of the U.S. male population. The only real clue—and it wasn't very strong—was Fuchs's impression that Raymond knew something about chemistry and engineering.

J. Edgar Hoover ordered Raymond be found regardless of cost. He called it Foocase. Alan Belmont, now assistant director of the domestic intelligence division in Washington, told Bob Lamphere that all the bureau's resources were at his disposal. Research was renewed, this time with an unlimited budget.

Dozens of agents were shifted over to work Foocase. They checked bureau files for subjects with a scientific background and came up with around a thousand possibles. Some photos of promising subjects were sent to London to be shown to Fuchs but he couldn't identify any of them. The bureau got so desperate they interviewed people at bus stops in New Mexico to see if they remembered any unusual characters from back in '45.

The big break came when agents on a hunch went back and reviewed Elizabeth Bentley's confession to the bureau. She had said that Jacob Golos introduced her to an engineer, Abe Brothman, in 1940 and that he gave her copies of documents he had stolen from Republic Steel in Philadelphia, his employer. Bentley and Golos then passed those documents on to Station One.[10] A further check of the files revealed that Brothman had connections to other chemists and engineers that the FBI had cards on.

Next, agents reviewed the testimony that Brothman gave to a 1947 grand jury investigating Bentley's claims of Soviet spying in America. Brothman testified that he had met Golos through a fellow chemist, Harry Gold. But there was a problem: Gold's photo had already been rejected by Fuchs.

Now a different tack was tried. Agents at the FBI's Philadelphia office secretly filmed Gold on the street to get a more natural view of the way he walked and held himself. They gave the footage to Lamphere and Hugh H.

Clegg, one of Hoover's top G-men from the thirties. Lamphere and Clegg then flew to London to interview Fuchs.

It was a delicate situation because MI5 didn't like Americans poaching on their estate. Nevertheless, on Monday, May 22, 1950, in Wormwood Scrubs Prison, Fuchs viewed the film and identified Gold as his courier Raymond.

Gold's apartment in Philadelphia was searched. He had earlier told the FBI he'd never traveled west of the Mississippi River. But when they found a street map of Santa Fe in his bookcase, he knew the game was up. He was the agent called Gus in that February 1944 message from Station One to Moscow Center that had been Bob Lamphere's first clue to identifying Fuchs.

Gold collapsed into a chair and told them he was their man.

Armed with the confession that Gold was about to give, Alan Belmont could begin a major roll-up of Soviet spies in North America.

Now Morris and Lona Cohen's remaining time in the United States was down to weeks.

HARRY GOLD (né Golodnitsky) had been one of Station One's best couriers. He was born December 12, 1910, in Switzerland to Russian Jewish parents who came to America in 1913 and lived in Little Rock and Chicago before settling in Philadelphia in 1914.[11] He developed an interest in socialism from his mother, and though he never joined the Communist Party, he believed the USSR was free from anti-Semitism and the only country standing up to fascism.

Gold worked in the laboratory of a sugar company during the Depression, and in 1935, at the age of twenty-five, was recruited for spying by an old friend. His controller was Sam Semyonov, the Cohens' first supervisor. Harry Gold was small and plump, with heavy eyes and a moon face, almost a Sad Sack. But he was energetic, dependable, and good-natured, and drew important courier assignments while being somewhat sloppy in *konspiratsia*, as evidenced by the map found in his apartment.

On May 22, 1950, Harry Gold told the FBI that he had traveled to Albuquerque in 1945 to pick up documents from Klaus Fuchs and another Soviet agent. He didn't know who the second agent was, only that he was in the army. Passwords and an identifier (matching pieces of a torn box top) were used in making the contact. After he identified the house where he picked up the documents, the FBI found it had been rented in '45 by David Greenglass and his wife, Ruth.[12]

Greenglass was picked up in New York, and on June 16, 1950, he confessed that he had passed information from Los Alamos to a Soviet courier (Gold). David told agents he had been indoctrinated into Communism at an early age by his sister, Ethel Rosenberg. He had been active in the Young Communist League, but never joined the CPUSA. David was an affable man, with dark wavy hair, a plump face, and a reputation for being honest, though not highly motivated. He had been fired from a job at the Federal Telephone Company for helping organize the shop for a union loaded with Communists. In 1943, at the age of twenty-one, he was drafted, the year after he married Ruth Printz, an attractive buxom brunette he had dated since he was fourteen.

David hadn't told the army about his radical background, and was assigned to the Manhattan Project with full security clearance. Ruth rented the house in Albuquerque and got a local federal job. She had been active in the YCL, too, and though she had reservations about Communism's atheism, she shared David's idea that the USSR was a utopian workers' society.

David's father had operated a machinery shop on the Lower East Side, and the boy grew up playing with machines. At Los Alamos, David was assigned to a machine shop that was forming high-explosive lenses for the first implosion bomb. Greenglass was an amateur sketch artist and made some rough drawings of the lenses. He admitted he gave the drawings to Gold for delivery to their control, Anatoli Yatskov, in New York. The Justice Department charged Greenglass with conspiracy to spy on July 6, 1950. Greenglass also implicated his wife Ruth, his sister Ethel, and her husband, Julius Rosenberg.

Ethel Rosenberg was a small, heavy woman with a talent for singing and acting. She was smart and probably could have done well as a performing artist if she'd had the money for a higher education. Julius Rosenberg, by contrast, was an electrical engineer who seemed content to plod along in shop work, never really getting ahead. Ethel and Julius both had parents born in Russia. They both became adamant Communists at an early age and were insulting toward people who disagreed with them. Julius was charged with conspiracy to spy on July 17, Ethel on August 11.

There has always been disagreement on exactly how involved Ethel was in the Rosenberg network. She wasn't in good health and couldn't go out on local missions the way Julius did, but David Greenglass testified in court that Ethel had talked Ruth into persuading him to spy. That made Ethel a Soviet recruiter. Greenglass also said Ethel typed up the notes he wrote to accompany his drawings.

Like the Cohens, the Rosenbergs were a close couple, and obviously worked together in their spy work. That's why Moscow Center preferred husband-wife teams. Beyond that, some have said that it was actually Ethel who ran the Rosenberg spy ring.

"It is the woman who is the strong and recalcitrant character; the man is the weak one," President Eisenhower wrote after refusing to intervene in the death sentences given the Rosenbergs. Perhaps referring to information not released publicly, Eisenhower added: "She [Ethel] has obviously been the leader in everything they did in the spy ring."[13]

By this time, perhaps some in Soviet intelligence were saying the same thing about Lona Cohen in the Volunteer network.

FROM THE DAY that Klaus Fuchs was charged to the day that Ethel Rosenberg was arrested, a little over six months had elapsed. Some other members of the Rosenberg network were also blown—Joel Barr, William Perl, Alfred Sarant, Morton and Helen Sobell, and Yatskov himself. It was an extraordinarily short period of time for a roll-up of that magnitude.

After Gold had been arrested and his picture plastered on the front page of newspapers, Station One tried to go into damage control by giving ten thousand dollars to the Rosenbergs and Greenglasses and telling them to leave the country. They took the money but refused to go, even though Julius had told David earlier that in the spy game it was acceptable to abandon one's family and go on the run. Moscow then wrote them off the way Washington had abandoned Xenophon Kalamatiano in 1918. Station One moved on to save the Cohens.

On a sweltering afternoon in early June 1950, Yuri Sokolov walked out of his air-conditioned office at the Soviet Mission to the United Nations, located in the Percy R. Pyne House at 680 Park Avenue and East Sixty-Eighth Street, a turn-of-the-century neo-Georgian mansion of red brick and white limestone. He walked up and down neighborhood streets to get clean of surveillance and then doubled back to the old brownstone on Seventy-First Street where the Cohens lived.

It was a dangerous move for a high-ranking Soviet spy to show up at the apartment of valuable American agents. Hoover's men were all over New York, knocking on doors and checking out leads pertaining to the Rosenberg network. If agents had been nearby and recognized Sokolov going into that building, they would have investigated to see who lived there.

Station One didn't send the Cohens' regular controller, Willie Fisher, perhaps because he was out of town on assignment. Or they might have decided it was simply safer to send Sokolov. If Yuri got into trouble, the most the U.S. government would do was declare him persona non grata and put him on a plane for Moscow. But Fisher, an illegal without diplomatic protection, would face the death penalty.

The Cohens didn't have air-conditioning. They were lounging around their apartment in shorts when Sokolov arrived. Yuri made some casual conversation first, in case the place was bugged. Then he took out a notebook and they communicated silently with pen and paper.

Sokolov told Morris and Lona they had to leave the country. Best to do it now, he said, before they got arrested. He emphasized that remaining might be dangerous. "It wasn't my aim to frighten them," he said in a later interview. "I tried to be delicate."[14]

Morris replied that if it only *might be* dangerous, then they still had a chance to do some more work for Station One. We're fighters, he insisted. "We'll fight on."

No, Big Yuri said. He had his orders. They had theirs.

"Well, that's that then," Morris said.[15]

Suddenly Sokolov jumped up. Smoke was coming out of the bathroom. He ran in to see what was the matter. Then he burst out laughing.

Lona, displaying her continuing ignorance of tradecraft, had been tearing off pages from Yuri's notebook and burning them over the sink. But she hadn't been doing it in the proper manner. Yuri showed her how. You roll the paper up into a tube and light it at the top. That way, it burns down and leaves nothing but ash. Even most valuable players need coaching once in a while.

Now go, Yuri told them. Don't take any suitcases. Don't tell the neighbors anything. Just walk out the door as if you were going to a movie. Close the door and never come back.

The Cohens followed their orders, but were a little casual in doing so. First they cashed their savings bonds. Then Morris went up to the Bronx to say goodbye to his folks. He told them he had been offered a good writing job in California, and that he and Lona were going out there. They told friends the same thing at a final dinner party they gave. Then he wrote a letter to the school board resigning his teaching job.

Then something must have spooked them. Maybe they had been in the park and came home to find some men in suits and snap-brim fedoras outside their building, and decided not to go in. Next thing, they were knocking on the door of Jack Bjoze, Morris's friend from Spain. Bjoze saw that they were in an awful hurry.

"They said they were going on a holiday, sort of a last-minute arrangement," Bjoze recalled. "Lona did not have proper clothes. She came to our apartment and asked my wife if she can pick up some things to wear, and my wife was happy to give them to her."[16]

Then they disappeared into the night. They would never see America again. They were gone, like a puff of smoke. Morris was forty years old, Lona thirty-seven.

Later on, Morris's mother, Sarah, went to see Bjoze. She asked if he knew where they were or if he had heard from them. No, Jack replied. But he was certain they were all right.

Some friends of the Cohens did receive postcards from them, mailed from California and Florida. The FBI took the cards in for handwriting analysis but couldn't be certain they had been written by either Morris or Lona. The cards might have been red herrings mailed by Soviet agents. After that, all communications dropped off.

Sarah Cohen went back to see Bjoze several times. But still no word had come in.

"She was devastated," Jack said. "She cried and then left."

The Cohens escaped to Mexico, probably by taking a train out to California and then crossing the border via the escape route that Willie Fisher had set up. Security was lax in those days, and all Morris and Lona had to do was to fill out tourist cards and look prosperous as they passed through for a day of tossing dollars about in Old Mexico.

For Soviet agents on the run, standard procedure was to take a bus down to Mexico City, check in to a modest hotel off the tourist track, and contact the Soviet embassy for passage out of the country. Then they would wait for new passports to be made up, and maybe go deeper into Latin America to board a ship for Europe. While waiting in Mexico City, the Cohens were protected by some members of the Spanish Communist Party in exile.

After they finally arrived in Moscow, in 1951, further trouble awaited them. Stalin had been on another witch hunt against Jews, and Moscow Center warned the Cohens to turn around and get out of Russia fast. They were sent to Poland, where the Center got Morris a job teaching English. That would be their cover while working new assignments.

"It was a complicated trip," Morris said.[17]

PART THREE **MASTERS**

15 WHISPERS OF SUSPICION

Peter and Helen Kroger were a seemingly harmless couple, not really old but definitely at an age when they no longer had much interest in what pop tunes were on the radio or which starlets adorned the pages of the tabloids. They sold rare books out of their comfy cottage in the northwest London suburb of Ruislip, Middlesex, which used to be a quiet hamlet noted for its verdant woodland that could feed fifteen hundred pigs, or so the story went. Hearty souls had been counted beneath these splendid elms as far back as the Domesday census of the British Isles commissioned by William the Conqueror almost nine hundred years before. Now in 1960 it was a postwar boomtown of seventy-two thousand, many of them connected to the British and American air bases down the road. Ruislip was considered a Conservative safe seat, represented in Parliament by an Old Etonian, a reference to the school, not the cocktail.[1]

The Krogers had been in town about five years. They occupied a sturdy bungalow they'd bought at the end of a quiet residential street off West End Road, a short walk from the local train station. They liked to travel a good bit, ostensibly on book business to the Continent. When in Ruislip, they dined out at fancy restaurants, attended the theatre, played a bit of cricket with friends, and during the week they threw parties, lots of parties—tea parties, cocktail parties, dinner parties, garden parties.

Peter and Helen had no children of their own, but they doted on the neighborhood kids, asking about their schoolwork and giving them treats when they made good grades. The children in turn adoringly called them Uncle and Auntie. They played in the Krogers' shady backyard and sometimes inside the house itself, sampling Helen's home-baked cookies and investigating the nuances of her Parisian perfumes. Occasionally they broke something, for which they were quickly forgiven. On the surface it was a quiet, peaceful scene built on affection and tolerance.

Except that some of the grown-ups in the neighborhood weren't so trusting. They didn't exactly suspect the Krogers of anything criminal, but they did harbor certain suspicions. For one thing, the Krogers claimed to be Canadian. Helen liked to reminisce about growing up on a farm in Canada, and seemed offended if someone confused her for an American. But she and Peter both spoke with thick New York City accents. If they had relocated to Canada for some reason, why not be truthful about it?

The second thing was the Krogers' obsession with home security. They had brought in a locksmith from the firm of S. W. Fallshaw to install heavy-duty Yale and Chubb deadbolts on all their doors and windows. Those were serious protective devices for Ruislip, which after all was not exactly the crime capital of Britain.

Helen, known to the neighborhood wives as Cookie, also had an interest in photography that was strange. The snaps she showed guests were embarrassingly amateurish, so why had she gone to the expense of converting a bathroom into a darkroom and outfitting it with expensive developing and printing equipment? With her apparent lack of talent, why not just drop the film off at a photo shop?

And despite Helen's reputation as the Perle Mesta of the neighborhood, the Krogers were never available for social engagements on Saturday nights.[2] They had no time for even a movie and a few pints with mates at a pub. After being repeatedly turned down, their friends had learned to not even ask.

Just how did the Krogers spend their weekends? They kept their lights burning late every Saturday night, sometimes until four in the morning. But filling orders for their moldy old book business shouldn't have required a long night *that* often. And there was nothing on the telly at that hour. What were they *doing*?

Did it have something to do with their mysterious visitor?

He came to visit the Krogers on Saturday evenings and stayed over until Sunday afternoon. He was a broad-shouldered gentleman in his late thirties, with gray eyes and a flair for fashionable suits, hats, shoes. He arrived and departed via a concrete walkway that connected the dead end of Cranley

Drive, where the Krogers' house was located, with another street, Willow Gardens, in the neighborhood to the south. The walkway was for pedestrians only. It ran for almost forty yards, protected from view on both sides by tall wooden fences.

The man always came after dark. One neighbor thought he looked around furtively before approaching the Krogers' front door. Sometimes someone was waiting to let him in as he stepped up on the porch. At other times he knocked in a certain way. A code of some kind?

A secret knock?

The neighbors also noticed that the stranger chewed gum. Americans were famous—or infamous, depending on your point of view—for introducing British children to chewing gum during the war, so was this another Yank to deal with? The joke ever since the first war was that Americans were over-paid, over-sexed, and over here. With their loud music and souped-up cars they seemed to have the social graces of cowhands crashing a royal reception. But they did add a dash of glamour to the old town, and they spent their generous paychecks locally, so why be captious?

The Krogers had arrived in Ruislip with two suitcases, a trunk, and a small collection of cheap furniture. They bought nicer furnishings later on, but their odd arrival was the first brushstroke in a portrait of a couple of characters who were, well, just a little exotic for the time and place. Helen in particular drew attention by wearing men's slacks. Was she trying to be another Edith Summerskill?[3] Feminism was slow to invade outposts of suburban conformity like Ruislip, so some of the ladies in the neighborhood were prone to give Helen a sniff and a disapproving look.

Helen didn't care. As far as she was concerned, people like that were dull and unimaginative. "Meek" was the word she used.[4]

THE CASE of the mysterious stranger took a dramatic turn in the autumn of 1960 when still another unfamiliar face appeared in the neighborhood. This man was taller, thinner, and older, and sported a military-style mustache. He wore a floppy trilby and wrinkled overcoat, smoked a long-stemmed pipe, and carried a battered leather briefcase. When he got out of his plain-looking sedan, he looked around the neighborhood, as if sniffing the air for trouble.

He parked in front of a house on Courtfield Gardens belonging to Ruth and Wilfrid Search, at the intersection with Cranley Drive. It was a cold, blustery day in early November, and the man pulled up his collar as he walked to the front door of the Search residence. Courtfield Gardens, like Cranley Drive, was a clean, neat street of two-story, semidetached (duplex) cottages built during London's suburban boom after the war. Most were plain brown with white trim, and had television antennae growing on the rooftops. Some of the front yards had been paved for off-street parking. There weren't many trees around, but the sunshine was welcome on this raw afternoon.

Ruth Search answered the door. She was a pleasant lady, attractive for her age, the mother of a daughter and a son who were in high school. She looked up at the man who stood before her delivering a chilly wind into her home.

He touched his hat and introduced himself as Jim Skardon, of the Security Service. He showed Ruth his card and gave her a number to call if she wished to confirm his identify. Ruth might have recognized him. Skardon was a former detective with Scotland Yard's Special Branch. The public knew him as the man who finessed confessions out of Allan Nunn May and Klaus Fuchs, which had received extensive media coverage.

British intelligence agents had a reputation for sometimes not being able to talk easily with ordinary folk, and that was why Skardon, a skilled interrogator with a patient and friendly manner, had been brought into MI5 from the Yard. With his slightly disheveled appearance, Skardon was sort of a British version of Columbo. Meeting you in your home, he was always careful to wipe his feet on the mat so he wouldn't dirty up your floor. Then he would graciously compliment your garden, and pet your cat or dog, while accepting your offer of a cup, or glass, of whatever you were having. Receiving Jim Skardon was a bit like having a favorite cousin drop by for a chat, except that he wouldn't hit you up for a fiver.

That gentleness became businesslike, though, when he opened that old briefcase and pulled out some document that would give you a chilling look at the topic he had come to discuss.

In this case, it was the mystery man of Cranley Drive.

Skardon sat down with Ruth and her husband Wilfrid, known to his friends as Bill. Skardon showed them some surveillance photographs. The man in the pictures was of interest to the Security Service. Did they know him? Had they seen him about the neighborhood?

No, they had never seen him before. What was his name?

"Gordon Lonsdale," Skardon replied. At least, that's the name he was using.

Skardon asked Ruth and Bill if they would keep an eye out for Lonsdale. They agreed to. He then gave them an unlisted phone number. They could call him at any time.

Then, having won their confidence with that simple request, Jim skillfully segued to the next favor he wanted. This one was more complicated. He wanted to drop by again on Saturday and Sunday and borrow a room of their house for a surveillance operation. Upstairs, please, with a view of Cranley Drive, he said. Defense of the realm, you understand, very hush hush.

The request landed like a safe hitting the floor.

Ruth protested that the children would be in and out of the house all day Saturday and Sunday. And friends might come over. Skardon's request would be not just an inconvenience, but an intrusion.

Skardon was accustomed to talking people into doing things they normally wouldn't do. It was his job. He had been doing it since before the war. He started talking again, patiently, intelligently, reasonably. He appealed to the Searches' patriotism. He made them feel important, that they had been chosen.

Their resistance began to waver. Jim waited for the expected comfort questions: Just for the weekend, you say? And only during the day? No other interruptions?

Just what had this man done?

Skardon would only say that Gordon Lonsdale had entered the country illegally and was engaged in some illegal acts.[5] No, he was not dangerous. He didn't operate that way. He would do nothing to attract the attention of the police. The Searches had nothing to fear in that regard.

Ruth and Bill finally decided to trust him, and his service. They didn't like it, but they would go along with this somewhat troubling request.

Skardon thanked them and closed his briefcase. As he got up to leave, he cautioned them that no one could be told that a security officer was coming over. The Searches could not confide in any friends, relatives or neighbors—not a whisper.

But what about the children? Ruth asked. They would have to be told something.

Skardon suggested she say that he was just a sort of policeman, making certain inquiries in the neighborhood—collecting background information, that sort of thing. Jim pulled on his coat and walked to the door. Then he stopped and turned around. He had one final question: Did they know of any foreigners who lived in the neighborhood?

Foreigners? No, not unless you counted the Krogers.

The Krogers?

Ruth looked out a window. Peter and Helen Kroger lived right over there, across the road, at 45 Cranley Drive. They sold old books. They were from Canada, though they did speak with New York accents. But don't worry about them, she said. There was nothing suspicious about Peter and Helen. They were dear, sweet friends.

Skardon put his hat on. The Krogers were Canadian? He knew that Lonsdale had a Canadian passport, but he didn't say anything.

Skardon quietly left. With his briefcase and overcoat, he attracted no more attention than an insurance agent concluding a routine call on a client.

But the truth of the matter was that Skardon and his colleagues at MI5 and the CIA and the FBI and British Naval Intelligence were deeply involved in a very serious espionage case called Operation Whisper. Foreign spies, possibly Soviet, were stealing top-secret information from NATO in England. This Gordon Lonsdale was the key to breaking up the ring. The Security Service had given him the code name Last Act.

Operation Whisper was the biggest Western counterintelligence case in ten years. Skardon and his team were working literally around the clock to bring the curtain down on Last Act before more damage could be done to Western security. To do that, he desperately needed the cooperation of Ruth and Wilfrid Search.

OPERATION WHISPER had begun two years earlier, when Ted Shackley, a CIA field officer assigned to the Berlin station, examined a letter that the agency's mail intercept program had flagged. It was written in German, but in some impenetrable doublespeak. It was signed "Heckenschütze," German for "sniper." Shackley reported the letter to Howard Roman, a German-speaking oss veteran and former head of the cia's Polish unit.[6]

Roman was interested immediately. A similar letter had been received by Henry J. Taylor, the U.S. ambassador to Switzerland. The author of the letter refused to give his real name or nationality but claimed to be a high-ranking intelligence officer for a Communist intelligence service. He was offering information. But was it real product, or disinformation? Was he an agent provocateur? An April Fools' prankster? Heckenschütze was given the address of a cia mail drop to which he could send further letters.

Howard Roman and fellow cia officer Tennant Bagley gave their odd new asset the code name Sniper, and began investigating his claims. A year later, in April 1959, Roman conducted a briefing in the fourth-floor headquarters of the Secret Intelligence Service (mi6) at 54 Broadway, opposite the Saint James Park tube station in Central London. It was a tall, imposing stone and brick building that had been elegant when built in the twenties. But these days it welcomed visitors with creaky floors, grimy walls, and echoes of a once glorious past tarnished by a plague of embarrassments in recent years, including the forced resignation of Soviet mole Kim Philby, who had been stealing Venona secrets from Bob Lamphere at the fbi in Washington. The sign out front said the building was the Minimaz Fire Extinguisher Company. During the war, the Germans had posted a spy by the front door, disguised as a blind pencil peddler.

"Sniper says the Russians have got two very important spies in Britain," Roman told the mi6 and mi5 officers assembled in the smoky room. "One in British intelligence, the other somewhere in the navy."

Roman said Sniper was almost certainly working for the ub (*Urząd Bezpieczeństwa*), the Polish security service installed by the Soviets to snuff out resistance to Communist rule in that country. Sniper's product was inside stuff, Grade 1, Roman added.

Sniper had given the two unidentified British spies the code names Lambda 1 and Lambda 2. It would take some time to identify Lambda 1, but Lambda 2 could be found more quickly. He was working for British Naval Intelligence, Sniper said. He had served in Warsaw in 1952 and was now on duty in England. He wasn't sure about the man's name. It was Horton, or something like that.

Naval Intelligence was brought in. Records were checked. A subject who fit the profile was Harry Houghton, stationed at the Royal Navy's Underwater Weapons Establishment on the Isle of Portland, down in Dorset. Portland was conducting top-secret submarine and sonar research for NATO while helping design HMS *Dreadnought*, Britain's first atomic submarine.

Houghton's name was checked in the MI5 central registry. Agents in D Branch (counterintelligence against the Soviets) discovered they had a card on him. Some time ago, Houghton's now-divorced wife had gone to the security office at Portland and complained that Harry had deserted her for another woman, was meeting regularly with foreigners, and had hidden large amounts of money in his garden shed. She suspected he was a spy. The interviewing officer thought this was just another matrimonial tiff. He passed his report to the Admiralty Security Division. They sent it along to MI5. They dropped it into a file and closed the drawer the way they and the FBI and the RCMP had done with the first hints about Klaus Fuchs.

Houghton was a high-school dropout who had served in the Royal Navy for twenty-four years, rising to master-at-arms, imposer of a ship's discipline, before retiring in 1945 with a pension. His early naval duties had included chasing opium smugglers in China (while secretly engaging in the trade himself). But officially his record was honorable during the war—his ships were bombed and torpedoed, and several of them were sunk with him on board. Harry had a surly, boastful side. He liked to tell the story of being on watch on a battleship with Prince Philip, who asked him to make some hot cocoa for the crew.

"I made the cocoa last night," Houghton replied. "Make it your bloody self."[7]

After the war, Houghton worked as a British naval attaché's clerk in Warsaw. It was a minor naval intelligence posting but it allowed him to make a tidy bundle as a spiv (black marketer) illegally selling English gin, cigarettes, and nylons to Polish buyers. Houghton also performed some courier runs for a man who called himself Al and spoke with an American accent.

Al had made his approach to Houghton in a Warsaw bar. He had heard that Harry was on the sniff for U.S. dollars, and offered him a job delivering packages to drop sites. But Houghton was warned that secrecy and danger were involved; if he got caught, he would be on his own. Houghton figured Al was CIA and that he had picked Harry because Polish security agents rarely tailed junior members of foreign delegations. Since the pay was five hundred dollars cash per trip, Harry signed on.

The packages were always delivered to Houghton's apartment by Al personally. Harry made several drops and each time brought back a smaller packet for Al. But then one day Houghton went out to the drop site and rolled aside the designated boulder. But instead of a return packet, he found a human hand that had been severed at the wrist.

"There was only one thing to do, to get the hell out of there," Houghton later recalled.

He found a river and tossed in the package he was supposed to deliver, and resigned from Al's courier service.

Houghton came from a working-class family in Lincoln, a picturesque old Roman city in Eastern England, famous for its cathedral, its castle, and William Foster and Company, builder of the world's first combat tanks. One of Harry's grandfathers was a founding member of the Fabian Society in London, a nonviolent revolutionary socialist club that aspired to be a think tank but which never seemed to get past the level of a noisy debate group. Harry's brother was named Ivor, which their mum thought was English for Ivan. But Houghton never joined the Communist Party. He later said he didn't have any political motives for his spy work. He admitted that he was in the game for the money, a hustler to the end.

At a party in Warsaw, Harry met Karytzia, a beautiful Polish girl who came on to him as sweet as creamed corn. She said she was a concentration camp survivor, and showed him a tattooed number on her wrist. Karytzia was slim, blonde, blue-eyed, and twenty years younger than Harry. He had a love-starved marriage and gratefully fell into her arms. Karytzia helped Harry in his black market sales and saved his life one night by shooting a man who attacked him during a deal gone bad in the rubble of the Warsaw ghetto. Harry and Karytsia parted after he was sent back to England in 1952 for alcohol abuse.

Houghton was given a job as a clerk at Portland. He and Karytsia corresponded for a while, but then her letters stopped. After that, Harry got a phone call. A man said he had just arrived from Poland. He had a message from Karytsia. They met at the Dulwich Art Gallery in London.

The man was an agent from UB, the Polish security service. Karytsia was under suspicion in Warsaw, he said. She had been found politically unreliable, meaning anti-Communist. But she might be shown leniency if good old Harry would provide the glorious fatherland with secret NATO information from Portland. Karytzia might really have been in trouble with the UB, but more likely she was a Communist agent herself and had lured Harry into a classic honey trap recruitment.

Houghton refused the offer. After that, some heavies came around to his caravan (mobile home) and gave him a couple of beatings. Harry then decided to get with the program. After all, money was involved. And he had a heavy drinking habit to support.

He was put into the hands of a succession of Soviet controllers. One of them, code-named Nikki, wearing a heavy overcoat and a hat as broad as Stalin's paranoia, lurked about in the shadows like a cartoonist's caricature of a Russian spy. In a scene reminiscent of John Buchan's *The Thirty-nine Steps,* a terrifying assignment came when Houghton helped two Soviet agents slip ashore one night from a Russian submarine.

First, Houghton received a certain advertising circular in the mail. That was a signal for him to go to his favorite Weymouth pub at 8:45 that night. After he arrived, a phone call came for him. The innkeeper said it was a cousin of his calling. But it wasn't. It was the voice of an unidentified man telling Harry to watch for another advert in the mail. The day it arrived would be the day for the landing.

"Be at Dorchester station at 11:00 p.m.," the voice added before hanging up. That was a coded reference to the time for the secret landing.

Church Ope Cove on the eastern coast of the Isle of Portland was the site chosen for the landing. The beach there had small pebbles instead of large rocks. It was also a secluded area out of sight of the coast guard station and the lighthouse. Harry arrived at the appointed time and parked his car on the cliff above the cove. Below him lay concrete steps descending to the beach. He turned on two battery-powered spotlights with red lenses and pointed them out to sea on a certain compass reading. Then he waited.

It was a miserably cold night and he turned up the collar of his heavy duffle coat. He smoked cigarette after cigarette. But nobody showed up. Finally he packed it in and went home.

He went back the next night at eleven o'clock and again set up his landing lights. This time he heard a motorboat approach. He went down the steps to the beach. Two figures got out of the boat and waded ashore. They wore Wellingtons and suits in an English cut. Houghton went to the prearranged parole.

"Did you get any fish?" he asked.

"None at all," one of them replied.

"What a pity."

They climbed the steps to the cliff while the motorboat turned around and went back to the sub. The two Russians got into Houghton's car. Their destination was a parking lot on the mainland where they would transfer to another car. Harry drove across the island through one town after another until he reached the causeway.

There he was stopped at a police roadblock.

The officers pointed flashlights into the faces of Harry and his two companions. The coppers gave the three men long, searching looks. Had the landing operation been blown?

"Nobody but me appeared to be breathing," Houghton later wrote.

Finally the police waved Harry on. They were looking for an escapee from one of the local prisons, and the men in the car didn't fit his description.

"Thank you, sir," one of them told Harry. "Goodnight."

But now in 1960, with Sniper's information, Houghton was placed under constant surveillance at Portland by naval intelligence agents and by detectives with CID, the criminal investigation department of the British territorial police. Section A4 of MI5, Jim Skardon's squad of about a hundred surveillance specialists known as the Watcher Service, would handle the London end. Skardon's watchers were chosen for surveillance duty because they looked ordinary. The clothes they wore were ordinary. The way they acted was ordinary. If you passed them on the street, you would barely notice them. When fresh faces were needed, their wives were brought in to help out.

The joint surveillance paid off in July of that year. Houghton was observed leaving Portland in his new Renault Dauphine. Detective Sergeant Leonard Burt of Dorset CID phoned up to London to alert Skardon. Houghton was then followed by three unmarked police cars as he and a woman drove to Marble Arch and bought train tickets to London. Plainclothes officers stayed with them on the train. Harry and his companion got off at Waterloo Station, walked to a small park opposite the Old Vic Theatre, and sat on a bench. The woman would later be identified as Ethel Gee. Her friends called her Bunty.

Bunty lived in Portland itself, a small, insular community off the southern coast of England. Basically, Portland was a block of limestone four miles long and a mile wide. It was famous for its Portland Stone, which had been quarried for construction of St. Paul's Cathedral in London and the United Nations building in New York. The NATO naval base was in Portland Harbor.

Bunty was the daughter of a blacksmith, and had left school at age fifteen to work at her uncle's sweetshop in Portland. As a girl, she had been a star player in the local badminton club. She was attractive in a handsome, strong manner. Some thought she was cheerful and gregarious; others thought her a bit of a snob. She had always enjoyed boyfriends, but lived at home and took care of her elderly mother, uncle, and disabled aunt. Aside from not having much time for a social life, she might have been simply bored by the selection of local boys.

Bunty worked at a defense plant during the war and went over to the Portland naval base as a clerk in 1950. She was conscientious and trustworthy, and rose to a position of top-level clearance where she was in charge of storing secret reports on NATO tests conducted at the base. Houghton didn't have a top clearance at Portland. Bunty was the source he needed. He began to romance her.

In 1960, Bunty was forty-six, and putting on weight. Harry was fifty-five and balding, no longer the handsome seaman he'd been during the war. Alcohol had ruined his looks and his temperament, and these days he was chunky, irritable, and cynical. But he knew how to charm a spinster like Bunty, taking her to London on weekends for dinners and shows. They were a frumpish couple who led dull, colorless lives. Bunty probably saw Harry as her last chance for real love.

Houghton paid Gee cash, supplied by the Russians, for photographing Portland documents. He told her the Royal Navy was cheating the U.S. Navy out of information from Portland. He convinced her that her efforts would simply facilitate the flow of information between Britain and America. It was what's known as a false flag recruitment. She thought she was helping the Yanks but was actually aiding the Reds.

Harry and Bunty met a man in the park that July afternoon in 1960. They chatted a while, and Houghton handed him a brown shopping bag. Harry then received a white envelope in return. It wasn't a very discreet pass. The man then drove off in a white Studebaker, a low-slung sports model with swept-back windshield, tail fins, and chromed fenders. It was a wave of American flashiness in a British sea of boxy black taxis and dowdy family sedans, and that made it easy to follow.

When MI5 ran the car's license plate number, they found it belonged to one Gordon Lonsdale, a Canadian who had set up shop as a businessman in London. He, too, was placed under twenty-four-hour surveillance.

Lonsdale was a stocky man with a broad, cheerful face, curly black hair, and bright, friendly eyes, handsome in a darkly Slavic way. When George Blake first met him, he thought that Lonsdale spoke English sprinkled with "transatlantic" (North American) expressions. Blake described Lonsdale as a charming raconteur, an affable hail-fellow-well-met.[8]

Lonsdale had rented office space in Wardour Street, a narrow lane between Leicester Square and Piccadilly Square in Soho. Back then it was a district of sex shops, greasy spoons, and pubs that catered to intellectuals, jazz musicians, and writers planning their next masterpieces while still trying to start their first. At number 19, a narrow three-story brick pile huddled next to the famous old Pinoli's Restaurant, Lonsdale's Automatic Merchandising Company Limited leased out American jukeboxes, slot machines, and gumball machines. Hence, Lonsdale's own chewing habit.

Lonsdale lived ten minutes to the north, in Albany Street, near Regent's Park in the Marylebone district. His address was the White House, a monolithic, stone-faced apartment block from the thirties that would have looked more at home in Miami Beach. It was expensive, but definitely several comfort levels above Soho.

Technicians were brought in from GCHQ (General Communications Headquarters), the equivalent of America's NSA. They broke into Lonsdale's flat and found a short-wave receiver, but no transmitter. They decorated the place with hidden microphones, then moved into the vacant apartment next door. One of the mikes was linked by telephone line to a tape recorder at MI5. There, the ladies who ran the transcribing service were entertained by the sounds of creaking bedsprings and heavy breathing at night as Lonsdale pursed his rather active love life.

Lonsdale was followed to the Midland Bank in Great Portland Street one day, and after he left town on a trip, his safety deposit box there was opened. Security Service agents found in it an impressive set of spy par-aphernalia—Minox and Praktina miniature cameras for photographing documents, a London street map, and a Ronson cigarette lighter with two books of one-time pads hidden inside.

Canadian, indeed. Jim Skardon knew they had a major spy for the Soviet intelligence and security service, now called the KGB (*Komitet Gosudarst-vennoye Bezopasnosti*), on their hands. Lonsdale was apparently a control officer running a network of illegals in Britain.

But where was his radio transmitter?

Once MI5 found the transmitter, they would undoubtedly discover clues leading to the identification of Lonsdale's local agents. This was the sort of thing in which Skardon had specialized for most of his career. He was confident the harvest would be abundant.

THE MI5 WATCHERS noted that Lonsdale had regular habits. He went to the office every morning and raked in money. He took calls, wrote contracts, signed out machines, then took off for lunch. Sometimes he came back in the afternoon. He dated glamorous women and went on singles excursions to the Continent. He seemed to spend most of his time waiting for the sun to go down so he could resume his nightly tours of the clubs and casinos.

Was there really that much money in gumballs?

Skardon noticed that Lonsdale sometimes broke his routine by driving out in a westerly direction in the evening. A tail was put on him, but with strict ground rules. First, no overt surveillance would be allowed: Don't let him see you, don't let him hear you, don't let him smell you. (That last rule was important because a watcher's well-chosen disguise as a beggar, for example, could be blown by the scent of his expensive cologne.) Second, the watcher teams would be rotated, with new faces every day. And third, it was possible that Lonsdale had a police monitor in his car, so radio silence had to be maintained.

The watchers used all sorts of cars—Humbers, Jaguars, an occasional MG. They all had finely tuned engines and were painted a different color and fitted with new license plates every three months. Lonsdale undoubtedly had been trained in evasive techniques, so the watchers used parallel streets when following him through traffic. One of the security officers, Arthur Martin, came up with a plan with an additional layer of security: Have a chase car follow Lonsdale for a short distance one night, then peel off. Next time, a different car with different agents inside would pick up at that point and again follow for a short distance. It was a tedious process, like building a patio by going out and buying one brick at a time. But at last the watchers pursued Lonsdale one night to his destination.

It was Ruislip.

Lonsdale parked in Willow Gardens, at the south end of that walkway that came down from Cranley Drive. Then he got out and walked up the alley. It was too risky for the watchers to follow. There was nothing they could do but watch as darkness masked him from view.

Obviously, surveillance of Lonsdale would have to be picked up at the other end of the walkway. But Cranley Drive was an open street that didn't offer much natural cover. A static observation post was needed, inside the house of helpful volunteers.

That's what had taken Jim Skardon to the home of Ruth and Bill Search on that cold November afternoon.

16 HOUSE OF SECRETS

When Jim Skardon first arrived in Ruislip he checked in at the local police station and briefed the chief constable on Operation Whisper. An important security case was under investigation. A house in Cranley Drive was needed for a stakeout. The chief phoned a trustworthy and discreet family that he knew. Certainly, they said, they would be glad to have a famous MI5 officer drop by for the weekend. At last, something interesting was happening in the old neighborhood.

But the results were disappointing. That Saturday night, as before, watchers followed Last Act (Lonsdale) to Willow Gardens and observed from a distance as he walked up the alley to Cranley Drive. However, Skardon, at the far end of Cranley, never saw him approach. Nor did he see him Sunday afternoon when he should have been walking back to the alley.

After all this surveillance work, the question remained: Where had he gone?

Obviously, Skardon was stationed too far away from the walkway. The host family suggested some friends of theirs down the street, Bill and Ruth Search.[1] Skardon drove down there and found that the side windows of the Search residence offered a clear view of Cranley Drive and Lonsdale's escape alley.

That was perfect.

Skardon ran a check on the Searches. The MI5 registry had a card on Bill. He had served with the Royal Air Force during the war and was now an aircraft engineer with Lucas Industries in Birmingham, a major British defense contractor. He worked on gas turbine engines, a classified job, and had signed the Official Secrets Act.

That made the Searches top-drawer recruits for Operation Whisper.

Skardon then checked real estate records. Yes, the house at 45 Cranley Drive belonged to the Krogers, just as Ruth Search had said. Skardon also confirmed that the Krogers sold old books. An advert in a trade journal, the *Clique*, announced that they specialized in "Americana from the North Pole to the South Pole." The Krogers had no police record in Britain, no card in the MI5 registry. They were just another quiet couple living a quiet life in a community of commuters, it seemed.

But there was an anomaly.

Security officers liked anomalies. They stood out like the sausage in a proper English breakfast. Anomalies drew attention to the unusual, the inconsistent, the little mistakes or contradictions that could open a window on things people were hiding. In this case, it was the nationality of the Krogers. Skardon had called the passport office, and his findings were curious indeed.

If the Krogers were Canadian, what were they doing with New Zealand passports?

And what about those New York accents?

Skardon put it all in his report and went back to Ruislip. But his first weekend in the Searches' home was no more productive than the two days he had spent up the street. Again on Saturday night the watchers followed Last Act all the way to Willow Gardens. But again they lost him as he walked up the alley to Cranley Drive. And because of MI5's radio silence on Operation Whisper, Skardon had not been advised of Lonsdale's approach, and missed him in the darkness.

Where the devil had Last Act gone?

Skardon could have sent out officers to knock on doors in the neighborhood and show photos of Lonsdale. But that would have tipped him off. It would be better to keep knowledge of this surveillance restricted to the Searches for the time being. Next day, Jim returned to his observation post in a second-floor bedroom of the Searches' home.

Skardon was used to the boredom of stakeouts. Cars drove by, children played in the street, somebody up the block worked in his garage. But he stayed with it, keeping his eyes on the street and writing down a description of every person and every car that passed. Then suddenly he spotted Lonsdale. Downstairs, Ruth Search looked out her kitchen window. She saw him, too.

But she was totally unprepared her for the rest of what she saw. It stunned her to the depths of her soul.

Lonsdale was coming out the door of the Krogers' home.

Peter and Helen Kroger were among Ruth and Bill's closest friends. Were the Krogers somehow mixed up in this strange affair being investigated by the Security Service?

Nice, sweet Peter and Helen, threats to national security?

It was unbelievable.

Skardon called his office to report the sighting, then sat down for a serious talk with the Searches. They were a handsome, settled couple, pleasant and unassuming, both wearing glasses as they approached middle age. Ruth had brown hair worn in a neat permanent. Her smile showed a slight strain caused by some health problems. Bill was tall, with an athletic build and thinning gray hair. His expression was thoughtful, undoubtedly suspicious of all this sudden intrigue occupying his quiet home.

Skardon still would not give up any details of the case but again emphasized the need for absolute secrecy. Yes, the Krogers were now subjects of interest to the Security Service. And Skardon wanted to continue using the Searches' house as an observation post, just for a while longer. The Searches didn't like that idea at all.

But there was more to come.

Skardon wanted to install watchers in their house for twenty-four-hour surveillance of the Krogers. A woman would come in during the day, for twelve hours, and another at night. Ruth was secretary of a local arts group, and Skardon suggested that she say the women were visiting club members, if anyone asked. But the Krogers must not under any circumstances find out they were being watched. No hints could be dropped, no jokes made. Life had to go on as normal.

That last part would turn out to be poison for Ruth. She spent a lot of time with Helen. They shopped together, they had coffee together, they spent hours in delightful conversation. Ruth would have to go on seeing Helen, pretending that nothing was wrong?

It was a lie, a monstrous lie.

She could not do it, absolutely not.

Why couldn't Skardon just walk across the street and knock up the Krogers and ask them what they knew about this Gordon Lonsdale? That was the last thing Skardon wanted to do. If the Krogers were spies like Lonsdale, they would all quickly skip the country. That wouldn't have been difficult in those days before heavy antiterrorist security was installed at airports and ferry terminals. You didn't even have to purchase an airline ticket in advance. If you were running late, just grab your passport, board the plane, and buy your ticket once you were seated.

Skardon also pointed out that if the Krogers were such sweet, close friends of the Searches, why had Peter and Helen never mentioned Lonsdale and his all-night visits?

But Ruth was adamant—no, no, no.

Finally, Skardon told the Searches, in a diplomatic but firm manner, that the government needed their house. The government was asking for their cooperation at the same time it was insisting upon it. He also reminded them of the Official Secrets Act. Under that law, it was illegal for anyone to communicate to anybody else any information that might be useful to an enemy. In other words, the Searches should not divulge any word about this operation to anyone, least of all the Krogers. A violation of the secrets act could send them both to prison.

With that, the Searches realized the enormity of the situation. There was no use arguing about it, they were in this thing whether they liked it or not. They decided to do their duty and cooperate.

AS THE SEARCHES had feared, the stakeout turned into a grind. The weekend stretched into a week, the week into a month, that month into another. The surveillance team watched the Krogers' house and everybody on the street. They made notes. They took pictures. They reported in on a special hotline. The Searches marked the days, and nights, with growing tension and anxiety.

Complications arose several times when Helen Kroger popped in for a visit. Ruth had to make certain that Helen didn't go upstairs for any reason whatsoever. On one such occasion, the operation was almost blown when

Helen strolled into Ruth's kitchen and noticed a purse on the kitchen table. Helen didn't recognize it as being one of Ruth's. In fact, it belonged to the watcher hiding upstairs. Ruth gave Helen a quick smile, scooped up the purse, and tossed it into a cupboard.

"That daughter of mine never puts anything away," she said.[2]

Meanwhile, MI5 investigated the background of the Krogers. Official records could only provide clues to the truth that waited somewhere out there. To get the kind of results that would stand up in court, they would have to follow the procedure that had served detectives so well from time immemorial: knocking on doors and talking to people.

When the Krogers applied for a mortgage on the Cranley Drive house early in 1955, they had listed their address as 18 Penderry Rise, in Catford, Southeast London. Officers drove down there and spread out to canvass the neighborhood. Catford was another suburb of duplexes, short on trees but heavy on TV antennae, with streets beginning nowhere of interest and ending no place of importance.

The Krogers had rented the furnished house, through a real estate agency, from a doctor who was going to the United States for a while. They introduced themselves as Canadian book dealers relocating to England for a better climate. They had been staying in a hotel while house hunting. When asked for references, they had none except for a letter from a Swiss bank guaranteeing the weekly rent of five guineas. That was good enough for the doctor. He liked Peter and Helen.

Peter rented temporary office space nearby and began selling books there. He left the house early and returned late at night, so he didn't have much time to socialize with the neighbors. But Helen introduced herself to everybody in sight. Her openness was a shock to suburban Brits who hadn't been around North Americans before. Soon she was a popular addition to the block. Children and dogs loved her.

But while Peter worked during the day, Helen drank. Gin it was, all day long. When a neighbor stopped by, she would offer the bottle instead of the teapot. Still, despite her coarseness and her sometimes-violent temper, Helen was described as a kind and considerate sort, always ready to lend a hand or an encouraging word. But she was also observed crying in her backyard several times. Acquaintances could see she was under a terrific strain. They attributed this to the couple's not having children of their own.

The suburbs were no place for an ambitious antiquarian book dealer. Peter knew he had to get to Central London, where the big auctions were held. He rented space at 190 the Strand, an aging, soot-stained brick building across from St. Clement Dane's Church, which had burned during the war. Detectives found Peter's office to be one large room at the back of the building, down a long hallway past a tobacconist's shop. Shelves held hundreds of books. A glass partition separated his space from that of a secretarial agency that provided a constant symphony of noise from typewriters, ringing phones, and copy machines.

Peter's closest friend in the book trade was Oswald Frederick Snelling— Freddie, to all who knew him. Snelling was an auctioneer's clerk at Hodgson's in nearby Chancery Lane, one of the top auction houses in London. An auctioneer's clerk was more important than the auctioneer himself. The clerk knew the books, he knew the sellers, he knew the buyers. He kept the records and offered advice (and warnings) to his customers, some of whom were regulars, while others were just in off the street.

Snelling had written three books on boxing, and was one of Ian Fleming's author friends. Snelling would soon become famous himself, for turning out the first critical analysis of Fleming's spy books, titled *Double O Seven James Bond: A Report*, published under the name O. F. Snelling (London: N. Spearman, 1964). Freddie would admit it wasn't very well written. But he would beat Kingsley Amis to the starting gate, and make millions.[3]

That was a little in the future. Now, in the autumn of 1960, Snelling described to security officers his first meeting Peter Kroger. It was back in July of '55. Kroger had walked into Hodgson's and introduced himself as a recently arrived Canadian who wanted to set up an antiquarian book business. Peter was a striking looking man, Snelling recalled. He had a deep tan and spoke educated American English, though with a working-class New York accent. His hair was white and wrapped around his head like a turban. He wore a pale-blue double-breasted suit with wide lapels, a white nylon shirt with long collar points, and polished brown shoes in a basket weave.

"If his object was to draw attention to himself as an obvious American," Snelling later wrote, "he could have done no better."[4]

But as far as the book trade was concerned, it was painfully obvious that this intelligent, witty man didn't know a bleed from a block.

In ways, Snelling was just the opposite of Peter. Freddie's suits were conservative and fashionably Continental, offset by a starched shirt and club tie. He wore a modern style of glasses, and a mustache. His vocabulary showed that he was a well-read man, but he spoke in a staccato voice like a sportscaster. An old friend of Freddie's described him as a "die-hard royalist forever loyal to the crown," a man who had married several times but was absolutely devoted to his last wife, Molly, a Jamaican.[5] Freddie liked eccentrics and innocents, and took an instant liking to this odd North American who stood before him. Snelling took Peter back to his musty, dimly lit office, where he kept a high chair above a scarred and sloping mahogany desk like some latter-day Bob Cratchit. There the lessons began.

At first, some sharpies recognized that Peter Kroger was a rube, and took advantage of him. One of them sold him an entire basement full of old books which turned to be imperfect and not marketable. But Peter took it in stride, and with Freddie's help he learned to make crafty buys. Freddie and Peter played darts together and drank pint for pint at the Mitre. They played cricket in the annual booksellers' match between the Bibliomites and the Guv'nors, where Peter entertained everybody by swinging the bat like Babe Ruth. In time, he was elected into the prestigious Antiquarian Booksellers' Association and became one of the top dealers in London. Soon he and Helen were regularly seen in evening dress as they made the rounds of clubs and theatres in the West End.

But maintaining a shop in the Strand was expensive, Peter soon told Freddie, and he was losing time in his daily commute. He wanted to work at home. So in October of '55, he and Helen bought the bungalow in Ruislip from a former policeman for four thousand pounds. They had the entire house rewired, central heat installed, comfortable new furniture brought in, and those heavy locks installed. Peter began moving books into the house, and in 1958 he left the Strand. Thereafter, he ran a catalogue business from home. One of his favorite expressions was, "Well, what's new?"

Some of Peter's other associates in the book trade told security officers that Kroger's passions in life, aside from his books, were his wife and his 78-rpm phonograph records. Helen was overheard saying at a party once that Peter was "the perfect lover."[6] He never discussed politics but admitted to an admiration of Russian history and Russian composers. Tchaikovsky was a favorite. So was Verdi. Peter also favored the works of Stephen Vincent Benét and Sir Walter Raleigh.[7]

Investigating MI5 officers made a note of that: Subject liked music and poetry by foreigners.

Other security officers questioned people in Ruislip who knew the Krogers. Neighbors and shopkeepers were reminded of the Official Secrets Act, and sworn to absolute secrecy about the inquiries. They all mentioned Helen's brilliant blue eyes. Those eyes had grabbed Peter's attention immediately they first met, she liked to say. Her figure had also attracted him, she would add, performing a little pirouette. But she was putting on weight these days because of her drinking, and tried to hide it by wearing a baggy barn jacket. She also dyed her hair brown to hide the gray. She was a short woman with red-painted nails, a coffee-grinder voice, a brassy manner, and a vocabulary to match. Imagine Thelma Ritter at a Manchester United football match.

Yes, everyone agreed, Peter and Helen were a bit odd. But you often saw that in childless couples. And yes, they had suddenly appeared in Ruislip as if out of nowhere, with no friends or family in tow. They didn't talk much about their past. They didn't even have pictures from their wedding. Like instant coffee, they seemed to have been a creation of the moment.

But London was a grand Old World capital finally throwing off her shawl of prewar provinciality and postwar austerity. The city was becoming a cultural center for music, art, writing, fashion, and cinema. The Swinging Sixties had arrived, and people were flocking here from all over the world for all sorts of reasons. London was growing accustomed to the sartorial misadventures of mods and rockers, and Elvis movies and British beat music brightening up the entertainment landscape. Now there was even talk of color TV coming to the old BBC. Some thought it all rather intriguing.

Oh, one more thing: The Krogers had a big multiband radio receiver in their living room in Cranley Drive. It was an expensive, top-of-the-line model with wonderful speakers. Peter liked to keep an ear on foreign broadcasts while playing bridge at home Wednesday nights with Snelling and other friends. He especially liked Radio Moscow. They had some of the best music shows on the air, including a jazz show that was popular with Western listeners.

That went into the notebook, too. Subject listened to a Communist radio station.

PETER WRIGHT, a brilliant electronic surveillance agent, was added to MI5's Operation Whisper team. He had studied farming at Oxford, then did radar research for the Admiralty at the Marconi Company until 1954, when he joined the Security Service. His vetting consisted of an interview by a personnel officer who gave him a Masonic handshake, asked if he had ever been a Communist or a queer, then sent him along for two days of counterintelligence training. There was one other recruit in the class.

Wright was a stooped man with bad teeth, a long hooked nose, thinning gray hair, and eyebrows as unruly as a briar patch. He was one of the oldest men in his service. Like many of his associates at MI5, he was a heavy smoker, and he spoke with something between a lisp and a stutter. He was assistant to Hugh Winterborn, director of A Branch (the technical department), and was MI5's first bona fide, full-time scientist. As the office techie his mission was to advise branch directors on how to drag musty MI5 into the twentieth century.

Peter Wright and Jim Skardon clashed several times. One of their arguments involved Wright's suggestion that a man and a woman working together as watchers would draw less attention than two men. Therefore, more women should be hired. Skardon opposed the idea on the grounds that the wives of the male agents wouldn't like it. Then they bickered over Wright's suggestion that three watchers in a surveillance car were too many. They made the vehicle easy to spot by the opposition. But Skardon insisted that three agents really were needed: one to drive, one to read the map, one to take radio calls.

Wright had also shown the audacity to suggest that something be done about the MI5 registry, on the ground floor of headquarters. For one thing, the registry had no fingerprint files. And their American counterpart, the FBI, had been using UNIVAC computers for at least six years, while MI5 officers still wrote reports on paper and stored them in file cabinets, hundreds of them. To find a certain file category, a steel rod was inserted through punch holes in a master index card. Then after the files were located, they were sent upstairs to the offices by dumbwaiter (a lift, not an employee description). But Peter was quickly informed that computerization would mean that the army of attractive young debutantes who worked as file clerks would have to be laid off.

Wright later admitted that he made a crucial mistake in Operation Whisper. It happened after he made an important trip to Washington to report to the FBI on a new system of radio surveillance he had developed.

Peter didn't like the big Justice Department building on Pennsylvania Avenue where FBI headquarters was located. Wright thought it looked like a mausoleum. And he said that the dictatorial J. Edgar Hoover suffered from "God disease." But Peter got along instantly with Alan Belmont, who was now supervisor of all major-case investigations and was about to be promoted to the number-three spot at the bureau.

Everything passed across Belmont's desk—case summaries, requests for more manpower, inquiries from associated agencies. Belmont was known as an agent's agent. If something good happened, he saw to it that the field agents got the credit. If something went wrong, he took responsibility for it himself. Wright and Belmont retired to Al's office, sent up a bank of cigarette and cigar smoke, and swapped spy stories. Al brought Peter up to date on one of the most important cases the bureau had ever cracked.

The subject was Willie Fisher, still known to the FBI in 1960 by his cover name of "Colonel" Abel. Fisher had arrived in New York in 1948 and posed as an aspiring artist, living in a dirty thirty-five-dollar-a-month studio apartment on the top floor of a brick pile at 252 Fulton Street in Brooklyn. His sooty window, and the copper antenna wire he had strung outside for his shortwave radio link to Moscow, faced the federal courthouse across the street. Willie's acquaintances in the local artistic colony, including the painter Burt Silverman and the cartoonist Jules Feiffer, knew him as Emil Goldfus.

Willie Fisher was no longer the brisk, tailored young army officer who had saved Gordon Lonsdale's skin during the war. He still exuded Old World charm and was only in his early fifties, but stress and time had not been kind to him, and in New York he acquired the graying, seedy look of a man who'd come back from being on the bum. Drawings in his sketchbook showed old men in parks playing checkers—forsaken loners, adrift in the middle of a big city. Perhaps that's how Willie, away from home and family for years, saw himself.

"There's something about guys like that," one of his acquaintances said. "No matter how much their look improves, they never lose that look. And he's got it."[8] Willie might have been stuck with the face of a starved eagle, but his voice and his confidence were still strong. That confidence, and his spy career, were shattered by Reino Hayhanen, a Latvian sent by Moscow to work as Willie's assistant in 1952.

Hayhanen's code name was Quebec. He knew Fisher only as Mark. Hayhanen was tall and overweight, a generation younger than Fisher, with pale blue eyes, sloping shoulders, and hard workman's hands. He dyed his hair, mustache, and eyebrows jet black, which made him look a little like King Farouk. Willie sent him on missions to Colorado and Massachusetts, and they made other trips together to Atlantic City and Poughkeepsie.

Hayhanen would later complain that Fisher looked down on him as an intellectual inferior and treated him like a chauffeur. But Hayhanen's main problem was vodka. He drank it every day. He beat his wife. He blew assignments for Willie. Finally after he stole $5,000 in KGB funds, Fisher sent him back to Moscow, ostensibly to deliver some product. Let the Lubyanka deal with him.

Hayhanen got as far as Paris and sobered up long enough to figure out the real reason why he was being sent to Moscow. He walked into the U.S. embassy and gave himself up as a Russian spy who had been trying to steal atomic secrets in America. But the legal attaché on duty didn't know, or care, anything about spy cases. In a scene reminiscent of the Gouzenko case, he put Hayhanen in a taxi and sent him to the CIA station. Over there, the duty officer shook his head. No, this was an FBI case. He sent Hayhanen back to the embassy. This time, the legal attaché cabled FBI headquarters, which he should have done in the first place, and Belmont told him to put Hayhanen on a plane for Washington.

Hayhanen identified Fisher as his control. Aside from his Brooklyn studio, Fisher was found to have a room (10 by 13 feet, $29 a week) at the Hotel Latham, 4 East Twenty-Eighth Street. He was registered as Martin Collins. When FBI and U.S. immigration agents raided the room and arrested the naked Fisher at 7:00 a.m. on June 21, 1957, they found $4,000 in cash wrapped in brown paper.

The parcel also contained two photographs. One was a photo of a man. On the back was written: "Have you taken a trip to Frisco since we last saw you?" It was signed "Morris." The other photo was that of a woman. On the rear was written: "How are Joann's murders [sic]?" Signed, "Shirley."[9]

Informants who knew the Cohens identified the pictures as those of Morris and Lona. The messages on the photos were paroles to be used for identification. It's a mystery why Fisher would have been holding cash for two agents who had left the country seven years before. Possibly one of Fisher's agents was going to meet the Cohens somewhere, maybe at a Canadian or Mexican airport, and deliver the cash to them as they passed through on one of their missions for Moscow.

The photos, the paroles, and the cash all confirmed to Belmont that the Cohens were indeed Soviet spies. Their connection to Fisher meant they were major players. He ordered their file brought up and sent out a small army of agents to knock on doors again. Belmont got the Cohens' wartime fingerprints from the files, added those two more recent photographs, and sent out wanted flyers to FBI offices in Rio, Paris, Bonn, London, Rome, Madrid, Tokyo, Havana, Ottawa, and New York. From those legations, leads were pursued in ten additional nations. The International Criminal Police Organization was not brought in because some Interpol members were from Communist countries.

The worldwide manhunt for Morris and Lona Cohen was on. They had made fools of the American, Canadian, and British counterintelligence agencies for too long. Al Belmont, the FBI's Inspector Javert, was not going to let them get away this time.

But where did Peter Wright make that crucial mistake in Operation Whisper?

He later described it this way: While he was in Belmont's office, he volunteered that MI5, too, was working on a major Soviet spy case, in Britain. He described Lonsdale, Houghton, and Gee. Belmont didn't know anything about them.

But when Wright described Peter and Helen Kroger, their approximate ages, and their New York accents, Belmont sat up.

Maybe they're the Cohens, Belmont said. Check the flyer we sent you in '57.

Wright made a note of that, and failed to follow up on it.

17 LOCK, STOCK, AND BARREL

British Security Service headquarters were located in Leconfield House, Curzon Street, Mayfair, an anonymous-looking triangular office building with wide windows that burned like Arctic ice in the wintery sunlight. For those who worked there, its mystery was the mystery of secrets themselves. It veiled and suckled them, and cried for bigger and bigger appropriations to nourish them. The premises included a private bar, the Pig and Eye Club. There MI5 staff could relax for drinks without running the risk of leaking any of those treasured secrets to barmaids at nearby pubs.

It had been twenty-one months since Howard Roman of the CIA first gave MI5 the clues that led to the identification of Harry Houghton and the opening of Operation Whisper. Now, in January 1961, the stakeout of Peter and Helen Kroger's house had reached its ninth week. Roger Hollis, director general of MI5, called for a full review of the case.

Jim Skardon, Peter Wright, and other top officers working Operation Whisper gathered in the director general's outer office on the fifth floor, standing and smoking in the midst of secretaries, typewriters, and wall-mounted safes. Finally the light above the DG's door turned green, the electric door lock snapped open, and they were admitted into the inner sanctum. It was a sunny, high-ceilinged office with antique furniture and cushioned chairs that stood at attention around a polished conference table. Coffee and tea were served, and the men settled in.

Hollis stared down at them from the head of the table. He was a tall, hunched man with thick black eyebrows that stood out as last bastions of resistance against his encroaching baldness. He had just turned fifty-five, and wore his signature starched white shirt, pin-striped suit, and club tie. The son of an Anglican bishop, his penchant for partying had resulted in his rustication from Oxford before he could graduate. He then worked seven years in Shanghai, for the British American Tobacco Company and the *Shanghai Morning Post*, before returning to England with tuberculosis. The *Times* and MI6 turned him down for employment but MI5 hired him in 1938 on the basis of his knowledge of the Chinese language and the Far East business climate.

Hollis liked to pinch women's rumps at MI5 and tell bawdy jokes, for which he seemed to have a talent. Some of the officers under Hollis saw him as an uninspiring hack, an aloof, condescending man with a lopsided, silly smile and the parade-ground manner of a passed-over major. But his closest friends knew that many of his personality problems were caused by his being trapped in an unhappy marriage, and that he was having an affair with his secretary, whom he intended to marry.

Hollis had been one of the senior officers who approved Klaus Fuchs for duty with the Manhattan Project in the United States. That, and claims by Soviet tipsters that a Communist mole had burrowed his way into the very top of the British intelligence community, had convinced Peter Wright that Roger Hollis was Moscow's most dangerous double agent in London. Years later, that suspicion would be echoed by Robert Lamphere, who wrote that "there remains little doubt that it was Hollis who provided the earliest information to the KGB [NKGB] that the FBI was reading their 1944–45 cables."[1] But to be fair, Lamphere's accusation was based on a book he had read about Hollis (Chapman Pincher's *Their Trade Is Treachery*). If Lamphere had accessed FBI or MI5 sources for his information, he didn't name them.[2]

Another new addition to the Operation Whisper team in Hollis's office was Special Branch Detective Superintendent George Gordon Smith, a blustery self-promoter who had racked up an impressive record of arresting Nazi and Soviet spies and Irish and Israeli terrorists in Britain in the past. Commander Evan Jones, head of Special Branch, had instructed Smith to have his detectives help the MI5 watchers monitor the London activities of Houghton, Gee, and Lonsdale. In Portland and Weymouth, their movements would continue to be followed by naval intelligence agents and Leonard Burt's squad of CID detectives.

Superintendent Smith was tall, stout, and balding, a well-dressed gentleman with a beautiful daughter who (luckily, he admitted) had inherited his wife's looks. George was the son of a Wiltshire farm laborer. His first job, at age eight, was delivering milk before dawn. He spent years working as a pantry boy and a footman before joining the Metropolitan Police in 1926. Smith's lack of formal education belied his natural intelligence, his keen eye for details, his ability to lead complicated street ops. He was quickly moved up to Special Branch, which had been founded in 1883 as the Irish Branch, charged with countering terrorism by the Fenians.

Smith was the same age as Hollis, and had been a copper for thirty-four years. He had a close professional relationship with J. Edgar Hoover and was one of the few Yard men allowed access to MI5 and MI6 secrets. Like Skardon, he had a reassuring, amiable manner about him that hid an inner toughness. Fleet Street loved him. He was always good for a quote or a tip. They called him Moonraker, a popular nickname for men from Wiltshire.[3]

Superintendent Smith was necessary to Operation Whisper because MI5, unlike the FBI and the RCMP, had no powers of arrest. When it came time to prefer charges against the Portland spies, Special Branch would do the honors. Smith intended to slap on the cuffs himself, accompanied by his usual entourage of adoring reporters and photographers.

After Moonraker was welcomed to the Portland spy case, Hollis reminded everyone in the room how much Operation Whisper was costing the government. Exactly where did they stand? He was quickly brought up to date on the surveillance results:

—The first time Harry Houghton and Gordon Lonsdale met after
their July 1960 rendezvous was on Saturday, August 6, of that year. As
before, Houghton came up on the train, but alone this time. He got off
at Waterloo Station, in southeast London, and met Lonsdale at the same
time and place, 4:00 p.m. outside the Old Vic. But on this occasion,
instead of going to a park, they walked four blocks over to Lower Marsh,
a crowded market district just off Waterloo Road. They went into
Steve's Restaurant at 30 Lower Marsh, a small eatery barely wide enough
for a row of tables, tucked in between a low-end men's store and an
ironmonger's shop. A cigarette machine stood guard out front beside the
greasy window.

They took a table and ordered a pot of tea. Two detectives with tape recorders in their pockets sat down at an adjacent table. The conversation between Lonsdale and Houghton was clearly heard, and recorded.

"You seem to have plenty in there," Lonsdale said, grinning and pointing at Houghton's brown suitcase that sat on the floor by the table. "It certainly is fat. I reckon you've got a lot of work for me to do tonight."

Houghton laughed. "You're right," he said. "You'll have to burn some midnight oil to get through it all in one go."

They agreed to meet again on the first Saturdays of October and November, and then they finished their tea and left. They walked over to Baylis Road, and Houghton stepped into a red phone booth. Passing documents openly in a public park was bad enough, but now they showed another amateurish display of tradecraft. Houghton took a parcel and an envelope from his suitcase, wrapped them in a newspaper, and left them on the shelf in the booth. This, while Lonsdale was standing just outside. Then Houghton stepped out, and Lonsdale stepped in to take the bundle.

—The second meeting was Saturday, November 5. The scheduled October meeting had been canceled because Lonsdale went on another trip to the Continent. (He later said that some of his trips over there were to spend a few days with his Russian wife in one of the East European capitals.) The November meet was at 6:30 p.m. in the Maypole public house, in Ditten Road, Kingston, a southeast London suburb. It was a traditional English pub, with fireplaces, a dartboard, rooms to rent upstairs, and a bar as wide as Soviet ambitions in Britain. They drank scotch, exchanged briefcases, and then Lonsdale got into his Studebaker and drove up to Ruislip, followed discreetly by three MI5 chase cars. The next day, Sunday, was when Jim Skardon and Ruth Search spotted him leaving the Krogers' house.

—The third meeting was Saturday, December 10. Lonsdale was waiting at Waterloo Station when Houghton and Bunty Gee got off their train at 4:15. Bunty was carrying a bag. Again, they went to that little park by the Old Vic. The tops of the trees were barely catching the last afternoon light, and the sidewalk was crowded, so the watchers weren't able to see a pass. But Lonsdale drove to Ruislip that night, indicating he had picked up new product to pass on to his people up there.

Hollis digested the report, then turned to Charles Elwell, from D Branch (the Soviet problem). Elwell, too, had gone to Oxford, where he read modern languages. He joined the Royal Navy in 1940 and smuggled Special Operations Executive agents into occupied Europe for two years until he was captured by the Germans and locked up in Colditz Castle, a prison for "incorrigible" Allied POWs.

Elwell had grown up with a pretty face, curly blond hair, and a delicately formed mouth. That led him to be cast as women in two plays staged by Colditz prisoners—as Lady Bracknell in *The Importance of Being Earnest* and as Mrs. Eynsford-Hill in *Pygmalion.*[4] He turned down further such prison roles because he did not wish to be typecast as old bags. Like Hollis, Elwell dressed elegantly and spoke in a direct, military manner. But Elwell had an infectious sense of humor, which unfortunately never seemed to infect the DG. Elwell had joined MI5 in 1949 and quickly became one of the service's most dedicated Red hunters. Like Wright and Hollis, he was a farmer at heart.

Hollis had a question pertaining to Elwell's participation in Operation Whisper. It involved a photograph that MI5 officers found in Lonsdale's safety deposit box. The picture showed Elwell and his wife at a party together. The person with them was none other than Lonsdale himself. Spy meeting counterspy and having a lovely time, it seemed.

Hollis *was* rather curious about that.

All in the line of duty, Elwell assured him. His wife had enrolled in a Chinese language course at the School of Oriental and African studies at the University of London. Lonsdale was in the class, too. The picture was taken at a party for students. Elwell had attended the party so he could observe Lonsdale close-up.

(Lonsdale would later say that he had taken the language course because the class was packed with Western agents and he hoped to pick up information by eavesdropping on them. One day an American student in the class turned to him and said: "Listen, Gordon. Except for you and me, they're all spies in here!")

Right. Back to business then. What about the Krogers in Ruislip?

Skardon, Wright, and Elwell laid their bones on the table, as bare as they were. The Krogers worked at home. They brought in groceries, they took out the garbage. They mailed out books, they entertained friends. They went out to dinner parties, restaurants, and plays, and returning home they didn't even run a red light. Except for those all-night visits from Lonsdale on Saturdays, all seemed dull and ordinary at 45 Cranley Drive.

But there was one thing new, Wright added. All heads turned toward him, expecting another one of those anomalies that hungry spies like on their plates. Wright reported that some residents of the neighborhood had complained of some kind of strange interference to their radio and television sets. Investigators from the General Post Office, the agency that regulated broadcasting, had visited the complainants and listened to the loud squeals blasting out from their speakers. They knew immediately what they were—oscillator interference. An illegal radio transmitter was operating somewhere in Ruislip. Its signals were so powerful that they were stepping on the regular broadcast bands. The GPO had sent a detector van with signal tracers to Ruislip and was trying to locate the source of the illegal transmissions. Wright was betting that the transmitter was Lonsdale's secret link with Moscow, and that it was hidden inside the Krogers' house.

The frustrating thing was that the more they found out about Lonsdale, the more apparent it became that his secrets were as deep as a writer's imagination. Who the bloody hell *was* he? Elwell reported that Alan Belmont at FBI headquarters had requested that the RCMP run a background check on Lonsdale. The Lonsdale in London had a legal Canadian passport, but was he the real Gordon Lonsdale? He might have been a ghoul who used birth and death records to obtain a dead double passport. Elwell was standing by for answers.

There was also the continuing problem of the Search family, Skardon reported. They had been putting up with surveillance agents in their house for over nine weeks now. They had had enough. To be precise, they had had enough eight weeks ago. Bill and Ruth Search were not counterintelligence agents trained in techniques of deception. Sooner or later, an accident was bound to happen. A word, a look, a tone of voice could tip off the Krogers.

But the Searches weren't the only ones having trouble keeping secrets. Freddie Snelling and the other bridge players at the Krogers' house (all of whom had been questioned by MI5) couldn't help making spy jokes from behind their cards when Peter got up to tune in Radio Moscow. And at a party given by the Krogers' friend Frank Doel, a bookseller with Marks and Company and the subject of *84 Charing Cross Road*, Helen Kroger had arrived looking exotic in a long black evening gown, which prompted Doel's wife Nora to remark:

"Helen, you look just like a Russian spy!"[5]

Hollis looked around the table at his officers. What do you recommend? Arrest the five Portland spies now? Or wait for their next scheduled meeting?

Arthur Martin spoke up. It was too early for a roll-up, he said. Lonsdale was probably the illegals control officer for other Soviet agents in Britain. Some of them might be highly placed in the government. Continued surveillance was needed. He was adamant about that.

Martin was also in counterintelligence at MI5. A former army signals officer in the war, he had worked the Klaus Fuchs case with Skardon. Arthur had never attended an exclusive public school, and so, with Wright, he had little use for the British class system that had propelled souls like Hollis into the upper echelons of government.[6] Martin was a short, balding man who liked his scotch. He was also a quiet observer of body language. If the subject of an interrogation twiddled his thumbs, Arthur made a note of it. If he looked out the window, he made another note. An old friend of Martin's described him this way: "He was the consummate professional, with a permanent air of the slightly disappointed, mildly lugubrious, but not entirely without a sense of humor."[7]

But like the others present, Martin was tired and frustrated with Operation Whisper. Still, he argued for staying the course. Lighters came out, and pipes and cigarettes were lit again. The others backed him up with a chorus of concurrences.

But the pressure to do something had arrived at Hollis's desk in a sealed envelope. The message was from Cleveland Cram, PhD, the plump, amiable CIA deputy station chief in London. Cram was a Harvard man and Anglophile who worked as CIA liaison officer with Britain's intelligence services. Later on, he would find himself part of a CIA plot to render MI5 irrelevant by flooding London with American agents, money, and computers.[8] But his communiqué to Hollis was about to save Operation Whisper.

Cram's note concerned Sniper, the CIA's Polish source in Warsaw whose tip had led to the discovery of the Portland spy ring. The British had given him the code name Lavinia. Cram reported that a Soviet double agent somewhere in the West had alerted Moscow Center to the leaks that Sniper had been providing the CIA. The KGB had assigned Sniper himself to root out the pig (traitor) on the rusty side of the Iron Curtain. Fearing for his life, Sniper and his wife had defected to the U.S. military mission in West Berlin.

Sniper had finally identified himself. He was Michael Goleniewski, vice chairman of Polish military intelligence, and he said that the Soviet mole who had blown the whistle on him was in the CIA. But then he announced that Goleniewski was not his real name. To everyone's astonishment, he claimed he was actually Grand Duke Aleksei Nicholaevich Romanov, son of the late Nicholas II.⁹

What a day for Operation Whisper. But regardless of whether he was a madman or not, Goleniewski had put British, American, and Canadian agents on the track of the Portland spies. Now, though, as soon as Goleniewski's defection was discovered, Lonsdale, Houghton, Gee, and the Krogers would probably be warned by Moscow Center. Look for a late-night rush on plane tickets to the East.

Obviously, the Portland spy network would have to be rolled up right away. Lonsdale was due for another Saturday meeting with Houghton, Gee, and the Krogers in two days. The men in Hollis's smoky office agreed that it would be the day to bring down the curtain on Last Act and his supporting cast.

AS SOON AS THE OFFICERS working Operation Whisper left Hollis's office, they set to the tasks assigned to them. Superintendent Smith went to Bow Street Magistrates' Court and got search warrants for Lonsdale's office and flat, and the Krogers' house. His top aide, Chief Inspector Ferguson Smith, drove down to Dorset to brief Detective Superintendent Bert Smith of CID. Bert Smith got search warrants for the houses where Houghton and Gee lived. Naval Intelligence was contacted and they confirmed that Gee was being supplied with false "secrets" that wouldn't cause any harm to NATO. But time was a factor, they added, since Lonsdale sooner or later would figure out they were throwing him chicken feed.

That night, a joint MI5/CID team stationed themselves in the narrow lanes surrounding Houghton's house, a low-priced cottage in Meadow View Road, Broadwey, Weymouth. The town was a pleasant resort of yellow beaches and white seaside Georgian buildings just north of Portland.

Houghton had lived in the Weymouth house with his wife Peggy after he gave up his trailer home. Now that she had divorced him, he had the place to himself.

It was cold as frozen glass that night, but the watchers couldn't turn on their car heaters because the noise of the engines would alert the neighbors to the presence of strangers sitting out there in the dark. Sustaining themselves on hot tea and fish and chips, the men sat and watched the house all night. The interiors of the cars began to stink of fried grease and tobacco smoke.

At 6:30 a.m., a light was switched on in Houghton's bedroom. The watchers radioed a message to the duty officer in Superintendent Smith's department at Scotland Yard.

An hour later, they sent another signal: Houghton had just driven off in his red Renault Dauphine.

A third message was telephoned directly to Moonraker at his home in Hounslow, near Heathrow: Houghton had picked up Ethel Gee at her house.

Harry and Bunty crossed the causeway from Portland to the mainland and headed toward Salisbury, a larger town where they could board a train for London. The MI5 and CID watchers followed in chase cars. They had to be careful, though. The road was icy, and in the chalky morning light the slick pavement was joined, almost without horizon, into a sky the color of a dead man's pallor.

At nine o'clock, Moonraker's driver pulled into Victoria Street, Westminster. In the winter bleakness, London looked like a drained rock garden. Rain and frost had eroded last fall's repairs to rooftops and pavements, and the sharp edges of the city poked out through the gray mist blowing in from the river. A guard waved Moonraker's car into Scotland Yard, headquarters of the Metropolitan Police.

The Yard was an imposing complex of nineteenth-century stone and brick buildings whose colors had been stained and faded by a century of facing the elements. The buildings looked down on the river Thames from behind trees along the Victoria Embankment, and in the summer the smell from the water was sour and rotten. With all the turrets, ramparts, and spiked iron gates in there, one could almost expect the ghost of King Hamlet to appear. Headquarters got its name from its first building, which had originally been part of the old Whitehall Palace and was the place where royalty from Edinburgh used to stay on visits to London.

As Superintendent Smith entered the building he passed photographs, paintings and citations on the walls that recorded the history of Scotland Yard. The first detectives had taken over police duties from the Bow Street Runners established by Magistrate (and novelist) Henry Fielding. Charles Dickens admired the new force so much that he modeled his Inspector Bucket in *Bleak House* after a friend in the Yard. Arthur Conan Doyle wasn't so kind. His most famous Yard detective, Inspector Lestrade, was portrayed as a rat-faced, tenacious, nitwit. Queen Victoria wasn't impressed, either. After the Jack the Ripper murders, she ordered more detectives added to the force. The police commissioner went out and bought a pack of bloodhounds. They promptly got lost in a fog.

Moonraker's Scotland Yard was the modern version. It had helicopters, walkie-talkies, fingerprint files, and electric typewriters, though like M15 it was slow in coming to an understanding with the computer age. Nevertheless, when the superintendent swept into the detective section this morning he sprayed the office from his atomizer of energy and optimism. He had been up since six, eating breakfast, reading the morning papers, and selecting a disguise for the day. He had settled on a black French beret offset by a tan raincoat. But it wasn't a British trench coat. For a spy operation, that would be too clichéd, too obvious. He had chosen instead a tan raglan, a long baggy model with no epaulets or belt.

The rest of the morning was dominated by attention to details. Any more delays in the train? Yard cars gassed up, tires checked, radios working? For security reasons, the operatives assigned to the roundup were not allowed to leave the building or make outside phone calls.

Superintendent Smith stood by in the radio room and watched the big clock on the wall. Phone calls were coming in constantly—questions from officers, demands from press contacts, plus the usual criminal complaints of robbery and murder that someone had to address. Finally, Ferguson Smith's voice burst out from the radio speakers.

Icy roads had caused Houghton and Gee to miss the 11:50 train to London. They had just boarded the 12:50 at Salisbury. They were due to arrive at Waterloo Station at 2:45.

Superintendent Smith went back to the squad room. He called together the small team of men and women detectives he had assembled from the Yard. They were joined by Jim Skardon and a select group of MI5 apostles of bumper surveillance. In all, probably two dozen officers made up the team. Moonraker inspected their disguises, looking for obvious flaws. What was the use of dressing like a wino in old clothes when you were wearing polished black police shoes? And glue that mustache on straight.

The superintendent briefed them on the final stage of Operation Whisper. They would all go to Waterloo Station before Houghton and Gee's train arrived. They would fan out to their assigned positions covering the platform and the doorways. Unmarked radio cars would stand by outside to swiftly transport the prisoners to the Yard once they were in custody.

Superintendent Smith knew the three spies by sight. He would fall in directly behind Houghton and Gee as they walked out of the station to Waterloo Road. All the watchers should keep their eyes on him. As soon as Lonsdale met up with Houghton and Gee and took their bag of purloined product, Moonraker would pull out his handkerchief.

"As soon as I wave my handkerchief, get straight to me and grab the prisoners' hands," he told his headhunters. "Prevent them from destroying anything, and do not allow Gee to open her handbag. Maintain your hold on all three until we reach the Yard."

Once Lonsdale, Houghton, and Gee were in custody, Moonraker would send out a radio call: "Lock, stock, and barrel." That would be the signal that the first three subjects had been apprehended. Moonraker checked to be sure all watches were coordinated.

All right, then. Time to get on with it.

The agents and officers pulled on their hats and coats, picked up the various accessories necessary to their disguises, and went down to the garage. Some were teasing one another about their costumes. Others were more reflective, drawing on their pipes and thinking about the task that lay ahead.

But there was definitely a feeling of excitement in the air. This specially chosen team was on its way to break up the most dangerous Soviet spy conspiracy discovered in Britain since the Klaus Fuchs and Alan Nunn May cases. By the end of this day, the men and women of Operation Whisper would have traced their initials in the wet concrete of Cold War history.

They would find out later, just as Jim Skardon had expected, that today's raid was coming just in time. Up in Ruislip, the pressure of deceiving the

Krogers had turned Ruth Search almost hysterical. After each visit by Helen, Ruth would sit down and cry.

Ruth had almost blown the operation at a holiday party. She baked a pie for the Krogers, and then considered, but rejected, tucking a note inside with a warning to Peter and Helen:

"Go!"

18 A MACBETH MOMENT

Saturday, January 7, 1961, was the day the final curtain would be dropped on the KGB's London Players. In the morning, while Detective Superintendent George G. Smith was at Scotland Yard briefing his operatives for the impending Operation Whisper roll-up, Peter and Helen Kroger drove down to London in their Ford Consul and did some shopping. They met Gordon Lonsdale for lunch and gave him some letters on microdot they'd received from his family in Russia. He in turn gave them a letter he had written to his family that they could microdot and send along to Moscow. They parted expecting to see him that evening in Ruislip with another shipment of goods from Harry Houghton and Ethel Gee.

"Hello, my darling, I congratulate you on the past 43rd anniversary of the October [Revolution]," the letter from Gordon's wife Galyusha began. It was a stock Soviet greeting, like "Merry Christmas" in the West. Galyusha chatted about her teaching job. One day as she and her students were singing a certain patriotic song, she became overcome with sorrow that her husband was not with her. "It reminded me of our life in Prague and I felt very, very sad," she wrote.

Referring to the brief visits they had been allowed in Europe since Gordon had left Russia, she said, "Whenever we meet, we have to rush off and we are left with very little time." She was also "greatly distressed" about the grades their daughters Liza and Dina had made in school. She closed by saying that she had gone to a party given by some of their friends and they all toasted his health. "Everybody remembers you with good words," she said.

Liza in her own letter promised to improve her grades next term. "Winter has already set in here," she added. "Aunt Vera fell and broke a leg. The leg still gives pain. Grandma is well. Daddy, all of us are expecting you. Come home quickly. Trofim recently wrote a letter to you and kept on dictating to himself, 'Dear Daddy, come home quickly.'" She signed it, "Many, many kisses, your daughter, Liza."

Lonsdale's young son added a postscript: "Daddy, come home quickly, Trofim."[1]

Back in Ruislip that afternoon, Peter typed letters to some of his customers abroad. Then he wrapped a few books, put on his coat, and told Helen he was going to the post office.

Peter walked out his front door and down the steps to the short driveway in front of his garage. The weather had cleared up. Now it was cold and bright, a dazzling afternoon that offered a welcome break from the gloomy rain of that morning.

The Krogers' home had been built before the war. It was a white-stuccoed frame house with two bay windows in front, a high roof, and a dormer, a plain but substantial dwelling constructed in the days when a full cut of lumber was still a full cut. It sat quietly with curtains covering its windows like petticoats, and wood smoke rising from its chimneys to blend with the wintry smell of leaf mold.

The radio had warned of freezing rain or snow later on, so Bill Search across the road was washing his car before the weather turned. Peter called out to him. Bill looked up, gave a short, disinterested reply, then went back to work with his sponge. Normally, Bill would have stopped to joke around for a while. But today, for some reason, he just clammed up. He seemed distant, distracted.

Strange, Peter thought.

He walked up to Ruislip High Street, a broad avenue of trees, cottages, shops, a five-hundred-year-old pub, and a police station with an air-raid siren that was turned on for a test now and then, just in case. In the background, the sound of children running and laughing echoed up side streets beneath the roar of nuclear-armed strategic bombers taking off from the British and American airfields south of town.

It was an hour's hike to the post office and back. Peter liked the exercise. Taking a walk also gave him a chance to think about another odd thing he had noticed—the appearance of a certain vehicle in the neighborhood, an unmarked panel truck painted a forgettable shade of some nondescript color. But its anonymity was betrayed by its government license plates. Peter recognized it as a radio-detector van sent out by the General Post Office.

The sight of a detector van in itself was not unusual. New families were moving into Ruislip every day, and the GPO drove through once in a while fishing for signals that indicated someone had not bought the license required for home use of a radio or TV. But this van had come down Cranley Drive several days in a row now. Was the Krogers' short-wave transmitter causing interference somewhere? One reason they had moved to Ruislip was because they thought their transmissions wouldn't be noticed in the crowd of military radio signals coming from the two air bases. The last thing they wanted was for government snoopers to come prowling around their house.

Then Peter was struck by two more peculiarities.

The first one occurred at the Ruislip post office, a three-story brick building nestled between other historic old treasures in the original core village. As Peter later described it, his sixth sense was activated as he approached on the front sidewalk. He got the distinct feeling he was being watched.[2] But when he looked around he didn't spot anyone paying any attention to him.

But was that a movement behind a window upstairs? Was somebody watching him from up there?

Maybe it was just his imagination.

Then again, maybe not.

The secret work that Peter and Helen performed behind the bolted doors of their house was not founded on certainties. It was based on deceit, distrust, doubt. Suspicion was a safe emotion for them. Suspicion kept them alert to early warnings of trouble. Suspicion provided an edge that they needed.

Peter posted his letters and packages and walked back to Cranley Drive. Arriving home, he saw that Bill Search was gone, leaving nothing behind but a puddle of soapy water on the ground.

Then he noticed something even more alarming.

Strangers were strolling up and down the alley that connected Cranley Drive to Willow Gardens to the south. Women wearing scarves and winter coats were carrying shopping bags. Men were toting packages. All of them looked very ordinary. The limited pedestrian and vehicular traffic at this end of Cranley Drive was a primary reason why the Krogers had bought this house in the first place. Why were there suddenly so many people down here? And up the street, a maintenance crew was working on the road. He hadn't noticed any pavement problems there before.

Peter felt danger in the air. He could smell it. He could taste it. The success of the Krogers' secret work depended on discretion, timing, and vigilance. One slipup and they could face the gallows.

Inside, Peter warmed himself and discussed the situation with Helen. Nothing threatening was happening at the moment, so they didn't panic. But if trouble really was brewing, if their amazing run of luck after all this time was about to end, then now was the time to get out. With the passports and the load of cash they kept hidden in their house, they could simply get in their car, use the evening traffic to get clean of surveillance, and head for Heathrow Airport.

They knew the drill for a getaway: no suitcases, no overnight bags, no parcels. Don't take anything that couldn't be dropped into a purse or pocket. Don't call a taxi, don't say anything to the neighbors, don't leave a note for the milkman. Keep the lights on and a radio playing. Walk out, drive off, don't look back.

But they hated to do that. They liked it here in England. They had renovated this house to their own tastes, their garden gave them flowers and apples every year, and the local train could deliver them to Central London in thirty-nine minutes (theoretically). They had a fairly new car, a cadré of loyal friends, and a good living selling old books. All in all, a comfortable, upwardly mobile life.

To flee, or to stay? They might be minutes away from disaster. They had reached a Macbeth moment. Turning back might be just as tedious, and dangerous, as continuing on.

They carefully considered their options. They were supposed to go down to the West End tonight to meet another book dealer for dinner and a play, Bertolt Brecht's *Galileo*, then return to Ruislip to conduct their late-night business with Lonsdale. He was coming over a little after seven o'clock and would be here waiting when they got back. If trouble was indeed afoot, the Krogers wanted to wait and talk with him before they left for the theatre. If Lonsdale agreed that it was time to get out, it would be better to coordinate their plans.

They phoned his Wardour Street office and his White House flat. They

got no answer at either location. They decided to cancel their dinner and theatre plans and wait here for Gordon. They would not abandon their friend.

DETECTIVE SUPERINTENDENT SMITH'S TEAM took their assigned
positions at Waterloo Station, Britain's biggest rail terminal. It was a heavy
stone Victorian building, with the main entrance, called Victory Arch, facing
Waterloo Road. The Old Vic, the Portland spies' favorite rendezvous, stood
off to the right in the next block. Moonraker paced the long concourse. The
steel girders overhead supported translucent roof panels that admitted an
eerie light that was not completely artificial, yet not truly natural. A vast and
gloomy shed, Robert Louis Stevenson had written about the place.

Peter Wright, Arthur Martin, and Martin Furnival Jones, head of D
Branch (Soviet counterintelligence) at MI5, were standing by at Leconfield
House. They had been in the third-floor operations room all night. It was
a small, brown-painted room not much bigger than a prison cell, with a
table, a bed, and pile of cables in the floor connecting them to the bugs
inside Lonsdale's flat and to hot lines coming in from Special Branch and
GCHQ. They had spent the night smoking, eating sandwiches from a pub,
drinking scotch, and listening to Lonsdale's bedroom exercises with a girl
he'd brought in.

At Waterloo, Superintendent Smith checked to be sure his people were
ready. Some were dressed as businessmen in suits and bowler hats, carrying
rolled-up umbrellas. Two wore old clothes like bums. Another pair was
disguised as railway porters. Others pretended to be peddlers, with boxes
of matches and shoelaces slung around their necks. They had all heard the
announcement that the train from Salisbury was late.

Smith took up position by gate 14. He stood reading a newspaper, trying
to appear inconspicuous. But the rakish way he wore his beret attracted
the attention of a charming young man who walked up and propositioned
him. Moonraker shooed him off and checked the big clock hanging from
the ceiling. It was 3:20.

The train from Salisbury finally rumbled into the station. The engine
stopped at the buffers, and passengers began getting off. Now they were
filing into the station. Superintendent Smith turned a page of his newspaper
as he watched.

Suddenly, Houghton and Gee were beside him, passing close enough to touch. Bunty held a shopping basket. Chief Inspector Ferguson Smith had gotten off the train behind them. In case the subjects turned and tried to go behind the train to an exit, he would be there to follow them.

But Houghton and Gee strolled out a side door to York Road and Superintendent Smith followed them up to Waterloo Road. Then the couple crossed the street and boarded a No. 68 bus that had stopped by the Union Jack Club. That was a surprise move. The superintendent looked around. Two of his men caught his look and got on the bus behind Houghton and Gee. Other officers followed in a radio car.

The subject of a surveillance is called a rabbit. The pursuers are hounds. At East Street in Walworth, the rabbits and hounds got off the bus together. They all meandered through the crowded market inspecting the fruit and vegetables for sale in the stalls. At 4:15 they all got back on the No. 68 bus and returned to Waterloo Road.

But the rabbits still had time to kill. They walked over to Lower Marsh, and back again, with Moonraker's team lurking in doorways and around corners. At 4:30, Houghton and Gee returned to Waterloo Road and stopped in front of the Old Vic, a plain-looking building, for all its fame, with dirty brick walls but featuring tall, impressive white windows that fronted the road.

Superintendent Smith spotted Lonsdale's Studebaker parked about fifty yards up the street. Lonsdale got out, stepped up on the sidewalk, and approached Houghton and Gee. The three of them then walked together down Waterloo Road.

Lonsdale was in the middle, with an arm around each of their shoulders. To a casual observer on the crowded sidewalk, just three mates strolling to a pub in the dying light of a winter afternoon. Superintendent Smith came up from behind, closing the distance.

After a few steps, Lonsdale reached down and took the shopping basket from Gee.

That was it.

The superintendent took out his handkerchief and waved it behind his back. Passersby stepped aside as a squad of porters, peddlers, winos, and suited gentlemen descended on the scene from all directions with pistols tucked under their belts.

Superintendent Smith trotted around the three spies. He got in front of them and stood blocking their way.

"You are all under arrest," he said. "I am a police officer."

"What?" Harry Houghton said in a weak voice.

"Oh!" was all Ethel Gee could manage. She thought at first that she was being accosted by a bunch of teddy boys, youngsters who wore rockabilly haircuts, dressed like American zoot-suiters of the forties, and liked to engage in the occasional street fight.

Moonraker introduced himself as Detective Superintendent George Smith of Scotland Yard. Houghton and Gee turned pale and looked like they were going to faint. Gordon Lonsdale, the professional trained for such contingences, did not open his mouth.

Three radio cars raced up and slid to a halt at the curb. Moonraker took the shopping basket from Lonsdale, and officers hustled him into the first car. Detective Sergeant Anne Winterbottom led Gee into the second car. Ferguson Smith guided Houghton into the third. The superintendent went to his own car.

"Lock, stock, and barrel!" he said into the radio mike.

The cars sped the prisoners off to the Yard. Superintendent Smith then sent his team on ahead to Ruislip to get into position while he went back to the office. He had enough time to question his three prisoners before he, too, headed for 45 Cranley Drive.

FOR THE KROGERS, the afternoon in Ruislip had dragged by as heavy as a pile of wet leaves. Peter watched out a window as the golden dusk winked out into a coal-black night. Up and down the street, lights came on. Children were called inside. Ruislip settled in for supper. But the quietness seemed unnatural. It felt as though the neighborhood were listening on behalf of some unseen audience.

Lonsdale did not arrive at the appointed time. Nor did he call to say why. Missing a scheduled meeting was not, by itself, cause for alarm. Gordon might have had car trouble. He might be sitting in a traffic jam. But still, his unexplained absence, along with those other things, made Peter and Helen nervous, as if they were standing too close to a cliff, looking over the edge.

They tried to relax. They ate, they read, they listened to the radio. Aside from following favorite shows on the BBC, they kept their big living room receiver tuned to Radio Moscow every night and listened for alerts aimed at them. An alert would appear as a seemingly innocent point of conversation in a program—perhaps a reference to a certain composer eight minutes into a nine o'clock music show. That would be a signal that Moscow Center had a message for the Krogers and they should tune their radio to a predetermined frequency at a certain time. And when the message came, it would be in the form of numbers that made up a ciphered message.

If this were an ordinary Saturday night, the Krogers' routine would have begun with the smiling Lonsdale coming in for dinner. He liked Helen's cooking. Gordon would have the film that Houghton had passed to him earlier in the day. The film contained Bunty's pictures of secret documents from Portland. Helen would develop the film in the bathroom, which she had converted to a darkroom. When the film was dry, she would put it under a microdot camera and photograph it again. When that film was developed, the result was a strip of microdots.

Peter would insert the microdots into the spines of books, wrap them up, and address them to some "special" customers he had on the Continent. Then he would write a message informing Moscow Center what he was sending this week. He put that message into code and used a one-time pad to further convert it into a cipher. After that, he took a telegraph key and recorded the ciphered message into dot and dashes on a tape recorder called a burst encoder.

The last step was to bring out his hidden shortwave radio transmitter and plug the burst encoder into it. Then he sent his message to Moscow, again at a certain frequency at a certain time. The burst encoder transmitted in a blast of speed, over two hundred words per minute, reducing the airtime needed to just a few seconds. He would hear a short response from Moscow, perhaps a coded letter R, if his message got through.

All this work took several hours, and that was why the Krogers never accepted social invitations on Saturday nights and why neighbors sometimes saw their lights burning until nearly dawn. After the night's work was done, Lonsdale and the Krogers would sleep late on Sunday, and after lunch, Gordon would drive back to London. Monday, Peter would mail his "special" books.

But on this cold night in January 1961, the Saturday routine had been disrupted by Lonsdale's failure to appear for dinner. Now it was getting later and he still hadn't phoned to say why. Peter and Helen thought about things over and over again. Suspicions stalked them like a sound of footsteps from behind on a dark street.

Then suddenly, a knock came at the door.

The Krogers had a heavy metal knocker, and tonight it sounded as loud as a hammer. Peter, settled in his favorite old chair in his private library, put his book down. He looked up at the clock. It was after seven.

It wasn't Lonsdale at the door. Peter knew that immediately. Nor did it sound like a neighbor. This knock had a businesslike tone. Peter waited a moment. Then he got up and walked up the carpeted hallway. He called out to Helen that he would get the door.

Reaching the front room, he turned off the radio and switched the outside porch light on. He had four locks on the door. He disengaged them one by one: snap, snap, snap, snap.

He cracked the door. A blade of icy air fell on his shoulder. Beyond the glow of porch light, wind moaned through telephone lines as a light snow fell. He pulled the door open a little farther. An ominous sight confronted him.

Two men in coats stood on the porch. Shadows from the overhead light hung from their faces like Venetian masks. Their breath steamed as they stared into Peter's eyes.

He had never seen them before. Their expressions, as bland as the bindings of law books, suggested official business. Peter kept his hand firmly on the door and fought an impulse to panic.

The one in front was a big, hefty man with heavy jowls and gray sideburns, wearing glasses with two-toned plastic frames, the kind you saw on counselors at the local labor exchange. But that image was contradicted by his black wool beret, which made him look a little, well, campy. Speaking in a soft West Country burr, he offered Peter Kroger a concrete smile.

"My name is G. G. Smith," he said. "I am a police officer making inquiries. May I come in?"

A simple copper, making simple inquiries? Peter didn't buy it, not for a second. This man was from state security. So was the other one. The way they stood, the way this one spoke, brought visions of interrogations, bright lights, and stenographers, a life unraveling like a spool of wire rolling across the floor.

What had happened?

For a moment, Peter forgot the first rule of the game, to act completely innocent, innocent and ignorant—know nothing, admit nothing, keep the burden of proof on the opposition. Most of all, stay calm. Plant an inscrutable expression on your face and keep it there.

But Peter no longer had the nerves of a younger man. In a moment of poor judgment he tried to shut the door. It was no use. Superintendent Smith blocked the door with his rather large shoe.

It was then that Peter saw strange cars pulling up in front of his house. Doors were slammed as other men, and women, got out and walked quickly through the headlights up to the porch and along the sides of the house toward the backyard. Additional figures emerged from a vacant house, from a mover's van parked up the street, and from that road-repair truck. They were surrounding the Krogers' house.

The crowd got bigger. Now there were people running down the street with cameras—press cameras and newsreel cameras, with flashguns and light bars. A plague of photographers and reporters was descending on 45 Cranley Drive.

No doubt about it, this was a raid—the stuff of extra editions with screaming headlines. Peter struggled to keep his composure. Now he realized who all those strangers were.

"Certainly," he told the superintendent.

He reverted to the emotional control—his wife called it coldness—that was his armor in times of danger. He stepped back and allowed the two men inside, then silently led them into his library. Turning around, he saw more detectives crowding in, also bundled up in winter coats and hats.

The thing that caught the detectives' attention was the number of books in the house. There were thousands of them, stacked everywhere, on tables, shelves, chairs, the floor. They included histories, biographies, and novels, stories of pride and humility, victory and defeat, smelling of mildew and red rot.

Peter offered the detectives seats. They preferred to stand. Peter sank into his chair again and waited for their next move.

"I would like to see your wife, as well," Smith told Peter.

He called to Helen. When she appeared, she looked concerned at the fact her house was suddenly full of strangers who frankly didn't look very friendly. Smith showed his police identity card.

"Detective Superintendent G. G. Smith, Special Branch," he said.

He introduced the detective who had been with him on the porch. He was a quiet Scot with blond hair, blond mustache, and eyes as sharp as they were blue. Chief Inspector Ferguson Smith was his name. Newspapers would later note that he was a recipient of the Distinguished Flying Cross for bravery in the Battle of Britain.

Superintendent Smith asked the Krogers for the name and address of the gentleman who came to stay with them on weekends. Peter and Helen exchanged glances but did not answer.

"Would you care to tell me?" Smith asked them.

"We have lots of friends," Peter replied.

The superintendent said he was referring to the man who came on Saturday nights and left on Sunday afternoon. The Krogers reeled off several names, but not the one he wanted to hear. To Smith, their lie was significant. It confirmed that the Krogers were involved in the illegal work that Lonsdale was doing. It was time to take them into custody. He showed the Krogers a document explaining the Official Secrets Act.

Under that legislation, a Special Branch superintendent had the power to ask questions about the identity of people seen in the company of others suspected of activities threatening the defense of the realm. Smith could arrest a person for refusing to divulge the name of someone that he or she was suspected of harboring. The Krogers' refusal to come clean gave Moonraker the grounds he needed.

He told them they were under arrest for conspiring to violate section 1 of the aforementioned secrets act—spying, that is. He produced a search warrant. He handed it to Peter, who read it to Helen.

When Peter was through, Smith told them both to get ready. Helen turned and marched down the hall into her bedroom. She was followed by Sergeant Anne Winterbottom, a small woman with short hair and keen, experienced police eyes.

Helen tried to close the door as she went in. Winterbottom caught the door and watched Helen pull a coat from the wardrobe. Then Helen leaned over a chair and reached for her purse. That was a normal thing for a woman to do. But why did she turn her back to Winterbottom first? Winterbottom had not made detective grade by missing things of significance.

Next, Helen wanted to go to the bathroom. Again, Winterbottom followed. Again, she held the door open. She noticed Helen making another suspicious move. It appeared she was trying to take something from her purse and flush it down the toilet. But seeing Winterbottom watching her, Helen straightened up, adjusted her hair, inspected her makeup, and came out again.

When they returned to the library, Helen asked Superintendent Smith, "As I am going out for some time, may I stoke the boiler?"

Winterbottom caught Smith's eye. Yes, he had seen it—Helen's right hand closing her coat over her left hand.

"Of course," Smith replied. He reached down and pulled Helen's coat open. That revealed her left hand clutching her purse. "But first, let me see what is in the handbag."

Helen glared at him. No cooperation was coming here, old man. A tug of war ensued. As a veteran of factory work during the war, Helen was strong. But Smith was stronger, and more determined. He yanked the purse away and pulled it open.

Along with the usual things a woman would carry in her purse, he found a white envelope. He held it up. "What is this?"

Helen kept to the rules. "I don't know."

Smith opened the envelope. Inside he found a list of London streets and map references. There was nothing illegal about that. He also found a six-page letter hand-written in Russian. There was no law against that, either. But then he hit pay dirt.

At the bottom of the purse were two glass slides, with three microdots sandwiched between them. In Britain, microdots were called duffs, a reference to raisins in a pudding called plum duff. There was also a page from a one-time cipher pad.

With evidence in hand, the superintendent held his hand out to direct Peter and Helen to the front door. They were escorted out of the house, put into separate cars, and driven five miles away to Hayes police station for booking.

Superintendent Smith gave them a satisfied smile as they disappeared from view. The Secrets Act was made for days like this. He stepped aside as an army of crime scene detectives tramped in to search the premises.

An impressive amount of spy paraphernalia was found: a microscope that could be used for reading microfilm, a flashlight containing 500 U.S. dollars, and a piece of Cellophane coated with silver bromide, suitable for making microfilm. Inside the base of a heavy cigarette lighter, more microdots and pages from a one-time pad were discovered. Also, a list of radio frequencies, days and times of broadcasts, and Russian call signs.

It got better. In the bathroom, another microdot reader was found in a secret compartment in a can of talcum powder. Hidden in the bedroom was a collection of passports from the United States, Canada, and New Zealand, all of them apparently legal, but in different names, and with the Krogers' pictures in them. In the attic, more money: $6,000 in twenties, $2,000 in small bills, and a fat supply of traveler's cheques.

A powerful shortwave transmitter was discovered hidden beneath a concrete slab under the house, accessible via a trapdoor under the refrigerator in the kitchen. A burst encoder was found with it. A long wire strung under the rafters in the attic turned out to be the antenna for the radio. Years later, new owners of the house would dig up a second transmitter, buried in the garden.

Superintendent Smith and the other spy catchers saw that the Krogers' antiquarian book business was a roof (front) for their spy operation. They knew from past experience how that kind of system worked. On one level, the Krogers' book business really was legitimate, with regular customers in the United States, Britain, and other countries. Those customers were separate from the Soviet sleeper agents who received the Krogers' "special" books with microfilm in the spines.

The sleepers had their own fronts, in countries like Switzerland and Austria, where a crosscurrent of mail between East and West was common and attracted little notice. After receiving the books, the sleepers cleaned them of identity by taking the wrappings off and sealing them in new mailers. Then they mailed them to a post office box in Moscow, where they were picked up by KGB agents. It was a system brilliant in its simplicity. It had worked perfectly for years.

But now, comrades, the show was over.

19 A MOST DISGRACEFUL CASE

Operation Whisper had been brought to a successful conclusion, showing MI5, the FBI, the CIA, the RCMP, British Naval Intelligence, and the Special Branch at what many thought was their very best—resourceful and focused, and mutually cooperative for a change. The British media covered the roll-up and trial in their unique style that was a mixture of the informative and the sensational. In the tabloids it was the "Secrets Case." The *Daily Mail* called the Krogers' home the "House of Secrets." The mainstream broadsheets papers referred to it simply as the "Portland Spy Case" and the "Naval Secrets Case." But even the normally sober *Guardian* couldn't help licking its editorial lips at the discovery of a "hidden cavity" under the Krogers' kitchen floor.

The public was fascinated, of course. The case was a real crowd pleaser before it ever went to trial. But this being the world of espionage, things were not quite as they seemed. Questions still remained. Who exactly *were* the Krogers? They certainly weren't British. Who was Lonsdale? He somehow didn't come off as a real Canadian.

How damaging had the Portland spy case been to NATO? How big was the KGB's current network in Britain? The exposure of the Cambridge spies in the 1950s had shown just how high up Soviet agents had once infiltrated the British government—Kim Philby and John Cairncross in MI6, and Donald Maclean and Guy Burgess in the Foreign Office. Were there more Soviet moles burrowing their way into Whitehall?

The case got more intriguing as it played out in court.[1]

THE PORTLAND FIVE went on trial together on March 13, 1961, in court-room No. 1 at the Central Criminal Court in London, known as the Old Bailey. The charge was conspiring to violate the Official Secrets Act of 1911. The courthouse was only fifty-three years old but looked like it had been there since the Gunpowder Plot. The neo-Baroque exterior was clad in Portland stone, and the tall gold-leaf dome supported a blindfolded Lady of Justice statue. Outside on the sidewalk, MI5 and Scotland Yard set up a display of dozens of spy cameras they had seized over the years.

The courtroom was small; barely a hundred could squeeze inside. It was luxuriously paneled with oak, and heavy railings separated the different sections. There were no windows, but the ceiling was dominated by a big skylight that admitted a weak, creepy light like that in Waterloo Station. All in all it was a cozy place, in a claustrophobic sort of way.

A loud knock at the door quieted the courtroom. The usher uttered something appropriate, and opened it. Representatives of the City of London strode in wearing furry robes. The presiding judge, Lord Hubert Parker, the lord chief justice of England, was draped in a crimson cassock and a white, shoulder-length wig. He adjusted his glasses as he and the lord mayor went to the far side of the room and took their seats on the throne. Behind them hung the royal coat of arms. A mighty sword was propped beneath.

Lord Parker was a slender, kindly looking man with a soft voice. But he was also known as a dispenser of stern justice, and his choice as judge indicated just how serious the government considered this case. Indeed, it was a cause célèbre, and the world press was on hand. Trials were supposed to be public affairs, and there was a visitors' gallery along the wall to the judges' left, but it had been taken over by new bleachers built for reporters. That left only a few seats for the public, in crannies here and there.

The jurors sat in their box along the wall to the judges' right. Fourteen prospective women jurors had been preempted by challenges from the attorneys, along with any men who looked like they had attended posh schools. That left twelve solid-looking blokes who might have been posing for a soccer team picture after they had retired and entered middle age.

Lawyers for both the defense and the prosecution occupied benches in front of and below the judges. The crown's case was presented by Sir Reginald Manningham-Buller, the attorney general, assisted by Mervyn

Griffiths-Jones and Alastair Morton. Sir Reginald was a huge, intimidating man. Some saw him as a character right out of an old Pinewood Studios courtroom melodrama, and called him "Bullying-Manner."

"I thought what an unprepossessing figure he cut, with his wobbling crimson cheeks and the apoplectic, bulging eyes of the over-indulgent," George Blake, the Soviet mole inside in MI6, would write after his own day in court here a few months later.[2]

Sir Reginald was famous for rambling, incoherent presentations, and when he had first taken the Portland spy case to a magistrate in February, his aides prepared a script for him to read. During this trial, the judge would correct him at least once as he got his facts mixed up.

Victor Durand and Robin Simpson represented Peter John Kroger, aged fifty, and Helen Joyce Kroger, forty-seven. James N. Dunlop defended Ethel Elizabeth Gee, forty-six, and Henry Palmer was counsel for Henry Frederick Houghton, fifty-five. John Maddocks and William M. F. Hudson represented Gordon Arnold Lonsdale, thirty-seven. Observing the rules of the spy game for illegal agents, Moscow Center apparently did not provide any financial assistance to the defendants. The Krogers raised money for their defense by selling their house and car. Houghton peddled his story to Sunday newspapers, while Gee used money she had invested from an inheritance. Lonsdale had cash on hand from his gumball business.

Most of the witnesses for the crown were the Special Branch officers who had worked Operation Whisper with MI5. Detective Superintendent George Smith, now more than ever the media's favorite Moonraker, was the star. He proudly presented the exhibits on the evidence table to the court in the manner of a TV game show host describing the prizes awaiting today's winners.

Smith testified that after Gee's arrest on January 7, he found Admiralty files and a can sealed with tape in her bag. Photo technicians opened the tin in a photo darkroom and found undeveloped film—310 exposures in all.

Confronted with that, Gee had snapped: "I've done nothing wrong!"

When Lonsdale was searched, they found a sealed envelope containing £125 in 5-pound notes. In another envelope, $300 in 20-dollar bills. When Smith asked for Lonsdale's name and address, he got this reply:

"To any questions you might ask me, my answer is 'No,' so you need not trouble to ask." Then Lonsdale's tone softened and he added: "As I appear to have to stay here all night, can you find a good chess player?" He smiled, and Moonraker found him a guard who would be a skilled opponent.

Houghton didn't say much at the time of his arrest, and nothing interesting was found on him. At first he had looked sullen and depressed. Then Harry turned clever. He asked Smith to bring in some pictures of suspected Soviet and Polish spies operating in Britain. He said he might be able to help MI5 by identifying some of them. Smith laid out a dozen photos and Houghton took a look. But now he wanted a "reward." If he cooperated, he said, he would turn queen's evidence and testify against the other defendants.

Smith got up and walked out. "I cannot bargain with you," he said.

Actually, some evidence against Houghton had been found. After Smith's "Lock, stock, and barrel" radio signal went out from Waterloo Road, detectives searched Houghton's cottage in Weymouth. They found secret Admiralty pamphlets describing the results of antisubmarine tests, along with charts of Portland Harbor, and an Exakta camera that Houghton admitted was given him by Lonsdale. In a shed in Houghton's garden, 650 1-pound notes were discovered hidden in an empty paint can.

In Gee's home, a two-story brick townhouse at 23 Hambro Road in Portland that fronted directly onto the sidewalk, detectives found a sheet of paper listing the numbers of eighteen Admiralty pamphlets missing from the naval base. They also discovered a questionnaire Bunty later admitted had been dictated to her by Lonsdale. Answers to the twelve questions would have given a good picture of NATO sonar developments.

When Lonsdale's flat in the White House was searched, Smith found $1,800 in cash hidden inside a Chinese scroll, and three one-time pads in a heavy table lighter. A phony battery inside a flashlight held a set of coded Moscow radio call signals that matched a group found in the Krogers' house. Lonsdale's portable typewriter was identified as the one on which the coded messages in Helen Kroger's handbag had been typed. And finally, a microdot reader and three negatives showing radio transmission schedules were found.

Operators at GCHQ listened in on the listed frequencies. At the designated times, they picked up the dot-dash signals for "277" and "Zebra." Other signals included "Rosa ya Fiaica" (Violet calling Rose) and "Lena ya Amor" (the names of Russian rivers). Direction-finding receivers traced the source of the calls. It was Moscow calling.

Lonsdale's attorney raised a point: Those signals were picked up *after* the

Portland suspects were arrested. The BBC had broadcast news of the arrests to the world, so Moscow could hardly have missed the publicity. Therefore, if Lonsdale was a Russian spy, why was Moscow sending him signals when they knew he was in jail?

Lord Parker dismissed that argument. Clearly, Moscow was broadcasting not just to the Portland spies but to other Soviet agents in Britain, he said. Undoubtedly there were additional Soviet networks operating in these islands.

But in the midst of all this, a bigger question loomed: Beyond information on sonar and other underwater weapons systems, what *else* were the Soviets after?

The answer was provided by that film Superintendent Smith had found in Gee's bag. When developed, the film showed pictures of the pages of a secret Admiralty book. The pages contained ship descriptions, fleet orders, and a particular drawing marked SH52CT. Captain George Osborn Symonds, director of the Underwater Warfare Division of the Royal Navy staff at the Admiralty, told the court that the information in those pictures "would be of great value to a potential enemy." More specifically:

"They also include details of the naval building program and details of HMS *Dreadnought,* the navy's first nuclear submarine."

There it was. Nuclear secrets were being stolen. Building nuclear submarines was a key part of the Cold War arms race. The United States had begun research on nuclear-powered submarines in the late forties and launched the world's first one, the USS *Nautilus,* in 1954. The American government then began sharing its research with Britain. The Soviet Union didn't launch their first atomic sub, the *K-3 Leninsky Komsomol,* until 1958.

Russia planned to build a large fleet of nuclear subs to compensate for America's increased production of intercontinental nuclear missiles. But Russia's nuclear subs were built in a hurry and were plagued with problems from the very beginning — radiation leaks, fires, and contamination — which in time would lead to many deaths.[3] By contrast, the HMS *Dreadnought* was being fitted with a reliable American Westinghouse reactor. The Soviets wanted to find out all they could about it.

Symonds's testimony confirmed that the Soviets were up to their old tricks again, infiltrating Western military installations for atomic secrets. It was 1945 all over again.

THE DEFENDANTS all sat together in a wide, glass-enclosed dock situated next to the main doors and facing across the room to the judges' throne. The courtroom doors to the dock were kept locked but an open stairway behind the defendants led down to holding cells in the basement. Each cell below was "small and dark, designed only to wait in, with just a wooden stool and a small table as furniture," George Blake recalled. "Dirty and damp, its walls were covered with inscriptions, some obscene, but most witnessing to the moods of despair, bitterness, defiance or hope of those who waited there."[4]

Ethel Gee appeared in court wearing glittering earrings above a sensible blue tweed jacket. Her black hair was tightly set. Bunty had an important job at Portland, managing the vault where top-secret documents were stored. It was a restricted section, and only those with clearance were allowed in. She tapped a pencil impatiently as she admitted she had taken Admiralty documents out of her office at Portland the day she was arrested. But she insisted it was an accident.

"I just put them in the official envelope, put the envelope under my arm, and walked out of the establishment," she said. "Harry picked me up in his car, and I put the envelope on the seat of the car and left it for him."

She "left it" for him? That didn't sound accidental.

Gee said she had first met Harry Houghton when he took an office next to hers at Portland. They discovered they were from the same hometown, and had lunch together with friends. She introduced him to her family, and he started coming over on Sundays to take them all for an afternoon drive. Soon Harry and Bunty were spending Saturdays together. It was a rather conventional courtship. They went shopping, they returned books to the library, they went to classical music concerts. Then she started helping him work on his cottage. That was followed by weekends in London for dinner and the theatre.

"I would have married him if conditions had been different," she told the court. "Conditions at home were the obstacle."

"Were you fond of him?" the prosecutor asked.

"Naturally."

"Was that reciprocated?"

"Oh, I am sure, yes."

"Were you happy?"

"Yes."

Bunty claimed, in her high-pitched, Hampshire-Dorset accent, that she had never been paid for what she did. Furthermore, she argued, her access to the documents room was no indication of anything sinister.

"Plenty of people used the strong room," she said. "You never knew who you were going to find in there."

"Khrushchev," somebody said from the back of the courtroom.

"At the time, I thought it was foolish, but I didn't think it was wrong," she said. "In the light of what has transpired here, I now realize I have done something terribly wrong."

Harry Houghton, a hefty man with a big nose and a clear, strong voice, tried to convince the court that he had been pressured into spying by Russian thugs who beat him up. Then once he was in the game he feared that if he tried to pull out, they would kill him with a booby trap or poison, and take care of Bunty with a letter bomb. Hearing that, Lonsdale buried his face in his hands and laughed. He knew Harry's motivation had not been fear, but cash.

Houghton, neatly decked out in a brown tweed suit, insisted that until the day of his arrest, the information he gave the Soviets was chicken feed, open intelligence taken from newspapers and service magazines. But he couldn't wiggle out of the questions posed in cross-examination:

"You are guilty of the charge preferred against you?" he was asked.

"In a way," he replied. "In that it was forced out of me."

"You are guilty of conspiring with others to communicate information which might be useful to a potential enemy?"

"I didn't conspire with the Krogers because I didn't know them."

"As far as your relations went with Lonsdale, you agree you conspired with him to supply him with information about the Royal Navy?"

"Yes."

Gordon Lonsdale's strategy was more interesting. He figured that if they all went to prison, he would get out first, in a swap arranged by the Soviet government. So, he tried to shift the blame onto himself and clear the Krogers. He and Peter agreed on this in talks before the trial.

Lonsdale was smartly turned out in a tailored gray suit. His voice was firm as he read from prepared notes. He had known the Krogers since 1955, he said. He often visited them in Cranley Road and stayed there to watch their books when they went out of town. He claimed he had hid all that spy paraphernalia in the Krogers' house without their knowledge. He said he dug that pit (the "hidden cavity") under the house and hid the radio transmitter there while Peter and Helen were on vacation.

But what about all that microdot equipment?

"I often used the Krogers' bathroom as a dark room. At the time, I was conducting some experiments in microphotography."

He also claimed he had brought in those foreign passports found in the Krogers' house. They would be used in case the Krogers got into trouble because of Lonsdale's activities and had to flee the country, he said. But he would not admit he was a Soviet spy or reveal his real name.

"I accept full responsibility for my actions, irrespective of the consequences to me personally," he said in closing. Reporters for a while thought he had some kind of muscular tremor in his jaw. Then they saw he was chewing gum.

Now it was time for the Krogers. With a suit and tie, and his turban of white hair, Peter really did look like what one might expect an antiquarian book dealer to look like. He talked like one, too. He held up copies of the *Clique* to show his adverts.

"What Lonsdale has just said is true, as far as I know," he read from a prepared statement. He and Helen had come to England from Canada to realize a "long-felt desire" to open an antiquarian book business, he said. His business was well known in America, Britain, and the Continent. "My wife helps me most faithfully in the business with the packing, invoicing, duplicating, and drives me around."

Kroger claimed he first met Lonsdale in 1955 when Gordon was a student in Oriental languages at the University of London and that "books entered our conversation from the outset." Then Lonsdale became a frequent guest in their home, he said. "It never entered our minds that he was engaged in anything suspicious." All the evidence recovered from Cranley Drive indeed belonged to Lonsdale, Peter insisted. Then he sat down. From his manner, some got the impression that he considered his trial an exercise in impertinence.

Helen wasn't so confident in her statement. She spoke in a nervous voice as she described herself as a simple housewife looking after their home as her husband sold his old books. Gordon Lonsdale had been their friend for years—just a kindly Russian who brought in coal, helped her cook, and even washed the dishes after dinner.

She wore a dark jacket, fawn-colored slacks, and flat shoes with ski socks. Ski socks? Reporters wondered about that. She and Peter had led a jet-set life of international spying, but here she was, dressed like some eccentric old lady who had wandered in off the street. They found out later that a policewoman had told her to wear something warm to court.

Continuing Lonsdale's strategy of shouldering all the blame himself, Helen said the envelope containing ciphered Russian messages found in her handbag had been given to her by Gordon the morning of the raid. He asked her to hold the envelope until later, she said. She had known nothing of the trap door in her kitchen floor until a plumber found it. She had never seen evidence of it being used.

"I know nothing of spying, and never had anything to do with such things," she said in closing. Some reporters thought that the audience seemed oddly sympathetic toward her.

Throughout the trial, Lonsdale sat quietly in a corner of the dock behind the iron bars, hunched and stoical, his face showing a Slavic indifference, except for those times when some statement by Houghton forced him to laugh. Lonsdale rarely said anything to the other defendants, but busily sent notes down to his attorneys. Houghton and Gee didn't say much, either. Houghton mostly seemed to enjoy being a center of attention.

The Krogers were more lively. They followed the proceedings closely. They held hands and laughed about the evidence being given. They smiled at friends in the courtroom and waved at some of them, including their friend Nora Doel, wife of Frank Doel, the bookshop owner. That resulted in Mrs. Doel being dubbed the mysterious "Woman in Blue" by the press. This, despite the fact she was just an ordinary suburban housewife like Ruth Search, with no particular secrets to guard except perhaps a recipe or two handed down from her grandmother.

AFTER EIGHT DAYS, the jury retired to reach their verdict. The hallway outside the courtroom and the windy streets around the Old Bailey were crowded with reporters, photographers, rubberneckers, and hawkers peddling newspapers, peanuts, and drinks. In the old days, Old Bailey juries were forced to deliberate in a room that was cold and dark, with no food or water. The idea was to speed up the wheels of justice. That seemed to be the case now, as a bailiff signaled that the jurors were returning after less than an hour. But all they wanted was clarification on a legal point. Then they went back to work.

The jury stayed out another thirty-three minutes. When they returned to the courtroom, the accused were ordered to stand. The verdict was delivered:

All guilty as charged.

The prisoners showed no emotions. They waited for their sentences to be handed down. But first, Detective Superintendent Smith returned to the courtroom and asked permission to make a statement. Lord Parker told him to take the witness stand.

After their arrest, the Krogers had been told they would be fingerprinted, Smith said. They refused. Only after they were informed that they would be fingerprinted one way or another, did they reluctantly agree. The prints were then delivered to the FBI's legal attaché at the U.S. embassy in London, who forwarded them to Washington.

But why were the prints sent to the FBI?

Superintendent Smith wasn't clear on that. But Freddie Snelling wrote in his reminiscences that after the Krogers were arrested, the *Toronto Star* did some research and discovered they were the Cohens.[5] Apparently the RCMP read that information in the paper and forwarded it to Scotland Yard. The Yard then contacted the U.S. embassy, and the embassy asked Alan Belmont for FBI verification.

Moonraker waved the results of the fingerprint query.

Peter and Helen Kroger, he announced, were, in fact, Morris and Lona Cohen, Americans who had spied for the Soviets in the United States and Canada during and after the war. Their spy network had stolen the secrets of the atomic bomb. Reporters noted that a collective gasp rose from the audience.

Smith went on for twenty minutes. The Cohens had fled New York in 1950 as the spy ring of their associates Julius and Ethel Rosenberg was being rolled up. They had been under investigation by the FBI since 1953. The

Soviets had placed them in Lublin, Poland, near the Soviet border, from 1951 to 1954, and Morris taught English there as a cover job.

While based in Poland, Smith continued, the Cohens went on foreign missions for Moscow. They left an American Express paper trail as they traveled to Japan, Hong Kong, Australia, New Zealand, Austria, Belgium, and the Netherlands. In Paris they went to the New Zealand embassy with birth certificates and a marriage license from that country, and obtained dead double passports in the name of Kroger. They made two trips to Canada and acquired more dead double passports there, in the name of Smith.

After the Cohens' last New York controller, Willie Fisher (still known as Abel), was arrested in 1957, the FBI sent wanted flyers on the couple to every NATO nation, plus a number of other countries. Why hadn't Scotland Yard acted on that information sooner? After all, the Cohens had been in Ruislip since 1955. The superintendent didn't address that point, either. Apparently, as in the Klaus Fuchs case, the wanted flyers were dropped into a folder and filed, somewhere.

The guilty verdicts were sensational news. Smith's identification of the Cohens was even more spectacular. The world's top Soviet atomic spies had been captured right here in London. Morris Cohen's attorney tried to do some fast footwork by saying the Cohens had been unjustly accused of being Communist spies. They were simply misunderstood liberals forced to flee the United States in the heat of early fifties McCarthyism.

Lord Parker listened patiently, then moved on to the sentencing. He emphasized the "gravity" of the case and said that "for peacetime, this must be one of the most disgraceful cases that has come before the court."

Lord Parker turned his eyes first on Lonsdale. "Gordon Arnold Lonsdale, you are clearly a professional spy. It is a dangerous career, and one in which you must be prepared, as you no doubt are, to suffer, if and when you are caught. I take the view that in this case, yours was the directing mind. You will go to prison for twenty-five years."

Low whistles swept through the audience. As Lonsdale was led away, a smile flickered on his face like a flash from a malfunctioning fluorescent bulb.

"Peter John Kroger and Helen Joyce Kroger, you are both in this up to the hilt," Lord Parker said next. "You are both professional spies. The only distinction I can see between you and Lonsdale is that, if I am right, yours was not the directing mind or minds, and you are older than he is. You each go to prison for twenty years."

Now voices could be heard from the shocked audience. Peter turned pale and walked quickly out of the dock. Helen was furious, and yanked her arm away from a policewoman.

"Harry Frederick Houghton, your conduct was in many ways the most culpable," Lord Parker continued. "You betrayed the secrets of your country by communicating secret information about Her Majesty's Navy. I've considered long what to do with you. You are, however, now fifty-six, and not a very young fifty-six, and it is against all our principles that a sentence should be given which might involve your dying in prison. But for that, I would give you a longer sentence. Fifteen years."

Houghton, already sweating, now swayed a little as he left the dock.

Lord Parker then turned to Gee. "Ethel Elizabeth Gee, you betrayed your trust. I am quite unable to think it is a possibility that you did what you did out of some blind infatuation for Houghton. Having heard you and watched your demeanor in the dock and in the witness box, I am inclined to think that yours was the stronger character of the two. I think you acted for greed. You will also go to prison for fifteen years."

Lord Parker's appraisal of Gee was a reminder of what President Eisenhower had said about the Rosenbergs—that Ethel, not Julius, was the dominant partner in their spy activities. Gee plunged her hands into her coat pockets and marched down the steps of the dock without looking back.

Reporters got up and rushed for telephones. Old Bailey was where spies were tried in Britain, and these were the stiffest sentences for espionage to ever come out of this courthouse. The determining factor had been the nature of the indictments. If the Portland five had been charged with one act of spying, the maximum sentence would have been fourteen years. But they had committed their offenses over a period of years, so they were charged with conspiracy. There was no maximum sentence for conspiracy.

EIGHT MONTHS AFTER THE TRIAL, Lonsdale's true identity was discovered by MI5 and the Yard. He was KGB Colonel Konon Trofimovich Molody, son of a famous Soviet scientist. In 1929, at the age of seven, his aunt took him to live with her in Berkeley, California. He was there nine years, going to school with local kids and immersing himself in American life. That's how he learned English so well. His son later said that Genrikh Yagoda, head of the NKVD, had helped Konon get a passport to go to America, suggesting that he was being groomed for spy work at an early age.[6] Konon went back to Russia in 1938 after being told he had to choose between the United States and the Soviet Union. He worked intelligence ops for the Red Army in the war, then signed on with the NKVD. His mentor was Willie Fisher, the Soviet agent who saved his skin during the war.

Moscow Center had introduced Molody to the Cohens in 1954. The three were told they would be working together on an important new assignment. While Lona was abroad on missions, Morris helped Konon fine-tune his English, and gave him a refresher course in how to dress, walk, gesture, and order meals like a North American. All that was done at a *dacha*, a country house, outside Moscow. Thus, Moscow Center referred to the Cohens as *Dachniki*.

Morris and Lona, posing as the Krogers, moved to England in December 1954. With Moscow's financial backing, Morris set up his book business. Molody went to Canada in 1955 on a false passport and acquired a copy of the birth certificate for the real Gordon Arnold Lonsdale, born 1924 at Cobalt, a mining town in Ontario. Armed with that document, Molody then got a valid driver's license and passport in the name Lonsdale. With funds supplied by Moscow Center, the resurrected Gordon Lonsdale entered England and set himself up as a Canadian businessman and a silver-tongued roué pursuing a James Bond lifestyle of cars, casinos, and girls.

When the RCMP investigated, they interviewed two references Molody had given when he applied for his passport. Those Canadians said they had never heard of Gordon Lonsdale. And those weren't their signatures on the application. Then the RCMP interviewed the doctor who had delivered the real Gordon Lonsdale. He told them the child had been circumcised.[7]

In London, Moonraker told *their* Gordon Lonsdale to drop his pants. It was another bad day for the Soviet ringmaster.

HARRY HOUGHTON'S FIRST CONTROL OFFICER, the mysterious Nikki, was identified by MI5 as Nikolai B. Korovin, a KGB legal *rezident* whose cover job was first counsellor at the Russian embassy in London. Korovin was above Lonsdale. That meant other spy rings were probably operating in Britain, as Lord Parker had suspected. Korovin hastily left England in order to avoid the messy publicity of being identified and deported.

Still, the Portland spy case set off repercussions on both side of the Atlantic, resulting in more bad press for everyone involved.

Prime Minister Harold Macmillan described the Portland spy case as a "terrible blow" to Britain. He set up a committee of inquiry, headed up by Sir Charles Romer, a retired lord justice of appeal, to find out what had happened. But first, a little whitewash: Macmillan claimed, contrary to evidence given in court, that there was no possibility that any information on nuclear research had been betrayed by the Portland spies. The opposition immediately jumped on him. So did the *Guardian*: "That something at Portland was badly wrong is clear," a leader (editorial) said. "How else could Ethel Gee have taken away classified papers every weekend much as a housewife takes home groceries?"

The Romer Committee attached no blame to the British immigration service for allowing Lonsdale and the Krogers into the country. They had entered on valid passports, and immigration officials had no way of knowing those documents had been fraudulently obtained. Nor was MI5 blamed for any failure of liaison with U.S. authorities.

"Indeed, the circumstances in which Lonsdale and the Krogers were eventually detected and brought to justice are in themselves a convincing example of close and effective international security liaison," the report concluded.

The blame was placed on "certain defects" in Admiralty policy that had allowed Portland officials to ignore Houghton's record as a drunkard, along with a report that he was taking secret papers off the base. But the report did not blame the Admiralty for appointing Houghton to Portland, despite his drinking problem.

Criticism in the United States was more severe. Members of the Joint Congressional Committee on Atomic Energy cited the Portland spy case as reason why no more nuclear secrets should be shared with European allies. Four years before, Senator Clinton P. Anderson of New Mexico said, the committee had warned President Eisenhower against turning over information on the USS *Nautilus* to Britain, a nation with "chinks" in her security wall. The committee had further cautioned Eisenhower about his secret agreement to aid Britain in building the HMS *Dreadnought* and his plan to give NATO four submarines capable of firing Polaris nuclear missiles.

And now a new agreement would allow President Kennedy to give information on nuclear weapons to Italy?

The committee was aghast.

In 1960 the Cold War had entered another stage of hot war through surrogates. There had already been one of those surrogate wars, in Korea. Then President Eisenhower sent U.S. military advisers to South Vietnam to pick up where the French had left off in their war against the North, and now the CIA was plotting an invasion of Cuba. Both the NATO and Warsaw Pact powers were pulling out all stops to spy on one another. The Soviet Union was trying to catch up with the West, particularly in the nuclear arms race.

Atomic subs were especially attractive to the Soviets because they could be positioned in international waters off the coast of the United States, Britain, and France as mobile launching pads for nuclear missiles in case of direct war. The West, at the same time, was trying to counter Moscow's efforts at every turn. It was a classic case of intelligence versus counterintelligence. That was why the Portland spy case was such an embarrassment. The counterspies claimed victory in their roll-up, but the ring had been operating undetected for five years.

The fallout from the Portland spy case would continue for years. Shortly after the trial, at a meeting in Washington of the National Security Council, the U.S. Navy sought to push through a complete break in the Anglo-American exchange of intelligence. Al Belmont of the FBI was one of those present who spoke up to defeat that notion. But then within months of the Portland spy trial, British intelligence suffered another humiliation as George Blake was exposed as a longtime Soviet mole in MI6.

Blake (né Behar) was the son of a Turkish father and a Dutch mother, with some Jewish ancestry. While growing up in Holland he wanted to become a pastor, but turned his back on that. After his father died he went to live with a rich aunt in Cairo. There he came under the influence of an older cousin who had founded the Egyptian Communist Party. The daily contrasts that Blake saw between the wealth and poverty of Cairo influenced him deeply.

Blake ran messages for a while for the Dutch Resistance during the Second World War, then escaped occupied Holland for England in 1943. He served with British Naval Intelligence and the SOE before joining MI6 in 1947. They sent him to study Russian for three years at Cambridge. There he came under additional communist influence from one of his language instructors. In 1948, MI6 sent Blake to their Seoul station. During the Korean War he was arrested by enemy forces and interned for three years. He later said that the sight of American warplanes bombing North Korean villages convinced him that he had been fighting on the wrong side. He offered his services to the Soviets.

"Nobody recruited me," he said later. "It was my decision." He further stated, "I view communism as an attempt to create the Kingdom of God in this world. The communists are trying to do by action what the church has tried to achieve by prayer and precept."[8]

In the early fifties the CIA and MI6 hatched a plot, called Operation Gold by the Americans, and Operation Stopwatch by the British, to dig a tunnel from West Berlin into the Soviet zone of that city and tap the underground phone lines of the Soviet Army. Blake was assigned to keep the minutes of the planning session in London. He photocopied his notes and turned them over to his Soviet control officer. After the tunnel was dug successfully in 1955, the Soviets "discovered" it and exposed it to the world press. It was another embarrassment for the West.

Blake had been under suspicion at MI6 for some time. Michael Goleniewski (Sniper), the Polish intelligence defector who led MI5 to Harry Houghton, said that an MI6 officer in Berlin—he called him Lambda 1—had given up British agents working in Poland. That tip led to the identification of Blake. He was recalled to London, and under questioning in 1961 he confessed to spying. He was convicted in a trial before Lord Parker in the Old Bailey and sentenced to an astonishing forty-two years in prison.

Blake's most catastrophic damage to MI6 had been his betrayal of British agents working in East Germany. When the *Daily Telegraph* ran the story in 1961 they printed silhouettes of 40 figures in trench coats across the top of the front page, one for each agent that Blake allegedly had identified. Blake himself claimed he blew "maybe 500, 600" agents. But in 2015 an intelligence researcher dug through the records of the Stasi, the East German secret police, and estimated the figure was more like 100.[9]

Blake joined the Cohens and the other Portland spies in prison. Apparently he had not been involved in the Portland case, but in later interviews and writings he offered insights into the characters of the Portland spies and the way they handled their incarceration.

The roundup of Soviet spies in Britain didn't end with the Cohens and Blake and the others. The arrests continued into 1962. The next one apprehended was William John Christopher Vassall. Like Harry Houghton and Ethel Gee, Vassall was an employee of the Admiralty. His control officer was code-named Nikki. That caught Moonraker's eye because Harry Houghton's control was also named Nikki.

Had John Vassall been involved with the Cohens? Was he a sixth member of the Portland spy ring?

Smith said that of all the spies he had known, Vassall was the one who least looked the part. Smith described him as a "slim, softly good-looking, dimpled 'mother's boy' . . . fastidious, sensitive, weakly vacillating."[10] His luxurious flat in London was furnished with antiques, French perfumes, big cuddly toys, and photos of handsome rugby players. His mother was a beautiful nonconformist who had converted to Roman Catholicism, while his father was a Church of England vicar. The family had been in England since the sixteenth century. The family motto was "Often for the Throne, Always for the Country."

During the war, Vassall was turned down for RAF flight training, though he found satisfaction working as a photographer. He then spent several years in boring jobs at the Admiralty, but in 1953 was posted to Moscow as a clerk for the naval attaché. He was immediately captivated by Old Russia. He went to diplomatic parties and made friends easily. His gay lifestyle caused him to be noticed by Sigmund Mikhailski, a spotter for Soviet intelligence. After a drunken party with Mikhailski and two other Russians, Vassall was photographed naked on a sofa with another man. Then he was shown the pictures. Under threat of blackmail, he agreed to spy for the Soviets.

Vassall stole documents from the British embassy in Moscow in 1955 and turned them over to Russian agents who then photographed them and returned them. In 1956 he went back to London, worked as a naval intelligence clerk, and continued to steal documents. But Detective Superintendent Smith had been tipped off to the presence of a mole in the Admiralty, and narrowed his search down to Vassall. He confessed readily after his arrest.

As it tuned out, Vassall apparently had no connection to the Cohens and the other Portland spies. There were, in fact, two Soviet controllers in London code-named Nikki and that's where the confusion had arisen. The first Nikki was Nikolai Korovin, Houghton's controller. The second was Nikolai Karpekov, Vassall's controller.

In October 1962, John Vassall was convicted in the Old Bailey of spying. Lord Parker sentenced him to eighteen years in prison. "The whole of my blackmail experiences and my life as a spy had suddenly come to an abrupt end," Vassall told Smith. "I felt a lost soul who could not look to anyone for a word of comfort."

Then he added: "I'm glad it's all over."[11]

20 SWAPS AND A DARING ESCAPE

As far as Freddie Snelling, Morris Cohen's closest bookdealer friend, was concerned, British prisons were all about the same—gloomy, ghastly, brick monstrosities built in the last century. He figured he ought to know, because over the next few years he would visit the Cohens (still known in Britain as the Krogers) at some of England's most infamous slammers.

Snelling said he always had to enter through a fortified front door in an arched gateway. Then he was escorted to a waiting room, for some reason always on the left. There visitors sat in hard chairs amidst blowsy peroxide blondes holding squalling brats in their laps, and waited for someone to call out the name of the prisoner they'd come to see. When "Kroger" was called, Freddie would get up and slink out of the room with all eyes staring at him.

"Gawd, I imagined those blondes saying to one another, 'D'you reckon 'e's a bleedin' spy, too?'"[1]

Snelling had first gone to see Morris at Brixton Prison in London, where the male Portland spies were being held while awaiting trial. Lona Cohen and Bunty Gee were at Holloway women's prison, a former debtors' house called the Castle. Freddie and Morris sat in a small room called the solicitors' box. Morris wore street clothes, but without tie or belt. A guard sat with them to be sure they didn't discuss the upcoming trial. Cohen was anxious that his business affairs be wrapped up so that his (legitimate) costumers would get their orders. Snelling volunteered to do that in the following months.

When Konon Molody (still known as Gordon Lonsdale) was first taken to Brixton, he accused Moonraker of having stolen his gold lighter. Lona said the police swiped a diamond necklace of hers. Molody said he was told by policemen who were in prison for theft that the coppers routinely stole 10 to 15 percent of the value of a subject's possessions.

After the trial, the three male prisoners were sent to Wormwood Scrubs in Hammersmith, London. "Did any house of detention bear a more suitable name?" Snelling wrote. By comparison, he said, Strangeways Prison in Manchester sounded "almost romantic."

CELLS IN THE SCRUBS were cold and damp, and young offenders were routinely mixed with hardened criminals. Molody claimed that the breakfast porridge was made from sacks of Canadian pig meal, despite the fact the bags were labeled "best quality." He also complained about the chamber pots the prisoners had to use instead of a proper loo. Imagine, he said, the smell of thousands of men in a badly ventilated building all slopping out their pots at the same time. For washing up, they were given a jug of cold water and a bowl. They used the water to wash themselves and the floor.

"I find it hard to imagine anything more cruel and pointless than the British penal system," Molody wrote later.[2]

"Every person has a handbook," Morris recalled. "It tells the prisoner what he or she can do, what they cannot do. I tried to read it. I couldn't understand it. It took three days." Finally he figured it all out, he said, and life became more livable after that.

Despite press reports that the Portland spies were closely guarded by armed officers, Molody strolled into the visitors' room one day without escort, and Morris introduced him to Snelling, who would later help Konon write his memoirs. Meanwhile, Molody kept busy by translating English books into Russian and making plans to write a history of the wartime British SOE. He also got a bill from Inland Revenue for £108 in income taxes. He replied that he would be delighted to pay after he got out of prison in 1986.

"He bore his fate with remarkable fortitude and was invariably in good spirits," George Blake wrote of Molody in his memoirs. "He was an excellent story teller and I found his company in those first weeks of my imprisonment a great morale booster."[3]

It was during one of those prison visits that Morris offered Freddie a brief clue to his politics. "As you'll have gathered by now," Cohen said, "I'm for the ordinary Joe."

Morris constantly ordered books through Snelling. It was the heaviest and dullest stuff going, Freddie said, with no fiction, no "literature." Cohen preferred two-volume histories and titles containing words like "metaphysical contradictions." He especially liked books that advanced his personal commitment to Communism.

Lona, on the other hand, wanted feminine things like house slippers and hair curlers. After Lona was sent to Winson Green Prison in Birmingham, Snelling had a bouquet of flowers delivered to her once a week from a shop across the road. He also kept her supplied with cigarettes. Morris quit smoking while in prison. What Ethel Gee missed was her glass of sherry each evening.

Molody was the first of the Portland spies to be released. On the morning of April 21, 1964, he was called from his job in the paint shop at Strangeways and told he was being exchanged for Greville Wynne, a forty-two-year-old British electrical engineer held by the Soviets. But before Molody left prison, he told Morris: "Our comrades will take care of you. It means you just have to wait."[4]

Wynne, a short, balding, dapper dresser with an Errol Flynn mustache, had been doing business in the Soviet bloc for years. He had also been picking up papers from Colonel Oleg Penkovsky of Soviet military intelligence and smuggling them out to MI6. Some of those documents had aided President Kennedy in his handling of the Cuban missile crisis. Wynne was arrested at a trade fair in Budapest, convicted of spying in Russia, and sentenced to eight years in prison. Penkovsky was shot.

Molody was flown to West Berlin for the swap. Next day in an early morning fog he got out of a black Mercedes-Benz on the western side of the Heerstrasse checkpoint, a small shack in the middle of the wide street that flowed into East Berlin. Wynne got out of a car on the other side of the frontier. They walked toward one another, and two minutes later both men were on their way home to their families.

"Lonsdale swapped!" prisoners inside Strangeways cheered. Morris was exhilarated. "Like a drink of water to a thirsty man," he said.

When the Portland spies first went to prison, security was lax. Snelling said it was a long-standing British tradition of locking up the stable after the horse has gone. That was illustrated by George Blake's daring escape on October 22, 1966.

Three young radicals opposed to the presence of nuclear weapons in Britain engineered Blake's breakout. They were former guests of the Scrubs themselves, locked up for their antinuclear protests, and they knew the prison's routines. They liked the bearded, amiable George, and thought his sentence of forty-two years was unreasonable. That was their motive for helping him break out. They would strike a blow against the Establishment.

Blake was liked by the prison authorities, too, and was given freedom to move about. One Saturday night, while most of the prisoners and guards were watching a movie, he wiggled out a window, climbed over the wall, and was sped off to a safe house. His liberators smuggled him into East Germany in a false bottom built into a camper van.

His daring escape shocked the government. The authorities feared that a KGB gang had sprung Blake and that the Portland spies would break out next. They were all declared high-risk prisoners and placed on escape lists. High-speed convoys of police vehicles swept them to maximum-security prisons all across the country.

Upon arrival at their new digs, Morris Cohen and Harry Houghton were humiliated by being forced to dress in clownish harlequin uniforms. Then all of them, men and women, were thrown into solitary confinement at the different prisons where they were held. They were given only thirty minutes of outside exercise each day. Lona was not allowed to touch the letters she received in prison. A guard held each letter up against a wall, and she had to read it from a distance. Houghton called it the Blake Penance.[5] It went on for years.

Houghton spent time in Winchester, Durham, and Maidstone prisons. At Maidstone he was beaten regularly by skinheads. That continued until the gang tried (unsuccessfully) to burn down the prison shop, after which the authorities split them up. Harry spent most of his time sewing mailbags and attending Alcoholics Anonymous meetings, which amused him since there was marijuana available in the prison, but no booze.

After Holloway, Bunty was assigned to Styal, where she eventually got a job as a librarian. But after closing the library one night at eight, she found she was locked out of her cellblock. It was an open prison, and she could have simply walked out. But she went to look for somebody to let her in. For that, they took her radio away and threw her back into solitary.

Bunty, though, refused to look at solitary as punishment. "I am on my own most of the time, which means much in these places," she wrote in a letter to Houghton. "I do not have to listen to hard-luck stories. One can become so weary hearing how well-off and what big shots these people were outside. If one believed it, they are doing us a favor by letting us mix with such people."[6]

In a letter to a London friend, Morris said he had spent the 1968 holidays in the Parkhurst Prison "monastery" by watching two films on TV, *Scrooge* on Christmas and *The Apartment* on New Year's Day. "The shroud of melancholy which hung in our common room was too formidable for the artists to break through," he wrote.[7]

Morris and Lona were allowed to meet occasionally for a long talk at a neutral prison, supervised by seven "chaperones." But those visits were so infrequent that Morris feared they would lose their bond to one another. Helen developed back trouble. She was measured for a corset, and slept on a board. She also had sciatica and an infected kidney. Then boils, and stomach and gall bladder pain. She also incurred injuries fighting other women prisoners, once "defending her honor" against a lesbian.

Morris had surgery on a leg and both hands. Meanwhile, he was a popular prisoner. He conducted himself as a gentleman, taught prisoners to read and write, and helped them write letters to their families (and their lawyers).

THE COHENS were freed in a swap for Gerald Brooke, a twenty-seven-year-old British lecturer arrested by the KGB in 1965 while leading what he called a discussion group of students and teachers in Moscow. The Brooke case was a revealing one, showing how frustrating East-West relations could be in the Cold War.

Brooke was accused of anti-Soviet activities, passing propaganda material to antigovernment dissidents. A show trial was held in a movie theatre before TV cameras and an audience of six hundred spectators. He was sentenced to five years in prison.

When MI5 investigated, they found that the handsome, well-dressed young man with a winning smile had become involved with a Russian émigré group, NTS (*Narodnyj Trudovoj Soyuz*, the Popular Labor Union). The group smuggled in books by writers banned by the Soviets, and operated Radio Free Russia from Frankfurt. It also ran secret ops against the Soviets, MI5 said. Brooke was described as a foolish young man, deeply religious, who had been duped into passing NTS documents to Russians.

Moscow proposed a swap early on: Brooke for the Cohens. London said no. The Cohens were big fish caught in a serious espionage case and still possessed damaging information they could deliver to Moscow. They were in no way comparable to the gullible young Brooke. Also, MI5 denied that Brooke was a spy. He "was not working for HMG [Her Majesty's Government] in any capacity," the Security Service said.[8]

British defector Kim Philby, in Moscow, disagreed. The NTS was a CIA project, he said. "It used to be financed by the SIS [Secret Intelligence Service, aka MI6] but it was handed over to the CIA. This certainly makes Brooke some kind of Western agent, doesn't it?"

The Soviets twice more offered to swap Brooke for the Cohens. Twice more, Britain refused. Relations between the two countries worsened after the Soviets invaded Czechoslovakia in 1968. Then Moscow escalated the conflict by threatening to extend Brooke's sentence. There was also a veiled threat against his wife. That didn't work, so they announced they were going to bring a more serious charge against Brooke—spying. A conviction would add fifteen years to his sentence.

The U.S. State Department joined the bickering by telling the Soviets that the Cohens were "not available for exchange."[9] Washington wanted to extradite the Cohens to America and try them for spying once they had served their time in England. But the Cohens were British, not American, prisoners, and London kept control of the negotiations. All this, while Brooke languished in a Soviet labor camp in declining health. Macmillan's cabinet secretaries finally yielded to pressure from public opinion and hammered out a deal: the Cohens would be swapped for Brooke and two other British subjects, Michael Parsons and Anthony Lorraine, who were serving drug-smuggling sentences in Russia.

For their part, Parsons and Lorraine considered the swap a "fair deal," and added: "Spies play one game, we play another."[10]

While awaiting release, Morris was treated to a farewell dinner organized by some of his mates at Parkhurst, on the Isle of Wight. A number of Britain's most notorious murderers, robbers, and rapists saved up their shop wages so they could lay on a spread of chicken, ham, and fish. The guest of honor's chair was draped with a handmade Soviet flag. Morris made a short, mostly apolitical speech, and received a round of applause.[11]

Queen Elizabeth II signed the Cohens' release papers and they were reunited back at Brixton Prison in London on October 21, 1969. "Hello, sweetie pie," Lona said as she embraced her husband. After lunch together, they met with Tadeusz Piwinski, a Polish consul in Britain. The Soviet government for some time had been trotting out Polish citizens who swore they were long-lost relatives of the "Krogers" and that "Peter and Helen" were legal citizens of Poland. It was an attempt to block their possible extradition to America.

In order to provide some privacy for the couple as they departed Britain, Piwinski announced that no Polish visas would be issued to Western journalists for the next few days. Nor would the Cohens' flight number be revealed. It didn't work. Journalists booked seats on every flight to Warsaw the day of the release. They planned to sit with the Cohens on the plane over, then take a return flight without going through immigration.

But first, a glitch, as usually happens in an affair of this magnitude. Lona announced she did not want to go "home" to Poland. She didn't want to be back in the USSR, either. She wanted to go to America. If that weren't possible, she would stay in England. She liked it here.[12]

Morris said no. He had been working to establish their Polish "identity." All that work would be lost. And he had no intention of sitting in prison for the remaining years of his term. The British government also weighed in. Gerald Brooke had been returned to England three months before. If the Cohens backed out now, that would queer the rest of the deal: to allow four Brits to marry Russians, which was usually taboo in those days, and to allow more consular visits to Western prisoners held by the Soviets.

It must have sounded to the Cohens like they were back in New York in 1950, being told by Big Yuri that they had to go, whether they wanted to or not. So here the message was again:

Walk out and don't look back.

THE COHENS' DEPARTURE was surrounded with the kind of security one might expect if the crown jewels were being flown out of Britain. It was raining the morning of Friday, October 24, 1969, as Morris and Lona walked out into the Brixton Prison yard and climbed into a police van with blacked-out windows. Death threats had been called in, so two police cars and a motorcycle outrider accompanied the van as it took off with headlights on. Morris and Lona had five hundred pounds between them. Morris wore the suit in which he had been arrested nine years before, along with a hat and topcoat. Lona looked fetching in a fashionable new coat.

Traffic was stopped for the convoy as it raced through London out to Heathrow. When they reached the airport, the Cohens found their flight had been delayed by a bomb threat. A cordon of Scotland Yard and CID detectives and uniformed bobbies closed around them as they walked out to the waiting British European Airways plane. Journalists who weren't taking the flight were kept behind a barrier.

Morris carried an album of music from *Zorba the Greek,* a gift from the gang back in stir. Women prisoners had given Lona a blue teddy bear. They had bought their tickets themselves. First class, it was.

The Cohens walked up the steps to the plane, paused at the top, turned around, and waved goodbye to England. Inside, they took their seats, and a bottle of Champagne was opened for them. They held hands and joked about their prison experiences as the Trident took off and turned toward Warsaw.

"It's wonderful to see men again," Lona said as she chatted with reporters and the BEA crew. She turned to Morris. "We were allowed to meet occasionally before we were freed. And all those times he saw me, he never said he loved me."

Morris laughed. "All right, then. I love you."[13]

They refused to discuss their future plans. But over a dinner of grilled salmon, Lona said: "We want to see no more war. Only peace."

Morris was fifty-nine years old, Lona almost fifty-seven. Five notebooks Morris had filled with writings while in prison were seized by the Home Office, but he was allowed to keep more than twenty other notebooks containing copies of letters he had written. The Cohens had left some assets behind, mainly books, and the government announced they would be sold and the money donated to holidays for poor children.

A BBC correspondent stationed in Warsaw was at the airport when the Trident touched down. But all he saw of the Cohens was a fleeting view of two figures descending the steps and getting into a white van that whisked them away.

"After that, there was bedlam as what seemed to me to be most of Fleet Street, as well as all the world's TV, poured off the plane," he recalled.[14]

The Cohens had announced they were going to settle back in Lublin, an old Jewish town where they had lived before. After the war, it had been the seat of the puppet government the Soviets set up in Poland. But that BBC reporter found no trace of the Cohens there. They had, in fact, checked into a Warsaw hospital for a medical checkup.

With the Cohens' arrival in Poland, most of the Portland spy gang had been removed from England. That meant that after all those years of work, the spy catchers at MI5, Scotland Yard, British Naval Intelligence, the FBI, the CIA, and the RCMP had run out of worthy opponents with whom to match wits. They were left with Harry Houghton and Ethel Gee, who would go on to serve out most of their sentences, then get married and fade away into the English fog. After a while, there would be George Blake and John Vassall to deal with, but that was about it for the time being.

"Now the cupboard is bare," a member of British intelligence lamented. "All we have left are the amateurs and idealists."[15]

"DURING THE FIRST WEEKS after our return," Morris wrote in 1970 to Sheila Doel, daughter of Frank and Nora Doel, "we were treading on clouds. Then the reaction came—with a terrific sock!" They were no longer in their beloved England or America. Like it or not, after years of enjoying the high life in the West, they were back in Poland. Furthermore, they had to adjust to one another again after being separated for nine years.

"Each of us got upset most easily," Morris said. "Our individualities found it painful to accept and respect the desires of the other. At the same time, correspondents from various newspapers abroad continued to bother us . . . and memories of the abnormal and subnormal characters we had daily mingled with continued to spring up afresh night and day."[16]

Morris developed a stomach ulcer, and in the harsh Polish winters he was plagued by bronchitis and rheumatism. Their Polish doctors recommended a long rest for both of them, so for the next two years they relaxed in a series of sanatoriums. In 1972, Morris took a job in Warsaw teaching English to seventeen-year-old Polish kids.

"What about Hemingway?" once of them asked in a brassy voice.

"I pondered a moment," Morris wrote. "Suddenly I recalled that once upon a time I'd been close enough to Hemingway [in Spain] to be able to say something about the man as well as the author. Then their ears pricked up and we were taking the hurdles with mutual interest."

Morris was called to give guest lectures at the KGB training school in Moscow. But he suffered health problems again, this time in a series of heart attacks. Lona had a hard time, too. Sciatica caused her to fall and break her wrist. They were brought to Moscow, and given a small, furnished apartment in the Patriarchy Pond district near the American embassy. Then as they became frail, they were moved to a KGB nursing home.

Konon Molody, too, was treated well upon his return to Russia, at least at first. He was hired as a KGB consultant and was given a big apartment for his family. But then official sentiment turned against him and he was treated shabbily, his son Trofim Molodiy said. (Trofim used the family's ancestral Ukrainian spelling of his surname.)

Moscow Center didn't trust Konon. They bugged his phone and followed him. He was forbidden to talk with other spies he had known. Molody grew further disillusioned with the Soviet system because he was able to judge it by Western standards. He was also angered by the fact that after Michael Goleniewski (Sniper) defected, Moscow Center could have warned him he was in danger. But they didn't.

Molody died October 9, 1970, on a picnic with his family outside Moscow. Trofim said he could not rule out the possibility that the KGB poisoned him.[17] Konon Molody was later honored with his picture on a postage stamp. So was Willie Fisher, his mentor.

Both the Cohens were given the Order of the Red Banner, the top Russian award for valor in combat and for spying during the war. Yuri Andropov, chief of Soviet intelligence, made the presentation. That put the Cohens in the same company as Stalin and Kim Philby. They were also given the title of Heroes of the Russian Federation by the government of Boris Yeltsin. And Morris, too, got his picture on a Russian stamp.

Lona died on December 30, 1992, at the age of seventy-nine, and Morris two years later, on June 23, 1995, at eighty-four. They were buried in the KGB's Novokuntsevo Cemetery, with the words "To Love and To Be Loved" inscribed on Lona's tombstone.

AFTERWORD

A summing up of the Cohens' espionage career might read this way: They were talented, dedicated, worldly spies—an urbane, jet-set couple loyal to their service, and very good at their work. They were blessed with wit and charm, and loyalty to their friends. Most people they met seemed to think they represented the best of America. The Soviets certainly thought so.

But fighting the good fight against Nazis and Fascists was one thing. Choosing to spy against one's own country in the process was quite another. Morris and Lona could not keep their idealism in perspective. They made the conscious decision to devote their lives to working for a political system that was just as evil as the ones they had sworn to defeat.

When the Cohens' controller Willie Fisher went on trial in in 1957 in New York, his lawyer admitted that he was a spy for an enemy power but insisted that he was also a dedicated servant of his country, deserving the same legal compassion as an American agent who might get caught in Russia. And when Konon Molody was tried in London, the court was told that although he was the directing mind in the Portland spy ring, his conduct was not stamped with dishonor. What he did, he did for his country. His arresting officer, Detective Superintendent Smith, admitted that he liked the man.

The Cohens did not receive such an agreeable appraisal. They were branded turncoats by the public, the press, and the governments of Britain, the United States, and Canada. Their treachery had betrayed the entire Western alliance. They were attacked in a torrent of hatred and obloquy. In a word, they were dirty Reds.

But Morris and Lona never saw it that way. They were convinced that during the war, the Soviets hadn't been on the wrong side any more than the British were, or the French. They felt they were just as American as anybody else; that they had not spied to harm their country but to assist a wartime partner in attaining nuclear parity so that a balance of power could be assured and another world war prevented.

This, despite the fact that Morris, as far back as 1954, admitted that Stalin had made certain "mistakes." It wasn't much of a criticism but it was an improvement over the days when the Cohens faithfully defended Uncle Joe at every turn. And their suspicions toward the Soviet system grew as they got older.

"When it comes to freedom, there were certain shortcomings in the Soviet Union," Morris told a KGB interviewer four years before his death. "In the past ten years, life was much more difficult than before. The past ten years revealed a great deal that we did not know about deeply."[1]

"They were politically disillusioned," said Svetlana Chervonnaya, a Russian historian who befriended the Cohens after they went into the KGB nursing home. Chervonnaya heard Lona denounce the Soviet system as "outright totalitarianism."[2]

Still, the Cohens were proud of their role in stealing the secrets of the atomic bomb. They felt they had done the truly dangerous work of traveling across wartime America to recruit assets and pick up stolen documents at a time when people were being pulled off trains and arrested just because they somehow didn't look right. They worked under a shadow of the gallows while Ethel and Julius Rosenberg stayed in New York and served mostly as a conduit for goods brought in by other agents.

David Greenglass, the Rosenbergs, and Klaus Fuchs all made contributions to stealing Allied nuclear secrets, but the Cohens ran the only Soviet network dedicated to atomic spying, and Lona's famous Kleenex box contained Ted Hall's complete diagram of the first A-bomb. That's what Lona meant when she told Chervonnaya the Rosenbergs got the "credit" for stealing the atomic bomb, while the Cohens were overlooked.

The Cohens knew they were historical figures who had pulled off what was undoubtedly one of the most damaging espionage coups of all time. But as their lives drew to a close they came to miss America and their families. It tugged at them like the cry of a sick child.

They tried to regain their American souls. They wanted to be Americans again, to die as Americans, to be buried in America. But the time had long since passed when they could have gone home, under any circumstances. A sister came to visit Lona in the Moscow nursing home, but that was the only contact she had had with her family since she and Morris left New York forty-two years before.

"Am I a traitor?" Lona asked Chervonnaya one day from her hospital bed.

She and Morris both had become obsessed with that word. They spent hours analyzing its nuances. Morris, the dependable intellectual, talked about the relativity of history, how an act denounced as a betrayal might someday be vindicated by history. He wanted someone to write about Lona and himself, or make a film about them, to tell their story once the Cold War was over.

Lona, as always, saw it from the emotional side. On a gray December afternoon as she lay dying of cancer, she again denied she was a traitor. "I didn't kill anybody and I didn't destroy any American life," she told Chervonnaya. "No American soldier died because of what I have done."

But the word stayed with them to the end.

ACKNOWLEDGMENTS

The bibliography lists the major sources I consulted during my research, but I owe special thanks to certain individuals who were of particular assistance. These include my agent, Don Fehr, and his assistant, Brittany Lloyd, at Trident Media, and my editor, Stephen P. Hull at the University Press of New England, all of whom had faith in this project from the very beginning. Rosemary James and Joe DeSalvo at the Faulkner Society in New Orleans were consistent in their support, as were the following: Gail Malmgreen at the Abraham Lincoln Brigade Archives at New York University; David M. Hardy and Dr. John Fox at the Federal Bureau of Investigation; Mike Ballard, Amanda Carlock, Ryan Semmes, John R. Dickerson, Neil Gilbeau, and Dr. Roy H. Ruby at Mississippi State University; and Erin McAfee at Rice University. Invaluable background information came from American historians Dr. Richard Spence, Edward Jay Epstein, J. Mitchell Johnson, Joseph Albright, Gary Kern, Peter N. Carroll, Eugene Michalenko, Paul E. Richardson, and Christopher Marcisz; and in Britain, Ronald Payne, Nigel West, Vin Arthey, and Dr. Roger H. Platt. Jeff Belmont was also of great help, as were Barbara Belmont, Nancy Ambrosiano, John Raughley, Lisa Roper, Matthew Lutts, Tim Davis, Philip Duerden, and Gay Search. Additional thanks go to the UPNE production and promotion team: Ann Brash, Cannon Labrie, Thomas E. Haushalter, Rick Henning, and Sherri L. Strickland.

NOTES

INTRODUCTION. THE LONG TWILIGHT STRUGGLE

1. George Blake KGB interview, *Red Files: Secret Victories of the KGB*, PBS, 1999.

2. Michelle Van Cleave, "Russian Spies Haven't Gone Away," *Wall Street Journal*, April 20, 2012. Van Cleave was chief of U.S. counterintelligence under President George W. Bush.

3. Bernard M. Baruch, *Baruch: The Public Years* (New York: Holt, Rinehart & Winston, 1960), 388.

4. Lenin to Comrades Kuraev, Bosh, Minkin, and other Penza communists, 11/8/18: "You need to hang (hang without fail so that the public sees) at least 100 notorious kulaks, the rich, and the bloodsuckers," *Revelations from the Russian Archives*, online exhibit, Library of Congress, Washington, DC.

5. Dmitri Volkogonov, *Lenin: A New Biography* (New York: Free Press, 1994), 123. Colonel-General Volkogonov, director of the Institute of Military History in Moscow, was the first researcher to gain access to secret party and state archives after the fall of Communism in Russia. But Russian counterintelligence agents as far back as 1917 had collected evidence of Lenin's dealings with Berlin. For photographs of some of the original "German Key" documents, see Edgar Grant Sisson, *The German-Bolshevik Conspiracy* (Washington: United States Committee on Public Information, 1918).

6. The term "soviets" originally referred to strike committees of workers organized during the Russian Revolution of 1905. Soldiers were included in the soviets during the second revolution, in February 1917.

7. A larger expeditionary force invaded Siberia at around the same time as the Archangel landing. The fighting in Siberia lasted longer than it did in Archangel, but the Siberian campaign had little effect on plans to restore the eastern front, which was the primary mission of the AEFNR.

8. Jerome Landfield to Third Assistant Secretary of State Breckenridge Long, July 13, 1918, Long Papers, Box 36, Manuscript Division, Library of Congress. Landfield was a State Department official who had lived in Russia and married a Russian, and apparently translated for Wilson and Botchkareva.

9. "The Russian Expeditions," *The Times History of the War*, vol. 21, chap. 292 (London: The Times, 1920), 155.

10. Letter to the author from Ray Heller, Case Corporation archivist, December 28, 2000.

11. R. H. Bruce Lockhart, *British Agent* (New York: G. P. Putnam's Sons, 1933), 8, 311. This autobiography by Lockhart focuses on his Russian adventures, but the reader should be warned that some of his claims of innocence in the Lenin Plot do not stand up to verification from other sources.

12. Andrew Cook, *On Her Majesty's Secret Service: Sidney Reilly ST1* (Stroud, Gloucestershire: Tempus, 2002), 131. Cook says in his introduction that Ian Fleming told a colleague at the *Sunday Times* that Reilly was the inspiration for the fictional James Bond. But on another occasion, Fleming said Bond was based on Dusko Popov, a British double agent working against the Germans in World War II. Bond's control officer "M" is modeled after "C."

13. Richard Spence, *Trust No One: The Secret World of Sidney Reilly* (Port Townsend WA: Feral House, 2002), xvi. See also Sidney Reilly and Pepita Reilly, *Britain's Master Spy: The Adventures of Sidney Reilly* (London: Dorset, 1985). Reilly's book is a somewhat fanciful "autobiography" that he penned with his last wife. Sidney was subject of a British miniseries, *Reilly, Ace of Spies*, which was also shown on U.S. television.

14. Will Stewart and Glen Owen, "Mystery of Nick Clegg's 'Mata Hari' Aunt and a Plot to Kill Lenin," the *Mail* (London), March 25, 2011. Moura's full name was Maria Ignatievna Zakrevska Benekendorff Budberg. She picked up the baroness title from her discarded second husband. Nick Clegg, a leader of today's Liberal Democratic Party in Britain, is a great-grandson of Moura's sister. Moura was mythologized in the 1934 movie *British Agent*.

15. Richard K. Debo, "Lockhart Plot or Dzerzhinskii Plot?" in the *Journal of Modern History*, 43, no. 3 (1971). Debo, professor of history at Simon Fraser University, says that two Cheka agents using the cover names of Shmidkhen and Bredis approached Reilly and Lockhart to offer assistance in a Moscow coup. Debo says they were sent by Dzerzhinsky and it was a "trap of monumental proportions." Among the sources that Debo cites is V. F. Kravchenko, "Pervye shagi VChK" in *Sovetskoe Gosudarsivo i Pravo* (March 1967), 97–102. Debo's analysis was amplified by Richard Spence, a professor of history at the University of Idaho who has researched elements of the Lenin Plot. Spence said in correspondence with the author that Kalamatiano had been under surveillance for some time and that Dzerzhinsky knew what the Allied plotters were up to.

16. Boris Savinkov, *Memoirs of a Terrorist* (New York: Albert & Charles Boni, 1931), 351. There were reports for years that Savinkov, after escaping from Russia, told friends in Paris that he had given the pistol to Fanny Kaplan. Joseph Shaplen, Savinkov's translator, verifies the Paris reports.

17. Author's conversation with a former KGB officer, February 1990.

18. Alexander Orlov, *The March of Time: Reminiscences* (London: St. Ermin's, 2004), 134. Orlov also seems to believe that Savinkov was behind Kaplan's shooting of Lenin. See p. 132 for his analysis of that.

19. Sergey Kobyakov, "Red Justice: How Soviet Russia's Secret Police Suppress the Foes of Bolshevism," *McClure's Magazine* 55, no. 22 (1923). Kobyakov was one of the defense attorneys at Kalamatiano's trial.

1. SECURITY MATTER C

1. Morris and Lona Cohen FBI file 100–406659, obtained through the Freedom of Information Act. Many of the details of the FBI's investigation of the Cohens, including interviews with people who knew them in the United States, are drawn from this file.

2. Senate Subcommittee of the Committee on the Judiciary, *Brewing and Liquor Interests and German Propaganda Hearings*, 65th Congress, January 21, 1919 (Washington: Government Printing Office, 1919), 2680.

3. "The Soviet Role in the Korean War," Central Intelligence Agency, top-secret summary of December 19, 1951, www.cia.gov.

4. Socialist Workers Party v. Atty. Gen. of US, 463 F, Supp. 515 (SDNY, 1978), filed December 15, 1978, lawjustia.com. In a deposition he gave in this case, Baxtrum admitted to between fifty and ninety burglaries against the SWP. Four or five agents would break into an office, he said, while five or six other agents remained outside on watch.

5. Courtland J. Jones, interview by Stanley A. Pimentel, February 8, 2008, Society of Former Special Agents of the FBI Inc., www.nleomf.org.

6. Author's conversation with a former reporter for the *Evening Star* (Washington, DC), December 2002.

7. Carlton C. Lenz, interview by John C. McAvoy, June 26, 2003, Society of Former Special Agents of the FBI Inc.

2. STUDENT RADICAL

1. The term "pushcart" refers to the wheeled carts from which fruit, ice cream, hot dogs, and snowballs were sold on the street. Sanitation crews armed with shovels and brooms also used pushcarts in cleaning streets.

2. Vladimir Tchikov and Gary Kern, *Comment Staline a volé la bombe atomique aux Américains: Dossier KGB No. 13676.* (Paris: Editions Robert Lafont, 1996), 107. Former KGB Col. Tchikov (Chikov) and U.S. historian Kern were given access to the Cohens' personnel files and a Soviet interview with them before their deaths.

3. The CPUSA closely guarded its membership rolls, but according to Morris and Lona Cohen's FBI file, Harry and Sarah Cohen were registered to vote in New York as Communists. Jack Bjoze, when interviewed for *Red Files*, said: "Morris came from a background, well, that is to say, his parents were communists. . . . They were involved in activities in the old country, and I suppose it rubbed off on Morris." Bjoze, like Cohen, was from the Bronx and fought in Spain. He was one of the spotters who recommended Cohen for Soviet spy work. Also, Joseph Albright and Marcia Kunstel in *Bombshell: The Secret Story of America's Unknown Atomic Spy Conspiracy* (New York: Times Books, 1997), 26, quote a Cohen family member as saying: "Moishe got communism as his mother's milk."

4. Hank Greenberg, *The Story of My Life* (New York: Times Books, 1989), 6.

5. Boria Sax interview, "Family of Spies," *NOVA: Secrets, Lies and Atomic Spies,* PBS, 2002.

6. Edward Lending to the *New Republic*, Washington, 1991, Lending Papers, Abraham Lincoln Brigade Archives, Tamiment Library, New York University. Lending's

comments regarding Morris Cohen in both New York and Spain are drawn from this unpublished letter to the magazine.

7. Greenberg, *The Story of My Life*, 7.

8. "Affable 'Unc' Cohen's Arrest Amazes His Acquaintances," *Commercial Appeal* (Memphis, TN), February 12, 1961.

9. Back issues of the *Reflector*, the Mississippi State student newspaper, are a good guide to what life was like in Starkville and on campus in those days.

10. "Mississippi State Confirms London Spy is Ex-Student," *Commercial Appeal*, February 13, 1961.

11. *Reveille* (Starkville: Mississippi State College, 1934), 155. University Archives, Special Collections Department, Mississippi State University Libraries.

12. "Building a Militant Student Movement: Program and Constitution of the National Student League" (New York: National Student League, 1934), Internet Archive, www.archive.org.

13. *Champaign and Urbana City Directory, 1937* (Champaign-Urbana: Flanigan-Pearson Co., 1937), Internet Archive, www.archive.org.

14. "6 Chicagoans Held, Suspected of Plan for Holdups Here," *Daily Illini*, University of Illinois, November 3, 1935, Illinois Digital Newspaper Collections, www.idnc.library.illinois.edu.

15. "Sachar Attacks 'War Interests,'" *Daily Illini*, October 11, 1935.

16. "Students Stage Own Pep Session, Crash Theater," *Daily Illini*, November 9, 1935.

17. "Police Corral Baby Rioters in Carle Park," *Daily Illini*, October 24, 1935.

18. "Voice Demands for Peace in U. of I. Meet," *Evening Courier* (Champaign, IL), November 12, 1935, IDNC.

19. After the NSL and the SLID merged to form the American Student Union in December 1935, Eleanor Roosevelt became one of the ASU's most energetic supporters, and a close friend of Joe Lash's. In later years Lash described himself as having been a full-time revolutionary in the thirties before he became a newspaperman. He went on to write a biography of the first lady, *Eleanor and Franklin*, which won a Pulitzer Prize in 1971. The American Student League died after Communists in the group pushed through a platform of official support for Russia's nonaggression and friendship treaties with Germany in 1939.

20. "Negro Students Sponsor Plan for Co-Operative Restaurant on Non-Discrimination Basis," *Daily Illini*, December 11, 1935; "Plan to Launch Eating Project," *Daily Illini*, December 13, 1935.

21. Tchikov and Kern, *Comment Staline*, 288–89.

3. SPAIN CALLING

1. New York Public Library to the author, January 11, 2010.

2. "Personal questionnaire of Morris Cohen," Historical Commission of the International Brigades, Mackenzie-Papineau Battalion, Albacete, Spain, August 1937, Morris Cohen file, ALBA.

3. "Confidential report on Edward Isaac Lending (aka Isaac Edward Lending)," U.S. War Department, Governor's Island, N.Y., August 18, 1943, National Archives

and Records Administration, FOIA; report on Lending from the Office of Camp Intelligence Officer, Camp Hullen, Texas, April 28, 1943, NARA, FOIA.

4. Rose Chernin, "Organizing the Unemployed in the Bronx in the 1930s," *History Is a Weapon*, www.historyisaweapon.com. Rose (née Rochele) Chernin was a Jewish immigrant from Russia who joined the CPUSA in 1932 and worked as an organizer in the Bronx. The government tried to deport her but the judge freed her, and in a landmark decision ruled the Smith Act unconstitutional. She wrote this reminiscence in 1949. For more on Chernin, see the Jewish Women's Archive, www.jwa.org.

5. *Wichita Eagle*, June 30, 1936, and the *Topeka Capital*, September 1936, Kansas State Historical Society, www.kshs.org.

6. Hugh Thomas, *The Spanish Civil War* (New York: Harper & Brothers, 1961), 142, 168. Baron Thomas, a British historian, quotes Spanish journalist Ramón J. Sender as saying that through mid-1938, 750,000 died by executions alone, and that was just in Nationalist Spain. Other sources he cited include the Madrid Council of Lawyers and the English Catholic College at Valladolid. Even accounting for exaggeration by partisan observers, the toll was high, considering that many deaths went unreported.

7. W. G. Krivitsky, *In Stalin's Secret Service* (New York: Enigma Books, 2000), 66, 70, 74, 76. Walter Krivitsky was chief of Soviet Military Intelligence (OGPU) in Western Europe and was one of Stalin's primary organizers of Russian intervention in Spain.

8. Earl Browder interview, radio station WTHT, Hartford, Connecticut, reported in *New Masses*, October 20, 1936.

9. Ed Lending FBI file 100–28887, FOIA.

10. Joseph J. Thorndike Jr., "'Cap' Rieber," *Life*, July 1, 1940, 57–68. Torkild Rieber, chairman of Texaco, sold $6 million in oil to Franco from 1936 to 1938, while supplying none to the Loyalists. That's nearly a billion in today's dollars. Rieber was a former sailor who ruled Texaco from his office in the Chrysler Building in New York. He was forced out of Texaco in 1940 because of his dealings with Nazi Germany and Fascist Italy.

4. DANGEROUS CROSSING

1. "98 Writers Score Spanish Rebels," *New York Times*, March 1, 1937.

2. "70,000 Here Mark Orderly May Day," *New York Daily Worker*, May 2, 1937.

3. "30% of U.S. Fighters for Loyalists Lost," *New York Times*, May 18, 1937.

4. "Personal questionnaire of Morris Cohen," Historical Commission of the International Brigades," ALBA.

5. This account of the rally is drawn from the *Daily Worker* of July 19, 20, and 21, 1937, and the *New York Times* of July 20, 1937.

6. Roger N. Baldwin, "Freedom in the U.S.A. and the U.S.S.R.," *Soviet Russia Today*, 1934, www.law.ucla.edu. Baldwin later renounced his Stalinist sympathies and purged the ACLU of Communists. President Jimmy Carter awarded him the Medal of Freedom in 1981.

7. Vladimir Chikov, "How the Soviet Intelligence Service 'Split' the American Atom," *New Times* (Moscow, Moskovskaya Pravda Press), no. 17, (1991), 36. Chikov quotes from the memoirs of Morris and Lona Cohen on file at Moscow Center.

8. Ibid.

9. Morris and Lona Cohen FBI file.

10. Senate Subcommittee to Investigate the Administration of the Internal Security Act and other Internal Security Laws of the Committee on the Judiciary, "Legend of U.S. Veterans of the International Brigade," *Scope of Soviet Activity in the United States Hearings*, 85th Congress, February 20, 1957 (Washington: GPO), A33.

11. Elizabeth Bentley, *Out of Bondage: The Story of Elizabeth Bentley* (New York: Devin-Adair, 1951), 94–95.

12. Ronald Liversedge, *A Memoir of the Spanish Civil War* (Cowichan Lake BC, 1966). Liversedge was a Canadian Communist who served with Morris Cohen in Spain. Unless noted otherwise, the account of the Mackenzie-Papineau's service in Spain in this and in succeeding chapters is based on his unpublished typescript, courtesy of the University of British Columbia Library, and on Cohen documents at ALBA.

13. Tchikov and Kern, *Comment Staline*, 289.

5. THE ELITE OF THE INTERNATIONALS

1. Richard Wright, *Pagan Spain* (New York: HarperPerennial, 1995), 7. Wright was an African American from Mississippi who joined, then rejected, the CPUSA before settling permanently in Paris as an expatriate writer.

2. Alexander Orlov, *The March of Time: Reminiscences* (London: St. Ermin's Press, 2004), 325–26. Orlov wrote that his marching orders from the NKVD were to organize an efficient intelligence service for the Loyalists and direct guerrilla training. He denied he was there to set up an NKVD operation.

3. Pavel Sudoplatov and Anatoli Sudoplatov with Jerrold L. and Leona P. Schecter, *Special Tasks: The Memoirs of an Unwanted Witness—A Soviet Spymaster* (New York: Little Brown, 1994), 45. Pavel Sudoplatov was in charge of special NKVD assignments such as the assassination of Trotsky.

4. John Costello and Oleg Tsarev, *Deadly Illusions* (London: Century Random House, 1993), 267. This book about Orlov's career was written by British historian Costello and former KGB First Directorate officer Tsarev.

5. Thomas, *The Spanish Civil War*, 777.

6. Ernest Hemingway, *For Whom the Bell Tolls* (New York: Charles Scribner's Sons, 1940), 419. Salvarsan (arsphenamine) was a treatment for syphilis before penicillin.

7. Philip Knightley, *The First Casualty: The War Correspondent as Hero and Myth-Maker from the Crimea to Iraq* (Baltimore: Johns Hopkins University Press, 2004), 231. Knightley is an Australian who was a special correspondent for the *Sunday Times* for twenty years and has authored several books on espionage and military matters. About Marty's kill claim of 500, Knightley writes: "Others would multiply that by five or even ten."

8. Hemingway, *For Whom the Bell Tolls*, 417.

9. Marion Merriman and Warren Lerude, *American Commander in Spain: Robert Hale Merriman and the Abraham Lincoln Brigade* (Reno: University of Nevada Press, 1986), 69. This chapter's account of Merriman's service in the civil war is based on recollections by his widow Marion, who was with her husband in Spain. Merriman went missing and was never heard from again, presumed to have been captured and executed by the Nationalists.

10. Morris Cohen to Jack Diamond, undated, Morris Cohen file, ALBA.

11. Edward Lending to the *New Republic*.

12. James Neuglass, "On the Road," *Salud! Poems, Stories and Sketches of Spain by American Writers* (New York: International Publishers, 1938), 12.

6. CODE NAME LUIS

1. Edward Lending to the *New Republic*.

2. Oscar Hunter to Services Sanitaires des Brigades Internationales, Sanatorio Quirúrgico de San Carlos, undated, Morris Cohen file, ALBA.

3. Jack Bjoze interview, *Red Files*.

4. Communist Party of Spain, Central Committee, Barcelona, to Comintern, Moscow, November 14, 1938, Comintern Archives, Fond 545, opus 6, delo 874, 100, Morris Cohen file, ALBA.

5. Orlov, *The March of Time*, 283–84, 293.

6. Tchikov and Kern, *Comment Staline*, 116–17. Orlov didn't mention Cohen in his published writings, so a corroborative account of this conversation is not available.

7. The tradecraft Orlov taught in Spain is described in his book, *Handbook of Intelligence and Guerrilla Warfare* (Ann Arbor: University of Michigan Press, 1963). Orlov says in his preface that this book is a recreation of a 1936 manual he wrote in Moscow. Orlov reportedly produced this U.S. version at the request of the CIA.

8. A. A. Konovalov and V. S. Sokolov, "Meetings with Agents," from a top-secret paper issued in 1960 by the Military-Diplomatic Academy of the Soviet Army, Department of Special Training, released by the CIA Center for the Study of Intelligence, www.cia.gov.

9. Victor Hoar, *The Mackenzie-Papineau Battalion* (Chicago: Copp Clark, 1969), 229.

7. VOLUNTEER ACTIVATED

1. Edward Lending to the *New Republic*.

2. "The Rise and Fall of 'Joe the Worker'" in *Biblion: the Boundless Library*, online exhibit of the New York Public Library, www.exhibitions.nypl.org

3. Pavel P. Klarin (Pastelnyak) FBI File 65–16825, Foreign Official Status Notification filed with the U.S. State Department, January 2, 1941, FOIA.

4. "Ford Plants Expel 51 Russian Experts, *New York Times*, October 19, 1939.

5. "Declares Russia 'Raids' U.S. Patents," *New York Times*, March 5, 1947.

6. John Earl Haynes, Harvey Klehr, and Alexander Vassiliev, *Spies: The Rise and Fall of the KGB in America* (New Haven: Yale University Press, 2009), xxx. Vassiliev was recruited into Soviet intelligence while he was a journalism student at Moscow State University. "The vetting process started," he wrote, "and I was 'clean': no Jews in either my background or my wife's. . . ."

7. Sherman W. Fleming, "Soviet Intelligence Training," CIA Center for the Study of Intelligence (Washington, 1995), www.cia.gov.

8. Report by Semen Semenov (Semyonov) to P. Fitin on his work, November 1944, "Vassiliev White Notebook #1," 209, in History and Public Policy Program Digital Archives, Alexander Vassiliev Papers, Manuscript Division, Library of Congress, 2009, www.digitalarchives.wilsoncenter.org.

9. Station One to Viktor at Moscow Center, undated, Cohen KGB File 13676, in Tchikov and Kern, *Comment Staline*, 105.

10. Joseph Albright and Marcia Kunstel, *Bombshell: The Secret Story of America's Unknown Atomic Spy Conspiracy* (New York: Times Books, 1997), 47. The authors were journalists in Moscow who interviewed a number of Russians and Americans who had known the Cohens before their deaths.

11. Lona Cohen interview in Chikov, "How the Soviet Intelligence Service," 37.

8. GHOULS AND DEAD DOUBLES

1. Eugene Michalenko and Ed Driscoll, "The Spy Who Lived Here," and John A. Bond, "Soviet Espionage and a Polish Girl from Adams," *Adams Historical Society Newsletter* (Adams, MA) 10, no. 7 (October 1983).

2. George Blake interview, *Red Files*.

3. Jack Bjoze interview, *Red Files*.

4. Some spy terms date back a hundred years and it's difficult to pinpoint their origin. Christopher Andrew, in his authorized history of MI5, *The Defence of the Realm* (London: Allen Lane, 2009), 486, refers to the Cohens' London control officer as having acquired a "dead double" passport in Canada in the fifties. In correspondence with the author, British spy historian Nigel West said the process of searching graveyards for dates of death is called "tombstoning" in the UK. For additional spy terms, see the "Language of Espionage" at the website of the International Spy Museum in Washington, www.spymuseum.org.

5. "Conspiracy to Act as Unregistered Agents of a Foreign Government, Violation of 18 USC §§ 371, 1956" federal charges filed June 28, 2010, www.justice.gov.

6. John J. Kearney, interview by Jack O'Flaherty, January 25, 2006, Society of Former Agents of the FBI.

7. John Edgar Hoover, "Present Status of Espionage and Counterespionage Operations of the Federal Bureau of Investigation, October 24, 1940," FBI, FOIA.

8. Chikov, "How the Soviet Intelligence Service," 37.

9. Svetlana Chervonnaya KGB interview, *Red Files*. Chervonnaya is a Russian historian who befriended the Cohens toward the end of their lives in Moscow.

10. "History of Russian Foreign Intelligence," Foreign Intelligence Service of the Russian Federation, svr.gov.ru.

11. Chikov, "How the Soviet Intelligence Service."

12. Alexander Feklisov and Sergei Kostin, *The Man Behind the Rosenbergs* (New York: Enigma Books, 2001), 82–85.

13. Albright and Kunstel, *Bombshell*, 49.

14. "Agent Network," February 1, 1945, KGB File 40594, vol. 7, 21–22, Vassiliev, *Black Notebook*, 120.

15. "History of Russian Foreign Intelligence," Foreign Intelligence Service of the Russian Federation, www.svr.gov.ru.

9. THE AGENT WHO NEVER WAS

1. Morris and Lona Cohen FBI file.

2. Accounts of Morris Cohen's service in North America and Europe are drawn from: Adjutant General, U.S. Army, "Historical Record, 3233d Quartermaster Service Company," NARA; Massachusetts National Guard, "Camp Edwards History," www .states.ng.mil; and Kenneth H. Brownell, "Historic Narrative of 3233rd Quartermaster Service Company (Company C, 241st Qm Battalion)," www.jraughley.com.

3. Morris and Lona Cohen FBI file.

4. Dorthea Calverley, "The Dawson Creek Disaster, February 13, 1943: A Personal Account of the Explosion and Fire," www.calverley.ca. This chapter's account of the fire is drawn from her first-person account.

5. Gus W. Weiss, "The Farewell Dossier," CIA Center for the Study of Intelligence, www.cia.gov. "Farewell" was Colonel Vladimir I. Vetrov, a KGB officer who photographed Soviet documents for French intelligence.

6. Semyonov to Fitkin, circa 1944, KGB file 40129, vol. 3a, 212–13, Vassiliev, *White Notebook #1,* 112–13, LOC.

7. William Wolfe Weisband FBI File 121–13210, FOIA; Weisband in Central Intelligence Agency reports, CIA Center for the Study of Intelligence, www.cia.gov.

8. William Wolfe Weisband FBI file.

9. Robert L. Benson and John R. Schindler, "LINK: The Greatest Intelligence Disaster in U.S. History," presentation at the National Security Agency Cryptologic History Symposium, October 31, 2003, NSA, FOIA.

10. William Wolfe Weisband FBI file.

11. William Weisband Jr. interview, *NOVA Online: Secrets, Lies and Atomic Spies,* PBS.

10. A BALANCE OF TERROR

1. Morris and Lona Cohen FBI file.

2. Joan Hall, "A Memoir of Ted Hall," History Happens, www.historyhappens.net, via www.web.archive.org. Mrs. Hall wrote this memoir in 2003.

3. "Family of Spies." Boria Sax talks at length about his father.

4. Richard Rhodes, *The Making of the Atomic Bomb* (New York: Simon and Schuster, 1986), 566–67. Rhodes quotes Robert Wilson, Cyclotron Program group leader, as saying that military police tried to close that particular dormitory. But after a "tearful group of young ladies" from the dorm appealed to the army, and were supported by a "determined group of bachelors," the matter was dropped.

5. Joan Hall, "A Memoir of Ted Hall."

6. Ibid.

7. Boria Sax, "The Boy Who Gave Away the Bomb," *New York Times Magazine,* October 5, 1997.

8. "History of Russian Foreign Intelligence," svr.gov.ru, ibid.

9. Boria Sax interview, "Family of Spies."

10. "New York to Moscow Center, BEK's report on Theodore Hall, 7 December 1944," KGB File 82702, vol. 1, 287–89, Vassiliev, *Yellow Notebook #1,* 19–22, LOC.

11. Boris Sax interview, "Family of Spies." Boria doesn't give the date this poem was written, but Savy was an active poet at the time he was Ted Hall's courier. According to Boria, Savy and Ted used a communication code based on Walt Whitman's "Leaves of Grass." Boria Sax is an author and a literature professor at Mercy College and the University of Illinois.

11. MISSION TO ALBUQUERQUE

1. Anonymous to Hoover, undated, received August 7, 1943, www.permanent.access .gpo.gov.

2. Sudoplatov and Sudoplatov, *Special Tasks*, 215.

3. Anatoli Yakovlev FBI File 100–81002, FOIA.

4. Bentley, *Out of Bondage*, 145–48.

5. Albright and Kunstel, *Bombshell*, 134.

6. This chapter's account of Lona's mission to Albuquerque is based on interviews the Cohens gave to the KGB before their deaths, as reported by Tchikov and Kern in chapter 4 of *Comment Staline*. Some details of Lona's trip were confirmed in the interview Morris Cohen gave to the KGB after Lona's death, as broadcast in *Red Files* on PBS. Lona might have made an earlier run to New Mexico in 1945, but reports of such a trip are sketchy and conflicting.

7. "Report on the Trinity Test by General Groves, Memorandum to the Secretary of War, July 18, 1945," www.atomicarchive.com. Groves apparently read the blind woman story in the *Albuquerque Journal*. The Associated Press picked it up and sent it to newspapers all over America, after which it was exaggerated. In 1993, Rolf Sinclair of the National Science Foundation identified the woman as Georgia Green, of Socorro, New Mexico, an eighteen-year-old university student in 1945. Green died before Sinclair could interview her, but her sister and brother-in-law said that she had been only partially blind and could distinguish light. The family was in a car when Green saw the flash. But she was more alarmed by the heat of the explosion on her face. That's when she said, "What's that?" See Rolf Sinclair, "The Blind Girl Who Saw the Flash of the First Nuclear Weapon Test," *Skeptical Inquirer*, 18 (1993): 63–67.

8. Michael Dobbs, "How Soviets Stole U.S. Atom Secrets: Ex-Kremlin Agent Reveals Unknown Spy in '40's Effort," *Washington Post*, October 4, 1992.

12. ALL NETWORKS BLOWN

1. Tchikov and Kern, *Comment Staline*, 296.

2. "Notes by Harry S. Truman on the Potsdam Conference, July 17–30, 1945, President's Secretary's File, Truman Papers," 5, Harry S. Truman Library and Museum, www.trumanlibrary.org, NARA.

3. Earl F. Ziemke, "Winter, the Season of Despair," chap. 23 in *The U.S. Army in the Occupation of Germany, 1944–1946*, (Washington, DC: U.S. Army Center of Military History, 1990), www.globalsecurity.org.

4. Nikolai Tolstoy, "Forced Repatriation to the Soviet Union: The Secret Betrayal," *Imprimis* (Hillsdale, MI: Hillsdale College), December 1988, www.fortfreedom.org.

5. Unless otherwise noted, details of the Gouzenko defection are drawn from "The CORBY Case: The Defection of Igor Gouzenko, September 1945," British Secret Intelligence Service (MI6), www.sis.gov.uk; and from a Canadian white paper, "The Report of the Royal Commission to Investigate the Facts Relating to the Circumstances Surrounding the Communication, by Public Officials and Other Persons in Positions of Trust, of Secret and Confidential Information to Agents of a Foreign Power, June 27, 1946," www.historyofrights.com.

6. Chester Frowde interview in John Sawatsky's *Gouzenko: The Untold Story* (Toronto: Macmillan, 1984), 22.

7. Cecil Bayfield interview, Sawatsky, *Gouzenko*, 34.

8. S. T. Wood to Norman Robertson, September 10, 1945, Library and Archives Canada. Wood was commissioner of the RCMP. In this report to the undersecretary for external affairs, he stated that protecting an individual in danger was the responsibility of the Ottawa police, not the RCMP.

9. Journalists and historians have spelled Nunn May's given name in two ways, as Alan and as Allan. Government documents at the British National Archives at Kew refer to him as Alan. See Records of the Cabinet Office, Agenda 1, February 17, 1959, www.nationalarchives.gov.uk.

10. John Edgar Hoover to Brigadier General Harry Hawkins Vaughan, November 8, 1945, FBI, FOIA. Hawkins was military aide to President Truman.

11. Unless otherwise indicated, these details of Elizabeth Bentley's life and her spy career for the Soviets are drawn from her confession of November 8, 1945, found in Silvermaster File 65–56402, FBI, FOIA; and the NKVD "Autobiography of Elizabeth Terrill Bentley" in Vassiliev's *White Notebook #2*, 212–85.

12. Message from X re M's work, 7.12.44, Vassiliev, *White Notebook #2*, 288.

13. Vadim to Center, November 27, 1945, Vassiliev, *White Notebook #2*, 33.

14. Yatskov, *The Man Behind the Rosenbergs*, 74–75.

13. A GRAVE SITUATION

1. J. Edgar Hoover to A. H. Belmont, December 7, 1940, in Alan Harden Belmont personnel file, FBI, FOIA. The account of Belmont's life and career are drawn from this file and from interviews with family members.

2. "Roger 'The Terrible' Touhy's Gang," *Famous Cases and Criminals*, www.fbi.gov.

3. "Colepaugh and Gimpel," in *Counterintelligence in World War II*, chap. 1, National Counterintelligence Center of the Federation of American Scientists, www.fas.org.

4. Louis De Rochement's film, *The House on 92nd Street* (1945) was based on the Duquesne spy case. It was made with the cooperation of the FBI and shows CI techniques in use at the time, including two-way surveillance mirrors and spectrographs for analyzing colors such as those left by lipstick traces.

5. G. A. Nease to Belmont, September 19 and 20, 1946, Belmont FBI file.

6. Ben Franklin High was later shut down as a failed school, then reopened in 1982 as the Manhattan Center for Science and Mathematics.

7. Feklisov, *The Man Behind the Rosenbergs*, 66, 99.

8. Sam Roberts, *The Brother: The Untold Story of Atomic Spy David Greenglass and How He Sent His Sister, Ethel Rosenberg, to the Electric Chair* (New York: Random

House, 2001), 176–77. Roberts, a journalist, based this book on conversations with Greenglass.

9. David G. Major interview, *Red Files*. Major is a retired FBI supervisory agent and founder of the Centre for Counterintelligence and Security Studies.

10. Center to Claude, 19.04.48, Vassiliev, *Black Notebook*, 107. Claude was Yuri Sokolov, the Cohens' control officer after Yatskov.

11. Center to Claude, 27.04.48, Vassiliev, *Black Notebook*, 118.

12. Charles Runyon to D. Rhoades, May 19, 1952, RG 59, NND 832933, Central Decimal File, 1950–54, Box 3814, Tab 13, NARA, FOIA; and CIA Supplement to Checklist of Soviet Officials Abroad, 1957, RG19, Boxes 1260 and 2624, NARA, FOIA. Runyon was acting assistant legal adviser for United Nations Affairs of the U.S. State Department. He wrote to Rhoades, a New York attorney, regarding fifty-eight copies of an industrial directory that Sokolov had ordered but not paid for. Industrial directories are a good example of open intelligence that can be acquired legally.

13. Center to Claude, 19.04.48, Vassiliev, *Black Notebook*, 127.

14. Center to Bob, 5.10.48, Vassiliev, *Black Notebook*, 208. Bob was Boris Mikhailovich Krotov, an intelligence officer at Station One.

15. Center to Bob, 5.10.48, Vassiliev, *Black Notebook*, 209.

16. Center to Bob, 5.10.48, Vassiliev, *Black Notebook*, 211. Hall and Sax were later reactivated by the Soviets, for a while, but had nothing to offer on the scale of the product they turned in from Los Alamos in 1945.

14. AGENTS ON THE RUN

1. Unless otherwise noted, information on Willie Fisher in this chapter is drawn from Vin Arthey's biography, *Like Father Like Son: A Dynasty of Spies* (London: St. Ermin's Press, 2004); and from "Famous Cases: Rudolph Ivanovich Abel," FBI History, www.fbi.gov. Although the FBI spelled the given name as Rudolph, Willie Fisher in a letter to his attorney used the Rudolf form. See James B. Donovan, *Strangers On a Bridge: The Case of Colonel Abel* (New York: Antheneum, 1964), 427.

2. Gordon Lonsdale, *Spy: Twenty Years in Soviet Secret Service* (New York: Hawthorn Books, 1965), 50. Gordon Lonsdale was the cover name used by Konon Molody in London when he worked with the Cohens. In this book he identifies Fisher by his code name, Alec.

3. Lamphere to Gardner, "'Emile Julius Klaus Fuchs, Karl Fuchs,' September 26, 1949," FBI, FOIA. Meredith Gardner was one of the top cryptanalysts working on Venona.

4. Rhodes, *The Making of the Atomic Bomb*, 650.

5. "Meeting between 'Gus' and 'Rest'; work on Enormous, February 9, 1944," Venona translation, www.mi5.gov.uk.

6. Lamphere to Gardner, "'Emile Julius Klaus Fuchs, Karl Fuchs.'"

7. Unless otherwise noted, information in this chapter regarding Fuchs's background and spy work comes from the confession he gave to FBI special agents Hugh H. Clegg and Robert J. Lamphere, and British Security Service officer William J. Skardon, at Wormwood Scrubbs Prison, London, May 26, 1950, FBI, FOIA.

8. Norman Moss, *Klaus Fuchs: The Man Who Stole the Atom Bomb* (New York: St. Martin's Press, 1987), 133. Journalist and broadcaster Moss quotes an interview with

Skardon as published in Peter Deely's *Beyond Breaking Point: A Study in the Techniques of Interrogation* (London: Hodder & Stoughton, 1979).

9. "Klaus Fuchs" in *The Cold War*, The Security Service, www.MI5.gov.uk.

10. "Abe Brothman" in Julius Rosenberg FBI File 100–365040, www.fbi.gov.

11. "Harry Gold" in Julius Rosenberg et al FBI file 65–57449, www.vault.fbi.gov. Details of Harry Gold's life and spy career are based on statements he gave the FBI.

12. Details of the David Greenglass case are drawn from documents in "Rosenberg Case Summary, Sept 25, 1963," FBI, FOIA.

13. Dwight D. Eisenhower to John Eisenhower, June 16, 1953, in Dwight David Eisenhower Diary, December 1952–July 1953 (2), Box 3, Dwight David Eisenhower Diary Series, Eisenhower Presidential Library and Museum, Abilene, Kansas.

14. Albright and Kunstel, *Bombshell*, 4–6.

15. Ibid.

16. Jack Bjoze interview, *Red Files*.

17. Morris Cohen interview, *Red Files*.

15. WHISPERS OF SUSPICION

1. An Old Etonian is a revered English cocktail made with one part gin, one part Kina Lillet, two dashes of orange bitters, and one dash of Crème de Noyaux, shaken with ice, and strained into a stemmed glass

2. Perle Mesta (née Pearl Skirvin) was a wealthy heiress from Michigan who was famous for giving fabulous parties in Washington. She was a member of the National Woman's Party and an early supporter of an equal rights amendment. President Truman appointed her ambassador to Luxembourg, where she amplified her reputation as "the hostess with the mostest." Her international soirées remained popular throughout the fifties and into the Kennedy years.

3. Baroness Edith Summerskill was a London physician and early advocate of women's rights in Britain. She was a committed socialist and at one time was chair of the Labour Party. She served in the House of Commons and then the House of Lords, 1938–1980.

4. Nancy Banks-Smith, "All Sweetness and Spies in Ruislip," *Guardian* (London), November 19, 1991.

5. Unless otherwise indicated, the details of Operation Whisper and the resulting trial, as related in this and succeeding chapters, are taken from first-person accounts published in the following books: Peter Wright with Paul Greenglass, *Spycatcher: The Candid Autobiography of a Senior Intelligence Officer* (New York: Viking, 1987); Norman Lucas, *Spycatcher: The Biography of the Late Detective Superintendent George Smith* (London: W. H. Allen, 1973); Gordon Lonsdale, *Spy: Twenty Years in Soviet Secret Service* (New York: Hawthorn Books, 1965); and Harry Houghton, *Operation Portland: The Autobiography of a Spy* (London: Rupert Hart-Davis, 1972). Also, trial testimony was consulted, as published in March 1961 by these London newspapers: the *Guardian*, the *Times*, the *Sunday Times*, the *Observer*, and the *Independent*.

6. Ted Shackley with Richard A. Finney, *Spymaster: My Life in the CIA* (Dulles VA: Potomac Books, 2005), 26.

7. John Bulloch and Henry Miller, *Spy Ring: The Full Story of the Naval Secrets Case* (London: Secker & Warburg, 1961), 125.

8. George Blake, *No Other Choice: An Autobiography* (New York: Simon and Shuster, 1990), 213.

16. HOUSE OF SECRETS

1. "Spies, Lies, and a Play That Slips Up," *Standard* (London), December 2, 1983. Investigative reporter Keith Dovkants interviewed MI5 sources who contradicted an earlier version of the Ruislip stakeout that said that Security Service watchers had seen Gordon Lonsdale enter the Kroger house before the surveillance was set up at the Search home.

2. Gay Search, "First Person," *Times*, October 21, 1983. Search, a BBC television presenter, describes the MI5 stakeout in her parents' Ruislip home.

3. Kingsley Amis published *The James Bond Dossier* (London: Jonathan Cape, 1965) the year after Snelling's book came out.

4. O. F. Snelling, *Rare Books and Rarer People: Some Personal Reminiscences of "The Trade"* (London: Werner Shaw, 1982), 206.

5. Author's correspondence with author and former *Sunday Telegraph* war correspondent Ronald Payne in London. He described himself as "Freddie Snelling's greatest admirer."

6. Bulloch and Miller, *Spy Ring*, 30.

7. Peter Kroger to Winnie, August 20, 1968, letter from prison, courtesy of the Imperial War Museum, London. Winifred Myers was a London friend of the Cohens.

8. Donovan, *Strangers On a Train*, 33. James B. Donovan was Fisher's court-appointed attorney after his arrest. He was a former naval intelligence officer, and charged no fee for his services. He wanted to show the Soviets that an enemy spy could get a fair trial in the United States, and he appealed Fisher's conviction all the way to the Supreme Court. Donovan is portrayed by Tom Hanks in the 2015 Steven Spielberg film *Bridge of Spies*.

9. Morris and Lona Cohen FBI file.

17. LOCK, STOCK, AND BARREL

1. Robert J. Lamphere and Tom Shactman, *The FBI-KGB War: A Special Agent's Story* (New York: Random House, 1986), 244.

2. Peter Wright, Arthur Martin, and others in MI5 pursued their suspicions of Hollis for years, based on several other points besides Sir Roger's approval of Fuchs. One was that when Hollis went to Canada in 1945 to debrief Igor Gouzenko, he was told about a Soviet mole in British intelligence code-named Elli, but did not report it. Another charge was that while he was in China as a young man, Hollis mixed with Agnes Smedley, a left-wing journalist and Comintern talent scout. "Every man is defined by his friends," Wright insisted. After Hollis retired, he was called back to MI5 for an interrogation by several officers, including Wright. But the evidence was circumstantial and no smoking gun was found. Hollis denied all allegations and the investigation ended without a conclusion that satisfied either side in the matter. See Wright, *Spycatcher*, 285, 288–90.

3. The term "Moonraker," so the story went, referred to some smugglers in Wiltshire

who had hidden contraband barrels of French brandy in a pond and were trying to retrieve them one night with rakes when revenue agents appeared. The lads acted dumb. They pointed to a reflection of the moon on the water and claimed they were raking in a big yellow cheese. The revenue agents dismissed them as stupid yokels and moved on.

4. Obituary of Charles Elwell, *Telegraph* (London), January 22, 2008.

5. Helene Hanff, *The Duchess of Bloomsbury Street* (New York: Avon, 1973), 40.

6. In England, the term "public school" refers to private, expensive, independent schools such as Eton that prepare students for college or public service.

7. Author's correspondence with Nigel West, British espionage historian and former BBC documentarian. Arthur Martin was West's mentor.

8. Harold Jackson, "Set a Spy to Catch a Spy," *Guardian*, January 19, 1999.

9. Edward Jay Epstein, "The Spy War," *New York Times Magazine*, September 20, 1980.

18. A MACBETH MOMENT

1. Lucas, *The Great Spy Ring*, 162–63.

2. Morris Cohen KGB interview, *Red Files*. His account of the Operation Whisper roll-up from his own point of view was given during an interview with KGB historians in a Moscow nursing home before his death.

19. A MOST DISGRACEFUL CASE

1. Aside from details of the trial as reported in the *Guardian*, the *Times*, the *Sunday Times*, the *Observer*, and the *Independent*, March 13–22, 1961, certain points in this narrative were amplified by Norman Lucas's biography, *Spycatcher*; John Bulloch and Henry Miller's investigative study, *Spy Ring*; and Morris Cohen's KGB interview in *Red Files*. Direct quotations from the trial, as presented in this chapter, are taken from the published testimony.

2. Blake, *No Other Choice*, 203.

3. "USSR's First-Ever Nuclear Sub Was Destroyed by Beer Bottle Cap," www.english .pravda.ru, May 4, 2015. In 1967, *K-3* was severely damaged by fire during a run through the Norwegian Sea and was knocked out of service for three years. The fire killed thirty-nine crewmen, and the incident was covered up by falsified documents. In 2012, a Russian investigating commission revealed that the fire started after a seaman tried to stop a hydraulic leak by installing a seal from a beer bottle. It didn't work, and leaking hydraulic fluid was ignited when it sprayed onto a lamp. The committee said that compensation would be awarded to the families of the crew members who were killed.

4. Blake, *No Other Choice*, 204.

5. O. F. Snelling, *Rare Books and Rarer People*, 218.

6. "At Last, the Truth Emerges about Gordon Lonsdale's Shadowy Life," the *Independent*, August 15, 1998. Interview with Trofim Molodiy, who was writing a book, *Dead Season: End of a Legend*, about his father. The title would have been familiar to those who remembered the Russian movie, *Dead Season*, a James Bond–type thriller based on Molody's exploits as a Soviet spy.

7. Nigel West, *Historical Dictionary of Cold War Counterintelligence* (Lanham, MD: Scarecrow Press, 2007), 183.

8. George Blake interview, "George Blake, Master of Moscow," *Storyville*, BBC Four, 2015, www.bbc.co.uk.

9. Ibid.

10. Norman Lucas, *Spycatcher*, 147.

11. Ibid., 162.

20. SWAPS AND A DARING ESCAPE

1. Snelling, *Rare Books and Rarer People*, 240.

2. Lonsdale, *Twenty Years in Soviet Secret Service*, 151, 155.

3. Blake, *No Other Choice*, 213.

4. Morris Cohen KGB interview, *Red Files*.

5. Houghton, *Operation Portland*, 147.

6. Ibid., 138.

7. Peter Kroger (Morris Cohen) to Winnie (Winifred Myers), January 3, 1968, Imperial War Museum.

8. Roger H. Platt, "The Soviet Imprisonment of Gerald Brooke and Subsequent Exchange for the Krogers, 1965–1969," *Contemporary British History* (London: Routledge Informa Ltd.), 24, no. 2 (2010): 197. Platt cites Foreign and Commonwealth Office 28/835, Macdonald to Gwynn, Sept. 1, 1965.

9. "U.S. Reportedly Rejected Spies-for-POWs Swap," *Baltimore Sun*, December 27, 1992. At one point, the Soviets offered to return five or six U.S. airmen shot down in the Vietnam War in exchange for the Cohens.

10. "Russia Frees Two Britons," the *Observer*, October 29, 1969.

11. "The Times Diary: Kroger's Farewell Supper," the *Times*, September 15, 1969.

12. "Kroger's Wife Wanted to Stay," the *Observer*, November 2, 1969.

13. "A Champagne Flight for the Krogers," the *Times*, October 25, 1969.

14. Robert Elphick, "Chasing Spies," *Historical Journal of Film, Radio and Television* 25, no. 2 (June 2005): 311.

15. "Mystery of Krogers' 'Lost' Years," the *Observer*, October 26, 1969.

16. "People: Letters from a Master Spy," undated British newspaper clipping, Imperial War Museum.

17. "At Last, the Truth Emerges about Gordon Lonsdale's Shadowy Life."

AFTERWORD

1. Banks-Smith, "All Sweetness and Spies in Ruislip." Banks-Smith quotes from an interview the Cohens gave for a documentary, *Strange Neighbours*, broadcast on Channel 4, London.

2. Svetlana Chervonnaya KGB interview, *Red Files*.

BIBLIOGRAPHY

Adjutant General, U.S. Army. "Historical Record, 3233d Quartermaster Service Company." National Archives and Records Administration, Washington, DC.

Albright, Joseph, and Marcia Kunstel. *Bombshell: The Secret Story of America's Unknown Atomic Spy Conspiracy.* New York: Times Books, 1997.

Andrew, Christopher. *The Defence of the Realm: The Authorized History of MI5.* London: Allen Lane, 2009.

Arthey, Vin. *Like Father Like Son: A Dynasty of Spies.* London: St. Ermin's Press, 2004.

Baruch, Bernard M. *Baruch: The Public Years.* New York: Holt, Rinehart & Winston, 1960.

Benson, Robert L., and John R. Schindler, "LINK: The Greatest Intelligence Disaster in U.S. History," National Security Agency Cryptologic History Symposium, October 31, 2003.

Bentley, Elizabeth. *Out of Bondage: The Story of Elizabeth Bentley.* New York: Devin-Adair, 1951.

Blake, George. *No Other Choice: An Autobiography.* New York: Simon and Shuster, 1990.

Bond, John A. "Soviet Espionage and a Polish Girl from Adams," *Adams Historical Society Newsletter* 10, no. 7 (October 1983): 1–2.

Brownell, Kenneth H. *Historic Narrative of 3233rd Quartermaster Service Company* (Company C, 241st Quartermaster Battalion), 1945. www.jraughley.com.

Bulloch, John, and Henry Miller. *Spy Ring: The Full Story of the Naval Secrets Case.* London: Secker & Warburg, 1961.

Calverley, Dorothea. "The Dawson Creek Disaster, February 13, 1943: A Personal Account of the Explosion and Fire." www.calverley.ca.

Chernin, Rose. "Organizing the Unemployed in the Bronx in the 1930s." *History Is a Weapon.* www.historyisaweapon.com.

Chikov, Vladimir. "How the Soviet Intelligence Service 'Split' the American Atom." *New Times* (Moscow: Moskovskaya Pravda Press), no. 17 (1991): 36–37.

Cook, Andrew. *On Her Majesty's Secret Service: Sidney Reilly ST1.* Stroud, Gloucestershire: Tempus, 2002.

Costello, John, and Oleg Tsarev. *Deadly Illusions*. London: Century Random House, 1993.

Debo, Richard K. "Lockhart Plot or Dzerzhinskii Plot?" *Journal of Modern History* 43, no. 3 (1971): 413–39.

Donovan, James B. *Strangers On a Train: The Case of Colonel Abel*. New York: Antheneum, 1964.

Elphick, Robert. "Chasing Spies." *Historical Journal of Film, Radio and Television* 25, no. 2 (June 2005): 311–14.

Feklisov, Alexander, and Sergei Kostin. *The Man Behind the Rosenbergs*. New York: Enigma Books, 2001.

Greenberg, Hank. *The Story of My Life*. New York: Times Books, 1989.

Groves, General Leslie. "Report on the Trinity Test, Memorandum to the Secretary of War, July 18, 1945." atomicarchive.com.

Hall, Joan. "A Memoir of Ted Hall." History Happens. www.historyhappens.net via www.web.archive.org.

Hanff, Helene. *The Duchess of Bloomsbury Street*. New York: Avon, 1973.

Haynes, John Earl, Harvey Klehr, and Alexander Vassiliev. *Spies: The Rise and Fall of the KGB in America*. New Haven: Yale University Press, 2009.

Hemingway, Ernest. *For Whom the Bell Tolls*. New York: Charles Scribner's Sons, 1940.

Hoar, Victor. *The Mackenzie-Papineau Battalion*. Chicago: Copp Clark, 1969.

Houghton, Harry. *Operation Portland: The Autobiography of a Spy*. London: Rupert Hart-Davis, 1972.

Knightley, Philip. *The First Casualty: The War Correspondent as Hero and Myth-Maker from the Crimea to Iraq*. Baltimore: Johns Hopkins University Press, 2004.

Kobyakov, Sergey. "Red Justice: How Soviet Russia's Secret Police Suppress the Foes of Bolshevism." *McClure's Magazine* 55, no. 2 (1923): 30–37.

Krivitsky, W.G. *In Stalin's Secret Service*. New York: Enigma Books, 2000.

Lamphere, Robert J., and Tom Shactman. *The FBI-KGB War: A Special Agent's Story*. New York: Random House, 1986.

Liversedge, Ronald. *A Memoir of the Spanish Civil War*. Cowichan Lake, BC, 1966.

Lockhart, R. H. Bruce. *British Agent*. New York: G. P. Putnam's Sons, 1933.

Lonsdale, Gordon. *Spy: Twenty Years in Soviet Secret Service*. New York: Hawthorn Books, 1965.

Lucas, Norman. *Spycatcher: The Biography of the Late Detective Superintendent George Smith*. London: W. H. Allen, 1973.

Massachusetts National Guard. "Camp Edwards History," www. states.ng.mil.

Merriman, Marion, and Warren Lerude, *American Commander in Spain: Robert Hale Merriman and the Abraham Lincoln Brigade*. Reno: University of Nevada Press, 1986.

Michalenko, Eugene, and Ed Driscoll, "The Spy Who Lived Here," *Adams Historical Society Newsletter* 24, nos. 5 and 6 (October–November 2002): 1–2.

Moss, Norman. *Klaus Fuchs: The Man Who Stole the Atom Bomb*. New York: St. Martin's Press, 1987.

Neuglass, James. "On the Road." In *Salud! Poems, Stories and Sketches of Spain by American Writers*. New York: International Publishers, 1938.

Orlov, Alexander. *The March of Time: Reminiscences*. London: St. Ermin's, 2004.

————. *Handbook of Intelligence and Guerrilla Warfare.* Ann Arbor: University of Michigan Press, 1963.

Platt, Roger H. "The Soviet Imprisonment of Gerald Brooke and Subsequent Exchange for the Krogers, 1965–1969." *Contemporary British History* 24, no. 2 (2010): 193–212.

Reilly, Sidney, and Pepita Reilly. *Britain's Master Spy: The Adventures of Sidney Reilly.* London: Dorset, 1985.

Rhodes, Richard. *The Making of the Atomic Bomb.* New York: Simon and Schuster, 1986.

Roberts, Sam. *The Brother: The Untold Story of Atomic Spy David Greenglass and How He Sent His Sister, Ethel Rosenberg, to the Electric Chair.* New York: Random House, 2001.

Royal Commission (Canada). "Report of the Royal Commission to Investigate the Facts Relating to the Circumstances Surrounding the Communication, by Public Officials and Other Persons in Positions of Trust, of Secret and Confidential Information to Agents of a Foreign Power, June 27, 1946." Igor Gouzenko case, www.historyofrights.com.

Savinkov, Boris. *Memoirs of a Terrorist.* New York: Albert & Charles Boni, 1931.

Shackley, Ted, with Richard A. Finney. *Spymaster: My Life in the CIA.* Dulles, VA: Potomac Books, 2005.

Sawatsky. John. *Gouzenko: The Untold Story.* Toronto: Macmillan, 1984.

Sax, Boria. "The Boy Who Gave Away the Bomb." *New York Times Magazine*, October 5, 1997.

Sinclair, Rolf. "The Blind Girl Who Saw the Flash of the First Nuclear Weapon Test." *Skeptical Inquirer* 18, (1993): 63–67.

Snelling, O. F. *Rare Books and Rarer People: Some Personal Reminiscences of "The Trade."* London: Werner Shaw, 1982.

Spence, Richard. *Trust No One: The Secret World of Sidney Reilly.* Port Townsend, WA: Feral House, 2002.

Sudoplatov, Pavel, and Anatoli Sudoplatov, with Jerrold L. and Leona P. Schecter. *Special Tasks: The Memoirs of an Unwanted Witness—A Soviet Spymaster.* New York: Little Brown, 1994.

Tchikov, Vladimir, and Gary Kern. *Comment Staline a volé la bombe atomique aux Américains: Dossier KGB No. 13676.* Paris: Editions Robert Lafont, 1996.

Thomas, Hugh. *The Spanish Civil War.* New York: Harper & Brothers, 1961.

The Times History of the War. "The Russian Expeditions," vol. 21, chapter 292. London: The Times, 1920.

Tolstoy, Nikolai. "Forced Repatriation to the Soviet Union: The Secret Betrayal." *Imprimis* (Hillsdale, MI: Hillsdale College), December 1988. www.fortfreedom.org.

U.S. Senate Subcommittee of the Committee on the Judiciary. *Brewing and Liquor Interests and German Propaganda Hearings.* 65th Congress, January 21, 1919. Washington, DC: Government Printing Office, 1919.

U.S. Senate Subcommittee to Investigate the Administration of the Internal Security Act and other Internal Security Laws of the Committee on the Judiciary. "Legend of U.S. Veterans of the International Brigade." *Scope of Soviet Activity in the United States Hearings.* 85th Congress, February 20, 1957. Washington, DC: Government Printing Office, 1957.

Volkogonov, Dmitri. *Lenin: A New Biography.* New York: Free Press, 1994.

West, Nigel. *Historical Dictionary of Cold War Counterintelligence*. Lanham, MD: Scarecrow Press, 2007.

Wright, Peter, with Paul Greenglass. *Spycatcher: The Candid Autobiography of a Senior Intelligence Officer*. New York: Viking, 1987.

Wright, Richard. *Pagan Spain*. New York: HarperPerennial, 1995.

Ziemke, Earl F. "Winter, The Season of Despair." In *The U.S. Army in the Occupation of Germany, 1944–1946*, chap. 23. Washington, DC: U.S. Army Center of Military History, www.globalsecurity.org.

INDEX

112, 134-35; 154, 186; controlled by Yuri Sokolov, 188-89, 192-93, 200-201; controlled by Anatoli Yatskov, 155, 185; cover names for, 51, 67, 107, 108; criticizes Soviet system, 288; cultural interests of, 228-29; deactivation, 172; death of, 286; decorated in USSR, 286; defends Stalin, 114, 170; denounced to FBI, 17; departure from England, 283-84; described, 29, 36, 66, 116, 119, 227, 266; develops assets, 109-10, 113, 115; discharge from army, 180; drafted into army, 128, 129; evaluation by Soviets, 90, 91, 93, 127; on fascism, 42, 57, 59, 64, 80, 93, 170; flees United States, 1-2, 202-3, 269; freed in swap, 281-83; growing up, 32-33; health problems of, 30, 63, 281, 285, 286; in high school, 36-37; identified by photo in US, 232-33; identified by fingerprints in England, 268; with international brigade in Spain, 68-69, 71-72, 74-92, 102-3; introduced to Lona, 66; job in England, 207, 223, 226, 227, 228, 247, 266; job in Moscow, 286; jobs in New York, 37, 51, 52, 107-8, 111, 185, 193; jobs in Poland, 203, 285-86; joins CPUSA, 50; and Judaism, 80; justification for spying, 3, 93, 123, 288, 289; leaves Spain, 103; lifestyle in England, 207, 208, 228, 238-240; and machine gun theft, 124-25; marriage of, 122, 123; at Mississippi State, 38-41; in National Student League, 41, 43, 44; at New York University, 36, 37; nicknames of, 36, 40, 43, 107; in Operation Keelhaul, 171-72; in Paris, 186; organizes for CPUSA, 61, passports held by, 67, 103, 156, 203, 223, 249, 258, 269; and Pavel Pastelnyak, 108-9; at Potsdam, 170; in prison, 277-81; problems with tradecraft, 239; in radar theft, 125-27; reactivation, 187; recruited for spying, 92-95; recruits assets, 109-10, 113, 115; recruits Lona, 123; relationship with parents, 35, 60; reprimanded by Soviets, 189; residence in Moscow, 286; residences in England, 207, 209, 223, 226, 228, 247, 249; residences in New York, 26, 27, 30, 32, 49, 67, 141, 181; residences in Poland, 269, 284-85;

sentenced to prison, 269-70; on Spanish Republic, 57, 66; sentenced, 269-70; and spy tools, 253, 258; and summer jobs, 37, 41; teaches at KGB school, 286; testifies at trial, 266; trains for army, 129-30; trains for spying, 94-101; at University of Illinois, 42-48; on USSR, 93; and Volunteer network, 115, 128; volunteers for Spain, 64, 65-66; wounded in Spain, 87, 88-90
Cohen, Sarah, 31-32, 34, 35, 202, 295n3
Cold War, 4, 13, 24
Columbia University, 45, 145, 177, 181, 185
Coulson, Fernande. *See* Gouzenko, Igor
Comintern (Communist International), 18, 33, 42, 48, 50, 53, 54, 57, 58, 76
Communist Party, Canada, 68, 175
Communist Party, France, 69, 70
Communist Party, Spain, 54, 91
CPUSA (Communist Party of the United States of America): agitprop techniques of, 51-52; appeals to immigrants, 33-34; and Earl Browder, 53; and Cultural Front, 61-62, 114, 120; damaged by Hitler-Stalin pacts, 114; in election of 1936, 57-58; growth of, 50; infiltrated by FBI, 27; and Popular Front, 48, 54-55, 57; as successor to American Communist Party, 67. *See also* Comintern
Construction (Orlov's spy school), 94, 95. *See also* Cohen, Morris
consulates (Soviet), 77, 94-95, 110-111, 121, 125, 149, 150, 152, 155, 178
Corby case. *See* Gouzenko, Igor
Cram, Cleveland, 240-41
Cultural Front. *See* CPUSA

Dawson Creek, Canada, 131-32
dead doubles. *See* passports
Debbs, Eugene, 39, 57
Doel, Frank, and Nora ("Woman in Blue"), 239-40, 267, 285
dubok (drop). *See* tradecraft
Dzerzhinsky, Felix, 11, 13, 151

Eisenhower, Dwight D., 171, 200, 272-73
Elwell, Charles, 238, 239